From Abraham to America

To Mike and
Janet — Once in a
while you get shown the
strangest look
of rivals if you
at it right....

Eric

From Abraham to America

A History of Jewish Circumcision

Eric Kline Silverman

ROWMAN & LITTLEFIELD PUBLISHERS, INC.
Lanham • Boulder • New York • Toronto • Oxford

ROWMAN & LITTLEFIELD PUBLISHERS, INC.

Published in the United States of America
by Rowman & Littlefield Publishers, Inc.
A wholly owned subsidary of The Rowman & Littlefield Publishing Group, Inc.
4501 Forbes Boulevard, Suite 200, Lanham, Maryland 20706
www.rowmanlittlefield.com

PO Box 317, Oxford
OX2 9RU, UK

British Library Cataloguing in Publication Information Available

Library of Congress Cataloging-in-Publication Data

Silverman, Eric Kline.
  From Abraham to America : a history of Jewish circumcision / Eric
Kline Silverman.
    p.   cm.
  Includes bibliographical references and index.
  ISBN-13: 978-0-7425-1668-7 (cloth : alk. paper)
  ISBN-10: 0-7425-1668-7 (cloth : alk. paper)
  ISBN-13: 978-0-7425-1669-4 (pbk : alk. paper)
  ISBN-10: 0-7425-1669-5 (pbk : alk. paper)
  1. Berit milah—History.   2. Circumcision—Religious aspects—Judaism.
3. Circumcision—History.   4. Antisemitism.   I. Title.
BM705.S55   2006
296.4'42—dc22   2006004450

Printed in the United States of America

♾ ™ The paper used in this publication meets the minimum requirements of American
National Standard for Information Sciences—Permanence of Paper for Printed Library
Materials, ANSI/NISO Z39.48-1992.

For my son, Sam, whose impending birth was greeted with the anticipation of a ceremony, and my daughter, Zoe, whose birth was not. I have yet to resolve fully this conflict. I hope someday that Sam and Zoe can do so for themselves.

Contents

Acknowledgments

This book was long in the making—eight years. I began the project about the time of my son's birth. Since then, he has been joined by a sister, and both of them have far more interest in Pokemon, Hello Kitty, and Harry Potter than in a topic they would surely greet with a resounding "yuck!" Over these long eight years, I benefited from many sources of support and advice, not the least of which came from the humbling experiences of parenting!

DePauw University graciously allowed me a sabbatical leave in 2000–2001 to begin this project and continued to assist my writing and research through its generous Faculty Development and Conference Travel Fund programs. I am also grateful to many of my students for tolerating a professor who introduced the most unlikely of subjects into many of his courses. The staff and librarians at DePauw, especially Kathryn Millis, continued their tradition of excellence.

The National Endowment for the Humanities kindly granted me a Fellowship in 2001–2002 to work on the book. I remain indebted for that wonderful opportunity.

I benefited from discussion of various aspects of the book and the topic more broadly with Sander Gilman, attendees at several annual meetings of the Midwest Jewish Studies Association (at which I presented preliminary thoughts on contemporary Jewish reactions to the rite), Stephan Bailis, Daniel Halperin, participants at the session "Male Circumcision, HIV/AIDS, and the Body in Africa and the West" at the 2000 Annual Meeting of the American Anthropological Association (at which I presented preliminary analysis of the image of the Jew in the contemporary opposition to medical circumcision), and an anonymous reviewer for Rowman & Littlefield, among others. In the earliest stages of the project, a DePauw University Collabora-tive Faculty-Student Research Grant allowed Jake Gross to spend a summer investigating for me the anthropological literature of circumcision rituals.

Some of the ideas in this book were anticipated by my essay "The Cut of Wholeness: Psychoanalytic Interpretations of Biblical Circumcision" in *The Covenant of Circumcision: New Perspectives on an Ancient Jewish Rite* (edited by Elizabeth Wyner Mark, 2003). I thank Elizabeth not only for inviting my contribution but also for offering sound advice.

I also included some of my findings in "Anthropology and Circumcision," *Annual Review of Anthropology* 33 (2004): 419–45.

For general collegiality and good humor during the project, I thank Tom Hall, Dave Berque, Paul and Yasuko Watt, Steve Wagschal and Sandy Shap-shay, Karen and Jay Adams (for Margaritas), and, for aesthetic advice, Roger Hirsch and Drew Souza. For those of you I unintentionally omitted, espe-cially folks who sent me e-mail jokes and unsolicited advice, please accept my thanks and apologies.

I want especially to thank Alan Dundes, one of the towering intellectual giants of the latter twentieth century, who suddenly died earlier this year. Alan unfailingly encouraged me to embark on this project, provided a detailed commentary on the prospectus with a characteristically detailed bibliography, and sent me many relevant jokes. I write this book in the spirit and shadow of his work.

My initial editor at Rowman & Littlefield, Dean Birkenkamp (now presi-dent and publisher of Paradigm Publishers), was a source of much advice and council. More recently, I acknowledge the great patience of Brian Romer, editor for Jewish studies and religious studies at Rowman & Littlefield.

Despite all this help, I take full responsibility for what I have written.

Among my family, I want to recognize, first, my parents, Phillip and Myrna Silverman, who taught me as a child about Judaism and then argued with me as an adult about everything they thought I should have learned! In all honesty, it was their response to my son's birth that spurred me to write this book. I also acknowledge the moral support of my in-laws, Pat and Gene Estess, and my broader kinship network, including Gary, Pete, Maureen, Jen, Pete W., Kate, Sharon, Bob, Aunt Faith and Uncle Irv, and a growing clan of nieces and nephews.

Again, I must acknowledge my children, Sam and Zoe. This book repre-sents my ongoing struggle to define what a moral, relevant, and truly inclu-sive Judaism should look like. I harbor no illusions that I will succeed. I hope

Sam and Zoe do so for themselves someday. If not, I hope they find the task rewarding and meaningful.

Finally, a few words about my wife, Andrea Wohl. As I was writing the dedication to my first book, she reflected on what it was like to live with me during the writing process, then said, "For that, you better dedicate all your books to me!" But when this book was entering its fourth year past due, for reasons I best not disclose, she asked that I *not* dedicate the book to her! Out of love, admiration, and gratitude, which I could never adequately describe, I respect her wishes.

And Abram was ninety and nine years old and the Lord appeared to Abram and said to him, "I am El Shaddai. Walk before Me and be blameless, and I will establish my covenant between Me and you, and I will make you exceedingly, exceedingly numerous."

And Abram flung himself upon his face, and God spoke to him, saying, "As for Me, this is My covenant with you: You shall be father to a multitude of nations. And no longer shall your name be called Abram but your name shall be Abraham, for I will make you the father of a multitude of nations. And I will make you exceedingly, exceedingly fruitful and turn you into nations, and kings shall come forth from you. And I will establish My covenant between Me and you and your seed after you throughout their generations as an everlasting covenant, to be God to you and to your seed after you. And I give unto you and your seed after you the land in which you sojourn, the whole land of Canaan, as an everlasting holding, and I will be their God."

And God further said to Abraham, "As for you, you shall keep My covenant, you and your seed after you throughout their generations. This is My covenant which you shall keep, between Me and you and your seed after you: every male among you must be circumcised. You shall circumcise the flesh of your foreskin and it shall be the sign of the covenant between Me and you. At eight days old every male among you shall be circumcised throughout your generations, even slaves born in your household and those purchased with silver from outsiders who are not your seed must be circumcised. My covenant in your flesh shall be an everlasting covenant. And a male with a foreskin who has not circumcised the flesh of his foreskin, that person shall be cut off from his kin; he has broken My covenant." (Genesis 17:1–14)

Introduction: Why *There?*

Of all the bodily locations where God could have marked a covenant with the Israelites, why the penis? And then why cut it? Why not a handshake, to be only slightly facetious, or an equally intimate or demanding gesture from women?

These are no trivial questions. After all, the rite of male circumcision is a key moment in the establishment of Abrahamic monotheism and so, as odd as it may seem, a pillar of Western religion, morality, and culture.

Circumcision is the premier "sign" of the covenant. The rite also exemplifies the values of biblical and, later, Jewish manhood—values that were and largely remain contradictory. To the extent that circumcision sacralizes male fecundity, the rite carves an image of Jewish men *against* women and uterine fertility. But circumcision, too, represents a masculine embodiment of female plentitude. The rite celebrates masculinity by sustaining male privilege and consecrating the male body while nonetheless hewing men into something other than themselves—*into a type of woman.* Circumcision trims the penis to contain but also to unleash phallic aggression and potency. The rite intentionally affixes an ever-present, lifelong, intensely physical reminder of the covenant on the most private part of a man's body. But circumcision, I hope to show, also enshrines far more ambiguity and ambivalence than either God or Abraham might willingly admit.

During the Hellenistic era, circumcision emerged as the paramount symbol of Jewishness.[1] The rite, what Jews eventually came to call *brit milah*, or "circumcision of the covenant," formed a "fence," to use a rabbinic idiom, or a boundary marker that separated the Jewish community from most other bodies and ethnic groups. In turn, ancient Greek and Latin writers relentlessly mocked the Jewish penis as aesthetically and erotically grotesque. The

Hellenistic ideal of foreskinned perfection, coupled to Platonic philosophy, shaped early Christianity into a preputial rather than foreskinless religion.

To Jew and non-Jew alike, normative Judaism became circumcised. Of course, not all Jewish bodies were circumcised. The phallic rite that cut down the phallus also cut out women from the typical idea and ideal of Jewishness. Even in biblical society, circumcision pushed women to the margins, seemingly casting the role and meaning of femininity and motherhood into uncertainty. But the rite also, if not more so, posed an equally ambiguous gender for men, albeit a blurred gender that, at least within Judaism, entailed a privileged access to legitimate power. The rite hallowed the penis, to be sure, but it did so through a gesture that symbolically feminized boys. Did not God promise fertility on the performance of a ceremony that opened and bloodied the genitals?

Circumcision often mediated the imaginative and real interactions between Jews and European Christians, who long ago abandoned the rite. Christ's genital pruning, to evoke biblical jargon, was the circumcision to end all circumcisions. The Crucifixion, in fact, as well as the Letters of Paul and the early church writings, all appear as responses to Jewish circumcision—rejoinders that eventually translated into an enduring image of the Jew as damaged and damaging. Circumcision diminished the Jew's body and mind: he was physically, sexually, and mentally deficient. To European theologians, kings, parliamentarians, and the folk, the "Jewish rite" was profoundly wrong. Circumcision threatened, moreover, to fatally wound the body of humanity united in Christ. No longer did circumcision circumscribe the covenantal community. Now the rite excluded Jews from the family of God as divine punishment for the betrayal and rejection of Christ.

The ritual performance and appearance of circumcision once intended and served, as it still often does, to "cut off" Jews from other ethnic groups. That's not all circumcision did, but it remained a powerful motivation. Today, the rite often rents the Jewish community in bitter debate. Scholars often remark on a similar feud that spurred the establishment of Reform Judaism in the late nineteenth century. But, oddly, academics today largely neglect recent, often impassioned discussions over the role of circumcision in defining or demeaning contemporary Judaism.

Scholars of present-day Judaism, too, fail to appreciate the significance of growing efforts to ban routine medical circumcision. This movement returns, again and again, to the venerable image of the circumcised Jew as psychologically and sexually wounded. So marred is the Jew's psyche, we often read, that he is unconsciously compelled to reenact his trauma by cutting others. In the United States and Europe, the Jew shrewdly inflicted circumcision onto gullible Christians for profit and even, it is said, to exact revenge for the Holocaust! In the Muslim world, the Jew insidiously introduced male *and* female circumcision to undermine the moral integrity of Islam. Then the Jew went from stealing Muslim foreskins to Palestinian land.

Despite a long, consequential, and sometimes tragic history, the symbolism and meanings of Jewish circumcision remain enigmatic to Jew and non-Jew alike. My goal in writing this book is to offer some insights into this ritual through a comprehensive analysis that extensively draws on a wide range of scholarly and popular sources. I view the rite from within Judaism and without. My focus spans the biblical through contemporary eras. I aim to appeal to academic specialists as well as to a wider readership by discussing biblical texts, rabbinic tales and legal codes, Renaissance paintings, and relevant scholarship from biblical studies, Jewish studies, gender, psychoanalysis, literature, and anthropology, as well as jokes, television shows, and postcards purchased on eBay. I also survey the anticircumcision movement and proponent voices, both medical and Jewish. Even readers who disagree with my interpretations will, I hope, concur that I offer the most comprehensive study (and bibliography) of Jewish circumcision published in English or perhaps any other language.

An anonymous reviewer of this manuscript for Rowman & Littlefield Publishers cautioned that "biblical scholars tend to be rather proprietary about their materials." Undoubtedly this is so. I respond by saying that my goal is not to invalidate or usurp their scholarly prerogatives. I have certainly not ignored them. My goal is far more modest: to offer novel, provocative interpretations that will complement, not replace, other perspectives. I trust that other scholars who are more familiar with biblical materials will view my interpretations through the spirit of intellectual openness and shared inquiry.

I strive for moral balance, arguing neither in favor nor against the rite. This strategy distinguishes the book from most other contemporary discussions of circumcision, especially books aimed at a broad readership. The earlier chapters, I hope, will clash with traditionalists who abide by circumcision with nary a thought for its violent tones, ambiguous morality, and gendered dilemmas. The latter chapters, I hope, will rile Jewish and non-Jewish opponents of the rite who commonly phrase their objections with intolerant, often medieval sensibilities. I aim, you might say, to unsettle all perspectives.

Symbolism and Ambivalence

Circumcision is a resolutely prismatic rite. Its meanings cannot be reduced to any singular or solitary message. I am not just saying that circumcision evokes multiple meanings. Rather, I want to anchor this multiplicity to a particular view of culture, religion, and human experience.

Circumcision exemplifies three properties of religious symbols identified by the eminent anthropologist Victor Turner (1962, 1967). First, the rite condenses a "fan" or "spectrum" of meanings. Second, circumcision unifies "disparate significata," that is, concepts normally associated with different domains of social life—connections that, outside the symbol, may even elicit strong denials. (Who would normally tie circumcision to fruit trees or mystical vision?) Third, circumcision lends abstract cultural values a tangible reality by linking them to basic bodily experiences, such as blood, milk, semen, and feces, and to basic physical acts, such as eating, sexuality, killing, and birth (Beidelman 1964:386). Nature and culture unite. The particularities of society appear innately connected to the natural order of reality. Our way of doing things seems not just another way but the only way.

I endorse this perspective on religious symbolism. But we need also to go beyond a framework that assigns to ritual only official meanings that sustain the dominant vision of social life. Instead, I see the power of circumcision and religion more generally to arise from the simultaneity of multiple, unstable, and irreducible meanings. For if bodily ritual transforms the ethereal conceptions of a worldview into everyday reality, then it also expresses contrary, often equivocal meanings. Ritual speaks with no single voice precisely because our commitments to social life are varied, uncertain, and frankly equivocal.

An effective interpretation of biblical and Jewish circumcision must therefore attend not only to symbolic plurality but also to contradiction and ambivalence. The bodily location of the covenantal sign bespeaks a concern with sexuality and reproduction. Insofar as the rite cuts around the penis, it circumscribes male sexuality within a moral framework. But as we learn from Freud (1913), collective morality never fully triumphs over the passion and the dissonance of human experience. Indeed, covenants themselves, Freud recognized, often derive their sacred character from otherwise immoral or taboo expressions of violence and intimacy.

Here, I draw not only on Freud but also on Mikhail Bakhtin (1984), the brilliant early twentieth-century theoretician of literature and culture. For Bakhtin, culture consists of contrary dialogues, both real and metaphoric, between voices dominant and submerged, authoritative and transgressive—voices, moreover, often spoken through bodily imagery. Together, these expressions form an endless conversation that anthropologists call culture (see Silverman 2001; Lipset and Silverman 2005). The irreducible dialogicality of culture captures what Bakhtin wonderfully called the "contradictory, double-face fullness of life."

Consider circumcision: an emasculating gesture of fertility, a fleshy covenant with an incorporeal god, a rite of wholeness that cuts a hole, a solemn pact received by Abraham in a paroxysm of laughter, and a sanctification of masculinity that emulates woman. In short, circumcision neither singularly sustains nor singularly subverts morality. Instead, circumcision is a bodily expression of profound ambivalence and moral struggle.[2]

My interpretive strategy is also guided by the anthropological project known as structuralism. Few paradigms in modern social science have received greater discussion and debate. To simplify, I will offer only the briefest remarks and then only aspects of structuralism that pertain to my own thesis.

Structuralism understands myth and ritual to communicate messages that are often obscured by the actual narrative or liturgy (Lévi-Strauss 1955). These messages, organized as binary oppositions, unconsciously express and seek to resolve ultimately unresolvable paradoxes of social life. Culture, to paraphrase Lévi-Strauss (1976), fails to answer our deepest questions and existential dilemmas. At some level, we know this failure. Yet we hesitate to admit it lest we call into question the social, cultural, and cosmological frameworks in which we ground our experiences. But myth and ritual *do* admit of this failure, "and there precisely lies their function." From this angle, circumcision is less a reflection of social values and more a fleeting glimpse into the limitations of our moral commitments.

Meaning and Midrash

Scholars generally parse the Five Books of Moses, what Jews call the Torah, into distinct "source documents," composed in different historical eras between, roughly speaking, the tenth and sixth centuries B.C.E. (Friedman 1987). Most references to circumcision occur in the so-called priestly compositions, dating to the Babylonian exile that followed the destruction of the first Jerusalem Temple in 586 B.C.E. Many scholars thus anchor the significance of the biblical rite to the social concerns of that particular era. The rite served as a broad marker of Israelite ethnicity and a more narrow token of priestly privilege (Eilberg-Schwartz 1990).[3] But while this interpretive strategy answers many questions, it also tends to dim recurring patterns and themes that lend the final version of the Hebrew Bible a sense of literary wholeness. My own approach to reading the Torah tends to eschew compositional chronology and focus instead on the totality of the text as a single narrative—albeit a narrative that contains fascinating gaps, contradictions, and dissonant and dissident voices. The Torah itself, we might say, encourages us to read much like an anthropologist studies ritual or a psychoanalyst interprets dreams. We read with and against the narrative grain.

There is another point of convergence between my anthropology and the sacred text. The classic rabbis codified their interpretations of the Hebrew Bible and Jewish traditions into recondite, often poetic, and always allusive conversations. The foundational colloquium of rabbinic culture is the Mishnah, a series of dialogues called the Oral Law. The Mishnah was compiled around the year 200. It runs, in standard English translation, to 1,100 pages.

Later rabbis offered detailed commentary on the Mishnah. These conversations formed the basis for the two Talmuds. The Jerusalem or Palestinian Talmud, redacted around the year 550, is the smaller compendium. Far more authoritative is the Babylonian Talmud, a vast encyclopedia of rabbinic law and lore, completed around the year 500. This massive work remains the paramount source of guidance on matters of religious law (*halakha*). Both Talmuds cover only a portion of the Mishnah. Nevertheless, the Babylonian work, which I often cite, exceeds 5,000 English pages.

Midrash forms another category of authoritative knowledge in Judaism. These conversations, recorded largely during the middle centuries of the first millennium, represent the height of the rabbinic imagination. Broadly speaking, midrash is an interpretive approach to the Torah that ascribes profound significance to literary idiosyncrasies such as unusual vocabulary, contradictions, missing information, and redundancies. Often, midrash probes the unconscious implications of the Torah, frequently focusing on issues that seemingly call into question the overt moral message. The logic of midrash is nonlinear, such that one biblical passage is interpreted through reference to other, noncontiguous phrases and events. This logic resembles anthropological analysis, which illuminates the meaning of ritual symbols through reference to wider aspects of the cultural system that are not immediately present during the ceremony. The premise of midrash, states Gruenwald (1993:11–12), is that "the [sacred] text is realized in being interpreted . . . the text lives in the interpretive mode . . . this is precisely the essence of Jewish religiousness."[4] I may lack the theological convictions of the classic

rabbis. But I find their interpretive strategies to anticipate symbolic anthropology with uncanny prescience.

History

Anthropologists characterize the first eleven chapters of Genesis as myth:
sacred tales detailing the creation of the world. These events occurred
nowhere and at no time. They reflect a way of thinking about the world, not
actual happenings. Traces of valid history in Genesis begin with the legends
of Abraham, which date to about the year 2000 B.C.E. But the ancients did
not, according to modern scholarship, compose the first narrative strands of
the Torah until the advent of the Israelite monarchy a millennium later, during the tenth century B.C.E. They continued to weave these tales until the
Assyrian destruction of the first Jerusalem Temple in 586 B.C.E. and the subsequent Babylonian exile. Shortly thereafter, the Torah was formally redacted
into its current form, more or less. The Torah, then, largely reflects the social
conventions and religious practices not of the patriarchs such as Abraham
and Moses, whose lives it details, but of the later society called ancient Israel.
And ancient Israel is *not* Judaism.

The Babylonian exile initiated the period known as ancient Judaism. This
long and tumultuous epoch included the construction of the Second Temple
and the canonization of the Torah as well as the rise of Hellenism, the Maccabean revolt against the Syrian Greeks, and the life and death of Jesus. This
era effectively ceased with the destruction of the Second Temple in the year
70 A.C.E.[5] Only then did rabbinic Judaism, which formalized the institutions
familiar to most Jews today, begin to emerge fully. Many characteristics of
rabbinic Judaism—especially synagogues, ordained rabbis, and scriptural
study—were unknown to the ancient Israelites, whose religious obligations
involved the Temple, hereditary priests, and animal sacrifice.

Rabbinic Judaism, in various historical formations, dominated Jewish life
in Europe for centuries. The hegemony of this rabbinic authority first started
seriously to fray with the rise of Hasidism in the eighteenth century. But it
was not until the mid-nineteenth century that the long era of rabbinic Judaism came to a close though the ascendance of Reform Jewry and, shortly
thereafter, the establishment of the Conservative and modern Orthodox
denominations. Needless to say, the twentieth century was even more consequential in shaping Judaism through the immigrant experience, the Holocaust, statehood, Palestinian aspiration, 9/11, the invasion of Iraq and the
"war on terror," and still-continuing debates over how best to define Jewish-

ness in terms of ethnic distinctiveness and assimilation. Without question, the meanings of circumcision have historically shifted.

Thematic Overview

History, however, cannot deny the persistence of religious and cultural conti-nuities. While each chapter of the book explores different facets and histori-cal aspects of circumcision, several common themes nevertheless emerge.

First, circumcision cuts a complex, contradictory relationship between masculinity and motherhood.[6] This strand of my argument draws on my prior anthropological research in a Papua New Guinean society (Silverman 2001).[7] The rite distinguishes men from women yet emulates female fertility, thus celebrating manhood while undermining its own masculine intent. From this angle, to borrow the terms of Boyarin (1997b), circumcision appears both phallic and counterphallic.

Second, circumcision offers another contrary message about the role of fertility and also sexuality in biblical culture and Judaism. The bodily loca-tion of the rite underscores the importance of fecundity and eroticism. Yet circumcision threatens to enact its own infertile punishment. "Cut off" or be "cut off." Circumcision thus exemplifies what D. Biale (1997) shows to be a wide-ranging ambivalence towards sexuality throughout Jewish history.

Third, circumcision flirts with taboo. The rite, for example, ensures male fecundity and upholds the heterosexual orientation of Judaism. Yet circumci-sion also, especially to the medieval mystics or Kabbalah, resonates with homoerotic themes and frankly violates several rabbinic edicts on the proper comportment for prayer. Here, I find inspiration in the work of recent schol-ars who read and counterread Jewish traditions and the Hebrew Bible (e.g., Bal 1985; Pardes 1992a; Boyarin 1993; Eilberg-Schwartz 1994). That is, I interpret the rite by focusing not solely on dominant meanings but also on tensions, paradoxes, and contradictions.

Fourth, numerous aspects of circumcision in its biblical, rabbinic, and folkloristic settings enable specifically women and mothers, despite their official marginalization, to call into question the authoritative meanings of Judaism and Jewish masculinity. That circumcision confers religious privi-leges to men seems obvious. I have in mind something akin to what Delaney (1991:78) observed while conducting fieldwork in another Abrahamic tradi-tion. As a small boy ran naked in a Turkish Muslim village, his grandfather pointed to the child's penis and asked, "What can men do that women can't?" The answer was no mystery to the boy. "Go to the mosque."[8] But it will not suffice, like the Turkish grandfather and child, to focus only on the androcentric meanings of circumcision. Instead, I equally focus on contrary voices and actions, especially those that allow women to express an otherwise muted subversion of the official gender hierarchy.

Fifth, I hope to show that circumcision was a central theme in anti-Semitic caricature since late antiquity. With the rise of Christianity, the rite shifted from a barbaric curiosity to a bodily blemish of sin and evil that violated even divine sensibilities. Anti-Jewish images and literature throughout European history conjured the figure of a knife-wielding Jew intent on cutting down Christendom and civil society. Today, we will see, this portrayal surfaces in many quarters of the opposition to medical circumcision. Only when the Jew restores his phallus to full size, in this view, can he join the rest of humanity.

As a final thesis, I show that circumcision since the nineteenth century has presented Jews with an opportunity for thinking through the tension between tradition and modernity. More than any other ritual, circumcision has argued both for and against full Jewish citizenship. For some Jews, the rite cuts Judaism *off* from the modern age—regrettably if you aspire to assimilation or laudably if you do not. Here, the rite is a barbaric religious impediment to the secular ideals of the Enlightenment and science, or an enlightened practice of divine imprimatur that eclipses the hubris of science and the Enlightenment. Still other Jews assert that the medical, hygienic, and moral benefits of circumcision uniquely cut the Jews *into* modern society—that science, in fact, has only recently discovered what the Jews knew all along! The rite remains the preeminent symbol of the Jew's precarious role, defined by himself and others, in a pluralistic world.

Chapter Summaries

The first chapter establishes my contention that the biblical meaning of circumcision makes sense only within the broader creation and structure of the Israelite cosmos. The physical act of circumcision, which halves unity into duality, parallels the unfolding of the universe in the early myths of Genesis. The Israelite penis, like the Israelite cosmos, attains wholeness through splitting.

Scholars typically divide Genesis into a primal history and the patriarchal narratives. While the early creation stories echo other ancient Near Eastern mythologies, the latter legends, which include the covenant and circumcision, uniquely apply to Israel. Consequently, nearly all scholarly discussions of biblical circumcision fail to connect the rite to the underlying themes of Creation. By contrast, I anchor circumcision to the biblical cosmology and, indeed, the opening phrase of Genesis. This strategy illuminates, among other symbolism, the relationship between circumcision and the paradox of a male deity creating the world.

Chapter 1 also introduces my argument that circumcision, as the quintessential rite of biblical and Jewish manhood, emulates female fertility, especially menstruation and birth. Finally, the first chapter discusses the mystical notion that circumcision effects an intimate relationship between man and God that poses homoerotic dilemmas for heterosexual masculinity.

Chapter 2 further situates circumcision in the early themes and events of Genesis. I explore tensions surrounding the idea of God's body as well as broader anxieties over sexuality and corporeality in biblical and rabbinic cultures. I also continue to link circumcision to wider notions of gender and reproduction, focusing on the extraction of a "rib" from the first human to form woman. This unnatural birth directly anticipates the removal of the infant's foreskin during circumcision.

The meanings of circumcision also take root in the infamous events in Eden, as I show in chapter 3, especially in regard to the symbolism of fruit, vision, eroticism, and the serpent. This chapter also ties circumcision to various markings of biblical bodies, beginning with the ambiguous sign that tarnished yet protected Cain after the first fratricide. Additionally, I establish a connection between circumcision and three themes of the great flood: incest, the prohibition on the consumption of blood, and, once again, the idea of male creation.

Chapter 4 analyzes the covenantal declarations that established circumcision during the life of Abraham and subsequent events that bear on the meaning of circumcision. These topics include the splitting of animals; the "cutting off" penalty that enforces circumcision; biblical notions of fruitfulness, wholeness, and castration; and an intergenerational saga of sex and violence that colors the covenantal lineage and circumcision with uncertain moral virtue. Finally, I explore the psychodynamic idea that circumcision feminizes men, and I show how Genesis occasionally allows biblical women such as Sarah to mock circumcision and other procreative boasts by God and man.

Chapter 5 takes up the issue of blood. Biblical circumcision draws meaning from the opposition between the positive male blood of sacrifice and the negative female blood of menstruation. Indeed, the rite resembles a menstrual sacrifice enacted by men. This interpretation explains the marginalization of women and mothers from circumcision. It also allows us to see a connection between circumcision and another biblical cutting of a child that ignored motherhood, namely, Abraham's near sacrifice of Isaac. Finally, chapter 5 explores God's enigmatic assault on Moses in Exodus 4. Moses survives only through the heroism of his wife, Zipporah, who swiftly circumcises their son, touches the severed foreskin to unknown male legs, and calls someone a "bloody bridegroom." This bizarre event subverts the masculine ideology of circumcision. Zipporah, almost literally, throws the rite back on men to ridicule the bloody, birthing fictions of monotheism. In more ways than one, the future of the covenant lay in the hands of women.

Chapter 6 turns from biblical culture to the folkloristic relationship between circumcision and the demoness named Lilith. In turn, this relationship illuminates playful and serious connections between circumcision and the evil eye, hair, skullcaps or *yarmulkes*, Hasidic earlocks, and women's wigs. I also explore the mystical notion that circumcision inscribes God's signature on the male body.

Chapter 7 probes the rules, prayers, and procedures of the formal circumcision ceremony that emerged during the rabbinic era and persists more or less intact today. My objective is to tease out the dissonant dimensions of the rite that both affirm and resist dominant meanings. Towards this aim, I focus on the symbolism of the knife, liturgical invocations of violence, sips of blood during the rite, and the former folkloristic practice by women to promote their own fertility by eating the foreskin. This chapter also explains the marginalization of motherhood during the rite in terms of the ceremonial usurpation of birth by men.

Chapter 8 shifts to Christianity. Despite the centrality of the rite in Judaism, it is really Christianity that might best be described as a culture obsessed with circumcision and foreskins. Yet circumcision in Christianity is no moral mark but rather a psychological and physical mutilation that betokens the Jew's exclusion from the covenantal community and, worse, threatens to slice away at the integrity of Christendom. The data in this chapter include the Gospels, Pauline Letters, and writings of the church fathers, as well as medieval devotions directed at Christ's circumcised foreskin. I also argue that a host of anti-Semitic canards throughout European history, including blood libels, coin clippings, and the notorious "pound of flesh" in Shakespeare's play *The Merchant of Venice*, all arise from a pervasive dread of Jewish circumcision.

Chapter 9 turns from Christianity to modern Jewish debates over circumcision since the rise of Reform Judaism in the late nineteenth century. I am

particularly interested in critically examining contemporary Jewish arguments against the rite, which typically evidence a poor understanding of biblical and rabbinic texts, and, more seriously, often rephrase long-standing
caricatures of the Jew as neurotic, violent, misogynistic, sexually perverse,
beholden to meaningless rituals, and lacking authentic spirituality. I also
explore modern endorsements of the ritual as well as alternative or noncut-
ting covenant ceremonies for boys *and* girls. The contemporary Jewish debate
over circumcision is deeply painful. Many Jews who refuse the rite feel
deserted by a tradition to which they stake enormous emotional attachment.
Yet other Jews see circumcision as encapsulating the very essence and survival of the religion. The continuing controversy attests to the still-undefined
role of the Jew in modern society and the meaning of Jewishness.

Chapter 9 also investigates different images of the Jew and "Jewish rite"
during the rise of routine medical circumcision in the late nineteenth century. In an era when, as I just noted, some Jews sought to diminish the importance and practice of ritual circumcision, other Jews promoted the medical
procedure. But the common assertion that the institutionalization of medical
circumcision was a Jewish effort is, I will show, misguided.

The final chapter of the book documents and analyzes references to Jews
in the growing opposition to routine medical circumcision, especially in the
United States. The central participants in this movement—physicians, lawyers, activists, and academics—often caricature the Jew in the most mainstream of publications and websites as psychologically and sexually wounded,
a tortured soul compelled to mutilate the bodies and psyches of others. It is
not the opposition to circumcision that I wish to challenge but, rather, a
persistent willingness to attribute the woes of modern society to the lost foreskin and a persistent anti-Semitism in doing so.

In the conclusion, I offer some thoughts on why it is difficult to write this
book and what I hope readers will learn from my effort.

Notes

1. Ashkenazic Jews, or those of European descent, often abbreviate the rite as *bris*.
2. For an earlier version of this thesis, see Silverman (2003).
3. Other discussions of circumcision and "source documents" include Hoffman (1996),
Blaschke (1998), Bernat (2002), and Warning (1999–2000, 2001).
4. For traces of oral tradition in the Hebrew Bible, see Niditch (1996) and Dundes
(1999).
5. For stylistic purposes, I will henceforth omit the "A.C.E." designation but retain
"B.C.E."

6. Women are not, nor have they ever been, circumcised in Jewish or biblical traditions despite an ancient report to the contrary by Strabo (*Geography* 16.2.37; 16.4.9; 17.2.5). Indeed, another ancient author, Philo, expressly discussed the *non*circumcision of Jewish women (*On the Special Laws* 1:1–11; *Questions and Answers on Genesis* 3:46–52).

7. As an anthropologist, I often draw on cross-cultural comparisons. For a broad review of circumcision around the world, see Silverman (2004).

8. Islamic circumcision (*khitān*, or "cutting") is one of several forms of moral-bodily cleanliness (Koran 30:30) called *fiṭra*. The Islamic rite lacks explicit mention in the Koran but is typically justified through the mandate "to follow the religion of Abraham" (16:123). As Bouhdiba (1985:182) put it, male circumcision is a rite practiced by Muslims, not a Muslim rite. For further discussion, often with comparison to Judaism, see Zaborowski (1897), Morgenstern (1973:chaps. 9 and 10), Chebel (1992), Kister (1994), and Dessing (2001).

Abbreviations and Sources for Classic Rabbinic, Mystical, and Jewish Texts

M	Mishnah
	The Mishnah: Translated from Hebrew with Introduction and Brief Explanatory Notes, by Herbert Danby (Oxford: Oxford University Press, 1933).
GR	Genesis Rabbah
ER	Exodus Rabbah
LR	Leviticus Rabbah
NR	Numbers Rabbah
DR	Deuteronomy Rabbah
EsR	Esther Rabbah
LamR	Lamentations Rabbah
SSR	Song of Songs Rabbah
ECR	Ecclesiastes Rabbah
	All the "Rabbah" texts are from *The Midrash Rabbah,* complete and unabridged English translated and edited by H. Freedman and Simon Maurice (Brooklyn, N.Y.: Soncino Press, 1977). (fifth to eleventh centuries)
PRE	Pirkê de Rabbi Eliezer
	Pirkê de Rabbi Eliezer: (The Chapters of Rabbi Eliezer the Great) According to the Text of the Manuscript Belonging to Abraham Epstein of Vienna, translated and annotated with introduction and indices by

Gerald Friedlander. (London: Kegan Paul, Trench, Trubner & Co., 1916). (eighth to ninth centuries)

RN   Avot de-Rabbi Nathan, Sayings of the Fathers according to Rabbi Nathan

The Fathers according to Rabbi Nathan: An Analytical Translation and Explanation, by Jacob Neusner (Atlanta: Scholars Press, 1986). (third to fourth centuries; redacted in the seventh to ninth centuries)

SH   Sefer Hayashar

Translated as *The Book of Yashar*, by Mordechai Manuel Noah (New York: M. M. Noah & S. S. Gould, 1840). (ninth to twelfth centuries)

PR   Pesikta Rabbati

Pesikta Rabbati: Discourses for Feasts, Fasts, and Special Sabbaths, 2 vols., translated by William G. Braude (New Haven, Conn.: Yale University Press, 1968). (third to fourth centuries; compiled seventh century)

PRK   Pěsikta dě-Rab̲ Kahăna

Pěsikta dě-Rab̲ Kahăna: Kahana's Compilation of Discourses for Sabbaths and Festal Days, translated from Hebrew and Aramaic by William G. (Gershon Zev) Braude and Israel J. Kapstein (Philadelphia: Jewish Publication Society, 1975). (fifth century)

T-Y   Midrash Tanhuma-Yelammedenu

Midrash Tanhuma-Yelammedenu: An English Translation of Genesis and Exodus from the Printed Version of Tanhuma-Yelammedenu with an Introduction, Notes, and Indexes, by Samuel A. Berman (Hoboken, N.J.: KTAV Publishing House, 1996). (eighth to ninth centuries)

TG   Tanhuma Genesis
TE   Tanhuma Exodus
TL   Tanhuma Leviticus

The three "Tanhuma" texts are from *Midrash Tanuma*, translated into English with introduction, indices, and brief notes by John T. Townsend. Vol. 1: *Genesis*, 1989; vol. 2: *Exodus and Leviticus*, 1997.

	(S. Buber Recension) (Hoboken, N.J.: KTAV Publishing House). (perhaps ninth century)
Babylonian Talmud	My source is the thirty-volume set issued by The Soncino Press, sometimes called The Soncino Talmud, translated by Maurice Simon, under the editorship of Isidore Epstein.
Kitzur	Kitzur Schulchan Aruch *Code of Jewish Law (Kitzur Schulchan Aruch): A Compilation of Jewish Laws and Customs*, by Solomon Ganzfried, rev. ed., translated by Hyman E. Goldin (New York: Hebrew Publishing Company, 1927).
YD	Yoreh Deah *Code of Hebrew Law. Shulan 'Aruk, Yoreh Deah, Yoreh Deah (sections from 260:1–266:14).* Two sources: "The Laws of Circumcision," translated by Boxman (1986), appendix 3, and www.torah.org/advanced/shulchan-aruch/classes/chapter20.html (sixteenth century). I also cited references to this rabbinic text as they occurred in other works.
HM	Mishneh Torah: Hilchot Milah, The Laws of Circumcision. Moses Maimonides. Eliyahu Touger, *Mishneh Torah: Hilchot Berachot, the Laws of Blessings, and Hilchot Milah, the Laws of Circumcision*, a new translation with commentaries and notes. (New York: Moznaim, 1991). (twelfth century)
Guide	Moses Maimonides, *The Guide of the Perplexed.* Moses Maimonides, *The Guide of the Perplexed*, translated with an introduction and notes by Shlomo Pines (Chicago: University of Chicago Press, 1963). (twelfth century)
SY	Sepher Yetzirah *Sepher Yetzirah. The Book of Creation*, rev. ed., translation and commentary by Aryeh Kaplan (York Beach, Me.: Samuel Weiser, 1997). (uncertain date, but pre-Mishnah)
Ibn Ezra	*Rabbi Abraham Ibn Ezra's Commentary on the Creation,*

translated and annotated by Michael Linetsky (Northvale, N.J.: Jason Aronson, 1998). (eleventh century)

Bahir   *The Bahir*, translated and commentary by Aryeh
                  Kaplan (Northvale, N.J.: Jason Aronson, 1995).
                  (twelfth century and earlier)

Zohar   *The Zohar*, vols. 1–5, translated by Harry Sperling and
                  Maurice Simon (London: Soncino Press. 1984). (com-
                  posed by Moses ben Shemtov de Leon, Spain, in the
                  latter thirteenth century)

Hebrew Bible. My translations derive mainly from three sources, as well as
my own referencing to the Hebrew itself: *Tanakh: A New Translation of the
Holy Scriptures according to the Traditional Hebrew Text* (Philadelphia: Jewish Publication Society, 1985), Robert Alter's *Genesis: Translation and
Commentary* (New York: Norton, 1996), and Everett Fox's *The Five Books
of Moses* (New York: Schocken Books, 1995).

Greek and Latin authors, including Philo and Josephus: I relied on the
numerous volumes in the Loeb Classical Library, published by Harvard
University Press, as well as L. Feldman (1993), Schäfer (1997), Signor
(1990), and especially Stern (1974–1984).

Church Fathers. I utilized several multivolume sets, including *A Select Library
of the Nicene and Post-Nicene Fathers of the Christian Church*, edited by
Philip Schaff (Grand Rapids, Mich.: W. R. Eerdmans, 1956); *The Ante-
Nicene Fathers: Translations of the Writings of the Fathers Down to A.D. 325*,
edited by Alexander Roberts and James Donaldson (Buffalo, N.Y.: Christian Literature Publishing Company, 1885–1896); and *The Fathers of the
Church Series* (Catholic University of America Press). Many of these texts
are now available online through the Christian Classics Ethereal Library
at www.ccel.org/fathers2.

CHAPTER ONE

Circumcision, Creation, and the Cosmic Phallus

When the Romans destroyed the second Temple of Jerusalem in the year 70, they razed the spiritual, ceremonial, and moral center of early Judaism. A century later, Rome again traumatized the Jewish community by routing the bar Kochba rebellion. Shortly thereafter, a conclave of Palestinian rabbis sought to reestablish order amid this chaos by authoring a massive compendium of religious regulation called the Mishnah. Judaism still remained true to its ancient roots of God, prayer, and divine law. Yet the old pillars of the religious system, namely, the Temple, hereditary priests, and animal sacrifice, were replaced by the synagogue, ordained rabbis, and scriptural study. The Mishnah, redacted around the year 200, imposes an exacting sense of biblical rule onto a nonbiblical reality.

In classic Jewish theology, God revealed *two* legal codes atop Mount Sinai. Moses transcribed one set of laws as the Torah, or Five Books of Moses. The other code, the Oral Law, remained unwritten, allegedly passing by word of mouth from Moses to Joshua, thence to generations of prophets, priests, and ancient scholars. Eventually, the early rabbis compiled this oral body of lore and legislation into the Mishnah. This complex series of colloquia offered practical guidance on how to apply often vague tenets of biblical law to everyday life in a nonbiblical reality. Although most people today, Jews included, trace Judaism only to the Five Books of Moses, it is the Mishnah that truly established the daily particularities of Judaism. And in the Mishnah, the rabbis pin the existence of the universe onto circumcision.

"Great Is Circumcision"

The Mishnaic tractate Nedarim clarifies formal vows. At one point, the rabbis ponder hypothetical oaths concerning people called "the uncircumcised" (M. Nedarim 3:11). Who are they? Uncircumcised Israelites? Circumcised Gentiles? And what about "the circumcised"? Drawing on various biblical passages such as Jeremiah 9:26, the rabbis understood the "uncircumcised" as non-Jews, while the "circumcised" referred to uncircumcised Jews but not circumcised Gentiles. The discussion ends with a rhetorical competition among the rabbis over the significance of circumcision.

Each rabbi's declaration begins "Great is circumcision." The culminating affirmation is "Great is circumcision, for if it were not for that, the Holy One, blessed be he, *would not have created his world.*"[1] For biblical prooftext, the rabbis cited Jeremiah 33:25, which they understood as "Thus saith the Lord, but for my covenant day and night, I had not set forth the ordinances of heaven and earth." God speaks to the same issue in Jeremiah 33:20, "If you [the Israelites] could break My covenant with the day and My covenant with the night," then "day and night should not come at their proper time." In the rabbinic imagination, circumcision sustains the existence of heaven and earth. The rite offers ritual reassurance despite historical catastrophe.[2]

Similar sentiments occur in the Babylonian Talmud. "But for the blood of the covenant," said the rabbis in tractate Shabbath (137b), "heaven and earth would not endure." The classic rabbis extolled the greatness of many things, including the Torah, knowledge, the Sabbath, repentance, and human dignity. Still, the rabbis again and again celebrated circumcision as vouchsafing the existence of heaven and earth. Why?

I answer this question by drawing on Leach (1962) and Carroll (1977) to uncover a dualistic pattern in the biblical cosmology. This binary structure shapes, through images of separation and division, almost all significant episodes in Genesis. My goal is to show that circumcision, as the separation of the foreskin from the penis, inscribes on the male body an image of the cosmos, humanity, and society. I also argue that the binary pattern underlying the covenantal rite and the Genesis cosmogony points to a central problem in biblical monotheism: masculine creation and male envy of female birth.

My final task in this chapter is to introduce the erotic and mystical dimensions of circumcision whereby the uncovering of the foreskin admits men into an intimate union with God, and represents the unveiling of hidden secrets in the Torah. Circumcision, too, attests to the importance of human sexuality and progeny in the biblical and rabbinic worldviews even as the rite dangerously flirts with reproductive disaster. By celebrating yet threaten-ing the penis, circumcision dramatizes a wide-ranging ambivalence about the role and value of men in the world.

Heavenly Paradoxes

The Hebrew Bible contains two accounts of creation (Genesis 1:1; 2:4; 2:4–25). For now, I concentrate on the first version. Beginning with its open-ing words, "When God began to create heaven and earth," the Torah affirms a dual cosmos.[3] The second phrase of Genesis is also binary. The primal con-ditions of the earth are *tohu* and *bohu*, two obscure Hebrew words that vari-ously connote unformed, void, dark, deep, windy, waste, watery, and barren. For some rabbis, *tohu* and *bohu* describe the initial state of the earth (see also Jeremiah 4:23; Isaiah 34:11). For others, *tohu* and *bohu* were the primal substances used by God to mold the world, perhaps allusions to ocean and land (Graves and Patai 1983:31, 47–53). In midrash, God created the cosmos from two orbs of fire and snow (GR 10:3; see also Psalm 148:4–8; Bahir 59). Even the first letter of the Torah, *bet*, which is the second letter of the Hebrew alphabet—a letter possessing the numerical value of two—conjures duality (Koren 1999). From various perspectives, the opening stanzas of Gen-esis establish a binary pattern.

Another dualism emerges on consideration of the relationship between God and the Torah in rabbinic culture. Traditionally, Jews treat the Torah, which is written by scribes on parchment scrolls, like female royalty, typi-cally, God's daughter or bride, but also a pious man's spiritual wife (ER 30:5; D. Biale 1997:117; see also chapter 7).[4] A female Torah moderates the mono-theistic dominance of men. But there is more to the Torah's gender than a muted sense of egalitarianism. For some rabbis, God created the Torah before he fashioned heaven and earth to consult with her (TG 1.5; ER 30:9, 47:4; PRE 3). Other rabbis said that God composed the Torah after Creation (Ginzberg 1909–1938:V:3–4 n. 5, 132–33 n. 2). This rabbinic debate entails two key questions. Was the world created by a divine unity or a divine dual-ity? This question is complicated by the word for God in these myths, *'elohim*, a masculine plural that is typically attached to male singular verbs. Although grammatical gender does not necessarily point to a sexual identity, the implied gender of God in most biblical passages is clearly male. So, does Cre-ation represent a masculine effort by God alone, or did he require a feminine presence? Paradoxically, the answer to both questions is yes. The God of bib-lical monotheism is dual *and* unitary, male *and* female. The same paradox informs circumcision. Both circumcision and creation entail a binary logic. Both circumcision and creation encode two modes of reproduction, one heterosexual, the other exclusively male. And both circumcision and creation reveal male envy of female fertility and birth, that is, a desire by men to assert covenantal reproduction in the absence of women.

Day One: Division and Transition

Let us return to the opening statement of Genesis, which implies the existence of a unitary god who generates a duality, namely, heaven and earth. God next creates light or Day, which he separates from darkness or Night. God "saw that the light was good," a self-congratulatory remark he confers onto nearly all his creations during the seven-day cosmogony. Binary oppositions are good.

Each day of creation generally entails the formation of unambiguous cosmological categories through separation and division. Yet Genesis also seeks to maintain a sense of continuity by bridging, or mediating, distinct categories—again, using dualities. Consecutive days are thus linked through a binary period of temporal transition phrased as "there was evening and there was morning."

Day Two: Aquatic Love

On Day Two, God created a celestial partition—a firmament, expanse, vault, dome, or heavenly sky—"in the midst of the water, that it may separate water from water." The rabbis parsed the Hebrew word for this sky, *shamayim*, into *'esh* and *mayim*, or fire and water (GR 4:7; Zohar ii:164b). Regardless, the sky divided primal fluid into upper and lower waters. Unity became duality.

The division of the waters has generated a wealth of rabbinic and folkloristic interpretations (see Ginzberg 1909–1938:I:14–15, V:17–19 nn. 50–53, 26 n. 73). Again, the rabbis are a useful interpretive source. In one view, the waters eagerly obeyed God and immediately divided. In another view, the waters stubbornly refused to budge (PRE 4; ER 15:22; Patai 1947:62–65). The mystics anthropomorphized the upper and lower waters into lovers who refused to separate from their passionate embrace (Zohar i:46a; Patai 1947:62; Wolfson 1995:110–11). These interpretations postdate by centuries the composition of Genesis. Yet they still elaborate on the biblical pattern of unity and division.

Day Three: Seeds and Sex

God gathers the lower waters to expose dry land on Day Three. This creative act parallels the division of light from darkness on Day One. It also generates the binary opposition of Seas and Earth, water and ground, salt and sod.

God also creates plants on Day Three (Genesis 1:11–12). Since the Hebrew syntax is ambiguous, there are two possible readings. The Jewish Publication Society understands the earth to sprout "vegetation," which is then divided into seed-bearing plants and seed-bearing fruit trees. But most other translations speak about three types of flora: grass, seed-bearing plants, and seed-bearing fruit trees. Either way, the cosmogonic logic of Day Three remains binary.

The seeds, says Bird (1981:146), foreshadow the future task of animals and humans to "be fruitful and multiply." By alluding to cycles of life and death, the third day hints at the opposition between change and permanence. Additionally, the self-germinating plants anticipate the reproductive strategy of animals and humans, who must mix their seed (Leach 1962). Circumcision encodes the same opposition, but with a twist I will later elaborate. The rite enables men to procreate *with* women and to reproduce *without* them.

Days Four and Five: Sky and Sea

God illuminates the heavens on the fourth day. Echoing Day One, he "separates" or "divides" day from night by creating "two great lights," the sun and moon. The moon is also paired with the stars. These lights are designated as "signs" for two "set times," days and years.

The next day, God populates two topographic realms, water and sky, with "swarms of teeming, living creatures" and "birds that fly." Curiously, fish are absent on Day Five. They do not appear by name until the sixth day. Perhaps this ambiguity, like the seeds of Day Three, allude to reproduction.

Biblical culture often linked water to devastation and chaos through images of the flood and, as in Habakkuk 3:8–15, sea monsters. But water was also rejuvenating, cleansing, and rebirthing. For example, the Nile famously saved Moses, and the Israelites waded through the Red Sea to freedom, whence they washed their clothes in preparation for the Sinaic revelation (Exodus 19:10). The Torah repeatedly mentions watery purification, especially in Leviticus.[5] Throughout Genesis, desert cisterns were sites of betrothal, miraculous nourishment, and conflict. If biblical water sometimes symbolized uterine fertility, then the presence of water in the myth of Creation, however necessary for verisimilitude, calls into question the creative primacy of a male God.

From this angle, we can turn to the missing fish. God created two categories of sea life on Day Five: "the great sea monsters," which evoke serpents, "and all the living creatures of every kind that creep [or teem, glide] which the waters brought forth in swarms." Biblical "swarms" tend to refer to insects, small reptiles, and other creatures that abundantly breed. Fish do seem to fit the bill, but these other animals, unlike fish, are largely prohibited by the later dietary code of Leviticus (11:29–43). Something seems amiss.

In later Jewish folklore, fish symbolize sexuality and fertility (e.g., B. Yoma 75a). This association may arise from a blessing in Genesis 48:16, which includes the phrase "May they multiply like fish in the midst of the land." Fish became a favorite Sabbath meal, a night when the rabbis recommended conjugal intercourse (Scholem 1965:43 n. 2; Chill 1979:111–12). Fish also symbolize the male reproductive organ (Patai 1945:208–9). If any of these meanings were relevant to the composers of Genesis, then the absent fish on Day Five may hint at the wider ambiguity concerning reproduction, and especially men, in biblical culture.

Day Six: The Limits of Male Birth

Cross-culturally, the ritual and mythic symbolism of manhood often reveals a desire to assert, mirror, and control female fertility and birth. This "womb envy," as Margaret Mead (1949) called it, is particularly pronounced in kinship-based societies where birth typically defines significant roles and relationships, such as clan and lineage affiliation. These societies pose a paradox for men since displays of male privilege and power are contested or counterbalanced by the reality of female childbearing. To overcome this dilemma, men symbolically assert that they and not women are ultimately responsible for reproduction.[6] With this in mind, let us return to Genesis. On the sixth day of creation, God attends to terrestrial creatures. He concocts three categories of land dwellers: cattle, creeping things (the same word that earlier referred to sea life), and wild beasts. This anomalous tripartite scheme foreshadows a cosmic disruption.

Further rupture in the binary fabric of Creation occurs during the birth of humanity (Genesis 1:26–28). "Let us make a human in our image, after our likeness," announces God. "They shall rule" the animals. Then "God created the human in his image, in the image of God he created him, male and female he created them." Finally, "God blessed them" and said famously, "Be fruitful and multiply and fill the earth."

Until now, God in Genesis operated as a peerless, masculine, cosmic singularity who effortlessly birthed the world. But as God prepares to create humanity, he utters a discordant statement: "Let *us* make a human in *our* image." At no other time during Creation does God invite the participation of others. Only during the birth of humanity does he seek partners. Who are they? Classic rabbis and modern scholars propose a variety of answers: a divine court, the Torah, angels, all of God's creation, vestiges of polytheism as reflected by God's plural name, and so forth. In my view, these responses overlook a key issue. The juxtaposition of the unknown plural with a unitary God further extends the dialectic between unity and duality. More important, the word "our" refers not to creatures or things but to a central predicament of masculine monotheism.

During the first five days, God amply, even limitlessly, demonstrated his ability to beget the world. But when God attempts to create humanity, he suddenly appears infertile or impotent. The biblical fiction of exclusive masculine creation, often called androgenesis, reaches the limits of plausibility. Genesis acknowledges its own failure. God requires a female. Of course, any explicit acknowledgment of God's dependence on a female partner diminishes divine omnipotence. God's masculine potency pales before the power of motherhood. In short, human creation subverts the ideology of biblical monotheism.

Women during gestation and birth transform their singular bodies into the mother–child duality. From one emerges two. This model of birth explains the binary pattern of the Genesis cosmogony. It also marginalizes men. For a male deity to assert omnipotence, then, he must claim uterine powers lest the female body undermine his monotheistic existence.

The rabbis explicitly imagined cosmic creation in terms of conception, birth, and uterine fertility (e.g., ER 15:22). God created the world "just as a child is born to a woman. . . . The formation of the embryo is like the formation of the world" (T-Y Exodus 11:3).[7] From one angle, this rhetorical flourish allows a male God and, by extension, men to incorporate female capacities within their own masculine bodies. From another angle, the persistence of uterine imagery attests to the inability of men to reproduce themselves and their social world in the absence of women. The Genesis creation of humanity, I contend, like circumcision, sustains and subverts the fiction of parturient masculinity.

Circumcision, promised God to Abraham, ensures male progeny. Of course, circumcision alone will not result in sons. Men must also unite with women. Likewise, God himself could only birth humanity with the assistance of others—women, really—a dependence Genesis and circumcision only begrudgingly admit.

The Gender of Humanity

In popular thought, God's first human in Genesis 1 was a man. Yet this reading is misleading. Although the Hebrew word for the human, *'adam*, is a masculine noun, many recent scholars argue that grammatical gender does not in this instance reflect anatomy. They translate *'adam* as "human" (Alter 1996), "it" (Kimelman 1998), "humankind" (Trible 1978), and "Earth-creature" (Boyarin 1993:36). Despite the dominance of men in ancient Israel, writes Bird (1981:151), maleness was "not an essential or defining characteristic" of humanity. The first human was a genderless androgyne.

For proof, let us examine closely Genesis 1:27. "God created the *human* in his image, in the image of God he created *him, male and female* he created *them.*" Notice how the masculofeminine "human," as Meeks (1973:185) calls it, seemingly splits into "male and female." The rabbis agreed. "When man was created," says midrash (LR 14:1), "he was created with two body fronts, and he [God] sawed him in two, so that two bodies resulted, one for the male and one for the female" (see also B. Berachot 61a; B. Erubin 18b; GR 7; 8:1; Ibn Ezra 1:27).[8] Unity begets duality. The creation of humanity mirrors the prior unfolding of the cosmos. More significant, the doubled gender of the first human suggests an originary state of egalitarianism. Yet the androgynous view of the first "human," however much it conforms to liberal sensibilities, including my own, is no less misleading than the more naive belief that the first human was biologically male. Throughout Genesis, God takes on a masculine gender and tone. Since the first human was created in the deity's image, it seems reasonable to interpret the initial gender of humanity as androgynous *and* masculine. Divine maleness encompassed "male and female" (Trible 1978:15–21). God's masculine gender reflected and legitimated the official dominance of men in politics and religion, while God's androgyny lent expression not to a muted sense of equality but to male envy of birth.

Some readers may object to this interpretation. To the ancient Israelites, writes Bird (1981:147–48), the idea of a sexed God was "an utterly foreign and repugnant notion." But I contend that no religious mythology speaks with a unified or unitary voice. For the composers of Genesis, God was male *and* female, phallic *and* uterine, sustaining *and* subverting his own moral order. The very same notion of parturient masculinity, in all its irreducible paradox, coupled to the very same dialectic between unity and duality, explains much about circumcision.

Day Seven: The Holiness of Creation

On Day Seven, "the heaven and the earth were finished," and God rested. The deity called the seventh day "holy." Why holy? Linguistically, Hebrew holiness implies "keeping distinct the categories of creation" (Douglas 1966:49–53). By resting, God separated the seventh day from the other six days of his cosmogonic toils.

The Israelites were also "holy." They were set apart from others (Leviticus 20:26). Circumcision contributed to this societal and cosmological holiness. The eighth-day performance of the rite, if not the physical outcome, separated the Israelites—mainly men, of course—from their ethnic neighbors. Even the actual procedure would seem to symbolize holiness and cosmic creation. By separating the foreskin from the penis, circumcision divides a male unity to engender masculine wholeness (see also Róheim 1945:22–23, 1955:195). This symbolism, too, evokes the division of the original androgyny into man and woman. In multiple ways, then, circumcision directly builds on the mythic creation of the world and humanity.

The Sabbath, Couvade, and Circumcision

The inaugural Sabbath afforded God a respite from his creative labors. Through comparison with other Near Eastern mythologies, the first humans in Genesis were perhaps created to cultivate God's food (Batto 1992:50–53). In this view, God rested on the Sabbath because he could.

Let me suggest an alternative interpretation. God announced the Sabbath immediately after creating humanity. He birthed, then rested. In many cultures, new or expectant fathers dramatize aspects of childbirth in rites known as couvade. Men may enter confinement, receive gifts and care, rest from work, and even pantomime delivery. Dundes (1983) argues that the biblical Sabbath is a form of couvade, which he traces to male envy of uterine fertility.

Men in ancient Israel dominated politics, law, social structure, and religion. Legitimate power was masculine. The Hebrew Bible refers to the "God of your fathers," not mothers (Eilberg-Schwartz 1994:83). In most biblical genealogies, fathers beget sons; mothers and daughters receive scant mention. God commanded both man and woman to "be fruitful and multiply" (Genesis 1:28). But the Torah, especially through circumcision, shifts this reproductive responsibility mainly onto men and male ritual.

The ancient Israelites, like the later rabbis, almost exclusively relied on birth to reproduce the community. Conversion and other social conventions were insignificant. Most Jews are born Jews. But the covenant, as I have said, associates fertility and reproduction mainly with men. The father–son relationship and male ritual such as circumcision eclipse motherhood as men seek to overcome their inability to directly reproduce society. But this yearning remains largely unconscious. For if men articulated outright a desire for uterine fertility, they would acknowledge the primacy of women and contravene the dominant ideology of manhood.

The Sabbath, I suggest after Dundes (1983), is a form of couvade, a type of laying-in that allowed God to rest after delivering humanity. Circumcision is another type of couvade (see also Boyarin 1992:496–97; 1994; Wolfson 1995). Only its symbolism is more apparent. Circumcision is a male-centered ceremony that closely follows birth. The rite does not, like the Sabbath, allow men to mirror postpartum motherhood. Rather, circumcision emulates birth and menstruation. Although I develop this theme in the next few chapters, some preliminary remarks are in order.

In the Torah and rabbinic Judaism, as in many cultures, the genital blood of circumcision is purifying, redemptive, and sacred. Circumcision welcomes a boy into the community. By contrast, menstrual blood and birthing fluids are polluting. They exclude women from the community. Circumcision, I contend, inverts the negative qualities associated with the reproductive aspects of the female body. Through symbolic projection, the boy's bleeding penis represents his father's successful ability to birth a son. The rite, too, guarantees the boy's future reproductive potential.

The Torah prohibits work on the Sabbath (Leviticus 23:3; Dundes 2002). In rabbinic law, the Sabbath constrains nearly all rituals and festivals. Even burial, which normally occurs within twenty-four hours after death, must pause for the Sabbath. The only rite that *regularly* annuls Sabbath prohibitions is circumcision (see also chapter 7).[9] The only thing Jews can cut on the day of rest is the prepuce (B. Yoma 73a). This exemption is hardly trivial. A Sabbath violator, commands the Torah, "shall be put to death . . . cut off from among his kin" (Exodus 32:14). The same fate awaits many other violators of biblical law, including Israelites who forsake circumcision: they, too, are "cut off" (Genesis 17). Yet one who cuts off foreskins on the Sabbath is *not* "cut off." Rather, he cuts boys *into* the community.

A man born on the Sabbath, declares the Talmud (B. Shabbath 156a), will die on the Sabbath. Why? Because his birth "desecrated" this "great day." Yet *ritual* birth from men, or couvade such as circumcision, never desecrates the Sabbath, only birth from women.

The Erotic Sabbath and Circumcision

By the Talmudic era, the rabbis required husbands to make love to their wives on the Sabbath eve (B. Ketuboth 62b, 65b; B. Baba Kamma 88a). During the week, pious men attended only to their studies. On the Sabbath, they embraced bodily desire. Since humanity was created in God's image, any failure to be "fruitful and multiply" necessarily diminished "the divine likeness" (GR 17:2). To the rabbis and mystics, argue many scholars (Boyarin 1993:46 n. 27), sexual intercourse resembled the *imago dei*.

Judaism is a bodily, sexual religion. In fact, rabbinic law interpreted two biblical passages as mandating a wife's legal entitlement to regular, nonreproductive intercourse and presumably orgasm (Exodus 21:7–11; Deuteronomy 24:5; B. Ketuboth 61b–62b; Boyarin 1993:chap. 5; Satlow 1995:chap. 7). The best assurance against illicit temptation was not carnal renunciation, the path chosen by early Christianity, but the promotion of sexuality within marriage. Since a husband's erotic obligations to his wife are distinct from God's command to procreate in Genesis 1, rabbinic culture could never outright condemn pleasurable sexuality (D. Biale 1997:80). Contemporary opponents of circumcision often interpret the rite as an attempt by traditional Judaism to impair pleasurable eroticism (see chapter 10). They err.[10] Rabbinic Judaism, like *all* cultures, offered an ambivalent view of human sexuality (D. Biale 1997). Not surprisingly, this ambivalence shapes circumcision.

Despite the prominence of female deities and cosmic copulations in the ancient world, Israelite monotheism precluded the existence of any such sexuality or goddesses. Nonetheless, rabbinic and mystical devotion often centered on images of intimacy. The goal of prayer was to unite with a female personification of God, called the Shekhinah. She was particularly attracted to circumcised men (see also chapter 6).[11] Rabbinic scholars consummated this mystical seduction on the Sabbath, when they slept with their wives. In so doing, they also united with the Sabbath (B. Shabbath 119a; Zohar ii:63b), whom Jews view as a beautiful queen, and allowed the male and female aspects of the godhead to come together (Ginsburg 1989:101–21; D. Biale 1997:chap. 5). In rabbinic culture, sexuality achieved wholeness.

The central text of mystical Judaism, called the Zohar, links Sabbath sexuality to circumcision. Isaiah 56:4–5 reads, "For thus said the Lord: As for the eunuchs who keep My sabbaths. . . . And hold fast to My covenant—I will give them . . . an everlasting name that shall not be cut off." The mystics interpreted these "eunuchs" as Talmudic scholars who shun their wives during the week to enjoy the male fellowship of textual study. On the Sabbath, however, these scholars turn to their wives (Zohar ii:89a, iii:82a; see D. Biale 1997:111).[12] The phrase "hold fast to My covenant" refers to the circumcised penis as a symbol of the phallic godhead. Mystically, pious men clasp God's penis. Circumcision here exhibits heterosexual and homoerotic tones, allowing devout men to join intimately with their wives as well as with God.

In Kabbalah, the mark of circumcision often symbolized the procreative potential of God (Scholem 1961:227; Wolfson 1987a:101–2, 1995:99–101). When men on the Sabbath united with their wives, human reproduction gained religious significance. At the same time, the mystical union between God and man denied yet obviously acknowledged the vital role of women in cosmic reproduction.

In this chapter, I offered three precise arguments. First, I paralleled circumcision with the binary structure of Creation in Genesis. More important, I introduced the thesis that circumcision expresses male envy of female fertility and parturition and enacts a wide-ranging ambivalence toward human sexuality. The quintessential rite of biblical and Jewish manhood is modeled after the female body. Finally, I started to build my case that the overt heterosexual orientation of circumcision often reveals a homoerotic countercurrent. I now turn to the creation of woman from the legendary "rib." This bodily extraction, much like circumcision, created a whole man who was really a type of woman.

Notes

1. All highlighting of biblical and religious texts reflects my own emphasis.

2. Some rabbis attributed the destruction of the First Temple in the sixth century B.C.E. to a lapse in circumcision (Ginzberg 1909–1938:IV:296, VI:388 n. 16).

3. The fourteenth-century text *Baal HaTurim* parses the first word of the Torah, *bereshit* ("In the beginning"), into "covenant" (*berit*) and "fire" (*esh*), or circumcision and the Torah (see Jeremiah 23:29), both of which offer salvation from hell. (Source: *The Torah:*

With the Baal HaTurim's Classic Commentary Translated, Annotated, and Elucidated by Rabbi Avie Gold [Brooklyn, N.Y.: Mesorah, 1999].)

4. The Torah in the Talmud is a female breast (B. Eruvin 54b).

5. Rabbinic Judaism prescribed ritual baths (*mikvah*) in connection with conversion, intercourse, certain festivals, and especially menstruation (Wasserfall 1999).

6. See also Bettelheim (1954), Meigs (1984), and Silverman (2001).

7. In mystical Judaism or Kabbalah, God etched the universe into existence through phallic writing on a cosmic "female principle" (Wolfson 1994b:178–80).

8. For centuries, Western science understood human anatomy not as two sexes, male and female, but as one sex, male, which became female through inverted yet stilted gestation (Laqueur 1990).

9. The Talmud, however, admonishes Jews to delay circumcision to inter corpses that would otherwise lie unburied (B. Megilah 3b).

10. For a popular version of Jewish sexuality, see Westheimer and Mark (1995).

11. Yet the Shekhinah shuns the circumcised man who "profanes . . . the sign of the covenant" by cohabiting with menstruating and non-Jewish women (Zohar ii:3a–b).

12. Actual eunuchs were forbidden membership in the Israelite community (Deuteronomy 23:2).

CHAPTER TWO

Covenantal Corporeality; or,
Was Adam Circumcised?

Bodies pose fundamental problems for biblical and rabbinic cultures. Divine incorporeality is a central tenet of monotheism. But this issue is fraught with paradox (Eilberg-Schwartz 1994). How can a bodiless God create humanity after the divine image? Conversely, how can humanity emulate an incorporeal deity and still obey God's command to be fruitful and multiply? And why would a disembodied God mark his covenant in men's flesh?

Rabbinic culture contained a similar tension by positioning men between the "contradictory demands of marriage and commitment to study the Torah" (Boyarin 1993:134). While Jewish history does contain ascetic traditions, renunciation was never a real option. Any abandonment of flesh would violate God's first charge to humanity. At the same time, unfettered sexuality was no better.

In this chapter, I explore tensions surrounding circumcision that arise from the idea of God's body and from the broader importance of corporeality in biblical and rabbinic cultures. I also continue to discuss gender and reproduction, focusing on the Genesis 2 creation of woman from the first human's rib, an unnatural birth that presages circumcision.

The Divine Physique and Biblical Manhood

The doctrine of a bodiless God arises more from Hellenistic Greek philosophy than from biblical culture (Eilberg-Schwartz 1994:73–74). In Hellenistic or Platonic dualism, mind is superior to body. Ultimate reality is nonmaterial. The physical world and sensory experiences are therefore illusory. This outlook achieved hegemony through the spread of early Christianity (Boyarin 1993:71). It defines the person as an eternal, pure soul seeking liberation from a mortal, loathsome body. The goal of life is achieved in death.

The Torah and most Jewish traditions define the person not as soul trapped in a body but as a body animated by a soul. Corporeal life, not bodiless death, matters most. Hence, God marks his covenant not through the resurrection of a heavenly son and the promise of spiritual rebirth but through a fleshy incision in mortal man that leads to the birth of sons.

Although the rabbis eventually absorbed a moderate form of Hellenistic dualism,[1] they rarely debased flesh. The moral status of the body hinged on what you did with it (Epstein 1948:chap. 1). Adultery is sinful, for example. Sabbath sexuality is not. To curb bodily excesses, the rabbis sought to circumscribe desire, not eradicate it, within an ethical system. This approach to human sexuality is best represented by circumcision, a rite that literally encircles the penis within the Law.

But what about the body of God? The Hebrew Bible offers myriad glimpses of the divine physique (Eilberg-Schwartz 1994; Gottstein 1994). Among God's many features are feet, hands, eyes, ears, nostrils, mouth, hair, face, and even his backside (Exodus 33:23). Divine corporeality was an essential element of Israelite cosmology. Yet God's body posed certain paradoxes.

The ideal roles assigned to biblical men were those of father, husband, king, and warrior. Behaviors that threatened these masculine ideals were strictly prohibited, including same-gender sexual relations (Leviticus 18:22; 20:13) and cross-dressing (Deuteronomy 22:5). Curiously, the Torah never condemns sexual relations between women. But the rabbis did so by looking to Leviticus 18:3, which warns the Israelites against imitating the Egyptians and Canaanites (Satlow 1995:88–91). Even so, the rabbis and ancient Israelites display concern mainly with defining the conventions of manhood, not femininity. Men were the real problem.

Like men, God in the Hebrew Bible is also a father, husband, king, and warrior. Divine roles legitimated biblical manhood. But these personifications of God also supplanted men, making them redundant, impotent, even useless (Eilberg-Schwartz 1994). Compared to women, Israelite men were dominant. They were men. Before God, however, Israelite men were less men. They were feminized.

When God said to Israel, "I will take you to be My people" (Exodus 7:1), he evoked a vow of marriage (Fox 1995:287). To whom was God speaking? To women? Not likely. In the main, Israelite society defined itself as a community of men. Leadership, religious authority, and even the social structure were all gendered as male. When God married Israel, he wedded men.

The Hebrew Bible often refers to Israel—principally men—as a woman. The prophetic literature equates the relationship between God and Israel with conjugal sex (e.g., Isaiah 62:5). Throughout Song of Songs, God and Israel embrace like naked lovers. Sometimes Israel clings to God's loins (Jeremiah 13:8–11; Eilberg-Schwartz 1994:102). At other times the deity withdraws (Hosea 5:6; Carmichael 1977:330). "My body yearns for You," sings Israel in Psalm 69:2–9, "I sing praises with joyful lips, when I call You to mind upon my bed." In these erotic passages, a male God unites sexually with Israelite men—men defined as men and as women.

The homoerotic relationship between God and man seemingly clashes with divine Law. The Torah censured homoeroticism, or at least a particular type of homoerotic encounter. "Do not," declares Leviticus 18:22 and 20:13, "lie with a male as one lies with a woman." This careful phrasing bans not homosexuality *in toto* but merely a single erotic practice, what the rabbis understood as male anal intercourse (Satlow 1995:chap. 5). This particular penetration violated two aspirations of biblical masculinity. First, the practice could not result in the birth of male offspring. Second, anal intercourse among men, as Leviticus makes clear, shamefully feminized the recipient (see also GR 63:10; Satlow 1995:213). Symbolically, homoeroticism transformed aggressive men who should sire sons into infertile and passive women.

The feminization of biblical men sometimes turns misogynistic. The prophets compared immoral and idolatrous Israelites "to a mangled, mutilated, ravished, raped, nude female body" (Weems 1995:66). God often chastised Israel as a whore, harlot, lecherous fornicator, and unfaithful wife (e.g., Isaiah 1:21; Jeremiah 2:20; Exodus 34:15; Hosea 4:12–15; Eilberg-Schwartz 1994:98–99). In one chilling passage, God threatened to lift Israel's skirt "over your face, And your shame shall be seen" (Jeremiah 13:15–26; see also Isaiah 47:3; Hosea 2:12; Nahum 3:5). In Ezekiel 16, God bedecked Israel with beautiful jewels and apparel. But Israel fashioned these gifts into "phallic images and fornicated with them . . . spread[ing] your legs to every passerby." God reacted with "bloody and impassioned fury."

This misogyny, argues Weems (1995), comments on the vulnerability of women in ancient Israelite society. I suggest another possibility. Biblical men feared feminization even as they envied uterine fertility. When this desire failed, as it must, envy gave way to rage. For this reason, Israel's transgressions were gendered as female and so aroused the hypermasculine fury of God.

Phallic Invisibility

God's masculinity legitimated male dominance yet also cast men aside as superfluous. Toward evading this paradox, argues Eilberg-Schwartz (1994), the Hebrew Bible bans divine images (Exodus 20:4). Scripture also, aside from a single reference to divine "loins" (Ezekiel 1:27), omits mention of God's penis and beard, two quintessentially masculine traits in the ancient world.[2] No man would see or even ponder God's penis.

The biblical deity clearly valued circumcision. But he expressed no interest in seeing naked men. Exposed genitals were banned from the alter and sacred precincts (Exodus 20:23; 28:42–43). Rabbinic law likewise forbids naked devotion (KSA 5:17). At the very least, a praying man should separate his penis and head with a belt or sash. The God who commanded circumcision wanted neither to see man's penis nor to expose his own.

The absence of God's phallus is no less dissonant than its presence. An emasculated or incorporeal deity implies that man only partly reflects the divine image. (Actually, this possibility implies something else: that *woman* is the true likeness of God!) That the biblical covenant is marked in the penis would seem to celebrate the phallic authority of man and God. But the invisibility of God's penis, like the actual cut of circumcision, symbolically threatens to castrate the very potency that defines human and divine manhood against femininity.

Biblical culture, writes Eilberg-Schwartz (1994), marginalized women not because they were alien to a male God. Rather, women and *not* men were God's fitting partner, especially in regard to covenantal reproduction, erotic intimacy, and the overall stress in biblical culture on male–female complementarity. Men responded to this alienation by dominating the religious system and denigrating the female body—the very body they envied. The penis alone, not some part of the female form, became suitable for the fertile "sign" of the covenant. But circumcision unmans men by flirting with castration and emulating uterine fertility, menstruation, and birth.

Insofar as circumcision symbolically detaches the penis, Israelite and Jewish men resemble an incorporeal God. Insofar as circumcision unleashes male "seed," men resemble a phallic deity. But circumcision also, continues Eilberg-Schwartz, allows men to do the one thing a bodiless God can never do, namely, procreate. Of course, another creature lacks a penis yet remains procreative: woman.

Human Creation, Again

Genesis 2 details a second creation of humanity. Why the redundancy? Most scholars assign Genesis 1 to the priestly source, a literary stratum of the Torah composed sometime after the Babylonian exile. Genesis 2 dates to the earlier compositions of the so-called Yahwist, sometime during the eighth to tenth centuries B.C.E. But more than chronology is at stake here.

The opening phrase of Genesis 2, "Lord God made earth and heaven," inverts the dual cosmos of Genesis 1, where God created "heaven and earth." This reversal foreshadows some disruption. The next sentence contains the first negative statement in the Torah, organized as two dualities: "no shrub . . . was yet on earth and no grasses . . . had yet sprouted." Why no growth? Because "the Lord God had not sent rain upon the earth and there was no human ('adam) to till the soil" (Genesis 2:5). Most recent interpreters understand this creature to represent a generic, nongendered humanity. But since men likely tilled the ancient soil, the early cosmos specifically lacked male labor. Indeed, the word 'adam will shortly denote a biological man (Genesis 2:25) who will eventually gain the name Adam. In Genesis 2, I propose, the human tiller called 'adam is a masculine androgyne.

In the absence of tilling, a "flow [wetness, surge] would well up from the ground and water the whole surface of the earth" (Genesis 2:6). Is there sexual symbolism here? The rabbis thought so. To them, the earth became "fruitful like a bride who conceives from her first husband" (PRE 5). No longer does Genesis emphasize that separation as wet and dry, interior and surface, male and female all combine into the fecund "dust of the earth." God molds this mixture into the first human, then animates the creature with "breath of life."[3]

Creative Naming

During the first six days of creation, said the rabbis, God made only pure creatures, not hybrids such as mules (GR 82:14). Apparently, the rabbis forgot about the human. This blended creature threatened to rupture any stable sense of cosmic order—and any stable sense of masculinity.

After planting "a garden in Eden," God grows trees that satisfy two modes of sensory delight, sight and taste. In the middle of the garden is a second arboreal category, itself a duality: the "tree of life" and the binary "tree of knowledge of good and bad." God places his human in the garden "to till it and tend it." The idea of a lone human cultivating the source of "his" own body suggests an image of self-reproduction. But this harvest was, with one exception, fruitless. The premier human did, as a male androgyny, success-fully birth woman. But he did so *only* to unite sexually with her. This way, Genesis expresses a masculine yearning for androgenesis while acknowledg-ing the necessity of uterine fertility.

God offers the human "every fruit of the garden" except for the "tree of knowledge of good and bad" lest the human die (Genesis 2:17). God then registers a second negative or absence in Eden, declaring the human's soli-tude "not good" (Genesis 2:18). To gain him a sustainer, God forms the ani-mals, which the human names. This naming echoes God's creative ability to speak the world into existence in Genesis 1. It also anticipates later biblical incidents of naming and especially renaming, as during the circumcision covenant in Genesis 17. Men in ancient Israel preserved their "names" through the birth of sons or male "seed" (Deuteronomy 25:6; Eilberg-Schwartz 1994:127). By naming the animals, the first human also anticipated this patriarchal obligation—a task shortly assisted by fertile circumcision.

The Circumcised Birth of Woman

When none of the animals sustained the human, God created the first woman, Eve, called *Chava* in Hebrew. She was born from a double negative, specifically, divine failure to remedy the first human's "not good" loneliness. In one midrash, the premier man tried unsuccessfully to copulate with the animals (GR 17:4; B. Yevamoth 63a). Only then did God create woman. The rabbis recognized well the reproductive dilemma of a lone human.

God induces the premier human into a deep slumber, extracts a body part called *tsel'a*, and fashions it into "woman" (Genesis 2:21–22). Linguistically, this "woman" (*'ishshah*) is an unambiguous adult female. But what kind of creature was the human from whence she came? In my view, "he" was an androgynous male, a type of pregnant man.

The withdrawal of a body part transformed the first human into a com-plete sexual and gendered adult (Trible 1983). Only through bodily loss did the masculine androgyne become wholly male. *Circumcision parallels the cre-ation of woman* (see also Reik 1960). The rite detaches the foreskin to reshape a feminine boy, as I will later describe him, into a fully male person who is now, as God said in Genesis 17, "whole." The rabbis *never* viewed circumcision as a mutilation. Instead, the rite perfected the male body (chapter 4). Ironically, this image of masculine perfection emulates woman.

The removal of the foreskin, states the covenant, also enables now-whole men to sire children. Similarly, the extraction of the rib, when fashioned into woman, allowed the first man to reproduce sexually. By replicating the primal creation of woman, circumcision, to repeat, models manhood after female fertility.

God, said the rabbis in midrash, fretted about a possible error of cosmic proportions (PRE 12). What if the animals mistakenly viewed Adam as the Creator? To prevent this blasphemy, God made Eve so the animals would see Adam in the act of intercourse, something God himself would never do! To the rabbis, in other words, God affirmed the male prerogative of asexual creation by creating woman and heterosexuality.

Linguistically, God in Genesis 2 shaped the first human from something soft, then "built" woman from the hard body part called *tsel'a* (Alter 1996:9). This word variously refers to a beam, plank, side, panel, and corner. *Tsel'a* also connotes an anatomical and architectural "rib." Readers who aspire to a nonsexist cosmos often prefer "side." I favor "rib," not because I wish to endorse monotheistic patriarchy but because the phallic connotations of this bone best fit the masculine dilemmas that are so integral to Genesis.

The "rib," I contend, represents an upward displacement of the male generative organ. Even the rabbis traced Eve's origin to Adam's "most private limb, from the thigh" (DR 11:11). I note, too, along with Bal (1985:323), that the vague penile allusion in Genesis 2 is no more euphemistic than the biblical use of "feet" for genitals (e.g., Judges 3:24; 1 Samuel 24:4; Ruth 3:4; Carmichael 1977:329; Eilberg-Schwartz 1994:78).[4] As a phallic rendition of birth, the creation of women from the parturient rib anticipates, if not establishes, the suitability of the penis as the site for circumcision.

From one angle, woman's birth symbolically emasculated the first human—much like circumcision. From another, woman's existence, again like circumcision, allowed biblical men to assert reproductive significance. Indeed, the image of the first human's "rib" disappearing inside woman evokes sexual intercourse. Both circumcision and woman, in this view, threaten yet validate the generative potential of man.

My interpretation of the "rib" as the male reproductive organ conforms to the overall theme of male birth in Genesis. The first man did not emerge from woman, as we might expect. Rather, woman emerged from man, specifically, from a boney detachment.[5] A fabled quest of medieval science was misdirected. Man does not contain one less rib than woman, a fallacy exposed by the sixteenth-century anatomist Andreas Vesalius in *De Humani Corporis Fabrica Libri Septem*.[6] Theologians were looking in the wrong place. The Edenic rib represents the penis—a uterine phallus, more precisely—the same organ to shortly represent the covenant.

Foreskinned Femininity

A Talmudic seminar on the ritual status of foreskinned men equates the prepuce with ambiguous sexuality (B. Yevamoth 70a–72b; Kraemer 1996). The gender of the uncircumcised is uncertain. Yet Genesis 2 evidences an idea of foreskinned femininity that long pre-dated the rabbis. For however much the creation of woman celebrated the reproductive potency of the phallus, the myth also demonstrates why biblical men must undergo circumcision.

Genesis 17 links masculine wholeness or completion to the removal of the foreskin. Why? Recall that God mixed the first androgynous human from dryness and moisture, or male and female. Yet the rest of the cosmos was born through separation and division. Circumcision, then, removes the feminine prepuce from the male body to remedy the blended origin of humanity, trims the male body into conformity with the cosmos, and mirrors birth.

Many cultures identify foreskins and precircumcised boys with femininity, women, and mothers (e.g., Beidelman 1964). In northern Sudan, where the prepuce encloses the penis in a feminine "veil," male circumcision exposes a boy's phallic masculinity (Boddy 1982:688). Throughout the Middle East, men scorn the foreskin as a sign of undesirable femininity (Granqvist 1947:207; Ammar 1954:121). Cross-cultural data thus support my view of biblical circumcision as symbolically separating female from male.

Psychoanalysts and anthropologists since Freud (1905) offer an explanation for this symbolism (see Silverman 2001). Two characteristics of early childhood in many societies are remote fathers and maternal intimacy. Consequently, girls and boys develop an initial female identity. Eventually, boys must renounce this femininity and identify with men, a process frequently enacted by traumatic initiation rites, which often include circumcision. The ceremony eliminates a physical symbol of the boy's feminine and maternal infancy (Róheim 1942; Nunberg 1949:145–46). These adolescent rites sear through blood and pain a masculine identity into the boy's psyche.

Of course, biblical circumcision occurs in infancy. In this case, I propose, the rite has two levels of meaning. On the one hand, circumcision swaps a boy's femininity for the promise of procreative manhood. On the other hand, the bloody pain is a form of couvade that represents the father's birth pangs. All told, the biblical rite celebrates the parturient vigor of manhood.

Procreative Wind and Mud

The myths of Genesis further reveal a theme of male parturition. Here are two examples. The first account of Creation concludes, "These are the generations (*toldot*) of heaven and earth when they were created" (Genesis 2:4). Nearly all other occurrences of the word "generations" in the Hebrew Bible refer to male descendants (e.g., Genesis 5:1, 10:1). Creation is tantamount to fathering sons. Moreover, when God created humanity after the divine "likeness" and "image," he anticipated the siring of male heirs since Adam begets Seth "in his likeness after his image" (Genesis 5:3). Here, again, divine creation parallels paternal procreation.

In Genesis 2, God molds the human from the "dust" or "trash" of the ground. The Hebrew Bible often equates womb and earth (e.g., Jeremiah 20:17; Psalm 139; Job 33:6). Jews and Muslims tell a tale in which an angel stole handfuls of mud from the maternal earth for God to mold into the first human (Rappoport 1928:I:141–42). This legend attributes the creative power of a male deity to a violation and usurpation of motherhood. The same theme, I am arguing, albeit in a muted form, weaves throughout Genesis.

Androcentric cosmologies often transform vaginal parturition into male bodily idioms (Dundes 1962, 1976; Silverman 2001). Cosmogonic clods, dust, soil, and dirt often represent feces to symbolize male anal birth. This way, gods create the cosmos by mirroring the emergence of a newborn from its mother. The parallelism between vaginal birth from women and anal exudations from men might offend some readers. But religious symbolism takes little notice of bourgeois etiquette. Mythic and ritual themes of anal fecundity allow men to emulate women and beget life.

A wind at the beginning of Genesis "hovers," "flutters," or "broods" over the primal waters. This image, after Deuteronomy 32:11, connotes birth and nurture (Alter 1996:3). God also breathes life into his first human. Both the "wind" and the breath are masculine agents of parturition. Isaiah 26:18 confirms this interpretation. There, the anguished Israelites resemble "a woman with child approaching childbirth, Writhing and screaming in her pangs . . . as though we had given birth to wind." Throughout global folklore and myth, winds impregnate animals (Zirkle 1936), women (Silverman 2001:chap. 4), and even, according to the Catholic Church and the Koran, the Virgin Mary. Cosmogonic wind symbolizes procreative flatus (Jones 1914; Dundes

1976). In Genesis, wind and mud transform heterosexual conception and uterine birth into an exclusive, anal idiom of masculinity.

Normally, human excrement in the Hebrew Bible is defiling, putrid, and insulting (e.g., Isaiah 4:4; Proverbs 30:12). Even God avoids stepping in it (Deuteronomy 23:14). A meal of feces punishes the sinful (2 Kings 18:27; Isaiah 36:12; Ezekiel 4:12). The rabbis expressed great concern about contaminating the sacred with shit (see Dundes 2002). They forbid flatulence while wearing phylacteries and prohibited prayer in the presence of uncovered feces, beneath soiled toilets in multistoried buildings, or when "there is a small particle of excrement in the anal orifice" (KSA 10:22). The manna fed by God to the Israelites was the food of angels (Ginzberg 1909–1938:III:246). It failed to produce feces.

During the creation of the first human, rubbish became reproductive. Conversely, the covenant construes Abraham's seminal "seed" as mere "dust" (Genesis 13:16; 28:14). Ordinarily, dust is contrary to nourishment. Shit is not seed. Yet male claims to reproduction often invert female parturition to displace uterine fertility with masculine fecundity.[7] Vaginal substances become defiling, as I detail in chapter 5, while male excrement gains procreative powers.

Lactating Manhood

While God in the Hebrew Bible is overwhelmingly masculine, he nonetheless possesses feminine qualities and bodily attributes (see also Trible 1983). The deity screams in labor (Isaiah 42:13–14), likens his mysteries to gestation (Ecclesiastes 11:5), births the Israelites (Numbers 11:5; Isaiah 46:3), and soothes his people "as a mother comforts her son" (Isaiah 66:13). God even exceeds a mother's own feelings in Isaiah 49:15, asking, "Can a woman forget her baby, Or disown the child of her womb? Though she might forget, I never could forget you."

Yet God's motherliness often appears in masculine guise.[8] Moses calls him a "nursing-father" (Numbers 11:12). A common moniker for the biblical deity is El Shaddai, which most scholars trace to the Semitic term for "God," or El, and the Akkadian word for mountain, shadu. But D. Biale (1982) controversially translates this divine name as "God with the breasts" (D. Biale 1982). The same fertile, maternal, lactating deity demanded circumcision in Genesis 17, thus linking the covenant to phallic nurture.[9]

The rabbis were also taken by male images of breast-feeding. Rabbinic literature contains several accounts of pious men who miraculously suckled their children (e.g., B. Shabbath 53b). One Talmudic passage (or *sugya*) contains what Boyarin (1993:chap. 7) brilliantly interprets as grotesque, male renditions of caesarian birth and menstruation (B. Baba Metzia 83b–85a; Boyarin 1993:chap. 7). All this imagery, I submit, reveals anxiety over the relationship between masculinity and motherhood.

God and men in biblical and rabbinic cultures symbolically lactated, menstruated, and feigned birth in order to demonstrate procreative independence from motherhood. A legend about the infant Abraham illustrates this very theme (Ginzberg 1909–1938:I:201; Graves and Patai 1983:134–38; SH 8). While *in utero*, Abraham was shielded by his mother's breasts from a murderous king and then, after birth, abandoned for safety in a cave. For nourishment, Abraham suckled milk and honey from his own finger or that of the angel Gabriel (SH 68:4). In another legend, Israelite mothers secretly gave birth in the fields to escape Pharaoh, then entrusted their newborns to God (ER 1:12; 23:8). The deity placed two stones in the infants' hands, from which they sucked oil and honey. These tales of lactating masculinity demonstrate the male desire to escape from yet appropriate female nurture.

In one tale about male breast-feeding (GR 30:8), the rabbis added a curious comment from the Mishnah, "The milk of a male is clean" (Makshirin 6:7). The original Mishnaic passage discusses the impurity of woman's milk. Although there is some disagreement concerning the extent of this pollution, the existence of the defilement is never questioned. By contrast, men's milk is always "clean." These instances of masculine motherhood, I suggest, allowed men to boast sole responsibility for the reproduction and care of the community.

I know of no biblical or rabbinic tale in which a woman gains a man's body and substances. Jewish women in Europe did once seek to ease labor pains by donning their husbands' garments (Trachtenberg 1939:105). Yiddish devotional literature did once liken pious women to the High Priest (Weissler 1989). But these women, however much they swapped gender, still retained their bodily sex. They acquired no penis.

A old rabbinic fragment from Cairo offers a glimpse into the torments of hell (Lieberman 1974a:37). Jewish men guilty of having sex with Gentiles dangle by their genitals and reattached foreskins. More significantly, Israelite women hang "by threads/nipples on their breasts, because they used to uncover their hair and strip the sides of their garments and sit in the marketplace and suckle, and lead men into sin." Rabbinic culture celebrated the male embodiment of motherhood yet construed mothers who suckle in public as dangerously licentious. The same ambivalent combination of envy and rejection suffuses the creation of woman from man's rib, as well as circumcision, which are but one and the same event.

The Mockery of a Parturient Slumber

God placed the first human, prior to extracting the female rib, into a "deep sleep." This trance-like slumber reminded Reik (1960) of a classic male initiation ceremony in which neophytes are symbolically killed and reborn as men, often through physical ordeals such as circumcision. I see the "deep sleep" as allowing the first human, as a masculine androgyne, to beget woman in the absence of sexual intercourse. Since male birth and asexual reproduction are humanly impossible, the creature enters an equally unreal state of reality. The "deep sleep" sustains yet subverts uterine manhood.

Reik (1960) also argued that Genesis depicts the birth of woman from man to supplant an earlier Near Eastern religion in which humanity was born from the union of a mother-goddess and father-god. Historical considerations aside, Reik makes a valid point. Two males, God and man, assume the creative roles normally associated with women and goddesses. Circumcision conveys a similar message.

Normally, male initiation rites boast only that men can birth men. Genesis, said Reik (1960:128–31), communicates something different: men birth women. Through "biting sarcasm," Reik continued, Genesis "sneers at the mothers who want to keep their children for themselves on the undeniable grounds that they gave birth to the boys." I offer another possibility. If the myth sneers at anything, it is the idea that men birth life.

Unity and Duality

The creation of woman symbolically divided a male androgyny. But the phallic detachment of femininity created masculine wholeness through sexual intercourse. This pattern of unity and duality, or sameness and separation, is especially evident in the first man's speech after meeting the first woman: "This one at last, Is bone of my bones, And flesh of my flesh. This one shall be called woman (*'ishshah*), for from man (*'ish*) was this one taken" (Genesis 2:23). The tale concludes with a further affirmation of this dialectic, stating that "man leaves his father and mother and clings to his wife, so that they become one flesh."

Circumcision entails a similar process. God promised Abraham wholeness through the loss of his foreskin. The deity also granted Abraham fantastic fertility, a pledge that obviously implies sexual intercourse. Here, again, the creation of women anticipates circumcision.

Planting the Foreskin

Abrahamic circumcision swaps the prepuce for multitudinous "seed." This horticultural idiom recalls the third day of Creation, when the earth sprouted seed-bearing fruits and flora. Plant-like, the premier human contained male and female reproductive substances within its body. Unlike plants, though, the human underwent division into two sexes that must unite for procreation.

Generally speaking, men alone contain seed in the Hebrew Bible and rabbinic culture. "Seed" and "semen," as in many languages, are identical. Men actively implant both types of spore, as Delaney (1988:86, 1991:32–33) discusses for Muslim Turkey, in the passive uterine soil of woman and the earth.

After circumcision, Jews traditionally bury the foreskin. Some European synagogues contain a vessel of sand or dirt for this very purpose. American *mohels*, as Jewish circumcision specialists are called, may plant the foreskin in their own backyard or beneath a flower bed at the child's house. Another custom is for the parents to bury the prepuce beneath a sapling whose branches will later be trimmed to support the boy's marriage canopy. Many of these gestures connect arboreal and human growth.

The rabbis often dated preputial burial to the exodus from Egypt, when the Israelites wandered the desert, planting foreskins in the sand. Biblical allusions to this practice include God's rhetorical question in Numbers 23:10, "Who can count the dust of Jacob, Number the dust-cloud of Israel?" (PRE 29; Hoffman 1996:101–2); Abraham's self-deprecation, "I who am but dust and ashes" (Genesis 18:27); and God's promise to multiply the Israelites like "dust of the earth" (Genesis 13:15–16; Bloch 1980:11; Dobrinsky 1980:63). Many rabbis also see foreskin burial as a reminder of human mortality or a propitiatory offering to evil serpents that prey on children (Pollack 1971:24–25; Chill 1979:303; Brauer 1993:167). I propose a different interpretation, one that turns on the matter of "seed."

The covenant promised Abraham vast fertility and land. He loses a part of his penis yet gains seed and soil. When Jews bury foreskins, they evoke the sowing of seminal "seed" in Israelite wombs and the planting of agricultural semen in a land that will later "flow" or "ooze" with "milk and honey." The Torah contains no mention of burying foreskins. Yet this postbiblical custom overtly expresses the biblical notion that circumcision assures men of fruitfulness when they plant seed in uterine bodies.[10]

A biblical law governing the cultivation of fruit trees supports a horticultural interpretation of circumcision and the burial of foreskins:

> Now when you enter the land, and plant any kind of tree for eating, you are to regard its fruit as foreskinned.[11] For three years it is to be considered foreskinned for you, you are not to eat it. In the fourth year all its fruit will be holy [set apart] for praise to the Lord. And in the fifth year may you eat its fruit, to increase its yield to you. (Leviticus 19:23–25)

The fourth year represents an arboreal circumcision that prunes foreskinned fruit from young trees as an offering to God. Only then is the fruit suitable for human consumption. The penile foreskin, especially to the rabbis, is a similar gift to God (see also DR 3:5; SSR 2:13:2; PR 15; B. Shabbath 108a). The biblical prepuce—human and horticultural—is called a barrier ('orlah). It bars fruitfulness. Juvenile trees and uncircumcised boys are barren, hence excluded from the covenant and table (Eilberg-Schwartz 1990:151–52; cf. Carmichael 1997:113–18; Bernat 2002:199–207). Both fruit trees and penises require a fertile pruning—and a foreskinned gift to God—to yield a full harvest. Once buried, the foreskin represents the reproductive sowing of Abrahamic "seed."

Horticultural references to circumcision equate the penis with fruit and sexuality with food. After Joshua led the Israelites across the Jordan River into the land of "milk and honey," God told the prophet to fashion "flint" or "sharp" knives and "proceed with a second circumcision of the Israelites" at a place called the "hill of foreskins" (Joshua 5:2–9).[12] Afterward, God declares, "Today I have rolled away from you the disgrace of Egypt" (Joshua 5:9). This rolling evokes the physical removal of the foreskin from the glans as well as the liquid imagery of the fabled milk and honey the Israelites will shortly taste.[13]

Afterward, the Israelites performed the annual Passover sacrifice and dined on "unleavened bread and parched grain" from "the produce of the land" (Joshua 5:10–12). The very next day, God forever ceased to provide manna. Henceforth, the Israelites eat only the fruit of the land, the same land promised to Abraham during the circumcision covenant. In Joshua, then, circumcision is no longer linked just metaphorically to fruit trees. Now the Israelites directly consume the fruit of their circumcision.

Adam's Foreskin

Was the first man created with or without a foreskin? This is no silly question (Eilberg-Schwartz 1994). The answer illustrates the varied symbolism of circumcision.

Rabbinic and mystical texts affirm the foreskinless birth of a dozen or so biblical men, including Noah, Jacob, Joseph, Moses, Samuel, and David (RN 2:5; GR 43:6; ER 1:20; LR 20:1; NR 14:5; Zohar i:161a; ii:11b; Kalimi 2002).[14] The logic behind this conclusion wonderfully illustrates the brilliant creativity of midrash. The Torah characterizes certain men as righteous, flawless, good, obedient, and so forth, moral qualities that reminded the rabbis of the perfection promised to Abraham through circumcision. Consequently, certain biblical heroes were aposthetic, that is, born with absent prepuces. To some Jews, congenital foreskinlessness also points to messianic stirrings. The winter 1981–1982 issue of the *Journal of Jewish Communal Service* reported the birth of a circumcised boy in Israel, an event said "in some religious circles" to herald the "immanence of the advent of the Messiah."

The first man, said the rabbis, like some of his righteous descendants, also lacked a prepuce. Rabbinic culture viewed the foreskin with abject disgust. It was simply inconceivable that a prepuce would so blight the initial condition of man, which, as Genesis tells us, mirrored divine perfection. Adam, then, was foreskinless—and so, apparently, was God.

After the expulsion from Eden, concluded the rabbis, Adam gained a foreskin. This way, Adam sunk to the immoral level of two other loathsome figures in the rabbinic imagination, Esau and the lesser-known Achan (Joshua 7). All three apostates, said the rabbis, reversed their circumcisions through epispasm (B. Sanhedrin 38b, 44a; LR 191:6; Zohar i:35b; Ginzberg 1909–1938:V:99–100 n. 78; VI:175 n. 2). By rejoining the foreskin to the Israelite penis, these scoundrels symbolically regressed the holy separations of Creation back to primal chaos.

Epispasm is not merely mythic. In late antiquity, some Jewish men physically reversed their circumcision to assimilate into the wider Hellenistic cultures of Greece and Rome that viewed foreskinlessness as a humorous vulgarity (Hall 1988). Epispasm variously allowed Jewish men to attain full citizenship, to avoid the "Jewish tax" imposed by Rome in the first century (see chapter 8), and to enter public gymnasia and baths to nakedly pursue politics, business, and athletic fame.[15] Aulus Cornelius Celsus, a first-century Roman physician, described epispasm or "decircumcision" in his encyclopedic work *De Medicina Libri Octo* (7:25; Rubin 1980). An incision circled the penis, just behind the glans, and the skin of the shaft tugged forward to form the new foreskin. The penis was bandaged and plaster packed between the stretched skin and the glans to prevent adhesion. Healing was aided by "cold water effusions" and fasting, "lest satiety excite that part."

The rabbis bitterly denounced epispasm. The procedure signified danger-ous assimilation and the willingness of a Jew to abandon God and tradition. Many of the same themes animate discussions about circumcision today, as I discuss in the final chapter. Epispastic Jews cast themselves out of the reli-gious community, much like Adam, whom God cast out of Eden with a fore-skin.

For all its emasculating imagery, biblical circumcision ritually assured men of reproductive fruitfulness. From this angle, it is *un*circumcision, not cir-cumcision, that truly castrates men by denying them fertility and, more broadly, the existence of an ordered world in which to be "fruitful and multi-ply." By defying God, Adam gained a phallic excrescence. Later, Israelite and Jewish men would cut down this besmirched phallus, thus restoring the cosmos.

"If circumcision is so precious," asked Abraham to God in midrash (GR 46:3), "why was it not given to Adam?" God deigns to offer no answer. Instead, the deity scolds Abraham for his cheekiness, saying, "It should be enough for you that I have asked you to do this." If Abraham refuses circum-cision, God promises to destroy the world.

In this chapter, I illustrated the logic that underlies the biblical connec-tion between Creation and circumcision, a connection the rabbis themselves so often understood. This logic, I argued, consisted of binary oppositions, processes of division and separation, and a dialectic between unity and dual-ity. I also argued that these themes pertain to, perhaps even arise from, the reproductive dilemma of men and a male deity birthing the world and humanity. In short, I began to construct my argument that the meanings of circumcision argue both in favor of yet against the dominant phallic narra-tive of biblical culture, myth, and ritual.

Barth (1991:50–51) interprets the rabbinic debate between Abraham and God as "an inner Jewish opposition" to circumcision (see also T-Y 3:19; Zohar i:93b; TG 3.24). Yet another midrash (GR 11:6) provides an answer to Abraham's audacious query: everything created during the first six days requires completion. To eat, humans must grind wheat. To see, we trim our hair. The penis, too, requires refinement.

But no such improvement is apparently necessary for women. Perhaps woman was simply irrelevant. Or maybe she was deemed too coarse for any such perfection. There is another possibility, as I also argued in this chapter: woman is the ideal that God and man strive to attain through circumcision but that they can never bring themselves to admit.

Notes

1. More radical forms of Jewish dualism were advanced by Philo of Alexandria and especially Maimonides, whom I discuss later.

2. Despite the aniconic tradition, visual experience was central to biblical, mystical, and rabbinic devotion (Boyarin 1990; Wolfson 1994a).

3. The rabbis interpreted the first human in Genesis 2 as a blend of male and female, animal and divine, earth and empyrean (GR 8:11, 12:8, 14:3; LR 9:9). In the Zohar (i:49a), God's breath "impregnated" the earth like semen.

4. Rabbinic law interprets Ecclesiastes 4:17, "Guard your foot when you go to the house of the Lord," as a recommendation to urinate before prayer (ECR 4:17; KSA 12:3).

5. Why, asked the rabbis (GR 17:8), do women perfume their bodies? Because bone, but not earth (the source of man), putrefies. Why is woman's voice shrill? Because bone sizzles in a cooking pot. This unusual misogyny in early rabbinic Judaism, argues Boyarin (1993:88–94), reflects the broader cultural milieu rather than an inherent Jewish sexism.

6. For the Genesis 2 rib as the *baculum*, a small penile bone present in most mammalian and primate males except humans, see Dundes (1983, 1988) and Gilbert and Zevit (2001).

7. Parturient mud also shapes the famous *golem* of Jewish mysticism and folklore, a man-like creature formed from clod and magically enlivened.

8. For another perspective on nurturance and biblical men, see Forster (1993).

9. Kabbalah valorized breast-feeding "as an aspect of the phallus" (Wolfson 1995:102).

10. Some Australian Aboriginal groups buried the prepuce in a pool of water lilies to promote growth (Frazer 1904:210–11).

11. Literally, a "foreskin a foreskin."

12. The first collective circumcision occurred just prior to the inaugural Passover sacrifice (Exodus 13:43–51). But the rite lapsed in the wilderness (Joshua 5:4–5), necessitating the second mass ceremony (cf. Finkel 1974; Gooding 1977).

13. The rabbis paralleled the splitting of the penis during circumcision with the parting of the Red Sea (TE 4.12).

14. Later, angels were said to be foreskinless (Jubilees 15:26–27), as well as, in Islamic legend, Muhammad.

15. At least one ancient Jewish athlete did bravely bare his circumcision (Kerkeslager 1997; see also chapter 9).

CHAPTER THREE

Circumcision and the Mark of Cain

The first humans in Eden were unashamedly "naked" ('*arumin*), a foreshadowing wordplay on the "cunning" ('*arum*) serpent, who taunts the woman. "Did God really say: You shall not eat of any tree of the garden . . . ?" No, woman clarifies, God forbid only the tree in the middle of the garden. Woman then *enlarges* this prohibition. Not only must we refrain from eating the tree, but we may not even touch it. This way, suggests Trible (1978:110) provocatively, the first woman initiates a major task of the rabbis. To prevent Jews from inadvertently trespassing the Law, the rabbis expanded many commandments or, as they said, "built a fence around the Torah." Male authority emulates the first woman. But masculinity refuses to abide by this feminine primacy.

Undeterred, the serpent continues. "You are not going to die," it says to woman. Rather, "your eyes will be opened and you will become as gods knowing good and evil." The forbidden fruit mediates between moral opposites and collapses the distinction between human and divine. It also represents taboo sexuality as vision and food. Eventually, of course, this culinary eroticism leads to the expulsion from Paradise.

Circumcision responds to these themes of sight, sexuality, and exile. The rite confers authorized vision since God, as the rabbis stressed, "appeared" to Abraham when delivering the covenantal declaration in Genesis 17. Circumcision also releases covenantal "seed," thus allowing for legitimate or reproductive sexuality. Last, the rite redresses the expulsion by promising land and divine protection. We can discern another allusion to circumcision in Eden through the image of woman plucking the forbidden fruit, a gesture that also recalls her own surgical birth and the later Levitical law concerning juvenile fruit trees. Beginning with Eden, then, my goal in this chapter is to further show how the opening myths of Genesis establish themes and patterns that frame circumcision.

Maternal Apples and Circumcised Wheat

Eve succumbs to the serpent's culinary seduction. She eats the fruit and offers a taste to the man. Their eyes "opened," and they viewed their nakedness with shame. The humans sew fig-leaf garments.

Genesis fails to identify the infamous fruit. Yet biblical fruitfulness often refers to human fecundity, as when Psalm 127:3 refers to children as "the fruit of the womb." European lore sees an apple. Many scholars attribute this identification to medieval confusion between or a pun on the Latin words for "evil" and "apple," which are spelled the same (*malum*) but pronounced slightly differently. Dundes (1991a:345–48) offer an alternative explanation after surveying European folklore, literature, and Christian iconography. The legendary apple symbolizes the female breast. This interpretation suggests to some psychoanalysts that the myth expresses anxiety over weaning and independence (Róheim 1940:196–98; Rubenstein 1963:145). Eden represents an ideal of infancy we must all renounce for adulthood. But we only partly overcome this desire, continues Róheim (1940:198). Through the maternal symbolism of the biblical earth (chapter 2), humans return to a nurturing body during cultivation and burial, two punishments resulting from the trespass in Eden.

There is also an erotic component to Eden. Song of Songs likens female sexuality to a "locked garden" (4:12). "Under the apple tree I roused you," states another passage. "It was there your mother conceived you" (Song of Songs 8:5). This verse explains why guests at Persian circumcision ceremonies dine on apples (Krohn 1985:170). In Song of Songs 2:3, an apple tree symbolizes the penis during intercourse. Its "fruit" is "sweet" to the lover's "taste."

Culinary metaphors for sexuality are common in the Torah and rabbinic culture (Boyarin 1993:chap. 4; Satlow 1995). Devout Jews carefully restrict eating and intercourse. "A man," says the Talmud, "shall not drink out of one cup and think of another" (B. Nedarim 20b). Some rabbinic texts identify the forbidden fruit as a fig, which sometimes symbolized the genitals (Levy 1917–1919b:26–27). Other texts specify grapes since wine offers humanity drunken sin or ritual salvation (PRK 20:6). In Kabbalah, apples represent breasts and sometimes testicles (Wolfson 1995:109, 226–27 n. 156).

Still other rabbis identified the taboo fruit as "wheat" (*chittah*), which in Hebrew resembles "sin" (*chattah*). Wheat, too, unlike grains such as barley, contains a cleft. While barley is foreskinned, said the rabbis, and so symbolizes promiscuity, circumcised wheat represents self-restraint (PR 18; Braude 1968:387 n. 25). The rabbis also claimed that Song of Songs 7:3 likens Israel's "belly" to "a heap of wheat" because "the circumcision at the middle of Israel's belly is like the split down the middle of a grain of wheat" (PR 10). When Song of Songs elsewhere compares Israel to nuts (6:11), the rabbis once again gendered all Israelites as men and detected another allusion to circumcision (PR 11). The two shells of a nut must be "peeled away to expose the kernel" much like "two layers of skin are cut away so as to expose the glans."[1] The myth of Eden mentions no apples, breasts, or penile trees. Yet the rabbis correctly interpreted the tale in terms of eroticism, female fertility, maternal nurture, and a foreshadowing of circumcision.

Serpentine Symbolism

The rabbis recognized the serpent in Eden as Satan, often called Samael (Lachs 1965; Dan 1980). In punishing the reptile, God declared "On your belly shall you crawl" (Genesis 3:14), implying that the serpent originally walked upright (GR 20:5; Ibn Ezra 3:1; PRE 13; Bahir 200). God amputated its limbs, reducing the beast to filthy slithering. While the transgressive serpent thus endures eternal flaccidity, the circumcised penis represents the covenantal erection of Israelite society and the ability of men to "walk."

The mystics and rabbis understood an enemy of Israel named Amalek (Exodus 17) as an "evil serpent" who "planned to uproot the sign of the covenant" (Zohar ii:194b–195a). In some texts, this serpent actually hurls circumcised penises toward heaven in a rebuke of God (PR 12; NR 13:3).[2] Long before Freud, I am suggesting, the rabbis connected serpents to circumcision. Genesis implies the same symbolism.

The Eastern Iatmul people of Papua New Guinea, whom I have studied since the late 1980s, tell a legend in which frogs die while snakes shed skin to regenerate anew. Unfortunately, humans resemble frogs. The serpent in Eden represents a similar yearning for immortality (Frazer 1918:45–77). Yet the Genesis snake also portrays a male yearning for self-reproduction. This masculine pursuit gains ritual reality when God attaches an everlasting covenant and fantastic fertility to the phallus through circumcision. The shedding of penile skin confers immortality (La Barre 1962:80). Circumcision allows men to escape the inevitability of death and a dependence on women for their own existence and the birth of their sons.

Some passages in the Hebrew Bible hint at a snake-god tradition (Numbers 21:8–9; 2 Kings 18:4). The serpent's symbolic evasion of death through regenerative molting accords with this divine status. After the taboo snack in Eden, however, the god-like snake was cast down to dirt and stomped by humans (Genesis 3:15; Niditch 1985:35–36). The snake's molted skin now symbolizes a sloughing away of divine grace. Conversely, the human sloughing of the foreskin represents God's favor.

By shedding skin, the serpent also symbolically casts off modesty. Contrariwise, Adam and Eve gain shame and "garments of skins" (Genesis 3:21; Eilberg-Schwartz 1994:88–90). The humans repudiate animalistic nature and cover themselves with culture, while the snake loses culture—it never again speaks—and slithers naturally unclad. Circumcision also builds on these themes. The rite undresses the glans. But a circumcised man, said the rabbis, is never fully naked (B. Menachoth 43b). He is always clothed with a covenantal garment of holiness.

Phallic Ambiguities

Sexuality in Jewish traditions is originary and Edenic, even messianic, and not, as in Christianity, immoral (Anderson 1989). The sin of Adam and Eve was merely illicit sex, stresses Boyarin (1993), not sexuality entirely.

The serpent in one rabbinic view espied Adam and Eve in *flagrante delicto* (GR 18:6–19:3). Jealously, the snake lusted after Eve and schemed to murder Adam. The reptile apparently consummated its desire since God would find it necessary to separate serpents and women through mutual "enmity" (Genesis 3:15).[3] In a first-century composition, the serpent deflorated Eve (4 Maccabees 18). In the Zohar, he "injected" her with filth (1:126b; 3:79a). These rabbinic tales ultimately attribute dangerous desire to the phallus. So does Genesis.

The two humans in Eden eat the forbidden fruit and unsuccessfully hide in the trees. God interrogates the man. "Who told you that you were naked? Did you eat of the tree from which I had forbidden you to eat?" The man cowardly deflects responsibility onto his partner. Woman does likewise, pointing to the snake. Yet the snake symbolizes the phallus, and so the myth begins and ends with male desire.

The serpent, moreover, offered humanity a meal that confounded the boundaries between divine and worldly, celestial and terrestrial, life and death. Man, said God, has become "like one of us" (Genesis 3:22). If the phallic snake set in motion the transformation of dualities into unities, then circumcision later responds by transforming the phallus into a duality. In all these ways, Eden establishes the conditions for the bodily site of the covenantal sign.

God punishes the three transgressors. The erect serpent, now reduced to slithering, will henceforth eat dust (aphar), the same substance God earlier shaped into the human.[4] Next, God condemns woman to painful childbearing. Since creation was originally masculine, female birthing is a "male function passed on to women with some added disadvantage" (Adler 1977a:241). Male "seed" will now harm woman just as her "seed," or children, will stomp on the serpent (Trible 1978:127). Additionally, woman will "desire" her husband, who responds not with love but with domination or "rule" (cf. Trible 1978:118–19; Bal 1985:324; Kimelman 1998). It is man who stymies matrimonial wholeness. But, ironically, it is man who truly needs woman since the covenant stresses progeny. Eve's punishment makes men dependent on uterine fertility but then converts that dependence into a husband's rebuke of his wife's desire. God then turns to the man, afflicting him with the same "pains" ('itsavon) as woman, only in regard to agricultural toil rather than birth. God, too, will later suffer the same aches before unleashing the flood. Since the first appearance of these "pains" in the Torah pertains to birth, male work resembles a woman in labor. Finally, the ground will no longer yield human life. Hereafter, only women give birth. The earth is now humanity's grave, and men reproduce through sexual intercourse, aided by circumcision, not mud and ribs.

Dough and Bone

God banishes the two humans from the Garden, barring their return with a cherub who brandishes "the fiery ever-turning sword." Yet Jewish traditions rarely paint the expulsion with tones of gloom and guilt. Original Sin is an alien notion in rabbinic culture since sin is learned rather than innate (T-Y 1:7). Woman was the serpent's victim, claims Boyarin (1993:81–82), not the agent of humanity's ruination.

Nonetheless, Eve's role in the fateful meal negatively shaped the rabbinic view of women (e.g., PRE 13; GR 17:8; 18; Ibn Ezra 3:16; B. Sanhedrin 20a; RN 9:25; 42:117). Because of Eve, women suffer the pain and blood of defloration. They pierce their ears like slaves, cover their heads as "one who has done wrong and is ashamed of people," and, for introducing death into the world, walk in front of the corpse during funeral processions. Since Eve shed Adam's blood and extinguished his soul, women menstruate and light Sabbath candles.[5] And because Eve ate God's fruit, then corrupted Adam, the "sacred bread" of Creation whom God kneaded from the earth, women must set aside a "dough offering" when baking (GR 14:1; 17:8; T-Y 2:1; TG 2:1; after Numbers 15:17–21).[6] These unsavory passages reveal considerable rabbinic ambivalence toward women and the female body. Why? Midrash supplies a clue. During the shaping of man from the earth, God resembled a woman who mixed flour and water, then separated the dough offering (GR 14:1). The supreme act of God's monotheistic power is thus likened to female baking. Underlying this midrash is the theme of male envy, a jealousy that explains biblical and rabbinic moments of misogyny as well as the exclusion of women from many rituals.[7]

Once the misdeed in Eden was discovered, man responded by trying to distance himself from woman. He betrayed the intimacy of their shared meal—an intimacy that he himself, in the guise of phallic desire, initiated. Man no longer referred to his partner through bodily idioms of sameness such as "bone of my bone and flesh of my flesh." Now she is simply "woman." No longer does man say "we," only "I." Man needs woman, the myth seems to tell us, yet marginalizes her existence. Not surprisingly, circumcision expresses the same contradiction.

The Blood of Man

Eve's Hebrew name, Chavah, resembles "life" (*chaim*) and "to live" (*chaya*). As Adam comments, "she was mother of everything that lives" (Genesis 3:20). But however much Eve exemplifies life-giving motherhood, she births no daughters, only sons (Williams 1977). The Mother of All Life is really the mother of male "seed."

The name Chavah also conjures phallic transgression. In midrash, Eve or Chavah lent Adam poor "opinion," or *chavveh* (GR 20:11), much like the snake, called *chivya* in Aramaic.[8] Snakes symbolize not only death, danger, and desire. They also represent eternal cycles of life. For this reason, a Palestinian mother who suffered the loss of a child hung a snake's head around her next born's neck since the Arabic serpent, *haiyeh*, gives life, *haiâh* (Canaan 1929:68). The ambiguous relationship between Eve and the serpent, I am suggesting, doubles for the equally complex relationship between masculinity and motherhood.

The first man's proper name, Adam, derives from the generic term for "human" ('adam). Adam's name refers to the soil of his birth, I noted earlier, and the creation of humanity after God's "likeness," or demut (Miller 1972:299–304). Adam's name also evokes "blood" (dam), the biblical source of life, an attribution that explains the prohibition on the consumption of blood (Genesis 9:4–7; Leviticus 17). From this angle, Adam's name foreshadows the importance of blood in Israelite religion, especially animal sacrifice but also circumcision. These rites, as I will argue at length later, transform polluting menstrual blood into blood that is sacred, life giving, and covenantal. If it is valid to propose that Eve's name alludes to the serpentine phallus she once possessed but lost, then it seems equally valid to suggest that Adam's name hints at the bloody fertility ascribed to women that men lack but yearn to emulate.

Eve, notes Pardes (1989:171–73), receives her motherly name *after* creation. Any earlier acknowledgment of the "Mother of All" would have challenged the "parturient fantasies" of God and man. Still, Eve does respond to male procreative boasting. After birthing Cain in Genesis 4, she exclaims, "I have got me a man with the help of the Lord." Not only does Eve omit mention of her husband, but she construes God as her mere assistant! Furthermore, Eve announces the birth of a man ('ish), not an infant, thus answering Adam's announcement in Genesis 2:23 that "she shall be called woman ('ishah) because she was taken out of man ('ish)." The symbolism of circumcision must be anchored to this early debate between man and woman over the ultimate repository of procreative power.

Siblingship and Sexuality

Human creation inside the Garden was asexual and male. Yet masculine birth is difficult to reconcile with human experience. The expulsion from Eden seeks to overcome this contradiction (Leach 1962). But it failed. Eve, we just saw, attributes the birth of her son to God, not Adam, thereby blurring the distinction between human and divine and especially confounding sexual reproduction. The unreality of Eden persists.

Eve's firstborn, Cain, tills the soil, much like his human father.[9] Abel, Cain's younger brother, tends sheep. Cain offers God the "fruit of the soil," the exact same bounty that enticed his mother in Eden. Abel presents "the choicest of the firstlings of his flock." God spurns Cain, who kills Abel.

The first fratricide establishes a tragic pattern of sibling strife that recurs throughout Genesis. In most instances, younger sons triumph. Yet Cain is the firstborn, and so his crime seems anomalous. Cain's atrocity, as Lévi-

Strauss (1955) suggested for Oedipus, was "the underrating of blood relations." Cain treated Abel like a stranger, not a sibling.

Cain also erred by overvaluing the intimacy of kinship, much like his human parents. In the Garden, Adam and Eve were ambiguously and impossibly related as brother and sister, father and daughter, husband and wife. The fateful meal in Eden culminated this dangerous confusion of kinship categories. Cain's fratricide blurred the same moral boundaries. Both Adam and Cain, writes Leach (1962), swapped a sibling for a wife. To both men, God posed the question, "What have you done?" The deity then asked, "Where are you?" or "Where is your brother?" Both men were disciplined with exile and agricultural hardship. Afterward, each "knew his wife, and she conceived and bore" a son (Genesis 3:20; 4:1). Prior to this acknowledgment of matrimonial reproduction, Adam and Cain each committed a type of incest (Leach 1962). To the extent that the illicit encounter between Cain and Abel (brothers born from the same mother) thematically parallels the intimacy between Adam and Eve (siblings who acted like spouses), then Cain, like Adam, symbolically copulated with his own body. Like God, Adam and Cain represent male desire to self-reproduce, thus denying the procreative reality of woman.

Cain's misdeed also hints at same-gender male sexuality. The regulations of Leviticus 17–26, also known as the Holiness Code, often reflect Creation by lending concrete expression to the principle of categorical separation. Biblical law prohibits many mixtures, including incest, bestiality, cross-dressing, everyday wool-and-linen garments, animal crossbreeding, mixed-grain fields, and, as we saw in chapter 2, a particular mode of homoeroticism. These forbidden unions blur distinctions. Biblical law also banned men from sexual encounters that lacked the potential to reproduce sons. This edict pertained to menstruating women in addition to other men.

Yet same-gender male sexuality, while strongly censured, evoked the homoerotic relationship between men and God, a devotional intimacy that undermined the official ideology of biblical manhood (chapter 2). As in many societies, biblical and rabbinic cultures strongly valorized heterosexual marriage and denounced homoeroticism while nonetheless institutionalizing intimate male fellowship that appeared strikingly homoerotic. Maimonides, the great medieval philosopher, recognized this very theme in regard to circumcision in The Guide of the Perplexed (3:49). This male ceremony centers on the naked penis but creates only nonsexual "love."[10] I will later say more about the muted eroticism of circumcision. For now, I want only to suggest that the early episodes of Genesis speak powerfully to the instability of the two basic institutions of biblical society: marriage and male fellowship.

A Mark of Infamy or Divinity?

God punishes Cain for his homoerotic, incestuous, self-reproducing fratricide with restless wandering (Genesis 4). Aghast, Cain cries, "Anyone who meets me may kill me!" To deter would-be executioners, God promises "sevenfold vengeance" and adorns Cain with a "mark" or "sign . . . lest anyone who met him should kill him." This bodily warning is the first appearance in the Hebrew Bible of many divine signs called 'ôt, a term that also refers to circumcision (Genesis 17; Fox 1974). Cain's badge signals punishment and exile yet reward and shelter.

Divine insignia often adorned biblical bodies. In Ezekiel 9, God evokes Cain when instructing the pious to mark the center of their foreheads with another indeterminate sign, again to avoid slaughter. More famously, God commanded the Israelites to "bind a sign on your hand and . . . between your eyes" (Exodus 13:9; 16; Deuteronomy 6:8; 11:18). On this basis, devout Jewish men enwrap themselves daily in phylacteries (tephillin) during morning prayer.[11] Some Israelites inscribed or tattooed "of the Lord's" on their arms (Isaiah 44:5). God's own palms were similarly engraved with the word Zion (Isaiah 49:16). In fact, the Almighty seemed particularly enamored of bodily ordeals. God befouled Moses' hand to demonstrate divine power (Exodus 4:6–7), induced ecstatic speech (1 Samuel 10:9), opened and closed wombs (e.g., Genesis 29:31), and promised prodigious fecundity on the performance of circumcision. Not all bodily signs were holy and authorized. The Law repeatedly forbid funerary gashing and other markings (e.g., Leviticus 19:28). Idolaters "cut themselves with knives and spears" (1 Kings 18:28). Sham prophets flaunted stigmata (Zechariah 13:6). The Hebrew Bible frequently denounced jewelry (chapter 4). Cain's mark, it seems clear, established a moral ambivalence of bodily brands that extended to circumcision.

The rabbis (and modern psychoanalysts) elaborated on Cain's mark. Some rabbis saw a horn (GR 22:12; T-Y 1:11; SH 1:26–32). Others suggested that his forehead was etched with a letter from the divine name (PRE 21; GR 22:12–13). This proposition echoes the Kabbalistic view of circumcision as God's signature (chapter 6). Reik (1917–1919) analyzed Cain's mark as a self-inflicted, castrative circumcision enacted as penalty for incest. Indeed, rabbinic legends tell that Cain and Abel married their own twin sisters (PRE 21–22; Zohar i:36b, 54b; Ginzberg 1909–1938:I:108; V:138–39 n. 17). Many of these themes also pertain to circumcision.

Cain's mark announced exile. Circumcision admits men into the Promised Land. Both marks, however, betoken divine custodianship. We can discern further symbolic parallels by drawing on Aycock's (1983) comparison of Cain's mark and Christ's wounds. All three bodily brands have sacrificial tones. Christ died for the sins of humanity. Cain offered his brother to God. And, circumcision, we will see in chapter 5, resembles an animal sacrifice. Last, all three bodily marks point to an existential paradox. The killer Cain is not himself to be killed. The mortal wounds of Christ attest to his immortality (John 20:19–31). And Abraham's near-castrative cut confers endless progeny while only begrudgingly acknowledging the reproductive role of women.

In paralleling the "signs" of Cain and circumcision, I am not endorsing the anti-Jewish sentiments of the church fathers such as St. Augustine, who wrote, "Only when a Jew comes over to Christ, is he no longer Cain" (*Contra Faustum* 12:13). Nothing could be further from my intent. Rather, I am merely proposing that the early tales of Genesis establish a thematic and narrative context that helps explains circumcision. And in these tales, as in the rite of circumcision, we can discern considerable moral ambivalence.

Circumcision and the Flood

The biblical flood also helps establish the meaning of circumcision. In most flood tales, male deities destroy the world to punish humanity. Yet a male survivor repopulates the earth. Typically, women figure insignificantly in these tales, which instead stress the role of men and gods in the watery death and rebirth. Flood myths, argues Dundes (1988), are an aquatic expression of male birth envy. The biblical flood (Genesis 6–10) conforms to this pattern.

Religious cosmogonies often model creation after childbirth. At the beginning of Genesis, God's breath hovered over the uterine-like primal waters. Then, mirroring the infant's movement through the birth canal, God declared, "Let there be light." Other male images of watery birth include Isaiah 48:1, where the house of Jacob "issued from the waters of Judah," and, much later, "rivers of living water" that in John 7:38 flowed from Christ's "belly" (*koilia*)—a Greek word that also means "uterus." These floods all evidence the transfer of uterine fertility to male bodies.

The flood narrative in Genesis begins with an illicit intermingling between "the sons of god," or "divine beings," and "the daughters of men"

(Genesis 6:1). Not incidentally, these women were as visually delightful as the forbidden fruit in Eden (Genesis 3:6; 6:2). The resulting offspring were the Nephilim (Genesis 6:4), or "fallen ones," who later appear as cannibalistic giants (Number 13:33; see also Deuteronomy 2:11; Joshua 12:4–6; 13:12; 1 Enoch 6–11). In other words, the flood was spawned by wanton sexuality that blurred the boundary between humanity and God, the same transgression that befouled Eden and the birth of Cain.

Genesis neglects to mention the specific wickedness that prompted God to drown humanity. Midrash is more explicit. The flood narrative begins, "When men began to increase on the earth." To the rabbis, this phrase implied that men "spilled their semen upon the trees and stones . . . because they were steeped in lust" (GR 26:4; PRE 22; Zohar i:56b). The antediluvians also committed incest and "composed nuptial songs in honour of pederasty and bestiality" (GR 26:5; 31:6). Clearly, the sexual confounding of categories threatened the authoritative structure of biblical society.

To save the world, God selects Noah, a man who "found favor in the eyes of the Lord" (Genesis 6:8). This optical intimacy, suggests Dundes (1988), like that between Moses and God (Exodus 33:12–13), hints at sexual desire. Since Genesis describes Noah as "blameless" or "whole" (tamim), the same word that describes the benefit of circumcision (Genesis 17), the rabbis concluded that Noah was born circumcised (T-Y 1:1; Zohar i:58b). Perhaps this foreskinlessness explains why God looked on Noah with such favor, even promising him a "covenant" (Genesis 6:18). But the homoerotic relationship between Noah and God is not solely sexual. Rather, Genesis construes Noah as God's wife, for it is Noah who in essence gestates and rebirths the world. The ark, as a masculine womb, shelters life.

The biblical word for "water" (mayim) also denotes "urine" (2 Kings 18:27; Isaiah 36:12). "Anyone who holds his penis while urinating," says the Talmud, "is as if he brings a flood into the world" (B. Nidah 13a–b, 43a; B. Shabbath 41a). This exclamation, like those rabbis who boasted of never looking at their own circumcision (ECR 9:10:2), may seek to curtail the masturbatory squandering of procreative seed. Or it may warn men against trying to conceal their circumcision (Finkel 1974:205–7; Satlow 1995:246–64). Regardless, rabbinic culture linked the penis to water. Indeed, when the prophet Elijah appealed to God for rain during a dry spell and "crouched on the ground, and put his face between his knees" (I Kings 18:42), the meaning of this gesture was unmistakable to the rabbis: "Sovereign of the Universe! If we have no merit, then look to the covenant of circumcision" (LR 31:4; PR 52; ER 11:2; SSR 7:6:1).[12]

Biblical "water" also refers to "semen" (Isaiah 48:1). The rabbis, in fact, described the flood as hot and viscous, like ejaculate (B. Sanhedrin 108a). Rabbinic exegesis, then, supports an interpretation of the deluge as seminal rain expelled by the divine phallus.

After 150 days of rain (Genesis 8:1), God quiets the storm with "wind." The famed eleventh-century Rabbi Shlomo ben Yitzchak, better known as Rashi, equated this interval with the duration between conception and fetal formation.[13] At any rate, the same procreative gust that ceased the flood also initiated Creation. It is unclear exactly how long Noah and his charge remained in the ark. But the first signs of land appeared in the tenth month (Genesis 8:5), which is suspiciously close to the length of human gestation. By now, my point in this section should be clear: biblical and postbiblical sources encourage an interpretation of the Genesis flood as a masculine idiom of reproduction and birth.

Sacrificial Birth

The earliest biblical compositions hint at matriliny (e.g., Genesis 4:1). The later priestly narratives, however, stress patrilineal descent as well as the performance of animal sacrifice.[14] Cross-culturally, argues Jay (1992), men often forge bonds of ceremonial kinship through animal immolations that eclipse or invalidate the bonds of maternal kinship. The blood of slaughter replaces the blood of childbirth.

The flood myth fits this pattern. When the waters recede, Noah lets fly a raven, then a dove. This binary opposition heralds a new cosmic era. On emerging from the ark, the survivors present God with "burnt offerings" (Genesis 8:20). Death follows rebirth. More precisely, blood shed by men substitutes for the blood of birth. Circumcision, we will see, evidences a similar theme.

After the flood, God "blessed" Noah and his sons, commanding them to be "fruitful and multiply" (Genesis 9:1). But God neglected to mention by name any mothers, daughters, or wives. Similarly, the lengthy register of Noah's descendants in Genesis 10 includes no women, thus, as in circumcision, subordinating motherhood and uterine fertility to paternity and masculine fecundity.

There are further parallels between the flood myth and circumcision. God establishes a covenant with Abraham, of course, but also with Noah, promising, "Never again shall all flesh be cut off by the waters of a flood" (Genesis 9:11). Both pacts were announced to men. Both are perpetual. Both make

negative reference to "cutting off." Both refer to the body. And both covenants conclude with a phallic "sign." Admittedly, this symbolism might seem
unclear in the flood myth, until we recognize that rainbows around the world
often represent serpents (e.g., Róheim 1945:184–99). The Jewish mystics
were more to the point (Wolfson 1994a, 1995:87). They expressly identified
Noah's bow with the curvature of the penis, circumcision, and even God's
own phallus.

Scholars of the Hebrew Bible attribute the Noachide covenant to the
source called J, for whom "flesh" (bāśār) refers to humanity. The later priestly
compositions use "flesh" as a metaphor for kinship and the penis (Eilberg-
Schwartz 1990:170). By promoting vast paternal fertility, circumcision
makes good on God's message in the rainbow to never again "cut off"
humanity or "flesh." Yet Abraham's circumcision also subverts the Noachide
covenant by cutting off flesh so that "flesh" is never again "cut off."

Bloody Human

After Noah's sacrifice, God permits humanity to consume meat. With one
proviso. It is forbidden to eat "flesh with its life-blood in it" (Genesis 9:4), a
rule often repeated (Leviticus 7:26–27; 17:11; Deuteronomy 12:16, 23–25;
15:23). The legal code known as the Noachide Laws also prohibit murder, a
decree typically traced to linguistic similarities between the words "human"
('adam), "blood" (dam), and God's "image" (demut; see Miller 1972). But
this explanation does not attend to the full spectrum of bloody meanings in
ancient Israel.

Menstruating and postpartum women were polluted and polluting in the
Levitical purity code. But as I argue in chapter 5, the bloods of sacrifice and
circumcision were sacred, moral, and purifying. The male bloods were positive transformations of the female bloods. Indeed, men cut both themselves
and animals to reproduce the community as if they were menstruating
women and birthing mothers. Genesis thus legislated the forbidden status of
blood after the deluge not only to affirm the sanctity of life, as most commentators aver, but also to continue the dialogue established in Eden over the
gender of human and covenantal reproduction.

Incest Redux

The mythic origin of humanity in the Bible and beyond contains a moral
problem since, logically, incest taints the original act of human reproduc-

tion. Adam and Eve are no exception. Of course, incest is a poor exemplar of social life. Consequently, myth must split the original ancestors from their descendants while nonetheless preserving genealogical continuity (Leach 1962; Moore 1964). This is one explanation for the expulsion from Eden. But it failed to cut off humanity from illicit desire. So God initiated another cosmic rupture, the great flood. Yet it, too, only partially washed away immoral sexuality.

After the flood, Noah planted a vineyard, quaffed his wine, and "became drunk" (Genesis 9:20–27). In Hebrew, Noah's name resembles "console" or "comfort" (Genesis 5:29; Ibn Ezra 5:29). The toil suffered by man on account of the forbidden fruit is now eased by the consumption of another fruit. One fruit was wild, raw, and eaten; the other is domesticated, cooked, and imbibed. Both fruits led to carnal shame.

In his stupor, Noah passed out and "uncovered himself within his tent" (Genesis 9:20–27). Noah's youngest son, Ham, "saw his father's nakedness." But Ham's brothers refused this spectacle. They grabbed a cloak and "walking backward . . . covered their father's nakedness." On awakening, Noah "knew what his youngest son had done to him." He cursed Ham's own son, Canaan, to be "the lowliest of slaves."

Clearly, Ham "saw" Noah in the same way that the taboo fruit in Eden "opened" the eyes of Adam and Eve. In both passages, to "see" is to "know," and "to know" someone is to have sexual knowledge of them (Bassett 1971). Additionally, the expression "to see a man's nakedness," like mention of a son who "removes his father's garment," refers to adultery (Leviticus 18:7; 20:11; Deuteronomy 27:20; Bassett 1971). The possibility that Ham "knew" his mother would certainly explain why Noah cursed the fruit of this illicit union.

Alternatively, the rabbis claimed that Ham sodomized or castrated his father, perhaps assisted by Canaan (B. Sanhedrin 70a; GR 36:7; T-Y 2:15; PRE 23). Since Ham thus presented an oedipal threat to fatherhood, Noah cursed Canaan to deny Ham the future honor of ascending to his own position of patriarchal leadership.[15]

Senior men in Genesis, as in many other cultures, uncovered their genitals for juniors to swear an oath, saying, "put your hand, pray, under my thigh" (Genesis 24:1–4; 47:29–31; Eilberg-Schwartz 1994:154; see also Róheim 1945:28, 1949:326; Patai 1959:167–68). Yet as Ham learned, subordinate men are permitted this privilege only when invited. To do otherwise is to emasculate paternal authority. The punishment? To be "cut off" from the community.

Of course, the "cutting off" penalty is the very same fate that befalls men who refuse to cut off their foreskins. As a rite that permits elder men to view youthful penes, circumcision now appears as a moral inversion of Ham's illicit grasp of the patriarchal phallus.

After the flood, the inhabitants of Shinar aspire to the loftiness of God. They erect the tower of Babel "to make a *name* for ourselves; else we shall be *scattered* all over the world" (Genesis 11:4). But God thwarted this hubris, which threatened yet again to blur the distinction between human and divine. The deity strew humanity into polyphony. The tower was cut off.

Circumcision also trims a phallus, albeit less severely than at Babel. The covenantal cut enables, not scatters, social continuity. Moreover, circumcision accomplishes what the tower did not. The rite allows men to acquire a name. Many rabbinic and modern commentators discern parallels between Eden and Babel. But no scholar has noted the obvious similarities between the tower and two other phallic images in Eden, the serpent and tree. These symbols, like the tower, all represent dangerous desire and cosmological chaos. They require, like Israelite penises, a lawful trimming.

Not all readers, I recognize, will agree with my specific interpretations of Babel, Eden, Cain, and the flood. But I do hope that readers will accept my wider argument in this chapter that the early tales of Genesis establish a thematic context in which three aspects of circumcision make sense: the location of the covenantal sign on the male genitals, the act of dividing the penis, and the meaning of the rite as it pertains to a wide-ranging debate in Genesis over the bodily location of reproductive primacy.

Notes

1. For the symbolism of nuts, circumcision, and the divine chariot in mystical Judaism, see Wolfson (1987a:89–96). Interestingly, the word "glans" derives from the Latin for "nut."

2. For a linguistically complex castrative response by Samuel to Amalek, see PRE 3:6.

3. In Talmudic thought, a woman confronted by a snake can protect herself by uttering "I am menstruous" (B. Shabbath 110a).

4. Levy (1917–1919b:28) and Róheim (1940:177) detect an image of incest as the serpent creeps through and eats the maternal land.

5. Islam has a similar view (Delaney 1988:79).

6. Women who neglect menstrual prohibitions, dough offerings, and Sabbath candles may die in childbirth (M. Shabbat 2:6).

7. Women's private devotions, though, often challenged this marginalization (Weissler 1992; Hoffman 1996:chap. 10).

8. Despite Eve's poor advice, the personification of wisdom in Proverbs is female (e.g., 1:20, 8:22–31). Proverbs also speaks about a seductress called the "strange woman."

9. Rabbinic tales variously trace Cain's conception to Satan, the serpent's slime, and demons (PRE 21; Zohar i:36b, 54a, 55a; GR 22:2).

10. Maimonides also saw circumcision as uniting Jew and Muslim in the "Abrahamic community" (Kasher 1995).

11. A set of *tephillin* consists of two small boxes, each containing biblical passages (Exodus 13:1–10, 11–16; Deuteronomy 6:4–9, 11:13–21), attached to leather straps. One piece is wound around the left arm and hand; the other is wrapped around the head.

12. Persian Jews sought to alleviate drought by reciting rain prayers after circumcision ceremonies (Patai 1947:160).

13. Source: *Rashi 'al ha-Torah: The Torah with Rashi's Commentary, Translated, Annotated, and Elucidated.* Yisrael Isser Zvi Herczeg (Brooklyn, N.Y.: Mesorah, 1994).

14. The current rule of matriliny in Judaism is postbiblical, although its origins remain unclear (compare Cohen 1985 with Sorke 2002).

15. For neglecting "to cover his naked father," adds midrash, Ham "went about naked, with his prepuce extended" (T-Y 2:13). Ham's immoral penetration, like that of Adam, resulted in a foreskinned phallus. When Nebuchadnezzar, reports the Talmud, became aroused at the thought of sodomizing an imprisoned Israelite, "his membrum was extended three hundred cubits" (B. Shabbath 149b; Satlow 1995:218).

CHAPTER FOUR

The Life and Times of Abraham

"Go forth from your land and your birthplace and your father's house," commands God to Abram, "to the land I will show you" (Genesis 12:1). This paradoxical invitation to exile and home introduces the covenant and essentially establishes monotheism. God also offers Abram vast fecundity and renown. He will become a "great nation" and a "great" name. Finally, God promises to bless those who bless Abram and to curse those who curse him. Indeed, "all the families of the earth shall bless themselves by you."

Shortly thereafter, God "appeared" to Abram and declared, "I will assign this land to your seed" (Genesis 12:7). Abram, like Noah, responds by building an altar, thus exchanging blood for progeny. Later, Abram will offer God another type of blood, not from an animal but from his own penis.

This chapter focuses on Abraham and the circumcision covenant in Genesis 17. My goal is to interpret the rite against broader biblical themes but also to develop further my argument that circumcision is a dialogical response to uterine fertility that cuts an ambivalent ideal of manhood and society.

Triumphant Taboo and a Fragmented Family

Abram and his household flee famine for Egypt in Genesis 12:10. At the border, Abram fears that the Egyptians will kill him to abduct his beautiful wife, Sarai. So he tells her, "Please say that you are my sister, that it may go well with me." And it does. When Pharaoh escorts Sarai into the palace, unaware of her martial status, Abram gains "sheep, oxen, asses, male and female slaves, she-asses, and camels." In turn, the Egyptians suffer "mighty plagues." Furious at the deception, Pharaoh banishes Abram from Egypt.

This tale repeats almost exactly in Genesis 20 and then again in Genesis 26 with Isaac and Rebekah, Abraham's son and daughter-in-law.

In the second sister/wife tale, Abram reveals his true relationship to Sarai. She is "my father's daughter though not my mother's daughter" (Genesis 20:12). Although half siblings were then legitimate spouses, the relationship still, as the rabbis noted (Firestone 1993), flirted with taboo and confounded social roles. The sister/wife tales thus resemble the myths of Adam and Eve and Cain and Abel.[1]

The sister/wife tales, too, represent male desire to reproduce "seed" and society in the absence of wives. Symbolic marriage to a sister, or reproductive unity, repudiates true marriage, or reproductive duality. Indeed, the sister/wife tales never censure near incest or male reproductive autonomy. Quite the contrary. They conclude with fantastic prosperity.

A similar moral ambiguity besets the relationship between Abraham's cowives (Genesis 16). Infertile Sarai implores Abram to marry her fertile slave, Hagar, saying, "I shall be built up through her." But household unity is soon halved through conflict. Hagar, now pregnant, mocks her barren mistress. Eventually, Sarah convinces Abram to cast out Hagar and his firstborn son, Ishmael (Genesis 21).[2] As Sarai and Hagar shift between the roles of reproductive spouse and nonreproductive kinswoman, Abram again appears unable to separate a wife from a sister. When it comes to clarifying the boundaries within his family, Abram proves impotent. The saga of Sarai and Hagar also emphasizes vision. When Hagar "saw" her pregnancy, Sarai became "slight in her eyes." Later, during a wilderness epiphany that promised Hagar a son and countless "seed," she called the deity El-roi, or "God Who sees me," explaining, "Did I not go on seeing after He saw me?" Finally, Sarah banished Hagar and Ishmael after she "saw" Ishmael "playing" or "laughing" (metsaheq), a word that evokes sexual fondling and erotic revelry (Stetkevych 1996:33). Whatever Ishmael did, it likely involved Sarah's son, Isaac.[3] Here, as in Eden and Noah's tent, eroticism is visual.

So is circumcision, as the rabbis repeatedly stressed (TG 3.26; NR 12:8). God "appeared" to Abraham when delivering the covenantal declaration (Genesis 17:1) and then again immediately after the rite (Genesis 18:1). The early events in Abraham's life, I contend, instance several themes—fertility, unity and duality, taboo, and erotic vision—that recall Creation and foreshadow circumcision.

Covenant of the Pieces

After the first sister/wife drama, a quarrel erupts between the herdsmen of Abram and his nephew, Lot. The group divides (Genesis 13:9), splitting a unified body of kin. A more vivid image of bodily bifurcation occurs in Genesis 15.

"Fear not," says God to Abram, "I am a shield to you; Your reward shall be very great." But Abram is unmoved. "What can you give me," he replies, "seeing that I shall die childless, and . . . my steward will be my heir." No, answers God, "he who comes forth from your belly shall be your heir." Since "belly" in Hebrew also refers to bowels, loins, and womb, God conjures an image of male parturition. Yet God then shifts to seminal fertility, promising Abram "seed" as numerous as the stars. Finally, God again offers Abram land.

Abram's theophany, argues Zeligs (1961, 1974:12–18), reveals several anxieties. The patriarch just sent away his nephew but now bemoans the lack of an heir. Yet several years will pass before Abram fathers a child, despite God's promise of a son—and then, Abraham will readily agree to sacrifice the boy! Lastly, Abram recently departed from his "father's house" and defeated several kings in battle (Genesis 14). Now, however, he looks to another father, or God, for protection. Plainly, Abram is ambivalent about fatherhood.

But Abram's anxieties are not so easily calmed. "How shall I know that I am to possess" the land? he boldly asks. God responds with a symbolic circumcision of animals. The deity tells Abram to cut in half a heifer, a goat, and a ram. Together, God and Abram arrange the split carcasses, "each half opposite the other." Just before sunset, Abram succumbs to a "deep sleep"— the same lexical slumber that allowed the splitting of the first human to form woman. At sunset, amid a "thick darkness," a smoking brazier mysteriously appears, and a "flaming torch" passes between the split animals. This way, "the Lord made a covenant with Abram" and assigned his "seed" the Promised Land.

Isaac (1964) sees this eerie event as the transformation of an earlier worldview in which deities are slain and reborn to signal the emergence of a new religion. Most scholars analyze the rite, often called the "covenant of the pieces," as a ratifying sacrifice or, more commonly, a conditional self-curse that typified ancient legal treaties (e.g., Frazer 1918:391–428). Violate the oath and suffer the same fate as the animals (see also Jeremiah 34:18; 1 Samuel 11:7). I prefer to stress the ritual creation of unity by dividing bodies.

In fact, ancient Israelites tended literally to "cut" their covenants. This idiom evokes the unity–duality theme that structured Creation.[4] It also mirrors the unfolding of ancient Israelite society through the mythic efforts to clarify what unites yet separates relationships between Adam and Eve, Cain and Abel, sisters and wives, Abram and Lot. Israelite society, too, preserved its sense of moral wholeness by repeatedly cutting away peripheral lineages in the figures of Ishmael, Ham, Lot, and so forth. The idea of creating coherence through division was central to the biblical outlook.

The "covenant of the pieces" also comments on the relationship between masculinity and motherhood. Róheim (1939:455–56) correctly sees an image of parturition as God and Abram symbolically pass through a bloodied, bodily opening. But this ritual of male rebirth and fellowship also represents a type of matricide. The sacrifice of the animals, which stand for the mother, allowed God and Abram to create an emotional state of security and communion that is prototypically associated with breast-feeding and the mother–child bond, which Róheim (1955:206) often called the "dual-unity." This bond, he proposed, served as the basis for all covenants formalized through blood and liquid (Róheim 1942:356; 1955:197–206). In short, God and Abram affirmed masculine unity through a sacrificial enactment of birth.

The same logic applies to circumcision, another bloody ritual whereby men split bodies to "cut" or deliver covenantal intimacy.[5] Circumcision cuts boys and men away from the mother's body, only to reunite them with a male figure of supernatural nurture and authority (see also Rashkow 2000). During circumcision, moreover, the "glans emerges from the foreskin," wrote Róheim (1955:207), "like the newborn from the mother." In this view, biblical men split animals and penises to emulate parturition and to forge an intensive bodily fellowship modeled after breast-feeding.

Cutting and Community

The "covenant of the pieces" is followed by the tale of Sodom and Gomorrah, two cities God intends on destroying for unspecified sins. Abram boldly haggles with God to save the innocents—neglecting to mention his own resident nephew, Lot. This way, Abram repeats Cain's misdeed by undervaluing the bonds of kinship.

Two angels, masquerading as travelers, arrive in Sodom. Lot invites them into his home. That evening, a mob of men demand the strangers "so that we may know them." Lot offers instead his own virginal daughters, saying that "you may do to them as you please" (Genesis 19:8). Luckily for the daughters, the mob refuses Lot's proposal. They pound on the door. Suddenly, the angels disorient the crowd with a blinding light and bid Lot to flee with his family. Later, God "rained upon Sodom and Gomorrah sulfurous fire" (Genesis 19:23). The angels caution Lot's group against witnessing

God's wrath. But Lot's wife foolishly stole a glance and turns into a pillar of salt. The message seems clear, at least to an anthropologist familiar with the secrecy and brutality that surrounds men's ceremonies in Melanesia: uninvited women who glimpse male ritual are severely punished.

The tale of Sodom and Gomorrah parallels the deluge. Fire doubles for rain. Women are nameless. Illicit eroticism is cataclysmic. And God saves a male protagonist who then succumbs to wine and incest. When Lot and his daughters escape to a cave, the eldest sibling says to her sister, "Our father is old, and there is not a man on earth to consort with us. . . . Come, let us make our father drink wine, and let us lie with him that we may maintain seed through our father" (Genesis 19:31–32). The daughters do as they scheme, bearing their father's children. This oedipal immorality cuts off Lot's descendants from the covenantal lineage (Prewitt 1990:26–27). It also allows the daughters revenge on a father who valued hospitality over parenting (Bronner 1994:116–17; see also Dundes 1980:246). Thematically, the tale reenacts previous episodes, including the sister/wife tales, Ham's penetration of Noah, Cain's murder of Abel, and the taboo meal in Eden.

A more brutal version of the scene at Sodom occurs in Judges 19–21. This time it is the guest who violates the trust of kinship. He pushes his concubine-wife into a mob of Benjaminites who "raped and abused her all night long." At daybreak, the victim crawls back to the house and dies "with her hands on the threshold." The husband "picked up a knife"—a phrase repeated only when Abraham prepared to sacrifice his own son (Trible 1983:80)—and cut his wife "limb by limb," which he sent throughout Israel. Outraged, the Israelites slaughter the Benjaminites, then offer the few male survivors some virgins from another massacre and the "annual feast of the Lord" at Shiloh. This way, writes Trible (1983:83), the rape of one becomes the rape of many. The rent body politic of Israel regains masculine wholeness by cutting and penetrating female bodies. This theme of bodily cutting and feminine exclusion recalls the "covenant of the pieces" as well as circumcision, to which I now turn.

Introducing the Covenant of Circumcision

The centerpiece of the Biblical covenant is Genesis 17. "Walk with Me," proposes *El Shaddai*, or "God with the breasts," to Abram, and become "blameless" or "whole" (*tamim*). The androgynous deity promises to make Abram "very very numerous," an exceptional doubling of masculine fertility (Eilberg-Schwartz 1990:147). Abram drops to the ground, hiding his face.

"You shall be the father of a multitude of nations," continues God, who then renames Abram as Abraham. (This event serves as prooftext for the later Jewish custom of bestowing Hebrew names onto boys during the *brit milah* ceremony.) God repeats the promise of vast paternal fecundity, this time through an image of regal birth—"kings shall come forth from you"—and asserts the eternity of the covenant. The deity also cedes the land of Canaan to Abraham's "seed." Finally, God specifies Abraham's sole covenantal obligation:

> You shall circumcise the flesh of your foreskin and it shall be a sign of the covenant between Me and you. At eight days old every male among you shall be circumcised throughout your generations.

As for those who fail to cut this pact, they "shall be cut off" from their kin.

God next turns to Sarai while nonetheless continuing to speak solely to her husband. God changes Sarai's name to Sarah, then promises Abraham a son "from her." To this, God adds that Sarah will "give rise to nations; rulers of peoples shall issue from her." Abraham again falls to the ground, this time while laughing. He even offers God a way out of this absurdity by mentioning Ishmael, the son already born (Alter 1996:75). But God is unswayed. Ishmael will also be blessed but the covenant passes to "Isaac, whom Sarah shall bear . . . next year."

God's pledge to open a barren matriarch's womb parallels the demand that an elderly patriarch open his penis (Kunin 1995:96–97, 221). Covenantal fertility hinges on the real and metaphoric cutting of Israelite genitals by human and divine males. But there is an important nuance. Uterine fertility requires the prior and more important hallowing of the phallus—recall Sarai's inability to conceive while her husband remained foreskinned (Hoffman 1996:38–39). Yet the imagery of circumcision itself, I suggested earlier, seems partly modeled after birth.

At any rate, Abraham, the near centenarian, circumcises himself, his thirteen-year-old son, Ishmael, and his entire household. Like Noah, Abraham established a new line of human descent. Both lineages were cut off from previous generations by either a flood or a foreskin (Eilberg-Schwartz 1990:167). Adam, I add, anticipated this pattern of patrilineal rebirth when his phallus was cut away to create woman. Abraham's circumcision, together with the "covenant of the pieces" and the fate of Lot, symbolically cut away potential claimants to the divine patrimony (Eilberg-Schwartz 1990:168; Prewitt 1990:24–33). Circumcision promises a "multitude of nations." Yet the rite restricts the covenantal community to one lineage (Lupton 1999:196–98). For those within the covenant, circumcision unleashes fantastic fertility. For those who reside outside it or refuse the rite, circumcision seems castrative.

The widespread practice of circumcision in the ancient Near East linked Abraham's deity and lineage with an older, pan-tribal worldview (Jeremiah 9:24–25; Propp 1987; Sasson 1966). Nevertheless, the rite also divided the Abrahamic pedigree from all other nations. Abram's name change, which entailed the addition of only a single letter, also symbolized separation and sameness (Fleishman 2001).

Surprisingly, scholars largely miss the parallel between Abraham's circumcision and the earlier splitting of animals. Both rites affirm Abraham's fruitfulness. Both rites deed land and divine favor to Abrahamic "seed." Both rites lend a physical expression to the promise of sons and soil (Hirsch 1988:78). And both rites commemorate the covenant through male acts of bodily cutting. In so doing, both rites cut *out* motherhood and uterine kinship from the foundational ceremonies of monotheism (Delaney 2001; see also Mark 2003). Covenantal reproduction is placed largely in the hands of men.

Twice in Genesis, as I mentioned earlier, subordinate men pledge fealty by clasping an elder's penis (Genesis 24:2; 47:29). They swear on the *yarek*, or "thigh," an anatomical allusion to reproduction (Genesis 46:26; Exodus 1:5; Numbers 5:21). Circumcision enacts a similar oath of loyalty (Paige and Paige 1981:chap. 4). The rite represents a father's willingness to entrust the reproductive potential of his son to elder kinsman. In fact, the Hebrew term for "circumcision" (*berit*) also means "covenant" and "pact"; the words "commemorate," "remember," and "male" all derive from the same proto-Semitic root (Eilberg-Schwartz 1990:172).[6] Not just any body part would suffice for the covenantal sign!

The Torah describes many things as a "sign" (*'ôt*) of the covenant (chapter 2; Fox 1974). Most of these signs are arbitrary. But not circumcision. The rite has a direct connection to its intended meaning. By removing the foreskin, circumcision symbolically readies the penis for reproductive intercourse (Eilberg-Schwartz 1990:148). With its barred glans, a circumcised penis *always* resembles an erection (Zimmerman 1951:109–10; Geller 1993:56). Fox (1974) even proposes that circumcision is a "sign" to God, not man. The deity sees the covenantal penis during Israelite intercourse and ensures a fruitful union. Only the penis, to repeat, sufficed as the bodily location for inscribing the covenant.

Many scholars rightly conclude that the neonatal timing of circumcision in some sense extends the birthing process. The rite further separates the boy from his mother as a type of secondary cutting of the umbilicus (see also TL 4.8; Róheim 1942:339–49; Pollock 1973; Van Gennep 1960; Kristeva 1982:100). I also see circumcision as a male rendition of birth. Similarly, the ritual opening of the penis and the inevitable, if not intentional, issuing of blood evoke menstruation. In most cultures that practice male circumcision, moreover, the rite contributes to the collective initiation of boys into manhood. But the biblical ceremony, like most puberty rites for girls, centers on the individual. I agree with Hoffman (1996) that circumcision separates male from female. But the rite also blurs that very same boundary. It masculinizes birth and feminizes men.

Humorous Fertility

Sarah's blessing and name change, while unique among biblical woman, amounts to only one verse in Genesis 17. She is a mere covenantal afterthought in comparison to Abraham. Her name translates as "princess," or perhaps "breasts" (Bakan 1979:74–77). Abraham is "father (*ab*) of a multitude of nations (*hamon*)." Sarah represents regal nurture. Abraham sires a world.

When God promises multitudinous "seed" to Abraham, the patriarch tumbles to the ground. He falls again on hearing the prediction of Sarah's pregnancy, only this time while laughing.[7] Abraham finds nothing funny about his own aged rejuvenation or the idea of cutting his penis to assist this renewal. He laughs only when God mentions elderly Sarah's fertility. However much this chuckle ridicules the female body, though, the covenant really passes *not* through Abraham, who has already fathered a son (Ishmael), *but through Sarah*. Despite circumcision and Abraham's laughter, uterine fertility is not so easily ignored. Sarah has her own moment of anticovenantal cackle. Three mysterious guests visit Abraham in Genesis 18 to augur the birth of Isaac. Abraham responds with a hospitable meal—bread, calf, curds, and milk—prepared by his wife. Yet Sarah's cooking is slyly subversive, noticed the rabbis, since the meal violated the later prohibition on mixing milk and meat (Ginzberg 1909–1938:V:235 n. 140). If Sarah's newly rejuvenated fertility implied the onset of menstruation, moreover, then the meal was also polluted (GR 48:14; ER 15:12). This aside, Sarah lurks outside Abraham's tent to eavesdrop on the conversation between her husband and the strangers. She "laughed to herself. . . . Now that I am withered, am I to have pleasure—with my husband so old?" While this "pleasure" ('*ednah*) evokes "sexual moistness" (Alter 1996:79), Sarah ridicules more than her own orgasm and menstrual flow. She mocks Abraham's virility and, more important, the efficacy of circumcision.

When Abraham scoffed at God's promise of covenantal fertility, he received only a gentle scolding. The scorn of woman is another matter. In Melanesia, men tell of a mythic era when ancestresses played sacred flutes. One day, jealous men stole the instruments. Ever since, they say, women give birth and men blow flutes. The melodies represent the voices of ancestral spirits who also govern pregnancy. During ritual, women must hear the tunes but never glimpse the flutes. Men enforce this rule with the threat of gang rape. Why? Because they fear that women may realize the true identity of the spirits and steal back the flutes.

Did sexual violence protect men's ceremonial privileges in ancient Israel? I already suggested as much for the deadly transformation of Lot's wife. Now I want to offer a similar interpretation of circumcision, a bloody and violent ritual enacted by men to sustain fertility. It is *not* unreasonable to see circumcision as a veiled threat to mothers: disrupt male ritual, and more than your son's foreskin will bleed!

Melanesian men also protect their ritual privileges with elaborate secrecy. They do so, argues Tuzin (1995), because they are unable to explain the seriousness of their rites without seeming foolish to women. By laughing, Sarah did precisely what Melanesian men fear. The rabbis might have agreed with this interpretation (SH 23:77; Ginzberg 1909–1938:I:278, V:250 n. 235). In Genesis 22, Abraham prepares to sacrifice his son, Isaac. At the last instant, an angel stays the knife (chapter 5). Shortly thereafter, Sarah dies—punishment, said the rabbis, for her disbelieving laughter outside Abraham's tent.

The narrative of Genesis positions Sarah outside Abraham's tent. But Sarah's laughter ridicules the marginalization of motherhood. The Semitic root of the word "laughter" (*t-s-q*) also means "to menstruate" (Stetkevych 1996). Sarah's chuckle, which immediately follows the narrator's comment about her postmenopausal age, is a self-parody. Yet Sarah also snickers at Abraham's elderly erection and the masculine inflection of covenantal fertility.

God tells Abraham to name his future son Yitshaq (Isaac). Most Jews tie this name to the cognate word for "laughter" (Genesis 21:6–7). But, linguistically, Isaac is no less menstrual. His birth, like Sarah's chuckle, represents a maternal rejoinder to circumcision.

Nature and Culture

Circumcision rites in south-central Africa promote male virility through tree symbols such as erect wood and semen-like whitish porridges (Gluckman 1949; White 1953; Turner 1962, 1967). Equally fruitful was the biblical rite (Eilberg-Schwartz 1990:chap. 6). The ancient Israelites, recall, circumcised both penises and trees since, in their worldview, foreskins impeded human and arboreal fruitfulness (chapter 2). Through circumcision, culture triumphs over nature, and nature validates the culture of male authority.

Maimonides, the great medieval philosopher, also tied circumcision to the nature–culture dichotomy. The pain of the rite, he wrote famously in *The Guide of the Perplexed* (3:35), inhibited the "violent concupiscence and lust that goes beyond what is needed" for procreation. Rabbi Isaac ben Yedaiah, writing in the thirteenth century, vividly expanded on this view (Biale 1997:94–95). The uncircumcised man pleasures his partner with an "iron" erection. He "thrusts inside her a great long time because of the foreskin, which is a barrier against ejaculation." When he tries to leave, his partner "brazenly grasps him, holding on to his genitals," and begs him for further intercourse. He relents, night after night, until, crazed and emaciated, "his heart dies within him; between her legs he sinks and falls." By contrast, the circumcised man ejaculates quickly, then remains satisfied for seven days. Since his wife rarely enjoys orgasm, she readily allows him to return to his studies.

An eighteenth-century Hasidic admirer of Maimonides, Nahman of Bratslav, also understood circumcision to dampen sexual desire. Jewish men experience "real suffering" during intercourse, he wrote, "like that which the infant undergoes when he is circumcised" (D. Biale 1997:135–36). Consequently, pious men unite with God, not women, except for lustless procreation.

These ascetic meditations on circumcision have more in common with Pauline Christianity than most rabbinic traditions. They certainly differ from the thrust of ancient Israelite religion. Nonetheless, this view does resemble the biblical outlook by positioning circumcision between nature and culture. These meditations also express rabbinic ambivalence toward sexuality—circumcised sexuality, more specifically.

Most rabbinic authorities believed circumcision to perfect the penis by removing a natural defect. Not so, said Maimonides (*Guide* 3:49). Since God created the foreskin, he argued, the uncircumcised penis is both natural and perfect (Stern 1993:133). Yet perfect nature is wild, thus necessitating the imposition of cultural rules and, in the case of circumcision, an intentional mar. While the uncircumcised penis is naturally perfect but morally imperfect, the circumcised penis is naturally imperfect but morally perfect. Here, again, the circumcised penis mediates between nature and culture.

"Cut Off" or "Cut Off"

Men who neglect to "cut off" the foreskin, as Exodus 4:25 describes circumcision, are themselves "cut off" (Genesis 17:14). The "cutting off" (*kārēt*) penalty refers to the divine annihilation of an Israelite family through the halting of future births. It applies to a broad array of violations that either disrupt cosmic order or confound the boundary between sacred and profane (Wold 1979:24; Frymer-Kensky 1983:405). These transgressions include the consumption of blood, working on the Sabbath, idolatry, child sacrifice, incest, and certain types of uncleanliness. The "cutting off" punishment seems especially fitting for noncircumcision since the rite symbolizes the binary structure of the cosmos by dividing the body into hallowed wholeness and impure prepuce.

Linguistically, the "cutting off" penalty resembles the "cutting" of covenants. Circumcision cuts men into the community by cutting away their foreskins. The fruitful slice of circumcision also symbolizes its own fruitless or emasculating punishment.

The dialogical meanings of "cutting off" resemble Amazonian penis sheathing (Lévi-Strauss 1988). The sheath advertises a man's entitlement to pursue sexual relations and marriage. Yet public displays of the glans are shameful. Consequently, the phallic sheath obscures the phallus it celebrates. The same paradox occurs in Melanesia (Gell 1971). On Melekula, for example, "circum-incision" exposed the glans, which men then covered with a pandanus wrapper (Layard 1942:chap. 18). A cultural foreskin clothed the naked, natural prepuce.

Circumcision also uncovers the glans, only to, as the rabbis saw it, enwrap men in a garment of holiness. In fact, the rabbis forbid prayer before an unclad penis (chapter 2). Yet they denounced men who concealed their circumcision in legitimately naked settings such as bathhouses. A covered circumcision is akin to a covered glans. Both transgressions result in the "cutting off" penalty. Despite the sanctity of circumcision, it resembles a sacred pun.

Castration?

We can also interpret circumcision as a dramatization of intergenerational male rivalry, often called the Oedipus complex (see, relatedly, Paul 1996). A father cuts his son's penis. Nevertheless, this seemingly aggressive slice actually ensures the father's legacy. Potential emasculation turns reproductive. For this reason, oedipal tension alone will not suffice to explain the rite.

The covenant promises progeny to men who symbolically sever their genitals. A circumcised man is thus a "fertile castrate" (Bakan 1979:144). Of course, another type of person lacks a penis yet remains reproductive: women. Indeed, I earlier remarked that the perfection promised by circumcision, which opens a man's genitals to blood and fertility, emulates the female body.

I also noted earlier that the Torah bans eunuchs. Celibacy violates God's repeated demand that humans procreate—an obligation incumbent mainly on men (D. Feldman 1975; R. Biale 1984). The Law also requires men, or at least new husbands, "to give happiness" to their wives (Deuteronomy 24:5). These dictums argue against any castrative intent to circumcision.

Still, circumcision comes perilously close to cutting off the possibility of reproduction and intercourse. Several episodes in the Torah, in fact, expressly link circumcision to castration. In Genesis 24, a Hivite named Shechem rapes Jacob's daughter, Dinah. Afterward, he proposes marriage. But Dinah's brothers refuse "to give our sister to a man who is uncircumcised, for that is a disgrace among us" (Genesis 34:14). Only circumcised men can enter Israelite women—and enter cult spaces (Ezekiel 44:7) and Jerusalem (Isaiah 52:1). But Dinah's brothers offer a compromise. They will consent to the marriage if the Hivites undergo circumcision. They agree. Three days later, while the Hivites are still "in pain," the brothers slaughter them and seize their wealth, flocks, children, and wives. This tale colors circumcision with deception, castration, and revenge. It construes the rite as a fatal, retributive rape.

A similar incident occurs later in the Hebrew Bible. God warns Moses against cutting covenants with local tribes lest the Israelites "lust after their gods" (Exodus 34:10–16). Of course, the Israelites do just that. As punishment, God orders Moses to impale the leaders of this sexual idolatry (Numbers 25). "Just then," an Israelite man brazenly escorts a Midianite woman past the contritely weeping people and into a tent for a tryst. So outraged is Phinehas, the High Priest's grandson, that he thrusts a spear through the

Israelite and his lover's "belly" (Numbers 25:6–8). God rewards Phinehas with an eternal "covenant of peace." This deadly penetration, I propose, which resulted from the sexual "cutting" of an illicit "covenant," makes sense only in reference to circumcision.

A clearer link between circumcision and castration occurs when Saul deceitfully offers his daughter to David in marriage (1 Samuel 18). Since Saul ultimately wants David killed, he demands a seemingly impossible bride-price: "the foreskins of a hundred Philistines." Yet David triumphs. He severs *twice* the number of Philistine prepuces.[8]

The covenantal cut also turns violent when, after a mass circumcision, the Israelites destroy Jericho (Joshua 5–6). Another aggressive circumcision occurs during Jacob's nocturnal tussle with a divine assailant in Genesis 32. One combatant strikes the "hollow" (*kap*) of his opponent's groin (Smith 1990; Eilberg-Schwartz 1994:152–58).[9] Afterward, Jacob is renamed Israel. Most readers understand the angel in this grammatically vague passage to wound Jacob, who then symbolically fathers the Israelites. Jacob's wound thus resembles Abraham's circumcision (Steinmetz 1991:132). Yet Eslinger (1981) provocatively sees Jacob smacking the angel, a type of below-the-belt blow that Deuteronomy 25:11–12 later deems unjust and unmanly. From this angle, the assault conjures a castrative rather than covenantal cut. Either way, the Israelite lineage receives its formal identity after a chop that resembles an ambiguous circumcision.

The Deuteronomy passage I just mentioned warrants further comment. It states that, if two men are fighting and one opponent's wife grabs the other man's genitals to save her husband, "you shall cut off her hand (*kap*); show no pity." Why? Perhaps a woman who seizes a man's groin appears to mock circumcision. She transforms the cut that promotes male "seed" into a slice that threatens masculine virility (cf. Carmichael 1977). The word for "hand" (*kap*) also appears in the account of Jacob's wrestling match, where it refers to the scrotum or "hollow" of the thigh. Through a double entendre, the same word also refers to the labia in Song of Songs 5:5 (Eslinger 1981). A woman who clenches a man's genitals, then, is bullied by the threat of her own circumcision!

Earlier, I argued that circumcision feminizes men so they can reproduce the covenant. Now it appears that, at least according to Deuteronomy, circumcision can also masculinize women, not to admit them into the covenant but to doubly exclude them from it. Male privilege is women's punishment.

Foreskins Foul and Feminine

Dinah's brothers viewed the biblical prepuce as a disgrace, reproach, or shame (*ḥerpah*). This disgust served as prooftext for the rabbis, who declared the foreskin "more unclean than all unclean things . . . a blemish above all blemishes" (PRE 29; GR 80:8). They associated the prepuce with dogs, carrion, corpses, sores, and inedible fruit stalks (M. Nedarim 3:10; B. Pesachim 92a; GR 46:1, 10; Kraemer 1996). Since God, moreover, restricted the first Passover feast and thus emancipation to the circumcised (Exodus 12), the biblical foreskin also connoted death and enslavement.

Ironically, circumcision also proclaims servitude—albeit to God, not man (Bernat 2002:81–105). The rite pierced the Israelite penis much like slaves were pierced through the ear (Exodus 21:6; Deuteronomy 15:17). Both marks inscribe the body within a regime of power and authority.

Foreskins blight more than penises and fruit. Immoral Israelites possess "uncircumcised hearts" (Deuteronomy 10:16; 30:6) and "uncircumcised ears" (Jeremiah 4:4; 6:10).[10] These foreskins thwart one from understanding and heeding the Law. The prepuce also connotes uncontrollability and wildness (Krohn 1985:80; Hirsch 1988:75–76). "I have never been a man with words," says Moses, "I am slow of speech and slow of tongue" (Exodus 4:10). Later, Moses refers to his stammering lips as "uncircumcised" or "foreskinned" (Exodus 6:12; 30). They spew nonsense. That which is foreskinned, summarizes Eilberg-Schwartz (1990:149), fails to perform its proper tasks. Israelites who abide by the covenant, states Leviticus 26, will enjoy rain, fruit, peace, fertility, and erect walking. Those with "uncircumcised hearts," however, will suffer consumption, fever, famine, pestilence, death, exile, cannibalism, and wild animal attacks on their children. Here the prepuce symbolizes a nightmarish world forsaken by God.

The biblical foreskin also represents feminine immorality. Jeremiah 3–4 likens sinful Israelites to a promiscuous whore. For atonement, they must "circumcise their hearts." While this metaphor opens the covenant to women, the language of redemption still privileges men and penises (Shields 1995). The many shifting meanings of foreskins and circumcision, like the marginalization of biblical and Jewish women, arise from an inability to create a stable sense of manhood.

Bodily Wholeness

The rise of Christianity aggressively charged the Hellenistic ideal of foreskinned manhood with theological imperative. To counter this hegemony, argue Barth (1991:50) and others, the rabbis defended circumcision as an ethical and bodily perfection. But this defense, I will now show, has earlier roots.

Foreskins, we have seen, inhibited the Israelites, especially men, from hearing, obeying, speaking, and reproducing the covenant. "He who separates himself from circumcision," said the rabbis, "is like one separated from the Holy One" (PRE 29). But any physical circumcision of a mouth, ear, or heart would result in mutilation, not wholeness, thus barring one from many devotional practices (GR 46:5; LR 25:6). Only the penile foreskin can undergo a literal circumcision.

The quality of wholeness (*tamim*) resulting from circumcision initially seems moral (Genesis 6:9). But biblical law mandated the same wholeness, or absence of blemish, for sacrificial animals (e.g., Leviticus 4:32). In this regard, circumcision promises both ethical and physical completeness (Hoffman 1996:35). Concern for bodily integrity also explains the exclusion of lame, blind, disfigured, and diminutive men from the priesthood. Likewise, temporary ritual pollution (*tamei*) and physical ailments barred priests from their ceremonial duties until after a ritual cleansing (Leviticus 21:16–23). Physical blemishes similarly polluted ordinary Israelites. Foreskinless wholeness, then, fits into a broader pattern of bodily purity in biblical culture.

No ritual cosmetically mends a blemished animal. But man can and must remedy his own corporeal defect through circumcision. In European—that is, Christian—society, persons are born physically complete, albeit undeveloped. But the biblical and Jewish body, as elsewhere (Ahmadu 2000:284), requires postpartum refinement. Indeed, many cultures liken uncircumcised foreskins to female genitalia (Turner 1967:265–74; Silverman 2004). Male bodily wholeness thus hinges on a penile extraction. The natural body of man is simply incomplete. A similar view likely shaped biblical circumcision.

When God invited Abram to become whole, says midrash, the patriarch wondered, "Surely, until now I have been whole in body, but if I circumcise myself I shall be incomplete" (T-Y 3:16). To this, God responded, "Why do you believe that you are whole? In fact you lack five limbs." The uncircumcised name Abram, spelled with four Hebrew letters (*alef, bet, resh,* and *mem,* or אברם), numerically totals 243. But humans possess 248 limbs, at least according to medieval anatomy. "Circumcise yourself and you will be whole," God continued, since the additional letter *heh* (ה), which equals five, transforms Abram into Abraham (אברהם), or 248, the full body of man (see also GR 46:3; NR 18:21; B. Nedarim 32b; TG 3.20; 5.6; Zohar 1:200b–201a).[11] In this worldview, circumcision perfects the male body.

Masculine Wholeness

The wholeness promised by biblical circumcision anticipated by centuries Jacques Lacan's controversial theory of psychoanalytic selfhood. At the same time, this theory helps us identify further nuances in the biblical rite.

The norms of social life, Lacan argued, must eventually shatter the intimate oneness of the mother–child bond. This way, children learn to seek fulfillment not through infantile desires but through cultural goals and conventions. Ironically, the primary drive of the self is to regain originary wholeness. But "if the self felt itself to become whole," writes Trawick (1990:145), "then human life would end, everything would stop." In this sense, culture must fail. Wholeness is illusory.

Biblical circumcision, like culture in Lacan's theory, inevitably fails. The recurrence of tragedy in Genesis, which I detail shortly, poignantly illustrates the impossibility of wholeness. Additionally, the biblical covenant seemingly offers wholeness to everyone. Yet circumcision privileges male bodies and paternal authority—much like Lacan's cultural norms (Lacan 1977:287; Carpenter 1988; Lupton 1999:196–97). Masculinity masquerades as universalism.

Lacan's theory stresses infantile loss. So did the rabbis. A lit candle atop the head of a baby, they said, which illuminates the passage of birth, extinguishes on delivery (B. Niddah 30b). The fetus, perhaps representing the ideal male scholar, learns the entire Torah from an angel, only to forget everything at birth. And infant boys, of course, experience the loss of their foreskins. At the end of life, moreover, men loose their libido—a depletion that, in the case of Abraham, circumcision apparently rejuvenated (GR 46:2; 85:1). The wholeness promised by circumcision, then, often addresses specifically male anxieties.

Despite its masculine inflection, circumcision in many cultures refers to motherhood. The severed prepuce in an Australian Aboriginal society represented the boy's separation from his mother (Róheim 1942:366). Yet the rite offered psychological restoration by identifying the boy with adult men and ancestor spirits—males who assumed the custodial role of a mother. The boy thus shifted from one "dual-unity" to another, thereby relinquishing masculine autonomy (Róheim 1945:101; see also Mehta 1996). Initiation gifts that embodied paternal potency, moreover, displayed uterine symbols (Róheim 1942:354–55; 1945:chaps. 5–6). Indeed, the boy "becomes the mother from whom the foreskin (child) is separated" (Róheim 1945:78). Aboriginal circumcision not only defined men as a mother but also celebrated manhood by recalling the importance of mothers during childhood.

Islamic circumcision in Morocco reveals similar symbolism (Crapanzano 1981). The boy is cut, then swaddled like an infant and returned to his mother, who consoles his tears and tends the wound. The Moroccan rite offers no transition to adult masculinity. Instead, the ceremony dramatizes male longing for motherhood. Anthropologists typically understand violent puberty rites to sever the mother–son bond, snap boys from their feminine identity, and imprint male youth with masculine ideas.[12] The rite is a type of adolescent weaning (Ammar 1954:122–23; Bilu 2000). But as Crapanzano and Róheim suggest, circumcision often thwarts as much as it enacts male emancipation from motherhood.[13] Circumcision, God implied to Abraham in Genesis 17, enables males to walk. This ability was a biblical sign of adulthood (Leviticus 26:3). But what did Abraham do on receiving the covenant and circumcision? He fell to the ground, thus regressing to infancy and undermining the circumcised erection of masculine wholeness.

Circumcision, Incest, and Freud

Freudians analyze puberty circumcision as a violent and castrative gesture that disciplines potentially unruly sons, legitimates paternal authority, and preserves the father's sexual monopoly over local women (e.g., Freud 1913, 1940).[14] So powerfully does circumcision arouse anxiety, wrote Freud (e.g., 1909, 1939), that the rite motivates anti-Semitism.[15]

Freud's oedipal view of circumcision remains controversial (e.g., Boyarin 1997b). But as I have shown, the Torah clearly links the rite to castration and aggression. Each major circumcision episode in the Hebrew Bible, moreover, seems to channel male sexuality to the fulfillment of God's plan (Goldingay 2000:13–14). The rite marks a turning point in the lives of the patriarchs. As a type of test, circumcision communicates the message that manhood is perilous yet safe (Levy 1973:371–73; Öztürk 1973; Rosen 1988). The circumcised penis, writes Paul (1990:328–29), is "heroically scarred." Masculine triumph, as Freud would agree, remains contained by paternal authority.

Two aspects of infant circumcision, however, diverge from the Freudian paradigm. First, newborns pose little direct threat to paternal authority. (Of course, children do represent a father's eventual replacement and death.) Second, infants lack the cognitive abilities to apprehend ritual messages. Many psychoanalytic interpreters thus see biblical and Jewish circumcision as reenacting the *father's* long-dormant oedipal conflicts, revived by the birth of his son and projected onto the child (Róheim 1945; Nunberg 1949; Reik

1951:105; Malev 1966; Kitahara 1976; Graber 1981; Rosen 1988; see also Benchekrouon 1982). Perhaps, then, it is prudent to view circumcision from a binocular perspective. The rite serves as a cultural enactment of unresolved paternal anxieties and, many years later, offers a reminder to the son of man's impotence before God and paternal authority (Schlossmann 1966:252–53).[16]

Biblical circumcision likewise complicates Freud's thesis that circumcision foils a son's incestuous desires. The rite admitted the Israelites into the Promised Land. Like a mother, this land flows or oozes (*zuwb*) with milk, a verb that also describes menstruation (Leviticus 15:19). Like a lover, the Promised Land drips with the sweetness of honey (Bal 1987). The covenant thus promises an erotic reunion with a terrestrial mother figure (Cronbach 1931–1932:637–38; Rosenzweig 1940:53–58; Zeligs 1961:177). From this angle, circumcision cuts taboo into, not out of, the covenant.

Zeligs (1974:30–31) argued that Abraham's circumcision aimed to "cut off" immorality from the patriarch's near-incestuous marriage to Sarah, thus allowing for the proper birth of Isaac and the covenantal lineage (see also Donaldson 1981). The rite split siblings into spouses. But this scheme actually renders circumcision a failure since Abraham, we saw earlier, later transforms his wife *back* into a sister. Here, again, circumcision inscribes on the penis no resolution but only an irreducible tension between desire and morality.

Feminine Men

Circumcision deeds a milky land to Israelite men so they, in turn, can nourish life like mothers (Bakan 1979:167; cf. Paul 1996:98–105; Pardes 2000:62–63). The rite also shapes men into an image of erotic femininity.

"Walk with Me," said God to Abraham when introducing circumcision, and become "whole" or "perfect" (Genesis 17:1). Here is Rabbi Levi's interpretation:

> This may be illustrated by a noble lady whom the king commanded, "Walk before me." She walked before him and her face went pale, for, thought she, who knows but that some defect may have been found in me? Said the king to her, "Thou hast no defect, but that the nail of thy little finger is slightly too long; pare it and the defect will be gone." Similarly, God said to Abraham, "Thou has no other defect but this foreskin: remove it and the defect will be gone." (GR 46:4)

Rabbi Levi equated circumcision with feminine beauty such that God viewed Abraham's penis with erotic innuendo.[17]

The rabbis similarly interpreted Psalm 45:3–4, "You are fairer than all men. . . . Gird your sword upon your thigh, O hero, in your splendor and glory," as expressing God's appraisal of Abraham. In their words, "perform the circumcision between your thighs, and it will add to your majesty" (T-Y 3:18).[18] The rabbis often construed circumcision as a wedding between God and his bride, Israel (NR 12:8; T-Y 3:17; Boyarin 1994:128–29). In rabbinic culture, circumcision distinguishes male from female (GR 46:5; LR 25:6; Hoffman 1996). Yet circumcision also confounds gender (Eilberg-Schwartz 1994:70–74). The rite feminizes men for God's pleasure. The rabbis formalized two stages of the circumcision procedure: excision of the foreskin, called *milah*, and exposure of the corona by peeling away the subcutaneous membrane, or *periah* (see chapter 7). In Kabbalah, these two stages represent the male and female dimensions of the deity (Wolfson 1987b:201–2). By thus uniting male and female within the penis, writes Wolfson (1994b:168), circumcision restores "the primal unity of God."

Additionally, Kabbalah associated the corona of the penis with the earthly and female personification of God, the Shekhinah, whom I discussed in chapter 1. Thus framed, circumcision represents the visionary goal of mystical devotion (Wolfson 1995:107, 2003). By implication, a glance at the "sign" of the covenant was tantamount to seeing God's phallus—a phallus that mirrored the masculofeminine qualities of the male body.

The mystics and rabbis also saw the circumcised penis as an eye onto God—an optical, erotic, and even vaginal opening through which men receive the divine presence (Wolfson 1987a, 1987b, 1994b:187–88).[19] Circumcision creates a "whole" body that is neither wholly male nor wholly female.

But if circumcision engenders androgyny, why not circumcise women? The theme of couvade offers a satisfactory answer. In a sense, women *are* circumcised but in the absence of ritual. Any comparable rite for women would seem redundant since they and not men are the true brides of God and the true begetters of children (Eilberg-Schwartz 1994). Male envy of female fertility explains the noncircumcision of women.

The Purloined Penis

Let us return to Genesis. The covenantal patrimony passes from Abraham to Isaac, then to twins who tussle in Rachel's womb, Esau and Jacob (Genesis

25). At birth, Jacob clasps his elder brother's heel or euphemistic genitals (Smith 1990), foreshadowing Jacob's later theft of the covenantal birthright. Since Esau hunts while Jacob farms, the twins inherit the conflict between nature and culture set in motion by Cain and Abel.

Esau's red hair illustrates his thirst for blood (see also GR 78:9; T-Y 8:4). Famished after a day of hunting, Esau famously swaps his birthright with Jacob for a bowl of "red red stuff" (Genesis 25:30). Despite this grotesque appetite, Isaac favors Esau, not Jacob, especially Esau's meat, much as God once enjoyed Abel's animals. The embodiment of biblical authority is not restraint and maternal nurture but devourment and paternal slaughter. Isaac knows this well since, as I discuss in chapter 5, he was almost sacrificed as a boy by his own father. Rebekah favors Jacob, not Esau. Meat and milk do not mix.

Isaac lays dying and near blind in Genesis 27. He asks Esau to prepare "a dish of the kind that I love . . . so that I may solemnly bless you before I die." Rebekah, emulating Sarah, eavesdrops on the conversation. Aghast at the thought of Esau inheriting the paternal blessing, she commands Jacob to fetch two lambs. She cooks Isaac's meal, then dresses Jacob in Esau's garments, slipping his arms into the lambskins to feign Esau's hirsute limbs. The ruse succeeds. Jacob feeds his dim-sighted father, who bestows the paternal blessing onto the wrong son. Jacob flees and is shortly renamed Israel. When Esau returns, he trembles and wails, but paternal blessings are irrevocable. The Israelite lineage, as Armstrong (1993) remarks, establishes its identity in a wrenching moment of matrimonial betrayal, paternal impotence, and filial pathos.[20] The future of circumcised wholeness hinges on a broken family. Jacob's duplicity inverts the morality of circumcision. The rite peels away a phallic skin of animality to signify filial and covenantal piety. Yet Jacob donned an animal pelt to deceive his father and purloin the covenant. Circumcision enhances vision. Yet Jacob exploited his father's ailing eyesight.[21] And while circumcision negates motherhood, Jacob's theft of the covenant hinged on a mother's sabotage of paternal authority (see also Reik 1951:229–51; Rashkow 2000:chap. 6). Within rabbinic culture, Jacob's symbolical reversal of circumcision seems particularly ironic since the rabbis often viewed Esau as the personification of the uncircumcised or epispastic apostate (Ginzberg 1909–1938:I:315, V:273 n. 25).

Jacob registers no qualms about his betrayal. Later, "Jacob's guilty conscious prompts him to shameful obsequiousness" and a compensatory offer of livestock (Genesis 33). Esau refuses, choosing instead to forgive his brother "wholeheartedly" (Graves and Patai 1983:233). The very man who embod-

ied uncircumcision to the rabbis lived the moral ideal of circumcised wholeness while the man named Israel succumbed to an immoral foreskin.

Dinah's Rape and Circumcised Retribution

The moral ambiguity of circumcision seems especially evident during
another episode in Jacob's life. In Genesis 29, Jacob asks to wed Rachel. He
toils in bride-service for seven years, then surprisingly awakens from the nuptial bed with Rachel's older sister, Leah! For having once deceived his own
father, Jacob is now duped by a father-in-law. So Jacob labors another seven
years and finally marries his beloved and beautiful Rachel. Alas, Rachel
proves barren while her "unloved" sister births three sons. Then, echoing the
entanglement between Sarah and Hagar, Rachel offers her slave girl to Jacob,
who also delivers sons (Genesis 30:3). As the two sisters vie for one husband's love, they mirror the earlier competition between two brothers "over
a blessing that cannot be halved" (Pardes 1992a:66; Alter 1996:178). Eventually, God "opens" Rachel's womb, and she births Joseph, the last born and
favorite of Jacob's twelve sons.

In Genesis 34, as I discussed earlier, a Hivite rapes Dinah, the daughter of
Jacob and Leah. Most rabbis blamed the victim for her immodesty since
Dinah "went out to visit the daughters of the land" (Genesis 34:1; Bronner
1994:118–21; GR 80:1–6). Yet some rabbis faulted Jacob for failing to
espouse Dinah "to one who is circumcised" (GR 80:4; 76:9). Either way, a
woman is raped to preserve male honor.

Jacob responds to his daughter's rape with silence, perhaps indifference.
But not Dinah's brothers. When the rapist proposes marriage, they demand
circumcision, a deception that linguistically echoes their father's guile when
filching Esau's patrimony. The brothers then slaughter the convalescing Hivites. Furious, Jacob scolds his sons for "making me odious among the inhabitants of the land . . . if they unite against me and attack me, I and my house
will be destroyed" (Genesis 34:30). Evidently, Jacob's concern with protecting his household did not extend to his daughter.[22]

Much later in the Hebrew Bible, King David's daughter, Tamar, suffers
rape by her half-brother, Amnon, despite pleading with him to marry her
instead, crying, "Where will I carry my shame?" (2 Samuel 13). Dinah, wrote
the rabbis, similarly pleaded with her own brothers to remain with Shechem
since a sullied woman attracted few suitors (GR 80:11). As an alternative,
Dinah's brother, Simeon, "swore that he would marry her." In reaching this
conclusion, the rabbis noticed that Genesis 46 reports an unnamed Canaan-

ite mother for one of Simeon's sons. In this reasoning, Dinah's rape and sexual immorality were so unworthy of an Israelite that she assumed a Canaanite identity. However obliquely, the rabbis here connected circumcision to incest.

This connection, though, extends to the biblical narrative. Rabbis and scholars have long pondered Jacob's silence after Dinah's rape, especially in contrast to his rebuke of the brothers after the circumcision massacre (e.g., Fewell and Gunn 1991). But no interpreter has looked to the logic of myth and drawn an obvious, albeit shocking, conclusion: Jacob raped Dinah. Often, myth simplifies psychological complexity by doubling or splitting individual personalities into two characters. Dinah represents the intergenerational double of her mother, Leah, the unloved wife of Jacob who thwarted his desire for Rachel. (Leah and Rachel are also doubles, much like the other siblings and twins in Genesis.) Shechem assumes a parallel role with respect to Jacob. Dinah's rape is Jacob's revenge.[23] But not for long.

On Rachel's death, Dinah's full brother, Reuben, "lay" with Jacob's concubine—a woman who also served as Rachel's slave girl (Genesis 35:22). Leah's sons further retaliate against their father by flinging his favorite son, Joseph, into a pit and dipping his garment in lamb's blood to feign an attack by wild beasts.[24] This plot mimics Jacob's use of lambskin to fool his own father. It also, I add, represents Esau's revenge.

Judah schemed the bloodstained cloak. His own son, Er, marries Tamar, a name later given to the daughter of David who suffered sibling rape. But God judges Er "displeasing" or "evil" and kills him. Judah tells his next son, Onan, to wed Tamar and sire a son for Er. But Onan refuses to cede "seed." He practices *coitus interruptus*, and so God kills him, too. Then Judah pledges his youngest son to Tamar. But Judah has no intention of keeping his vow. Humiliated, Tamar swaps her mourning garb for a veil and slyly waits for Judah. Thinking her a whore, he says, "Let me come into you." Tamar asks for payment, and Judah pledges a goat. But she knows well his promises and so demands a guarantee. Judah hands over his seal and cord (signet) and staff, two phallic tokens of masculine authority. After the tryst, Tamar conceives. When Judah later hears a rumor that his daughter-in-law "played the harlot," he demands her death—until Tamar reveals his gifts. Admits Judah, "She is more in the right than I."

In the twelfth century, Yehuda Halevi composed a liturgical poem in praise of circumcision that he called a "seal" and "cord" (Krohn 1985:140). Despite the poet's honorific intent, the allusion to Judah and Tamar argues against any simple morality by evoking a long family history of oedipal aggression, deceit, incest, rape, and fratricide. The covenantal lineage, sealed by circumcision, is a tale of woe and ambivalence, not moral wholeness.

In this chapter, I continued to argue that we can best understand the meanings of biblical circumcision through a lens hewn of symbolic anthropology and moderate psychoanalytic theory. More specifically, I provided further evidence that circumcision cuts an image of masculinity that opposes yet emulates female fertility, motherhood, and femininity. The rite, too, expresses considerable biblical and rabbinic ambivalence toward covenantal morality. How else can we explain the recurrence of themes of incest? How else can we explain that, despite all circumcision promises—wholeness, vision, progeny, land, and emancipation—the Israelites still needed to enforce its occurrence with violent intimidation? Cut, or die!

Additionally, I argued that circumcision seeks to mediate between nature and culture. The rite also expresses ambivalence toward sexuality. The Torah reports that, after the Hivite massacre, Dinah's brothers "took her out of Shechem's house" (Genesis 34:26). Why "took"? Because, reasoned the rabbis, "When a woman is intimate with an uncircumcised person, she finds it hard to tear herself away" (GR 80:11). The foreskin here symbolizes rabbinic uneasiness with eros despite the fact that the terms and the bodily sign of the covenant demand and celebrate sexuality.

The anxieties represented by circumcision help explain the persistence of familial deceit and tragedy in Genesis. They also account for the violence that suffuses many circumcision episodes. I discussed many such incidents. There are more. The "uncircumcised" emasculate Sampson by shearing his hair (Judges 15). Saul beseeches his arms bearer to "draw your sword and run me through, so that the uncircumcised may not run me through and make sport of me" (1 Samuel 31:3–10). Conversely, the "uncircumcised" themselves suffer violent penetrations by circumcised swords (Ezekiel 32; 1 Samuel 18:25). All this biblical aggression points to a profound ambivalence concerning the covenantal rite.

Shortly after Abraham circumcised his household, God dispatched three angels to announce the future birth of Isaac. In legend, the angels initially refuse this task (PRE 29; B. Baba Metzia 86b; T-Y 4:2; TG 4.4). Why such concern with a mere human, they asked God? Why descend to a place so defiled with stench and a "river of blood"? Because, answers God, "the savor of this blood is sweeter to me than myrrh and frankincense." Elsewhere, the rabbis imagined a "a hillock of foreskins" that putrefied in the hot sun, the odor ascending "to the Lord like sweet incense" (GR 47:7; SSR 4:6:1).

"When My children lapse into sinful ways," said God, "I will remember that odour in their favour and be filled with compassion." Surely, if circumcision presented the rabbis with no moral qualms, then they would have omitted mention of putrefying prepuces, rivers of blood, and foul fragrances. But they did not. Like the rabbis, then, my overall goal in this chapter was to demonstrate that, despite all efforts to shape circumcision into a moral exemplar, the rite admits of no such simplicity.

Notes

1. Anthropologists often see the sister/wife tales as reflecting the fragility of a kinship-based society that must balance endogamy and exogamy, or descent and alliance (Leach 1962; Carroll 1977).

2. In a Muslim tale, Sarah cuts off Hagar's nose, ear, and genitals, thus initiating female circumcision (Firestone 1990:67).

3. Teubal (1984:38–39) sees Sarah as a priestess from a noncircumcising matriarchy. Ishmael's laughter was a curious fondling of Isaac's foreskinned penis—the same penis that Hagar, as a circumcising Egyptian, wished to snip on behalf of Abraham's emergent, patriarchal religion.

4. They also "passed through" (Deuteronomy 29:11), "entered" (Ezekiel 16:8), and "stood in" (2 Kings 23:3) covenants. In 1 Kings 3:16–28, Solomon famously threatens to halve an infant to learn the whole truth.

5. The cutting, writes Issac (1967:54), represents not separation but the prior state of unity.

6. The Old and New *Testaments*, like the word testimony, derive from the Latin root *testi*, or "witness" and "testicles."

7. Some rabbis saw Abraham's two plummets as a rebuttal of God, necessitating as punishment two eras of noncircumcision: the Egyptian enslavement and the Sinaic wandering.

8. A twelfth-century inscription at the Great Temple of Karnak lists "uncircumcised phalli" as Egyptian war trophies (Breasted 1962:3:247–49). Biblical fingers, noses, and ears were similarly severed (Judges 1:6–7; Ezekiel 23:25). For additional castrative imagery in the Saul and David saga, see Paul (1985).

9. Jacob's sons drew on this very wounding, suggests Eilberg-Schwartz (1994:152–58), when plotting to avenge Dinah's rape.

10. Foreskinned Israelites were denied proper burial (Propp 1987:364–66; Ezekiel 28:10).

11. Circumcision reminded the rabbis of charity: loss perfects humanity.

12. Classic versions of this thesis include Whiting, Kluckhohn, and Anthony (1958), Burton and Whiting (1961), Harrington (1968), and Kitahara (1974); see also Silverman (2001).

13. For obvious reasons, Israelite and Jewish infants must return to the mother after circumcision; Genesis 21 mentions a weaning feast (Steinmetz 1991:188–89 n. 80; cf. Goldberg 1996:27).

14. For affinities between Freud and Maimonides, see Eckstein (1957) and Bakan (1997).

15. Many other psychoanalysts concurred (e.g., Fenichel 1946:27–28; Loewenstein 1951:34; Schoenfeld 1966).

16. Other Freudian analyses of circumcision include Reik (1915–1916), Daly (1950), Zimmermann (1951), Cansever (1965), and Heald (1999). For background to Freud's views on the rite, see Geller (1993, 1999), Gilman (1993a), Colman (1994), and Boyarin (1997b). Jungian approaches to circumcision include Hobson (1961), Dreifuss (1965), and Seligman (1965).

17. Another rabbinic tale similarly equates penis and finger. In it, Jacob avoids adultery by ejaculating through his fingers into the ground (GR 87:7, 98:20; B. Sotah 36b).

18. The rabbis (SSR 3:7:4) also identified the "sword" in Song of Songs 3:8 as a circumcised phallus.

19. The rabbis construed the vaginal imagery of Song of Songs 7:2, "Your rounded thighs are like jewels," as referring to circumcision (SSR 7:2:3).

20. So troubling was the idea of Jacob's thievery that some rabbis saw him as the rightful firstborn (Ginzberg 1909–1938:V:273 n. 22).

21. Psychoanalysts and Talmudic rabbis alike see eye loss as symbolic castration (B. Sotah 36a). Eye gouging was a biblical punishment (Numbers 16:14; 2 Kings 25:4–7).

22. Rabbinic texts also questioned the morality of the massacre—but not, again, the rape (T-Y 8:7; SH 34-35). Later compositions such as Jubilees sometimes omit entirely the circumcision episode.

23. David's inaction after Tamar's rape also hints at consent (Trible 1983:53–54). Later, Tamar's full brother, Absolom, kills Amnon and sleeps with David's concubines.

24. When the brothers eventually reunite in Genesis 45, says midrash, Joseph revealed his true identity by exposing his circumcision (GR 93:6, 10; T-Y 11:5).

CHAPTER FIVE

The Bloody Bridegroom

No interpretation of biblical and Jewish circumcision should neglect the symbolism of blood. Otherwise, we fail to realize that circumcision, like animal sacrifice, represents a positive and procreative spilling of male blood that inverts the negative qualities of menstrual blood. For this reason, both rites typically marginalized or excluded women and mothers. In this regard, circumcision resembles another sacrificial event during which a father wielded a knife above his young son, namely, Abraham's near sacrifice of Isaac. Blood, I will show, links circumcision to monotheistic terror as well as menstrual manhood. And how did women respond within the biblical narrative to this masculine symbolism? They subverted this ideology in the persona of Zipporah by throwing circumcision back on men, thus mocking the bloody, parturient assertions of God, male ritual, and the covenant.

Eight and Seven

Circumcision everywhere precedes marriage (Paige and Paige 1981). Many scholars assume that, since Ishmael was circumcised at age thirteen (Genesis 17:25), the biblical rite originally took place during puberty. Later, the ceremony shifted to infancy. Why? Perhaps the neonatal rite, among other possibilities, sought to include newborn boys in the covenant, shield them from demons, or guarantee a pleasant afterlife in the event of untimely death (Morgenstern 1963:36–39; Propp 1987:362–66). Since puberty circumcision often symbolizes a shift in responsibility for a boy's education from the household to a formal association of men, argues H. Goldberg (1996:27), the early age of the biblical rite stressed the importance of the family for socialization. Other scholars see the unusual timing of the ceremony as an effort to divorce circumcision from primitive notions of magical fertility (Fox 1974:589–95) or, by linking social status to birth, a validation of the hereditary priesthood (Eilberg-Schwartz 1994). But while these suggestions are useful, they provide little insight into why the biblical rite must occur on precisely the eighth day.

The number eight in the Torah frequently appears in connection with temple ritual. The High Priest, for example, wore eight vestments and mixed eight spices into the anointing oil. Eight-day durations typically pertain to sacrifice, consecration, renewal, and purification (e.g., Leviticus 9:1–6; 13–15; Numbers 6:10).[1] But the question remains, Why eight?

The biblical significance of the eighth day, I submit, pertains to the ubiquitous interval of seven, which signals rebirth and "the passage from sterility to fruitfulness" (Klingbeil 1997). The biblical phrase "for seven days" (šib'at yāmîm), which applies to cult ceremonies and rites of passage, suggests themes of purification, restoration, and holiness. This duration completes natural and physical cycles (Krohn 1985:61–62; Klingbeil 1997; Bailey 2000:165–69). The seven-day interval symbolizes worldly renewal.

But why seven? I alluded to the answer when interpreting Creation as a masculine rendition of childbirth. The source of the biblical seven-day interval is a typical menstrual period. Despite the attribution of contagious pollution to menstruating women, who were sequestered from the Israelite community for seven days (Leviticus 15:19–24), the female reproductive cycle nevertheless served as the schema for biblical notions of purity, creation, and male ritual.

Circumcision and Birth Pollution

After birthing a son, states Leviticus 12, a mother becomes "unclean for seven days, like the days of her menstrual impurity." On the eighth day, the boy is circumcised, and his mother enters into a thirty-three-day period of transition called "blood purification." The mother is no longer contagious. She may even resume conjugal relations. But she remains befouled and thus barred from sancta and holy spaces.[2]

The first week of a boy's life parallels the mother's seven days of impurity. Her pollution logically contaminates her son.[3] On the eighth day, the boy is cut off from this uncleanness by his circumcision. To the rabbis, in fact, circumcision resembled the ritual bath (mikvah) that cleanses women after menstruation (ER 23:12). The circumcised boy, like the woman emerging from her ablution, rejoins the community in a state of purity and real or symbolic fertility.

The eighth day is the earliest time when mother and son cease their contagiousness.[4] But this fact alone will not explain the timing of circumcision (cf. Bernat 2002:114–23). Instead, we need to consider that the ceremony occurs precisely at the start of the mother's postpartum "blood purification," a cleansing that, like the great flood, lasts forty days and concludes with an animal sacrifice (Leviticus 12:6–7; Whitekettle 1996).[5] Circumcision therefore represents a male abbreviation of the mother's purification and sacrifice (Eilberg-Schwartz 1990:175). What takes the mother a month, in other words, lasts but an instant for her son. The rite aims to separate boys from maternal defilement, the mother's body, and dependence on motherhood. What about baby girls? Are they cleansed from birth? No. Lacking circumcision or any comparable rite, girls were marginalized in biblical and subsequent rabbinic culture. Marginalized, that is, unless we view the monthly flow of menstrual blood as a natural cleansing that men devalued yet wished to emulate.

Circumcision and Menstruation

Both circumcision and menstruation, to state the obvious, issue genital blood. But there is a key difference. Female fertility is governed by monthly cycles that eventually ebb and vanish with menopause. For biblical women, the day after a menstrual period—the eighth day—merely renewed a temporal cycle. Circumcision mirrors uterine fertility. Yet circumcision also escapes the temporal limitations of human life by admitting men into an "everlasting" covenant (see also Bloch and Guggenheim 1981; Delaney 1988:76–80).[6] The eighth day signals the masculine transcendence of nature and its seven-day cycles of fertility (Morgenstern 1973:26; Hirsch 1988:99–111; Fox 1995:383).[7] After birth, biblical and Jewish boys *but not girls* enter a seven-day period of extrauterine gestation, then experience rebirth through circumcision into a timeless and divine fellowship. Nature conquers women, but circumcised men conquer nature.

For "seven days," commanded God, every male firstborn human and animal "shall remain with its mother; on the eighth day you shall give it to Me" (Exodus 22:28–29; Leviticus 22:26). The animals were sacrificed. The fate of the firstborn boys is less clear. As a gift to God, they were perhaps sacrificed, dedicated to cult service, or consecrated in some broad sense (Levenson 1993). For them, the eighth day represented escape from the normal rhythms of life. All boys, though, not just firstborns, were circumcised. From this angle, the eighth day signifies a separation from motherhood. But since circumcision also resembles couvade, the biblical rite, too, perfects birth.[8] "If thou refrain from sexual intercourse during the seven days of menstruation," said God in midrash, echoing Leviticus 12:1–3, "then I shall give thee a male child whom thou wilt circumcise on the eighth day" (PR 52; LR 14:7; PRK 28). While this statement postdates biblical culture, it reflects, in my view, a biblical worldview in which circumcision responds to or transforms menstruation and birth.

Blood, Pure and Impure

In the twelfth century, Rabbi Joseph Bekhor Shor equated the blood of circumcision with menstrual blood (Cohen 2003:40). Five hundred years later, Rabbi Nahman of Bratslav said something quite different. For him, the blood of circumcision atoned for menstrual blood (Deutsch 2002:204). But both views rest on the same assumption: circumcision does to men what naturally occurs to women. Plainly put, circumcision symbolizes male menstruation and masculine birth.[9]

Only once does the Hebrew Bible outright refer to circumcision blood, as I discuss shortly. Of far greater concern were the bloods of sacrifice and menstruation.[10] Sacrificial blood was male, covenantal, purifying, and controlled. Menstrual blood was female, polluting, and uncontrollable (Eilberg-Schwartz 1990:chap. 6; Delaney 1998:chap. 1). Circumcision fits into this system. After Rome destroyed the Second Temple in the first century, the rabbis abolished animal offerings. The blood of circumcision explicitly replaced the blood of sacrifice (GR 28:4–5; T-Y 4:2; TG 4.4; PRK 9:10; PRE 29; Goldin 1996:170–71). Both bloods arouse divine compassion (Zohar iii:14a). Both merited redemption from Egypt (ER 17:3; 19:12; PR 17). Indeed, some rabbis claimed that the blood daubed on Israelite doorways in Egypt to avert the "destroyer" was mixed from sacrifice and circumcision (PRE 29; ER 19:5; Zohar iii:95a).[11] These rabbinic statements, I stress again, are rooted in the earlier biblical worldview (cf. Hoffman 1996:chap. 8; Cohen 2003). Circumcision, menstruation, and sacrifice are all interrelated in a single system of blood and gender.

The Levitical purity code assigns varying degrees of impurity to certain bodily ailments and exudations. Leviticus 15 assigns temporary and contagious pollution (tamei) to ejaculate, nonseminal penile discharge, menstruation, birth, and irregular vaginal bleeding. This condition barred Israelites from sacred and communal spaces. It required some form of purification, typically a bath, and often sacrifice. Scholarly efforts to identify the logic behind the purity code generally turn on binary oppositions such as life/death, controlled/uncontrolled, contained/uncontained, and male/female (Douglas 1966; Milgrom 1976; Wenham 1983; Eilberg-Schwartz 1990; Hoffman 1996). Too often, scholars disregard the bloods of circumcision and sacrifice.

Let us return to Leviticus 15. At the cessation of major polluting conditions such as nonseminal discharge and menstruation, the still-defiled person must wait seven days, bathe, and, on the eighth day, offer two birds for sacrifice. But here's the rub: nonseminal discharge is the *exception* to male physiology, while menstruation is a *regular* event in a woman's life. Indeed, menstruation makes it possible for women to accomplish their primary covenantal task, namely, birth sons. Nonetheless, menstruation is highly polluting—so much so that it merited even its own term, *niddah*, translated as "impurity" or "being-apart" (Fox 1995:565). The Torah, I emphasize, assigns significant defilement to *abnormal* men but to *normal* women.

The Torah forbids menstrual and postpartum intercourse (Leviticus 18:19; 20:18).[12] Many scholars attribute this rule to the impossibility of conception (Whitekettle 1996). This decree, like prohibitions against incest, zoophilia, and same-gender male sexuality, prevents men from wasting seed (Eilberg-Schwartz 1990:183; D. Biale 1997:29). But intercourse with menstruating women is unique among all prohibited sexual activities since it results in *both* pollution *and* the "cutting off" penalty (Frymer-Kensky 1983:405). In the biblical purity system, menstrual blood creates unparalleled impurity.

The ancient Israelites, we have seen, assigned a "life force" to blood (chapter 3). But this symbolism fails to explain the aversion to menstruation since circumcision, like sacrifice, also spills blood (Eilberg-Schwartz 1990:179). But while these male bloods are pure, purifying, and covenantal, menstruation resembles illness (Leviticus 20:18), murder (Ezekiel 36:17–18), dirt (Ezekiel 16:3–7), and sin (Lamentations 1:18; Eilberg-Schwartz 1990:180–81).

For the sake of honesty, I must repeat that the Torah only once refers to circumcision blood. Still, I contend that the wider symbolism of blood and gender in the Hebrew Bible clearly positions circumcision as a pure antithesis of polluting menstruation. This proposition, moreover, explains why the Torah omits further mention of circumcision blood. To do otherwise would only serve to reveal masculinity as a variant of motherhood.

A brief reflection on Melanesia may offer some clarification. Men there often fear menstruation, birth, and vaginal secretions. Yet they infuse their rituals with elaborate reproductive and maternal symbols. Melanesian men, too, frequently purge their bodies of female contaminants acquired from birth and intercourse through urethral incision, tongue slashing, scarification, and other bodily mortifications. These same rites also mirror menstrua-tion and birth. The male blood that cleanses female blood emulates female fertility. And like Leviticus, Melanesian men are loathe to admit it—especially in front of women.

Male Menstruation

Sacrificial blood in biblical culture, as elsewhere argues Jay (1992), symbol-ized the death of birth—specifically, birth from women. This way, sacrifice allowed men to assume an identity as ritual life givers.

The biblical purification rite for skin disease in Leviticus 14 supports this interpretation. A priest slaughtered a bird over water. He then dipped a live bird into the bloody liquid, together with reddish plants (cedar, scarlet, hys-sop), and sprinkled the concoction seven times on the afflicted Israelite. This scarlet tonic evoked life-giving blood to counteract the deathly symbolism of the contagion (E. Greenstein 1984:95; Fox 1995:572). Seven days later, the priest performed the rite again. On the eighth day, he smeared sacrificial blood on the Israelite's ear, big toe, and thumb (see also Exodus 29:20; Leviticus 8:22–24).[13] It seems difficult not to discern a similarity between the purifica-tion ceremony and circumcision. Both rites represent male menstruation.

Lest my thesis on the menstrual significance of circumcision still seem tenuous, consider the curative for an Israelite contaminated by a corpse (Numbers 19). A priest slaughtered a red female heifer, then burned the car-cass. He also threw into the fire the same reddish plants used to purify skin disease. Finally, the priest mixed the ashes with water into a magical antisep-tic called the "waters of *niddah,*" that is, the "*waters of menstruation.*" Biblical menstrual blood that flowed naturally from women was polluting and deathly. When ritually concocted by men, however, menstrual blood was purifying and life affirming (Eilberg-Schwartz 1990:188). Circumcision is a variant of this theme.

To magically promote fertility, barren women in the Jewish communities of Kurdistan gazed at the circumciser's bloody hands (Brauer 1993:167–68). Sometimes they bathed in and even drank the water used to rinse the blood. More dramatically, these women swallowed the foreskins or inserted them into their vaginas. These ideas are not as alien to biblical religion as we might suppose.

As Moses prepared to ascend Mount Sinai to receive the decalogue, he ordered Israelite men to avoid women (Exodus 19:15). Moses also "dashed" half the blood from an animal sacrifice against the altar and read aloud "the record of the covenant" (Exodus 24:6–8). When the Israelites pledged their obedience to the Law, Moses "dashed" the rest of the blood directly on the people, declaring, "This is the blood of the covenant that the Lord now cuts with you." (I can not imagine Moses performing a similar gesture with menstrual blood!) Like circumcision, this ritual dashing validated the covenant by spilling male blood, splitting a body, and excluding yet emulating women.

Postbiblical tales elaborate on the foiled seductions of Joseph in Genesis 39. In one fable, banqueting Egyptian women are so besotted with Joseph's beauty that they slice bloody their fingers while peeling oranges. By casting female sexuality as menstruation, writes Hoffman (1996:168–69), the rabbis condemned women for their overflowing bodies and appetites.

In another tale of frustrated seduction, Joseph's "bow" became drawn, then relaxed. Joseph "examined himself and did *not* find that he was a man" (GR 87:7). Hoffman (1996:169–70) rightly suggests that Joseph gazed at his self-controlling circumcision. Yet this cut was also feminizing. Joseph was *neither* a foreskinned man *nor* an overflowing woman. Rather, circumcision created a man who was a better woman!

The Horror of Monotheism

Because Esau refused to spill the blood of circumcision, said the rabbis, God rebuked him with the words of Ezekiel 35:6, "I will doom you with blood; blood shall pursue you; I swear that, for your bloodthirsty hatred, blood shall pursue you" (GR 63:13; TG 6.4; NR 4:8). Another bloody passage from Ezekiel captivated the rabbis. Indeed, they incorporated it into the circumcision liturgy: "When I passed by you and saw you wallowing in your blood, I said to you: In your blood, live" (Ezekiel 16:6). The rabbis understood this statement as expressing Abraham's reward for circumcision. But the violence here and elsewhere in the Hebrew Bible is not so easily harnessed to moral purpose.

No biblical incident more dramatically expresses monotheistic terror than Abraham's willingness to sacrifice his own son (Genesis 22). Oddly, few modern scholars connect this event to circumcision.

God commands Abraham to slaughter Isaac, "whom you love," on a mountaintop in the land of Moriah.[14] The horror of this charge is deepened by the fact that it marks the first appearance of "love" in the Torah—a terror enhanced by Abraham's eager compliance. Earlier, Abraham was "distressed greatly" when asked by Sarah to banish Ishmael, "for it concerned a son of his" (Genesis 21:11). Now, Abraham voices no qualms about killing Isaac.

To the rabbis, in fact, Abraham's haste in departing for the grim task "early in the morning" (Genesis 22:3) exemplified true devotion. Abraham con-structs the altar, piles kindling, binds his son, and hefts a cleaver. At the last instant, an angel cries "Abraham! Abraham! . . . Do not raise your hand against the boy. . . . For now I know that you fear God" (Genesis 22:12). Instead of his son, Abraham slaughters a ram.

When medieval Jews bound a boy's legs for circumcision, they reflected on Isaac, tethered by his father for sacrifice (Goldin 1996:167–70). "If you had been thirteen years old" at your circumcision, boasts Ishmael to Isaac in midrash, "you could not have tolerated the anguish" (T-Y 4:18; SH 22:42–44; TG 4.42). To this taunt, Isaac replies with his own sacrifice. So troubled were the rabbis by this episode that they fashioned Isaac into a will-ing victim (PRE 31; T-Y 4:23; PR 40; TG 4.46). But the violence of this event, called the Akedah, or "binding," in Hebrew, resists this rewriting.

Typically, the Akedah is said to mark the superior morality of monotheism by substituting sacrificial animals for children. This interpretation, however, seems unduly moralistic, even naive. In fact, Delaney (1998) sees the Akedah as establishing the idea that children are suitable for sacrifice.[15] But it is the cut of circumcision that establishes or anticipates the Akedah. Lin-guistically, argues Alexander (1983), the initial formulation of the covenant in Genesis 17 was conditional. Circumcision only partly fulfilled Abraham's covenantal obligation. The sacrifice of Isaac completed it.

Both circumcision and the Akedah evidence the theme of divine rebirth (Leach 1983:53–54; Kunin 1994). Both rites dramatize male claims over uterine fertility (Róheim 1955:207). Both rites ask a father to lay down his son, grasp a knife, and cut the child (Brod 1995:288; Hansen 1995). And both rites so satisfy God that the deity honors or renews the covenantal promise of fantastic fertility.

The Akedah and circumcision enact the oedipal dilemma. Fathers fear death and generational succession and so seek to kill their sons, at least in ritual and myth. But they must fail since a son's maturity ensures his father's legacy (Paul 1996:54–55). Not surprisingly, the fate of Isaac is ambiguous. The Hebrew allows Abraham to sacrifice the ram "in place of" but also "after" (*tahat*) his son (Genesis 22:13; Spiegel 1993:60–61; GR 56:9). In rab-binic texts, Abraham actually shed Isaac's blood, much like circumcision. Only then did God spare the boy's life (Spiegel 1993, chap. 7; Hoffman 1996:107–10).

Most intriguingly, Genesis reports the return of Abraham *alone* from the sacrifice. There is no mention of Isaac. Where is he? The rabbis offered several charming scenarios (Spiegel 1993). Perhaps Isaac went home under cover of darkness to avoid the evil eye or traveled to study Torah. The rabbis also proposed more chilling possibilities, such as the son's death at the hands of his father. Later, the "dew of resurrection" revived Isaac's ashes.

During the Akedah, the first circumcised father agrees to fatally cut the first son circumcised on the eighth day. A devout father must not remain content simply to slice his son's penis. He must be prepared to cut even deeper.

Where Is the Mother?

Medieval Jews developed a ceremony to mark a boy's passage from his mother to the world of male fellowship and formal education (Goldberg 1987; Goldin 1996; Bilu 2000:48–49). During the rite, elder men feed boys biblical passages etched on sweet cakes and hard-boiled eggs. The boys also lick honey drizzled on the Hebrew alphabet. By ingesting divine words, the boys resemble Ezekiel, who consumed a scroll offered by God (Ezekiel 2:8–3:3). At the same time, the ritual casts male tutoring as a form of maternal nourishment. Yet a more violent image, one expressly recognized by medieval Jews, precedes this masculine portrait of moral mothering (Marcus 1996:94–101). When the father carries his son to the initiation ceremony, he resembles Abraham leading his own son to sacrifice.

In the school initiation ceremony, which many Jews continue to practice, men assume the role of mothers. During the Akedah, Abraham ignored motherhood entirely, never speaking with Sarah about the fate of her son. He simply whisked the boy away. Circumcision similarly marginalizes motherhood. In so doing, argues Delaney (1998:99–101), circumcision made possible the Akedah by inscribing a paternal seal of ownership into a boy's flesh. The rite allows God and fathers to do what they please to boys without consulting mothers. All three rites—the school initiation, circumcision, and the Akedah—deny the voices and emotions of women. All three rites emphasize the superiority of paternity over motherhood. And all three rites take sons from mothers so that, in two of the ceremonies, the father can cut the child.[16]

In one rabbinic tale, Abraham outright lied to Sarah (Spiegel 1993:48–49). "How long is your son going to hang onto your apron strings?" It's time for the boy to study Torah! Yet Abraham takes Isaac away to sacrifice, not schooling. When Isaac learns his fate, he weeps to his father, saying, "So this is the Torah you talked about to my mother!" Then, as Abraham begins to sob, Isaac assents. "Come now," the boy tells his father, "and carry out the will of your Father in heaven." These and similar tales establish monotheism as a deception of motherhood.

Sarah dies immediately after the Akedah (Genesis 23:2). The rabbis attributed her death to shock (PRK 26:3; SH 23:83–86; LR 20:2; T-Y 4:23). When she learned about her son's survival—or her husband's eagerness to kill the child—she drops dead.

The Rod of Moses

Despite the silencing of Sarah, motherhood eventually responds to covenantal patriarchy. As Genesis draws to a close, the sons of Jacob—now renamed Israel—reunite in Egypt. When Exodus opens, the Israelites prosper and proliferate, arousing Egyptian envy, then wrath, enslavement, and Pharaoh's decree to kill all newborn Hebrew boys (Exodus 1:15). To thwart this fate, an Israelite mother places her son in a basketry "ark" and sets him afloat on the Nile. Pharaoh's daughter discovers the basket, unwittingly hires the boy's mother as a wet nurse, and raises the child in the royal court. She names him Moses.

Years later, Moses kills an Egyptian who pummeled a Hebrew (Exodus 2:11). Pharaoh seeks revenge. Moses flees to Midian. He weds Zipporah, a priestly non-Israelite. Meanwhile, the enslaved Hebrews in Egypt beseech God for help. One day, while Moses tends flocks in the wilderness, God speaks through a burning bush and orders Moses back to Egypt to free the Israelites. But Moses is no hero. Again and again, he tries to duck God's charge. Not even several demonstrations of divine power—transforming Moses' rod into a snake, for example, and back again—calm his anxiety.

Moses even appeals to his foreskin, saying, "Please, O Lord, I have never been a man with words. . . . I am slow of speech and slow of tongue" (Exodus 4:10). Later, Moses will call this stammer his "uncircumcised lips" (Exodus 6:12, 30). But God dismisses the significance of this prepuce by essentially claiming ownership over Moses's phallus. "Who gives man speech? . . . I will be with you as you speak" (Exodus 4:11–12). When Moses still wavers, God angrily tells him to take Aaron, his brother, to Egypt since Aaron "speaks clearly." Finally, God offers Moses "this rod, with which you shall perform the signs," an order that evokes the phallic sign of circumcision.

Moses and Aaron arrive at the Egyptian court (Exodus 7). In a famous serpentine competition, the Mosaic rod "swallowed" Pharaoh's phalloi. Rashkow (1997:76–78) alerts us to an important nuance. Before the burning bush, Moses' rod mutated into a snake (*nahash*). At the Egyptian court, however, the staffs all metamorphosed into serpents (*tannin*), a word derived from the root "to elongate" (*tan*). Equally suggestive, the Hebrew for "swallow" (*bala'*) resembles "sexual intercourse" (*be'ilah*). The erect Mosaic phallus, empowered by God, thus devoured, raped, and emasculated Egypt.

Yet Pharaoh remains unimpressed, compelling Moses to unleash the ten plagues, often by pointing his "rod" (*matteh*).[17] During a later battle, the Israelites prevail only as long as Moses holds his rod aloft (Exodus 17:8–16). When it droops, the enemy dominates.

Moses' phallus was not only martial and consumptive but also aggressively nourishing. In the Sinai wasteland, God tells Moses to water the parched Israelites by striking the rod against a rock (Exodus 17:6). Water gushed forth. When the same situation occurs later, God instructs Moses merely to speak to the boulder. Instead, Moses impatiently strikes the rock—twice. For this impudence, God bars him from the land of "milk and honey" (Numbers 20:1–13). Moses dies in the wilderness. In midrash, these flowing rocks resembled menstruating women and a divine breast (ER 3:13; Ginzberg 1909–1938:III:319–20). Moses'swhacking thus hints at a sexual transgression as well as a violation of motherhood and a slap at God's ability to nurse his thirsty children (Zeligs 1983; Halperin 1995; Paul 1996:105–7, 168–69; Pardes 2000:chap. 3).

My point should now be clear. The varied symbolism and equivocal morality of Moses' rod makes sense only in reference to circumcision. And it is precisely in the context of circumcision, I now show, that Moses reveals his masculine inadequacy before the power of courageous motherhood.

The Bloody Bridegroom

The gender of Moses is no simple matter. On one occasion, Moses veiled his face like a woman (Exodus 34:34). On another occasion, as the Israelites "weep" for food in the wilderness, Moses grumbles to God, "Did I conceive all this people, did I bear them that You should say to me, 'Carry them in your bosom as a nurse carries an infant,' to the land that You have promised?" (Numbers 11:11–12). Moses here, suggests Pardes (1992b:96), assumes a maternal identity in order to berate God's own maternal failings.

Against this feminine symbolism, though, Moses presented four phalloi: penis, foreskinned lips, potent staff, and horns.[18] This hyperphallic body, Eilberg-Schwartz (1994:145–46) argues, sought to counter the feminization of biblical manhood, including circumcision. But all this machismo proved impotent when God attacked Moses in Exodus 4, sparing his life only when Moses' wife, Zipporah, circumcised their son. It is to this event that I now turn.

As Moses prepares for his return to Egypt, God instructs him on how to threaten Pharaoh. "Thus says the Lord: Israel is My first-born son. . . . Let My son go, that he may worship Me" or "I will slay your first-born son" (Exodus 4:22–23). Moses then departs. But,

> At a night encampment on the way, the Lord encountered him and sought to kill him. So Zipporah took a flint and cut off her son's foreskin, and touched it to his legs/feet, saying, "You are truly a bridegroom of blood to me!" And when He released him, she added, "A bridegroom of blood (*ḥatan damim*) because of the circumcision." (Exodus 4:24–26)

A more vexing passage in the Hebrew Bible scarcely exists. The puzzlement is heightened by the use of ambiguous pronouns. Who is the victim? Whose feet or legs are smeared? And what is a "bridegroom of blood"?

The rabbis offered a wide range of interpretations. In one scenario, Moses deemed it risky to circumcise his son and then immediately depart for Egypt since, as the Hivites learned in Genesis 34, the pain of the rite persists for several days (B. Nedarim 31b–32a; Vermes 1973). Of course, any delay in returning to Egypt would violate God's command—as would any delay in performing the circumcision. Unsure what to do, Moses began his journey, then stopped at the inn. But instead of circumcising his son, Moses tarried. For waffling, God attacked him.

In another rabbinic scenario, an angel swallowed Moses "from his head to his circumcised membrum" (ER 5:8). Moses' protruding penis pointed to the problem—namely, his son's foreskin—as well as to the "protective power of circumcision" since the angel "could not swallow him further than that membrum." Sometimes the angel assumed the form of a serpent (Ginzberg 1909–1938:II:295). For failing to cut a penis, we might say, Moses was consumed by a phallus that resembled his very own rod in the Egyptian court.

Some rabbis said that Moses neglected his infant son's circumcision to honor his Midianite father-in-law, who preferred foreskins or puberty rites (SH 79:8–12; Fink 1993). This reading, observes Vermes (1958:315–18), diminishes Moses's culpability, much like the introduction of the angel lessens God's capriciousness. Vermes also stresses that postbiblical texts tend to attribute Moses' salvation specifically to the blood of the circumcision (Vermes 1958:310–11). But the original passage, I emphasize, does likewise.

Rabbinic traditions disagree on God's victim, Moses or Moses' son. If the latter, then which son? Did Zipporah, moreover, smear the foreskin on Moses' feet or the assailant's legs? The rabbis also debated the meaning and recipient of the "bloody bridegroom" designation. Perhaps the phrase implies that circumcision formalized marriage? Or was a man so titled after his circumcision?

Modern scholars are no less befuddled than the rabbis. The "bloody bridegroom" assault is usually tied to other events in the Exodus saga, typically, God's preceding threat to kill Egyptian sons if Pharaoh fails to release God's son (Coppens 1941; Robinson 1986; Sarna 1991:24–26). In this view, God attacks Moses' son (or Moses himself as a symbol of Israel) in punishment for Moses' earlier refusal to emancipate the Israelites. We can also see the assault as yet another terrible father–son confrontation that marks or mars the moral tenor of the Torah.

After the circumcision, Zipporah touched the severed prepuce to unknown male legs or feet, whereupon God released the victim. For most scholars, this gesture foreshadows the protective painting of sacrificial blood on Israelite houses (Robinson 1986:453; Sarna 1991:25). It also evokes, I suggest, another protective sign linked to bloodshed, namely, Cain's quasi-circumcisional "mark" (see chapter 2). Propp (1993) underscores the use of the plural in Zipporah's utterance, or "bridegroom of *bloods*," a word that normally refers to the guilt of murder or some other heinous crimes. From this angle, Moses provoked God's attack by failing to redress the slaying of the Egyptian taskmaster.

Many modern scholars follow the rabbis and understand the "bloody bridegroom" phrase as recalling an era when the Israelites required circumcision for marriage—a rule Moses violated (Gunkel 1902–1903; Wellhausen 1957:340; Fox 1974:592–93; Propp 1987:358–61). At least two other biblical passages, recall, evidence a link between circumcision and matrimony, namely, the Hivite massacre after Dinah's rape and Saul's preputial brideprice request. Equally plausible, Zipporah simply phrased the covenant she cut between God and Moses through a marital idiom (Smith 1906:20–21; Cassuto 1967:61). By wedding Moses to God, Zipporah regained her husband.

Another modern line of interpretation, one yet again anticipated by the rabbis, focuses on Zipporah's non-Israelite heritage. In one view, "bloody bridegroom" is a loose Hebrew translation of a Midianite term that referred to a relationship defined by circumcision (Kosmala 1962; Sarna 1991:26). Others see the circumcision as an appropriate historical role for Midianites

(McNutt 1994) or admitting Zipporah and her children into the Israelite community (Maller 1993; Lehane 1996). Alternatively, the term "bloody bridegroom" might deride circumcision (Reis 1991; Frolov 1996; see also Gelernter 1988). If Zipporah hailed from a noncircumcising culture, then perhaps she hurled the epithet at Moses or God out of sheer disgust at the rite.

Some recent scholars see the "bloody bridegroom" incident as explaining why the sons of Aaron and not Moses assumed the priesthood (Propp 1993; Frolov 1996; Kunin 1996). Earlier generations saw the tale as recollecting a primitive tussle between a husband and demon over the privilege of nuptial defloration (Gunkel 1902–1903; Reinach 1908). Zipporah ruptured her son's penis to substitute for her own hymen, then smeared blood on the fiend whom she called a "bloody bridegroom."

The biblical term for "bridegroom" (ḥatan) actually refers more broadly to men related through marriage (male affines). The word, moreover, likely derives from the root (ḥtn), meaning to cut, circumcise, and protect. Originally, proposes Morgenstern (1963:45–46), a man was circumcised by his father-in-law or elder matrikin and thus cut into the lineage. Moses violated this custom, arousing the fury of a local deity. Zipporah swiftly assumed the role of her absent father or uncle, circumcised her son, and affirmed the legitimacy of the new relationship by declaring "you are truly a bridegroom of blood to me."[19]

The early anthropology of Palestine offers many connections between circumcision and marriage. Egyptian peasants, called Fellahin, greeted the birth of a child by "calling the blessing on the bridegroom or bride" (Baldensperger 1894:128–29). Sometimes the girl's father responded with an offer of betrothal. If accepted, the future wedding was formalized by an animal sacrifice. Similarly, a girl's navel chord was cut in the name of her future husband. Egyptian circumcision rites, moreover, thoroughly resembled marriage in garb, gifts, meals, and ruses against the evil eye (Granqvist 1947:96–97, 194, 201–5; see also Kennedy 1970:176–77). Despite wearing girls' scarves, the boys were addressed as bridegrooms (Ammar 1954:117). The "bloody bridegroom" similarly connects circumcision and marriage.[20] But it also comments on wider issues, as I now show.

An Ambivalent View of the Bloody Bridegroom

Zipporah's performance of circumcision is often characterized as apotropaic, not covenantal, and thus seems distinct from Abraham's rite (Alter

1996:73). Proponents of this view point to the fact that these two circumcision episodes were composed in different historical eras. Nevertheless, numerous parallels exist between Moses and Abraham. Both men experience in some capacity a unique circumcision. Both men were consecrated by this rite so they could fulfill their divinely appointed tasks (Houtman 1983:98–99). For both men, this task included real or symbolic fruitfulness: Abraham sired Isaac, and Moses birthed the Israelites into freedom. Both men voyaged. Both men underwent a wilderness theophany. Both men narrowly escaped sacrificing their firstborn sons (Róheim 1955:170). Finally, both men failed at fatherhood to the extent that Abraham expelled one son, then willingly agreed to slaughter the other, while Moses near fatally neglected to circumcise his own son (see also H. Goldberg 1996:28–30). All these parallels suggest that we view the "bloody bridegroom" incident as a wider comment on biblical circumcision.

Earlier, I mentioned Barth's (1991:50–51) interpretation of a genre of midrash as expressing an "inner Jewish opposition" to circumcision (chapter 2). I now propose that we extend this resistance back to biblical culture, which, after all, enforced circumcision through the severe threat of death: to cut off, to repeat, or be "cut off." In the absence of any equivocation toward circumcision, it is difficult to understand the rationale for mobilizing this terror to promote a rite that seemingly promised so much benefit. That God needed so aggressively to force Moses—the recipient of the Law and the liberator of Israel—to comply with circumcision further evidences this ambivalence.

A brief consideration of Jacob's nocturnal assault is now helpful. An angel, recall from chapter 4, possibly "touched" or "struck" Jacob on the thigh or groin. We can read Exodus 4 similarly, such that Zipporah touched her son's foreskin to Moses' feet or euphemistic genitals (de Groot 1943:13; Houtman 1983:85). Both gestures symbolize circumcision. Both occurred at the edge of daylight. Both allowed God to test a potential vehicle for the covenant. Both represent holiness as a blessing and wound (Róheim 1955:170; Geller 1982; cf. Kosmala 1962:15). Both betoken feminine submission before a manly God (Eilberg-Schwartz 1994:159–61). And both circumcisions, writes Robinson (1986:451–52), transform moral impotence into masculine heroism.

But neither Moses nor Jacob—that is, neither the liberator of Israel nor the man named Israel—received a normal, plainly stated, and uncoerced circumcision (see also Reinach 1908). Jacob and Moses were "touched," not "cut," by a woman or angel, not a man, on a body part that only alludes to the penis. No frank clarity and prideful declaration here. Rather, circumcision in both passages is represented through sly innuendo—an insinuation that seems best explained by a profound moral ambivalence.

Feminizing the Mosaic Phallus

The Exodus 4 incident, recognized Martin Buber (1946:58–59), contains many inversions. God tries to kill, not assist, his assistant. Moses, God's speaker, fails to speak. Moses, too, resists, not heeds, God. And a circumciser is female, not male. These inversions, I suggest, encourage a reading of the "bloody bridegroom" as a countertale that destabilizes biblical culture. First, Moses and Zipporah swap roles to confound the norms of gender. Second, the tale offers a feminine rejoinder to the uterine symbolism of circumcision. Third, the event dangerously blurs kinship categories. Finally, the "bloody bridegroom" demonstrates the importance of female agency. All told, the "bloody bridegroom" contributes yet another voice to the broad biblical conversation concerning circumcision, gender, power, and morality.

After the circumcision, Zipporah "touched" the foreskin to "*his*" feet or legs. Whose? Her son? Moses? God? The indeterminacy implies that the specific identity of the legs is less important than the fact that they are male and smeared with a severed, presumably bloody prepuce. Classic rabbis and modern scholars alike, as I mentioned earlier, commonly link this gesture with the daubing of sacrificial blood on Israelite doorways to save firstborn sons. Yet we need also consider gender. Biblical "legs" or "feet" often double as genitals (chapter 2). But do the limbs in Exodus 4 represent the penis or the vulva—better yet, do they represent both?

In mystical Judaism, circumcision carves an opening or doorway into the penis (Zohar ii:36a; Wolfson 1987b:204–5; Boyarin 1992:495). For prooftext, the Kabbalists cited Abraham, who sat in the entrance of his tent after his own circumcision (Genesis 18:1). According to this logic, bloodied doorways in Egypt symbolized the Israelites' newly circumcised sons. Male blood here is redemptive, and portals are phallic.

More commonly, though, biblical doorways and houses represent female genitals (e.g., Job 3:10; Song of Songs 8:9; B. Kethuboth 10a; B. Bechoroth 45a; PRE 30). If we assume a similar symbolism in Exodus, then the inaugural Passover sacrifice and the subsequent blood smearing enacted a type of ritual menstruation and birth. The "bloody bridegroom" incident speaks to the same theme.

God's attack feminized Moses. The bestaffed hero-to-be was impotent and immobile, unable to save himself by performing the signal duty of covenantal fatherhood. Indeed, Moses' ritual neglect almost "cut off" his own progeny from emancipation, resulting in real or social death. Luckily, Moses and his son were circumcised by Zipporah, who thereby assumed what biblical culture coded as a masculine identity in contrast to Moses' feminine submission. Like Abraham atop Mount Sinai, Moses was unable or unwilling to protect his son. Yet while Abraham's abdication of paternal duty pleased God, Moses' dereliction almost proved fatal. I am not just repeating my earlier claim that Moses and Abraham, the two great patriarchs of monotheism, failed at fatherhood. I am suggesting that this failure inverted the norms of gender.

What part of the body did Zipporah actually cut? This answer, too, resists simplification. Moses was blighted by many foreskins, including his lips and perhaps also his penis. Additionally, Moses' hesitancy about returning to Egypt bespoke a foreskinned heart, and his argument with God displayed uncircumcised ears. Only when cut by a woman, either directly or symbolically, could Moses live up to the moral and physical ideal of foreskinless Israelite manhood. In more ways than one, Moses' virility lay in the hands of his wife. Zipporah's slice thus restored and denied the masculinity of Moses. At the same time, Zipporah subverted, then reinstated, her own maternal and wifely norms. The role of circumcision in the "bloody bridegroom" episode casts doubt on any stable sense of biblical gender.

Circumcision and Maternal Empowerment

Let us return to the unknown legs besmeared by Zipporah. If the legs belonged to a foreskinned Moses, then Zipporah's gesture amounted to a symbolic circumcision—symbolic, writes de Groot (1943:14–15), because Moses was obviously too busy struggling with the assailant to undergo a proper circumcision.[21] Insofar as God punishes progeny for parental misdeeds, notes Cassuto (1967:60), a son's blood could surely "consecrate" a father. This logic of substitution reminded Reinach (1908:12) of the Akedah, when Abraham slaughtered a ram instead of his son. Today, Reinach's insight passes largely unnoticed. But it opens the way to interpret Zipporah's actions as a *response* to male ceremonies that exclude and devalue motherhood. Since the rabbis generally forbid women from performing circumcision, Zipporah proved perplexing. Perhaps, proposed the Talmud (B. Abodah Zarah 27a), she merely advised Moses on the circumcision of their son or simply initiated the rite, which Moses completed. Yet many modern readers, myself included, balk at attempts to divest Zipporah of her agency.

For example, Pardes (1992b) brilliantly situates Zipporah in a broader countermovement in Exodus in which women defy male authority. When Pharaoh decrees the death of Israelite newborns, he entrusts the gruesome task to a pair of Egyptian midwives. But they evade the task, saying that Israelite women breed too much (Exodus 1:19). This sly appeal to racism, Pardes argues, undermined Pharaoh and Egyptian hegemony by allowing the Israelites to multiply. I detect another irony. The midwives subverted the Abrahamic covenant by attributing fantastic fertility and covenantal conti-nuity to Israelite wombs rather than circumcised penises.

After the midwife fiasco, Pharaoh redoubles his murderous intent and decrees the drowning of newborn Israelite boys. But one child is set afloat on the Nile by his mother and sister, then rescued by Pharaoh's daughter. Once again, female agency disrupts paternal authority. Pharaoh's daughter names the child Moses since she "drew him out" (*meshitihu*) of the water. But this name also, remarks Pardes (1992b), hints at the boy's later role as "the drawer-out of the nation" (Isaiah 63:11). The future of the covenant yet again rests in the hands of women.

Zipporah continues this pattern of female subversion, argues Pardes (1992b:83), by marshaling maternal powerlessness to teach "weak and threatened young sons how to trick hostile oppressors, how to submit to paternal will and at the same time usurp the father's position."[22] Unlike Jacob, continues Pardes, Moses neither bested his divine adversary— Zipporah did—nor received a new name. When Zipporah called Moses a "bloody bridegroom," then, she scoffed at the failure of circumcision to sus-tain male privilege.

Zipporah did what Moses himself was unable to do: shed skin to save his skin. Through circumcision, Zipporah emasculated her already feminized husband while compensating for paternal immobility. Zipporah also mocked the procreative symbolism of circumcision. By seizing the rite, she reclaimed uterine fertility for motherhood and exposed the parturient fictions of male rituals that otherwise defined and celebrated biblical masculinity. Zipporah upheld male prerogative by liberating her husband so he, in turn, could liber-ate the Israelites and receive the Law. But Zipporah also showed that biblical manhood was not all it was cut—or erected—to be.

When Zipporah touched the bloody foreskin to male legs or genitals, she symbolically menstruated on man. This way, Zipporah offered a female rejoinder to the uterine and menstrual symbolism of circumcision, and responded to the monthly exclusion of women from the covenantal community. Regardless of who Zipporah bloodied, her gesture demonstrated that uterine fertility reigns supreme.

Finally, Zipporah's gesture anticipated the sacrificial splashes that later became central to the priesthood. She also established precedent, in a sense, for her husband's dashing of sacrificial blood on the community after the Sinaic revelation (Exodus 24:6–8). As much as Zipporah saves the covenant through circumcision, she also mocks it, thus challenging male privilege by showing the impossibility of silencing and marginalizing motherhood.

Oedipus Redux

To the extent that the ambiguous pronouns in Exodus 4 confuse the distinction between father and son (Pardes 1992b:84), Zipporah regressed Moses from patriarch to child. By so confusing kinship, she undermined the intergenerational and moral structure of Israelite society (cf. Kaplan 1981). Of course, this ambiguity beset Moses more than his son. The grown man failed to satisfy two important tasks of biblical masculinity, namely, martial triumph and ritual competence. Moses seemed little different than a child.

Earlier, Moses defended Zipporah from aggressive shepherds (Exodus 2:16–17).[23] Now, the hero is saved by the former damsel in distress. Twice non-Israelite women rebirthed Moses (Propp 1993:514). The first time, Moses was an infant. This time, he acts like one—doubly so given his foreskinned status. For her part, Zipporah resembles Isis, an Egyptian goddess, as I discuss in a moment, who resurrected her deceased husband's phallus to conceive a child (Pardes 1992b:89–93). Ancient iconography often depicted Isis as a bird. Zipporah, whose name means "bird," similarly revived a husband by attending to his penis.

By rebirthing Moses through genital blood, though, Zipporah also assumes the role of her husband's life-giving mother (Pardes 1992b:84–86). But Zipporah then shifts back to her role as a wife when she calls Moses "bridegroom" (Cassuto 1967:60–61). This exclamation attests to the indispensability of women as women for biblical men. That Zipporah takes on the active role in matrimony, however, simultaneously consigns men to a passive, normally feminine stance.

From another angle, Zipporah resembles Eve, who, on birthing a son, snubbed her husband by affirming a union with God (chapter 3). If Zipporah, in other words, calls God her "bridegroom" and not Moses, then she undermines male privilege since the Torah often phrases the covenant as a wedding between God and man (Eilberg-Schwartz 1994:160–61). But if Zipporah refers instead to Moses as her bridegroom, then she challenges God's matrimonial claims over Moses and Israelite males. Either way, Zipporah presents men with an irreducible image of womanhood.

Let us return to Isis, the Egyptian goddess. Isis married her own brother, Osiris, who was then murdered and dismembered by a jealous younger brother. Isis recovered all her husband's body parts except for his penis, which she fashioned from wood. This massive phallus became the focal object of Isis's devotees. But ancient women in the eastern Mediterranean lost control over the divine phallus, argues Rashkow (1997). For evidence, Rashkow points to the phallocentrism of Israelite society and religion and especially the importance of Moses' rod and Abraham's circumcision. Zipporah responds to this patriarchal theft (Pardes 1992b). Insofar as circumcision announces paternity, Zipporah denied Moses his son. Insofar as circumcision ascribes procreative power to divine and human males, Zipporah rebirthed Moses and then menstruated on male legs. And insofar as circumcision excludes women from covenantal reproduction, Zipporah demonstrated the impotence of men without women.

From a Freudian angle, the "bloody bridegroom" incident raises several oedipal themes. Zipporah symbolically castrated her son, then wedded the boy.[24] As an ambiguous mother-wife figure, such as we saw repeatedly in Genesis, Zipporah once again blurs normative kinship. But Zipporah's son overcame his incestuous and castrating mother since Zipporah all but disappears from the biblical narrative (Peto 1960:328–29). The "bloody bridegroom" now appears as a tale of male fantasy.

Yet we can also understand Zipporah to take up the paternal role in the Oedipus complex by symbolically sacrificing a son to reunite with her spouse (Peto 1960:326–27). Of course, she equally emasculated Moses, albeit ironically since the circumcision empowered him to perform his rightful heroism. Zipporah did what Leviticus forbid women: she grabbed male genitals. But Zipporah shrewdly skirted the law by grasping her son's penis, not the groin of her husband's assailant, or God. She then wiped the prepuce on legs, which, if attached to the aggressor, communicate another castrative intent. Here again, Zipporah sustains and subverts male authority. She secured the future heroism of her husband and the legacy of the covenant. But she left men with a bodily reminder that their masculine achievements ultimately belong to woman.

I began this chapter by anchoring circumcision and the seven-day biblical interval to a typical menstrual period. I then argued that various guises of female fertility establish the motive and model for circumcision. What women do naturally men did ritually. What's more, men devalued the very parturient potency they so desired. All this, I contended, rested on the varied biblical symbolism of blood.

Next, I argued for parallels between circumcision and the near sacrifice of Isaac by his own father, Abraham. Both rites silence and marginalize motherhood through a regime of paternal terror. Finally, I traced phallic continuities from circumcision and Abraham to the triumph and woes of Moses, ending with an extended analysis of the enigmatic "bloody bridegroom" episode as a maternal retort to the uterine boasts of male ritual.

After Exodus 4, Moses goes on to perform great deeds. He vanquishes Pharaoh, emancipates the Israelites, defeats an army, receives the Law, and guides the covenantal community to the Promised Land. Zipporah made all this possible. But she is denied her victory, disappearing entirely from the narrative after the "bloody bridegroom" incident save for one further insignificant appearance (Exodus 18:2). Why? Because Zipporah saved the covenant by rupturing the dominant meanings of circumcision and biblical patriarchy. She laid bare, in a sense, the parturient fictions of monotheism. For this reason, Zipporah is cut off from the exodus story, transformed into a minor figure whose silence stands as a masculine retort to male failure. However much the "bloody bridegroom" tale allows Moses and Zipporah to triumph, it also permits no stable heroics, only tragedy for men, mothers, and sons.

Notes

1. Eight figures prominently in postbiblical culture, including the length in days of Hanukkah and the number of fringes on a man's prayer shawl, called a *tallit* (chapter 6).

2. For the doubling of postpartum uncleanliness and "blood purification" after the birth of girls, compare E. Greenstein (1984:95) with Gruber (1989:68).

3. The rabbis (LR 25:8) equated menstruating women with "foreskinned" fruit (chapter 2).

4. The eighth day also ensures a festive mood, said the rabbis, since the boy's parents can resume intercourse (B. Niddah 31b).

5. When the Israelites renewed circumcision on the eve of the emancipation from Egypt, says the Zohar (iii:97a), "the uncleanness left them as the blood of uncleanness leaves a woman."

6. In Kabbalah, circumcision opens the "male" (*zakhar*) to memory (*zekher, zikaron*), thus again transcending time (Wolfson 2002).

7. The eighth day, said the rabbis, also allows boys to gain spiritual strength prior to circumcision by experiencing a Sabbath (DR 6:1).

8. The perfection-of-birth theme helps explain why rabbinic law relaxes the timing of circumcision after "unnatural" births such as cesarean delivery or medical complications (Hirsch 1988:109–10).

9. Likewise for Aboriginal Australian subincision (see Montagu 1974:320–21). For a critical historical overview of the circumcision-as-menstruation thesis, see Lupton (1993).

10. For a cursory version of this thesis, see Archer (1990), then Cohen's (1992) critique.

11. For the bloods of circumcision, sacrifice, and menstruation in Africa, see Gluckman (1949:155), Turner (1962), and de Heusch (1985:chap. 6).

12. Rabbinic law doubles this prohibition, echoing the biblical rule concerning nonmenstrual discharge (D. Biale 1997:55).

13. A mystical text advises a bride to fondle her groom's toe, thumb, and earlobe to "arouse his desire for honest procreation," to expel demons, and, if lucky, to birth a foreskinless son (Graves and Patai 1983:214).

14. Legends locate many events on Mount Moriah, including Abraham's circumcision (GR 24:9, 56:10; PRE 23, 31; Ginzberg 1909–1938:I:89).

15. Judges 11 is another wrenching tale of child-sacrifice, a practice mentioned throughout the Hebrew Bible (see Levenson 1993).

16. For mothers and the rabbinic "redemption of the firstborn" ceremony, see Hoffman (1996:chap. 10).

17. The biblical word for "rod" also means "tribe," thus providing a phallic backbone to Israelite society (Rashkow 1997:83 n. 9).

18. After receiving the Law atop Mount Sinai, Moses' face was *qāran*, or "radiant," a word similar to "horns," or *qeren* (Eilberg-Schwartz 1994:143–45).

19. Many scholars read Zipporah's second "bloody bridegroom" utterance as a later editorial insertion that seeks to clarify the meaning of the original phrase (e.g., Morgenstern 1963:67).

20. Central Australian boys were sometimes circumcised by their potential fathers-in-law, thus swapping foreskins for brides (Róheim 1945:72–73). In Amazonia, where penis sheathing entitles youth to intercourse and marriage, male initiates confronted a terrible spirit. The sheath was addressed as "wife." Since circumcision is the inverse of sheathing, argues Lévi-Strauss (1988), Zipporah addressed the severed prepuce as her "husband." At least one Kabbalistic text construes circumcision as a man's wife (Bahir 82; Kaplan 1995:146, 193–94 n. 62).

21. Others say Moses was circumcised as an Egyptian (Kosmala 1962:16) or, in midrash, born foreskinless (Robinson 1986; chapter 2).

22. Zipporah's heroism partly led Bloom to identify the J composer of the Torah as a woman (Bloom and Rosenberg 1990:245–47).

23. In legend, Zipporah was promised by her father to the man who could pluck a divinely hewn staff from the ground (SH 76–77; PRE 40; Ginzberg 1909–1938:II:291–94). The rod devoured those who failed. Only Moses triumphed.

24. Incidentally, one of the Egyptian midwives who saved Moses was named Shiphrah, which resembles Zipporah (Zeligs 1986:45).

CHAPTER SIX

Lilith, Yarmulkes, and the Eye of Circumcision

Lilith, a once dreaded demoness in Jewish folklore, now serves as a feminist heroine. Indeed, her name since 1976 identifies an important Jewish women's magazine. As Adam's legendary first wife, banished from Eden for demanding sexual equality, Lilith personifies women's rebellion against patriarchy. Or so it seems, for Lilith also represents male anxieties, at least in her earlier incarnations as a lustful creature who murders mothers and newborns, especially infant boys. Only circumcision offered protection from her deadly embrace.

Lilith emerged from different and often contradictory traditions. My goal in this chapter is neither to unify nor to comprehensively survey these exegetical and folkloristic sources. Instead, I want to interpret the relationship between Lilith and circumcision by focusing on the symbolism of hair, head coverings, and eyes.

Thwarting Lilith

The night preceding circumcision is fraught with mystical peril. Lilith, writes Gaster (1980:21–22) graphically, seeks to "plunge" a mother "into the sleep of death, take away her babe, suck its blood, drain its marrow and seal up its flesh." Jewish communities in Europe, North Africa, and the Middle East derived a rich magical repertoire to protect newborns and their mothers from Lilith and other demons (Gaster 1900; Patai 1967, 1983c; Dobrinsky 1980; Gaster 1980; Gutmann 1987; Brauer 1993; Klein 1998; see also Morgenstern 1973:chap. 4).[1]

Traditionally, for example, Jews etched magical circles around newborns with knives, swords, embers, and "nitre," impenetrable by Lilith and the evil eye (Patai 1967:228; 1983b:411–12). Moroccan Jews waved a sword about the child's room as if to slay invisible adversaries or tossed a knife against the wall while chanting Genesis 7:16, where God "shut" Noah safely in the ark (Dobrinsky 1980:62; Patai 1983a:289; 1983b:412). Other scriptural deterrents included Numbers 6:24–26, Psalm 121, and, among Hasidim today, Psalm 126 (Dobrinsky 1980:61; Klein 1998:chap. 10; Holtzberg 1999:7). In Kurdistan, Jewish infants slept in the laps of elderly women; midwives slapped mothers, then clapped three times, declaring "Depart, Lilith" (Brauer 1993:164). Magical inventories against Lilith, other demons, and the evil eye also included amulets, esoteric phrases, and henna patterns.

Circumcision was particularly prophylactic against nefarious spirits and powers (Trachtenberg 1939:170). The rite protected boys from danger, as did the circumcision knife when concealed beneath the child's pillow (Chill 1979:296; Patai 1983b:397–98). Some Jews even stuffed the severed foreskin into an infant's mouth to guard against Lilith's "possession" (Patai 1983b:406). The rabbis, alarmed that superstition might eclipse theology, protested against these magical interpretations of circumcision. But the folk accepted no such orthodoxy.

The Watch-Night

The Sabbath preceding circumcision acquired considerable significance by the medieval era. After the evening meal, family and friends gathered at the child's house for hymns, study, and refreshments. This convocation, called *Ben Zakhor*, or "child of remembrance," alludes to a tragedy of birth. *In utero*, as I mentioned in the previous chapter, infants learn the Torah, mystical secrets, even the future. But all is forgotten on delivery when an angel slaps the child on the mouth (B. Niddah 30b). The Friday night gathering consoled the infant for this lost wisdom. Visitors snacked on mourning foods as well as nuts, which, like the foreskinned penis, need slitting to reveal the kernel.

The Friday night festivity is also called *Shalom Zakhor*, or "welcome/peace to the male child." This greeting also comforts the newborn boy for his lost gestational wisdom and traumatic exodus from uterine tranquility into a turbulent world. It also reflects the Talmudic aphorism that "as soon as a male comes into the world peace comes into the world" (B. Nidah 31b; B. Berachoth 64a).[2] The gathering, too, joyously introduces the boy to the Sabbath Queen.

By the late medieval period, European Jews developed a circumcision eve ceremony called Yeshua Haben or, more commonly, the "watch-night" (vakh-nakht). This vigil protected boys from the murderous designs of Lilith and other scourges such as the evil eye (Trachtenberg 1939:171; Pollack 1971:19; Patai 1983a; Klein 1998:chap. 12).[3] The watch-night uneasily combined sacred and profane. Prayer joined with gambling, popular song, storytelling, masquerades, feasting, and drinking (Horowitz 1989). The raucousness lasted throughout the night until the circumcision in the morning. Interestingly, Italian statutes from the sixteenth and seventeenth centuries limited the extent of male participation in the watch-night. Perhaps its festive privileges initially favored only women (Horowitz 1989). At any rate, sumptuary legislation in the seventeenth century sought to restrain the unruly folk by curtailing the watch-night and other popular European festivals (Horowitz 1989:52). Rabbinic leaders welcomed these ordinances since the watch-night, like the Christian carnival, threatened religious authority at a time when theology was already besieged by the emerging secular ideal of the Enlightenment (Horowitz 1989:58). Once raucous and magical, the watch-night waned into a small gathering of men for sober prayer and study.

Today, many Jews continue the watch-night tradition. Yet its origins remain murky. The occasion may pertain to the post-Talmudic shift in the staging of circumcision from the synagogue to the home. Rabbis often look to Genesis 17:9, where God declared "thou shalt keep (tishmor)" or "watch My covenant" (Schauss 1950:309 n. 49). Or they cite Ecclesiastes 11:2, "distribute a portion to seven and/or even to eight," which seemingly alludes to a seventh-day feast before the eighth-day circumcision. Recent scholars trace the watch-night to a Germanic gathering on the eve of baptism (Gaster 1980:62; Gutmann 1983a:130–32). The question of origins aside, watch-night festivities both somber and gay alleviate anxieties over the possibility that demons or the circumcision procedure might harm the child.

The watch-night might also represent a folkloristic response to the "bloody bridegroom" incident of Exodus 4 (chapter 5), here understood as a nocturnal demon intent on preventing a father from circumcising his son. The watch-night also, at least in its earlier phases, permitted women, like Zipporah, unusual ritual license. Zipporah, as an uncertain heroine who preserved and subverted the covenantal cut, anticipated the rabbinic figure of Lilith, who imperils circumcision yet thereby compels the community to come together in defense of the rite. Indeed, both Lilith and Zipporah undermined male authority. But while Zipporah challenged patriarchy by performing circumcision, Lilith does so by threatening the rite.

The Origins of Lilith

Lilith's origins are no less hazy than those of the watch-night. She appears once in the Hebrew Bible when the prophet Isaiah paints a grim portrait of divine punishment. Amid a desert wasteland of blood and desolation, snakes and buzzards, "Wildcats shall meet hyenas, Goat-demons shall greet each other; There too the Lilith shall repose, And find herself a resting place" (Isaiah 34:14). Isaiah says nothing more about her.

The Sumerian counterpart to Lilith was a winged and taloned creature called Lillu, who sat astride a lion (Milgrom 1993). In the prologue to the famous Gilgamesh epic, Lilin is an avian demon who flees to the desert. The King James Bible similarly identifies Lilith as a "screech owl." But her name might also derive from "goat-sucker" or "night-jar," two evening birds that haunt the desert (Driver 1959). Popular etymologies derive Lilith from "night demon" (Trachtenberg 1939:36, 170; Patai 1983b:406). Schauss (1950:69) traces Lilith to a Babylonian spirit of the hot desert "wind," or *lil* in Sumerian. She later became identified with fatal pregnancies, birthing fevers, and "night" (*layil*).[4] These and other etymologies suggest that Lilith originated as a mysterious, predatory, airborne wilderness creature.

A different aspect of Lilith arose from a biblical puzzle. God created "male and female" in Genesis 1, then molded woman from the "rib" in Genesis 2. What happened to the first female? She became the Lilith of Jewish folklore. In one tale, the so-called first Eve was "full of discharge and blood" (GR 18:4; Zohar i:34b).[5] So repulsed was Adam that God returned her "to dust" and tried again. Another tale blames the first Eve for the quarrel between Cain and Abel (GR 22:7). After the expulsion from Eden and the death of Abel, goes yet a third tale, Adam and Eve embarked on solitary, celibate exiles, only to succumb to demonic seductions (GR 20:11; 23:4; 24:6; TG 1.26; Zohar i:54b, 55a, 169b; Zohar ii:231b). Succubi stimulated Adam to nocturnal ejaculation, then mounted him and conceived other spirits, some of whom were called Lilin. In many of these early rabbinic texts, Boyarin (1993:94–97) stresses, Lilith-like creatures are female *and* male, seducing Adam *and* Eve (see also 2 Baruch 10:8). Lilith is not yet the bloodthirsty witch who preys on uncircumcised infant boys.

Lilith makes several appearances in the Babylonian Talmud. She displays long hair (Eiruvin 100b) and wings (Nidah 24b), births demons (Baba

Bathra 73a)—sometimes by Adam (Eiruvin 18b)—and seizes sleeping men (Shabbath 151b). But here, too, Lilith lacks interest in circumcision and children.

Inscribed seventh-century bowls from Iraq portray a more vicious Lilith and her male double, Lili (Montgomery 1913; Patai 1967:212–17). These images roughly coincide with the final redaction of the Talmud. This Lilith preyed on menstruating, birthing, and virginal women. She provoked miscarriage and infertility and strangled children to suck their blood and gnaw on their bones. This Lilith, too, featured enlarged genitals and long, disheveled locks.

The first extensive account of Lilith in Jewish culture occurs in *The Alpha-Beth of Ben Sira*, a popular satire written during the ninth to tenth centuries in North Africa or Iraq. The book deploys the language of bawdy, bodily taboo to mock rabbinic authority. It also displays the assimilation into rabbinic culture of a wider, non-Jewish medieval misogyny (Boyarin 1993:94–97). In the story, Lilith is Adam's first wife. When she famously refuses to assume the passive position during sexual intercourse, her husband snarls, "I will not lie beneath you, but only on top . . . you are fit only to be in the bottom position, while I am to be in the superior one." Lilith responds, "We are equal to each other, inasmuch as we were both created from the earth." Adam remains adamant. So Lilith utters the ineffable name of God and takes flight to the sea. Three angels seek to retrieve her, but Lilith refuses. Enraged, God decrees the daily death of one hundred of her children. The angels also threaten to drown Lilith. "Leave me," she cries, "I was created only to cause sickness to infants. If the infant is male, I have dominion over him for eight days after his birth, and if a female, for twenty days." Only if Lilith sees one of the three angels, however, or the letters of its name will she surrender a child.

Lilith in *The Alpha-Beth of Ben Sira* did more than simply invert sexual norms.[6] She sought to upend a general conception of cosmic order (Kimelman 1998) that the rabbis, we saw in chapter 1, often linked to circumcision. Indeed, Lilith threatened to accomplish what fathers and *mohels* seemed poised to do: kill infants. By transforming the covenantal cut into a fatal grasp, Lilith expressed male anxieties about the performance of circumcision. As a prolific yet horrendous mother, she also personified male unease toward women and motherhood. Finally, since Lilith birthed hundreds of demon offspring daily, then slew them (NR 16:25), she mocked the promise of male fecundity contingent on the fulfillment of circumcision (Adler 1977b:22). In multiple ways, Lilith turned the tables on Jewish men and women.

From the Dregs of the Wine

The Kabbalistic Lilith was particularly fierce and carnal. Emerging from the "great abyss" (Zohar iii:19a), she aroused sleeping men to orgasm and thus to ritual impurity. When men make love to their wives, Lilith steals their seminal "sparks" to sire her own impious children. For protection, the Zohar (3:19a) prescribed a sprinkling of water around the bed, sexual modesty, and pure thoughts during intercourse.

In the thirteenth century *Treatise on the Left Emanation*, Lilith is married to Satan. From the waist upward, she resembles a beautiful maiden. Below, she is all aflame (see Dan 1980). Elsewhere in the mystical tradition, Lilith was born a snake from the "dregs of the wine" (Patai 1967:218–19, 233–35). She entwines with Satan and incestuously "makes sport" with her own off-spring. In a commentary to the Zohar, Lilith impersonates a harlot. After a tryst, she "turns into a menacing figure . . . clothed in garments of flaming fire . . . full of frightening eyes, in her hand a drawn sword dripping bitter drops" and "kills that fool" (Patai 1967:222). All of Lilith's Kabbalistic personifications express male anxieties over female sexuality and motherhood.

Erotic Tresses

Perhaps Lilith's most notable feature is her disheveled mop. Anthropologists and psychoanalysts have extensively pondered the cross-cultural significance of hair. Often, hair symbolizes natural appetites such as sexuality that require cultural restraint. Lilith's unruly tresses fit this pattern.

In 1922, Freud wrote a famous essay, "Medusa's Head." Why, he asked, should men turn to stone when glancing at this mythic woman's hair-like snakes? Freud offered two answers. First, Medusa's serpentine locks symbolized aggressive phalloi that subdue or castrate potential foes. (Her hair thus resembles Moses' staff.) Second, Medusa personified men's fright at the doubly castrative female body, a body that lacks a phallus and engulfs the penis during intercourse. How did men finally defeat Medusa? By decapitation, that is, emasculation.

Building on Freud's thesis, Ferenczi (1926) interpreted Medusa's head as the upward displacement of the vulva. Through an inverse symbolism, her snakes portrayed male horror at the absence of a penis.[7] But the petrification that resulted from a glance at her serpents alleviated this anxiety by restoring manhood to its solid, erect status.

Freud's approach to Medusa remains controversial. Yet many anthropologists agree that hair is a potent symbol. Long tresses frequently represent sexuality and social liminality (Hershman 1974; Obeyesekere 1981). Trimming may signify castrative renunciation (Berg 1951) or social reintegration (Hallpike 1969). Hair forms a symbolic boundary around self and society and so is frequently invested with notions of taboo, purity, and pollution (Douglas 1966). Many of these themes pertained to biblical and rabbinic cultures.

The Israelites abided by a precise shaving etiquette (Leviticus 19:27; 21:5; Deuteronomy 14:1). Ritual cutting and trimming generally marked changes in social status (Olyan 1998; cf. Morgenstern 1973:chap. 12). A trim coiffure indicated the acceptance of everyday gender conventions (Margalit 1995). Untidy or unfurled hair characterized Israelites such as the diseased and ascetics who, legitimately or not, rent the normal fabric of society.

Israelite culture regulated women's hair to symbolize a concern with governing female sexuality, a theme also present in Islam and Christianity (Delaney 1995:61; 1 Corinthians 11:2–16). Priests publicly shaved, unraveled, or uncovered the hair of suspected adulteresses (Numbers 5:18; see also Isaiah 3:17). To this disgrace, the Mishnah added the baring of the woman's breasts (M. Sotah 1:5). Public exposures of female hair were punitive and pornographic (see also Lieberman 1974a:52–56; Dobrinsky 1980:267). On the one hand, Lilith inverts this violence by exposing her own body and locks to dominate men. On the other hand, Lilith's hair represents the threat of unrestrained female carnality to ensnarl the norms of masculinity and motherhood—a fantasied threat, I add, concocted by men.

In a fascinating tale, Lilith is lured to the scent of breast milk. She assumes the form of a single black hair and falls into a glass of milk, just as a nursing mother is about to sip. The mother sees the strand and faints (Schwartz 1992:112; Klein 1998:179–80). This story portrays Lilith's hair as a force unto itself—a disheveled antithesis of nurturing motherhood.

The rabbis often linked maternal virtue and feminine modesty to bound and covered hair (B. Yoma 47a). They also imagined that God himself braided Eve's chaste, prelapsarian hair (B. Berachoth 61a; B. Nidah 45b). Lilith's unruly tresses could not be more different. So hairy is Lilith that, in one mystical text (Patai 1967:237–38), she is covered from head to foot.

Rabbinic authorities were somewhat divided on the specific hairdo of married women: covered or braided? Both rulings were justified with reference to the biblical humiliation of accused adulteresses (B. Berachoth 72a–b). Public displays of female hair in traditional and Orthodox Jewish cultures are dangerously erotic, like "the ways of the idolatrous women" (NR 9:16). Such lasciviousness was valid cause for divorce without the usual monetary compensation (M. Kethuboth 7:6).[8] Indeed, the Talmud (B. Berachoth 24a) admonishes men to shield their eyes from women's hair during prayer lest their thoughts stray from the sublime to the sensuous.

Jewish women during the Talmudic era cultivated "sumptuous" coiffures (Krauss 1970:455–60). Today, Orthodox women cover their hair with scarfs, hats, and wigs. In an earlier era, the practice perhaps avoided the impression that modest Jewish women emulated the habit of nuns (Epstein 1948:52–55). Still, the wig (*sheitel*) seems paradoxical when we consider the rabbinic edicts directing men to avoid the erotic allure of female hair. Wigs allow Jewish women to "circumvent custom" (Dundes 2002), to flirt with sexual taboo, and, since the rabbis once opposed the practice, to challenge religious authority (Bronner 1993:472). Like Lilith, wigs threaten male authority. Unlike Lilith, they represent erotic restraint by containing hair. Still, both Lilith and women's head coverings, I suggest, emerged partly from the same cultural concerns with male authority and female sexuality.

Haircutting: A Circumcision to Be Remembered

Hindu men in South Asia who renounce worldly pursuits also shave their heads. Muslim men are circumcised. Sikhs pare neither their hair nor their penes but enwrap their untrimmed locks in turbans and so stand apart from Hindus and Muslims (Olivelle 1998:27–28). Male hair in biblical and rabbinic cultures, I will now show, similarly relates to circumcision.

In the Book of Judith, a noncanonical Jewish text written in Greek, the Israelites refuse to join King Nebuchadnezzar in battle. As the insulted Assyrians prepare their revenge, Israel meekly offers to surrender. This passivity offends a beautiful widower named Judith, who opposes any submission to those who "have planned cruel things against thy [God's] covenant" (Judith 9:13). At a banquet, Judith seduces the Assyrian general Holofernes, who loses his head from too much wine. Judith decapitates Holofernes, and the headless Assyrians flee. (So impressed was the leader of the Ammonites, in the tale, that he threw himself on Judith's feet and performed his own circumcision!) Judith's beheading of Holofernes plainly alludes to circumcision (Levine 1995; Kim 1999).[9] Her swordsmanship recalls Zipporah's equally unorthodox slice and, more to the point, Lilith's locks and Medusa's snakes. These four phallic women cut down men, usurped masculine privilege, and, often like rabbinic tales about Esau (chapter 4), evidence a postbiblical connection between circumcision and hair.

This connection has ample support. Prior to the Exodus, said the rabbis,

Jewish men emulated the Egyptians by growing foreskins and long hair (PR 15; ECR 9:15:4). The "sons of Israel," declared another midrash, abided by three biblical edicts (SSR 1:15:2; PR 29/30A). They practiced circumcision, refused to trim their earlocks or "side-growth" of hair (Leviticus 19:27; 21:5), and adorned their garments with fringes (Numbers 15:38–39; Deuteronomy 22:12). The trimmed penis in these passages does not correspond to the wild tresses of Lilith. Quite the opposite. The penis here corresponds to controlled hair and hair-like, fringed apparel.

At the end of the twelfth century, northern Italian women abandoned earrings as tokens of un-Christian sensuality and vanity. Three hundred years later, earrings were imposed on Jewish women (Hughes 1986). These ornaments were also associated with gypsies, Moors, prostitutes, and the snouts of pigs and bulls.[10] In an Advent sermon, the Franciscan Giacomo della Marca referred to earrings as jewels "that Jewish women wear in place of circumcision, so they can be distinguished" from Christians (Hughes 1986:24). Not only did della Marca feminize Jewish men and associate all Jews with animalistic carnality, but he also identified the circumcised penis with an adorned head.

Lest the connection between heads and circumcision seem somewhat far-fetched in the Renaissance legislation, a famous biblical tale is more explicit. Ascetics such as Samson, called nazirites, refused to cut their hair as part of their dedication to God (Judges 5:2). Warriors sported a similar growth (Deuteronomy 32:42; Krauss 1970:427). Samson's untrimmed hair symbolized strength and renunciation (Judges 13–16). But despite this muscular piety, Samson craved Delilah, a woman from "the uncircumcised Philistines." Later, the same "uncircumcised" gouged out Samson's eyes and fatally snipped his hair while he slept "on" or "between the knees" of Delilah, a position connoting birth and rest after lovemaking (Bal 1987:58–63). Samson's castrative and infantilizing haircut was, as even the poet Milton recognized (Lieb 2000), a deadly circumcision.

Many Jews today, especially the Hasidic community, continue to dramatize a connection between foreskins and hair by celebrating a boy's first trimming, around the age of three. This haircutting festivity marks the child's emergence from infancy into the male world of formal education.[11] The rite, argues Bilu (2000), reenacts the child's earlier circumcision so that, this time, the boy consciously apprehends the ceremonial messages. (Recall from chapter 4 that "male" and "memory" are linguistic cognates in Hebrew.) The haircutting rite is a circumcision to be remembered.[12]

Long-locked Hasidic boys resemble girls (Bilu 2000:51). The haircutting

rite, like circumcision, snips boys from femininity and motherhood and teth-
ers them to adult men. Logically, boyish locks are female, much like foreskins. But the ceremonial trimming does not completely shave the child. In
accordance with Leviticus, the boy retains his earlocks (called *peyot* or *pey-
ess*). The exposure of these curls, once hidden by feminine hair, physically
attest to the boy's attainment of manhood. They make evident his earlier
and normally hidden circumcision. Indeed, both the haircut and circumcision remove an outer part of the male body to reveal an inner masculinity.
Ironically, though, the haircutting rite, like circumcision, also feminizes boys
through its visual reminder of the child's former feminine status.

The Hasidic haircutting rite makes sense only as a symbolic circumcision
that equates head and penis. Kabbalah is quite clear on this connection. The
mystics labeled the corona of the penis a "crown" (*'atarah*), the same head-
dress that adorns the female Torah scrolls and the feminine personification of
God, the Shekhinah (Wolfson 1994a:186–87; 1994b:358–59; 1995:86–89).
Why, asks the Zohar (i:162a), does Proverbs 10:6 speak about blessings
"upon the *head* of the righteous"? Because this "head" alludes to the Holy
Crown and the "place of the covenant." Hasidic men trim the penis but
allow for reproduction, and they trim hair but retain their earlocks (Bilu
2000:53). This way, Jewish men are twice distinguished from the untrimmed,
unholy, undomesticated passions of Lilith.

Hats and Penises

Muslim boys in rural Turkey enter the "gendered world" of adulthood by los-
ing their foreskins (Delaney 1991:87). Girls gain head scarves. Since Muslims shave their body hair, continues Delaney, especially the pubes, the
unpared head symbolizes the natural condition of the genitals. But while
women hide their sexuality beneath clothing, men triply flaunt it through an
exposed head, the growth of a virile moustache, and a public circumcision
ceremony that uncovers the penis (Delaney 1988:81–82). Judaism incorpo-
rates a similar dichotomy between men and women.

Devout Jewish men are often distinguished by a small hat, called a *kippah*
in Hebrew, or *yarmulke*. Cross-culturally, hats frequently serve as phallic
symbols (Dundes 1991a). Indeed, circumcision and the *yarmulke* form what
Boyarin and Boyarin (1995) call the "double sign" of Jewish masculinity. Yet
they fail to recognize the connection between these two signs, both of which
cover Jewish "heads."

Lest I seem to introduce an inappropriate Freudian symbolism into Jewish tradition, I immediately defer to the rabbis. For them, circumcision partly offered salvation from hell (TG 5.6; 3.27; Zohar ii:57b). Many biblical passages, when read through the lens of rabbinic logic, support this conclusion. For example, Ezekiel often reserves hell for the foreskinned (28:8–10; 31:18; 32:19–31). A question in Deuteronomy, "Who among us can go up to the heavens?" (30:12), contains the acronym *milah*, or "circumcision" (Wolfson 1987a:87–90). Many Jewish folktales, too, celebrate the redemptive power of circumcision. Long ago, a Jewish man slept with a betrothed virgin—on the Day of Atonement, no less! He was stoned to death, and his soul descended to hell (Gaster 1934:story 146). When the woman birthed a son, the community refused to sponsor the boy's circumcision. Later, the famous Rabbi Akiva rebuked the town for this injustice. He circumcised the boy, then taught him Torah. The father ascended to heaven.

But what happens to circumcised sinners? What is their fate? In some rabbinic texts, circumcised heretics and evildoers descend to hell after God or an angel restretches them new foreskins (T-Y 3:20; ER 19:4).[13] Rabbi Levi offered this view:

> In the Hereafter Abraham will sit at the entrance to Gehenna (a Jewish version of hell), and permit no circumcised Israelite to descend therein. What then will he do to those who have sinned very much? He will remove the foreskin from babes who died before circumcision and set it upon them [the sinners], and then let them descend into Gehenna.[14] (GR 48:8)

The text leaves unclear how Abraham places these foreskins on circumcised sinners. As a type of cap? If so, then this midrash attributes phallic symbolism to the Jewish head.

The skullcap, or *yarmulke*, became standard garb for Eastern European (Ashkenazic) Jewish men by the early eighteenth century. The origins of the practice, as well as the term, are somewhat unclear. Devout Jews often derive *yarmulke* from the Aramaic phrase "one who fears" or "is in awe of God" (*yarei me-eloheka*). Plaut (1955) offers a more prosaic explanation. In the sixteenth century, Jews were prescribed caps attached to small cowls. These garments resembled a late medieval priestly cape, or *almucia* in Latin. Through linguistic transformations, this term evolved into *yarmulke*.[15]

The Hebrew Bible mentions headgear for priests (Exodus 29:6; Leviticus 8:6; 13) and men during mourning, submission, and humiliation (1 Kings 20:31; II Kings 15:30; Jeremiah 14:3). There is no evidence that biblical men routinely donned caps. Nor does the Torah mandate male head covering as a sign of reverence before the Almighty (Lauterbach 1970; Krauss 1970). The Talmud, too, offers no uniform ruling on male headgear. For some rabbinic authorities, caps were optional (B. Nedarim 30b). Yet Rabbi Huna "would not walk four cubits bareheaded" in deference to the divine presence (B. Kiddushin 31a). By the eighth century, Jewish law required men to wear hats in some sacred settings. Medieval rabbis viewed headgear as a general token of piety, requiring no biblical precedent, yet expected only of religious authorities and scholars. It was not until the sixteenth century that head covering became the norm for Jewish men. Perhaps hats best ensured that no Jewish man required a foreskinned cap in death!

Jews as early as the ninth century favored distinctive attire (Kisch 1942:97). Otherwise, they might appear to imitate Gentiles and so violate biblical law (Leviticus 20:23; 28:3; Kisch 1942:98). Of course, it is one thing to self-select an emblem of ethnic identity, whether circumcision or clothing. It is something quite different to have this identity imposed by others, which is precisely what happened during the Lateran Council of 1215, convened by Pope Innocent III. This synod initiated a long era in European history that mandated distinctive and derogatory apparel for Jews (Kisch 1942; Zafran 1973; Marcus 1999). These tokens of opprobrium included caps, cloaks, kerchiefs, and the infamous "yellow badge."

The "yellow badge" first appeared in ninth-century Baghdad as part of a broader effort to separate Muslims from Jews and Christians (Lewis 1984:25).[16] When the insignia spread to England in 1217, thence to the rest of Europe, the badge aimed to mark only Jews. The European emblem was initially made from white linen or parchment and shaped to resemble the tablets of the Ten Commandments. The badge eventually turned yellow, a hue commonly used to tag medieval outcasts such as prostitutes, clerical concubines, insolvent debtors, and Jews (Kisch 1942:116–17). Later, the badge was rounded after the unholy money Jews reaped from the betrayal of Christ (Kisch 1942:16). This badge also recalled the Eucharistic host that medieval Jews, as I discuss in chapter 9, allegedly stabbed during their nefarious rituals (Trachtenberg 1943). Since Jews, from one angle, would not accept Christ into their hearts, they would wear him on their garments. From another angle, I suggest, Jews were forced to make visible on top of their clothing the *true* mark of Judaism that was ordinarily hidden beneath their britches.

In was only during the seventeenth and eighteenth centuries that European society began, after a shameful reign of 500 years, to rescind legal decrees that marked Jews—at least until a revival under Nazism. Yet Jewish men remained visibly distinctive since Christians largely abandoned beards in the thirteenth century to pilgrims, the elderly, and Jews. Even after assimilated Jewish men took up shaving in the seventeenth century, they still retained a bodily distinctiveness, albeit one hidden, namely, circumcision.[17] Beards, badges, hairstyles, and caps have waxed and waned over the past millennium. But circumcision continues to mark the body of the Jew.

Enwrapping the Body

Devout Jewish men over the age of thirteen enwrap themselves for morning prayers in a fringed garment called a *tallit*. Today, many women also enshroud their devotions with a prayer shawl. But my concern here is with tradition. The fringes of the *tallit*, like circumcision, serve a mnemonic function. The tassels evoke "all the commandments of the Lord . . . so that you do not follow your heart and eyes in your lustful urge" or, more literally, "go a whoring" (Numbers 15:39; Deuteronomy 22:12).[18] Like circumcision, too, as well as phylacteries, the *tallit* is a biblical "sign" that protectively surrounds the bodies of Jewish men (B. Menachoth 43b). Hair-like, the fringes of the *tallit* oppose all that Lilith represents.

Rabbinic culture shaped the prayer shawl into a symbol of cosmological order—again, like circumcision. The garment must be clearly marked so worshippers will not confuse its proper orientation. From each corner hangs an eight-stranded fringe (*tzitzit*), tied into five double knots and clusters of windings, typically, seven, eight, eleven, and thirteen (Bailey 2000:171–72). The rabbis saw a rich numerical symbolism in this pattern. Each set of windings, for example, represents a specific ritual practice. Not surprisingly, eight refers to the day of circumcision. The first three sets of windings, moreover, total the numerical value of the tetragrammaton ($7 + 8 + 11 = 26$). The final winding (13) equals the word for "one" to evoke the monotheistic creed (Deuteronomy 6:4). The numerical equivalent of word "fringes" (*tzitzit*), moreover, when added to the eight threads and five knots, equals 613, or the total number of laws in the Torah. By symbolizing the entire religious system, the *tallit* (something you put on) complements circumcision (something you take off) by further enveloping men within God's law.

When a father carries his son to the schooling initiation I discussed earlier, he often enwraps the child in a *tallit* to protect him from the evil eye and Gentile pollution (Marcus 1996:76–77).[19] During this procession, the *tallit* represents a masculine womb from which fathers rebirth their sons into the world of male study. Here, again, the prayer shawl resembles circumcision.

The *tallit*, too, mirrors circumcision by offering men protection from unholy female seduction and the lack of self-control. In one rabbinic tale, a devout Jew tests his piety by visiting a beautiful, Gentile harlot (B. Menachoth 44a; Satlow 1995:164–66). He is swiftly overcome with desire and almost succumbs to illicit intercourse when the fringes of his *tallit* slap him across the face. So astonished was the harlot that she converted to Judaism! A male Jew surrounds his body by a "fence" of circumcision, fringes, cap, and earlocks to bar the illicit desires represented by foreskins and Lilith.

Eyes Evil and Phallic

Lilith is the fearful double of a beloved female figure in Judaism, namely, the Shekhinah, who serves as the feminine personification of God (Patai 1967:242–45; Wolfson 1994b:189). The Shekhinah dwells on earth in times of righteousness. She offers humanity a warm, radiant, forgiving encounter with an otherwise awesome deity (Wolfson 1989:293–307). The Shekhinah does punish humanity for grievous sins (RN 34:8). But her maternal aggression, unlike that of Lilith, sustains divine morality.

While Lilith adulterously seduces husbands, the Shekhinah, as we saw in chapter 1, sanctifies marital intercourse (B. Sotah 17a). While Lilith seeks to thwart circumcision, the Shekhinah reveals herself mainly to circumcised men (NR 12:8; Wolfson 1987a). Indeed, circumcision opens the male body to an intimate union with God. The rite prepares men to receive the mystical secrets of Torah (Wolfson 1987b:190–98; Boyarin 1992:495; TE 6.3). The circumcised phallus thus represents a feminine eye, bestowed only onto men, that glimpses the divine presence.

"Before I became circumcised," said Abraham in midrash (GR 47:10), "travelers used to visit me; now that I am circumcised, perhaps they will no longer visit me?" God replied, "Before thou wast circumcised, uncircumcised mortals visited thee; now I in My glory will appear to thee." The rabbis corroborated the phallic vision of circumcision with reference to Job 19:26, "through my *flesh* shall I *see* God" (GR 48:21). Lacking a body—really, lacking a penis—God remains invisible and unapproachable (Boyarin 1994:127; Wolfson 1994a:342). Only through circumcision, exclaims midrash (NT 12:8), was Abraham qualified to behold the godhead.

These optical idioms recall the common belief in the evil eye. Like Lilith, the evil eye in Jewish folklore often threatened boys before their circumcision (e.g., Ohel 1973:67). In biblical and rabbinic cultures, the evil eye was rapacious, jealous, selfish, and hungry (Deuteronomy 15:9; 28:54, 56; Proverbs 23:6; 28:22; Elliott 1991; Ulmer 1994). These characteristics, Dundes (1992) shows, occur widely throughout Europe, the Middle East, and the Mediterranean.

Water in rabbinic culture confers immunity from the evil eye (B. Berachoth 20a; B. Sotah 36b; B. Baba Metzia 84a). The rabbis justified this belief by citing Genesis 49:22, where Joseph is described as "a fruitful vine by a spring (ayin)," a word that also means "eye." Jewish lore remedied the evil eye with spittle, drops of mother's milk, and the recitation of biblical passages such as Numbers 21:17–20 over cups of water (Trachtenberg 1939:109–12; Ulmer 1994:143, 155). Since the evil eye is everywhere thirsty, writes Dundes (1992), moisture is therapeutic.

Jews often associated the evil eye with witchcraft, menstruation, and the alluring gaze of women (B. Shabbath 62b; B. Sotah 10a; Ulmer 1994). As in the case of Lilith, postpartum mothers and newborns were especially susceptible to this optical scourge (Brav 1908:49). Nor surprisingly, the same virtues, humility and modesty, counteract both malignancies (Ulmer 1994:141–420). These resemblances do not seem incidental.

The Talmud reports a lewd prophylaxis against the evil eye: enclose the thumb within the opposite fist (B. Berachoth 55b). Other variants of this hand gesture include the Italian fica, or "fig," obscenity and the American extension of the middle finger. They all represent sexual intercourse and the membrum virile (e.g., Hirsch 1892:73). In Latin, in fact, the word fica also refers to the penis and vulva; fascinum, or "evil eye," likewise denotes an erection (Róheim 1952:217). Hand gestures thus suggest that genitals negate the evil eye. Why?

For an answer, I turn to Dundes's (1992) analysis of the evil eye as an Indo-European and Semitic expression of four folk premises. First, life depends on vital bodily liquids such as semen, milk, and blood. Second, the world contains a finite quantity of goodness; one person's gain is another's loss. Third, the ideal state of the world is equilibrium. Finally, the eye symbolizes the phallus and vulva.[20] This worldview, claims Dundes (1992:274), phrases envy in liquid terms. The evil eye represents a covetous glance that metaphorically dehydrates its victims. Liquid replenishment offers a logical remedy. The penis is an apt cure since it issues life-giving liquid. So does the vulva. But the vulva additionally "drinks" semen and exudes deathly blood and so appears depleting and dangerous in many folk worldviews.

The phallo-vaginal symbolism of the evil eye evokes the Kabbalistic imagery of circumcision as a feminine opening in the penis that enables men to see God and mystical secrets. Since the evil eye and circumcision represent

antithetical moral qualities in rabbinic culture, it seems reasonable to propose that they form a unified symbolic system. Circumcision, I add, serves as
an antidote to the seductive gaze of Lilith, who parallels the evil eye. Not by
accident do many premodern amulets offer protection against both Lilith
and the evil eye.

Chyet and Mirsky (1990:63) draw on Dundes (1992) to offer another connection between the evil eye and circumcision. Rabbinic culture, they propose, emphasized the extraction of blood during circumcision to compensate
the boy's parents for the loss of vital fluids such as semen and breast milk.
Since the birth of boys provoked envy (B. Baba Bathra 141a), moreover, the
rite dramatized unconscious hostility toward sons for placing parents at magical risk, which includes, of course, the evil eye.

I provisionally suggest that the folkloristic belief in the evil eye directly
influenced the rabbinic-mystical idea of Lilith and the visual dimensions of
circumcision. This suggestion allows us to recognize yet another, often
unstated dimension to the covenantal rite and to acknowledge the vital
importance of the "folk" and not just authorities in shaping Judaism.

The Divine Signature

The mystics also viewed circumcision as a literary "seal" or "letter," a type
of bodily writing that textualizes the penis and admits men into a theological
community of readers and writers (Wolfson 1987b:191 n. 6; Bilu 2000:36).[21]
Medieval Jews, in fact, placed Torah scrolls on newly circumcised boys, saying, "This one should fulfill what is written in this" (Rabinowitz 1972:191–
92). They also presented the child with an inkstand and pen.

The ritual opening of the penis to uncover the glans additionally represents the exposure of the hidden mysteries of Scripture (Wolfson 1987a,
1994a, 2003; Bilu 2000:43). Indeed, the Hebrew language itself conceals evidence of this connection through linguistic similarity between "circumcision" (milah) and "word" (millah; Bilu 2000:36) and numerical equivalence
between "circumcision" (milah) and "mouth" (peh). Both acts of revealing—
one bodily, the other hermeneutic—are traditionally accessible only to men.
The physical procedure of circumcision thus symbolized the ultimate goal of
male scholarship.

The mystics also saw circumcision as God's signature. The rite inscribed
onto the penis a particular name of God, Shaddai, the very same deity who
announced the covenant to Abraham (chapter 4). The Kabbalists often
expanded this text metaphor to encompass the entire male physique. They

spelled *Shaddai*—in Hebrew, שדי, or *shin dalet yod*—from the form of a man's nostrils, hand, and circumcised penis (Wolfson 1987a). Additionally, the mystics saw the letter yod, as an abbreviation of the Tetragrammaton—YHWH), spelled יהוה in Hebrew, or *yod heh vav heh*—in the circumcised phallus (Wolfson 1987a:109). Kabbalah, too, identified the four letters of the Tetragrammaton in the exposed corona of the penis, the space once occupied by the foreskin, the shaft of the penis, and the act of uncovering the glans.[22]

An early Kabbalistic work, *Sepher Yetzirah* (1:3), formed the letters of God's name from the juxtapositions of a man's fingers and tongue with his toes and circumcised penis (Wolfson 1987a:96–97). This equivalence of penis and tongue recalls the foreskinned lips of Moses. More important, it sexualizes the scholarly conversations of men. Oral exegesis penetrates the ear much as circumcision penetrates the mysteries of Torah. This way, men assume a privileged role in social reproduction through the analogous acts of intercourse and scholarship.

This chapter largely shifted my focus from the Torah and biblical culture to rabbinic texts and what, for lack of a better term, we can dub the Jewish "folk." I have little doubt that some readers will experience unease with my symbolic connections—here and in earlier chapters. But I have repeatedly argued in this book that we cannot reduce the meanings of ritual and religion simply to authoritative statements and ideologies. Culture is far too complex. I have also argued that, to the extent that the site of circumcision seeks to sanctify otherwise base bodily desires, the converse is also true: circumcision imbues the religious system with a sense of erotic taboo.

It was from this perspective that I sought to assert a connection between circumcision and other aspects of traditional Jewish lore, including beliefs in Lilith and the evil eye as well as Jewish mysticism. But while the content of this chapter stands alone, my underlying point regarding circumcision remains the same: the rite flirts with meanings and gendered anxieties that disrupt any official or authoritative convictions.

Notes

1. Lilith has a Muslim counterpart, Karine (Granqvist 1947:96–97).

2. On the Sabbath prior to circumcision, Kurdish Jews honored father and son (Brauer 1993:162–63). On the birth of a girl, however, the father was mocked.

3. For the obscure rabbinic festivals called *Shevua Haben/Habat*, or "week of the son/daughter," see Hoffman (1996:178–79).

4. The Talmud mentions two creatures named *lailah*, or "night," a protectress (B. Sanhedrin 96a) and an angel who overseas conception (B. Nidah 16b).

5. For the menstrual Zoharic demoness as a symbol of Christianity, see Wolfson (1998).

6. Rabbinic authorities were divided on the position demanded by Lilith, which they called "turning over the table" (Boyarin 1993:118).

7. Nunberg (1949:171) tells of an analysand who thought of a "bleeding vagina" while watching a circumcision and fainted.

8. For biblical veiling, see Epstein (1948:38–39) and van der Toorn (1995).

9. In Caucasia, uncircumcised Muslims spend eternity headless (Luzbetak 1951:142). The Ndembu of African also associate circumcision with beheading (Turner 1962:170).

10. When looped earrings again became fashionable for Christian women in the six-teenth century, they were prohibited to Jews.

11. Jewish fathers in Morocco trim their hair on the eve of a son's circumcision (Klein 1998:220).

12. That the haircutting ceremony may occur during a tree festival (Lag Ba'omer) recalls the Levitical association of youthful penes and fruit (chapter 4).

13. In one midrash, hell is a woman who hungrily "devours" men with newly "hanging foreskins" (ER 19:4).

14. Yet intercourse with non-Jewish women lies beyond this redemption (B. Eruvin 19a; Zohar i:8a–b; Stern 1994:163–64).

15. A Polish locution for masturbation, *kapucyna rznac*, or "to beat a Capuchin," refers to the distinctive cowl, or *capuche*, of Franciscan monks (Bryk 1934:193–96).

16. Since Jews and Muslims both circumcise, Jews were also required to wear a special necklace in public baths, something unnecessary for foreskinnned Christians.

17. An anticircumcision essay in *Esquire* magazine referred to the foreskin as a "skull-cap" (Raab 2000).

18. The fringes were once bordered with blue (*tekhelet*) that reminded some rabbis of dark circumcision blood (T-Y 7:5).

19. Thus enwrapped, the boy resembles a Torah scroll, which often symbolizes a child (Goldberg 1987). Men alone traditionally paraded the scrolls around the synagogue (Marcus 1996:77–78).

20. The evil eye, notes Dundes, is always singular. It is never an evil *pair* of eyes! Parenthetically, an American slang term for a circumcised penis is "blind."

21. Maimonides also viewed circumcision as a legal seal (*Guide* 3:49; Stern 1993:145). Pippin and Aichele (2000) relate circumcision to the macabre printing machine in Kafka's 1949 story "In the Penal Colony," which fatally inscribes death sentences into prisoners' bodies.

22. When circumcision is viewed as God's signature, sexual impropriety becomes patently blasphemous (Wolfson 1987b:207–8, 1987a:102–3).

CHAPTER SEVEN

The Jewish Circumcision Ceremony

The "whole tenor" of Judaism, affirms Isaac (1967:52–55), dissents from the bloody, mutilating rites of paganism. But then why should the premier sign of the covenant so obviously seem to cut against this principled grain? It does so, answers Isaac, to teach Jews "that morality must be understood as commanded rather than as part of a rational natural order." The moral inexplicability of circumcision, in other words, sustains belief in its own moral system.

In this chapter, I want to build on my previous arguments and offer a contrary view, focusing on the circumcision ceremony that developed during the rabbinic era and persists, more or less unaltered, today. Circumcision subverts its own sense of morality not to sustain a vision of social order but to confront the "dark side" of human experience that no religious system, heavenly or otherwise, can possibly erase or encompass.

The Consummate Cut

The formal *brit milah*, or "covenant of circumcision," ritual is rabbinic, not biblical. Indeed, the Torah records no pertinent ceremony or liturgy. The rabbis invested the rite with an almost unparalleled status, tolerating little disruption from any holy day, fast, feast, death, or festival. Only circumcision, recall from chapter 1, regularly annuls Sabbath prohibitions (B. Shabbath 130a–137b; B. Pesachim 69b).[1] As the first commandment given to Abraham, declares the Talmud (B. Shabbath 130a), the rite defines Judaism. The performance of circumcision gained enormous significance and prestige—so great that European circumcision specialists, called *mohels*,[2] once feuded in court for the honor (Rabinowitz 1972:192). A *mohel* who per-

117

formed the same number of rites as the numerical equivalent of his name, wrote Aurand (1939:49), "is thereby become intitled to a peculiar Blessing of Felicity, when he goes to a future State." Italian *mohels* saved their severed foreskins for a funerary necklace that ensured an immediate entrance into heaven (Patai 1983a:298). "I can still clearly remember when I first learned of this custom," wrote Patai (1983d:287 n. 4). "It was the late Rabbi David Prato who told me about it and showed me a sizable wooden box which he kept on top of one of his bookcases in his Tel Aviv apartment." In it, said the rabbi, was his "passport to paradise."

Circumcision equals all 613 religious obligations in Judaism (B. Nedarim 32a; Zohar iii:13b).[3] But circumcision is not the only Jewish practice that encapsulates the Torah. In a Kurdish folktale, an elderly midwife is awakened one stormy night to ease a difficult birth. "Such a great task," she says, "at such an hour and on such a night would be like fulfilling all six hundred and thirteen commandments at once" (Klein 1998:131). Perhaps the midwife wished to emulate circumcision. Or did she contest the rite, recognizing, as I have argued, that circumcision emulates birth? Jews often tell themselves that their steadfast adherence to circumcision has served as a moral anchor amid a tumultuous, often tragic history. But the ritual speaks with multiple, often contradictory voices.

Rabbinic Rules

The rabbis permitted little ambiguity in Jewish life. Myriad rules govern all aspects of human existence (Dundes 2002; see also Paul 1996:chap. 8). Circumcision is no different (see, e.g., B. Shabbath 131b–137b).[4] A proper rite occurs on the morning of a boy's eighth day—provided the child is healthy, full term, not born at dusk, and vaginally delivered from a Jewish mother. These stipulations aim to protect unhealthy boys and to avoid an improper circumcision, which, amounting to mutilation, the Torah forbids (see chapter 4). A delicate boundary separates the covenant from tragedy.

Rabbinic law, called *halakha*, forbids nighttime circumcisions since God commanded the rite to occur on the eighth *day* (Genesis 17:12). Ideally, as I mentioned in chapter 5, circumcision should take place in the morning, when Abraham prepared to sacrifice Isaac (B. Pesachim 4a). (Daylight, by the way, appears before sunrise yet after dawn, itself defined as the first streaks of visible light, or seventy-two minutes prior to astronomical sunrise.) This way, fathers demonstrate their zealous acceptance of the covenant.

The timing of birth, which the rabbis set as the appearance of the infant's forehead (B. Niddah 28a; 42b; B. Bechoroth 46b), is crucial to the scheduling of circumcision. The Jewish day ends at sunset. Since dusk lies at the ambiguous boundary between two days, a child so born is circumcised on the *ninth* day just in case his birth actually occurred at night, or the *next* day. Otherwise, a presumed eighth-day circumcision might actually fall on the child's seventh day and thus prove invalid. But if the ninth day is a Sabbath, the circumcision is delayed until the *tenth* day since only a normal eighth-day circumcision can disrupt the Sabbath. And should a holiday occupy the *tenth* day? Then the rite is further delayed until the *eleventh* day—unless that day is a two-day holiday, postponing the circumcision yet again, until the *twelfth* day!

Sabbath circumcisions never occur after conversion, cesarean birth, artificial insemination, or *in vitro* fertilization (e.g., J. D. Bleich 2001a). Rabbinic edicts also address the timing and procedure of circumcision for premature births, interfaith children, the sons of apostates, foreskinless infants (a few drops of blood are drawn), double foreskins and other genital abnormalities, and intersexed children. The latter do receive circumcision, but the ceremony omits certain benedictions to avoid wasting the utterance of God's name should the child later turn out female.

Circumcision is delayed for medical ailments.[5] In the case of minor complications such as jaundice or low birth weight (Bleich 1982), the ceremony immediately follows the child's recovery. But, again, the rite cannot occur on the Sabbath (B. Shabbath 134b). After a major illness or trauma, such as blood transfusion or artificial incubation, seven additional days must pass. If a boy's elder siblings died from circumcision complications, his own rite is deferred until adulthood.

An interesting case arose in Israel. A Jewish couple, unable to conceive, arranged an *in vitro* fertilization of the father's sperm and the mother's eggs.[6] The successful zygotes were implanted into a non-Jewish surrogate mother, who delivered twins by cesarean section. The boys were circumcised as converts.

Rabbis past and current hone these rules out of deep conviction and concern to prevent other Jews from inadvertently violating the Law. Nonetheless, even the devout find humor in the complexities of rabbinic discourse. The Yiddle Riddle Archives of Ohr Somayach International (www.ohr.org.il/ask/riddle.htm), an ultra-Orthodox organization in Jerusalem, offers this puzzle. Healthy triplets and their cousin are all born within a two-hour period. Yet the boys are circumcised on four consecutive days. Why? The answer wonderfully exemplifies *pilpul*, the hairsplitting logic of

Talmudic argumentation. One brother, born just before sunset, is circumcised on the *eighth* day. The second brother, born after dark, is circumcised on the *ninth* day—which happens to be a festival. The third brother, delivered at dusk, cannot be circumcised on the eighth day or the ninth day since only an eighth-day rite supersedes festivals. So his circumcision happens on the *tenth* day. The cousin is also born at dusk—in Johannesburg, a city located in the same time zone as Israel, where the triplets were born. Since festivals in the diaspora last for two days, his circumcision occurs on the *eleventh* day!

Gentile Genitals

Sometime between the mid-first and third centuries, the rabbis formalized a conversion ceremony, complete with immersion in water (*mikvah*), bird sacrifice, and circumcision (Porton 1994:60). But the exact role of circumcision during conversion remains unclear. Two rabbinic schools, the Houses of Hillel and Shammai, both demanded proselyte circumcision (B. Shabbath 135). But while the Shammaites saw the rite as a necessary condition for entrance into Judaism, the Hillelites understood it as a necessary sign of Jewish membership (Porton 1994:140–41). The rite of covenantal solidarity engendered disagreement.

Some modern scholars interpret another Talmudic debate (B. Yevamoth 46b) as specifying proselyte circumcision only during crises that threaten communal survival, such as war or assimilation (McEleney 1974:323; Smith 1980:14–15). The official governing body of Reform Judaism concurs, calling this type of circumcision a protective "fence" around Judaism, not an absolute requirement.[7] Yet most contemporary scholars understand classic rabbinic debates over circumcision to concern the exact moment of conversion, not the necessity of the rite (Nolland 1981; Boyarin 1993:232 n. 4; Porton 1994:94–95, 141–44). Even so, it seems curious that the precise role of circumcision would remain so unclear.

A minor post-Talmudic text (Gerim 1:1) fails entirely to mention circumcision when describing conversion, perhaps to advance an egalitarian covenant (Cohen 1990:190–91).[8] Porton (1994:152–54) offers a similar explanation for the Talmudic debate in tractate Yevamoth, mentioned previously. These omissions, I suggest, exhibit more than simply a lack of clarity about the role of circumcision. They lend voice to a wider moral unease.

Many rabbinic texts refer to "uncircumcised Israelites" (M. Pesahim 8:8; B. Pesahim 92a; 96a; M. Hullin 1:1; M. Nedarim 3:11; B. Yevamoth 46a–b). Who were they? McEleney (1974) sees them as Jews aspiring to assimilation in an era of public baths and naked athletics. Nolland (1981) argues that the "uncircumcised Israelites" were purely hypothetical persons conjured by the rabbis to advance certain legal concepts. To complicate matters, Hall (1988:79–81) notes that early Jewish literature and rabbinic texts viciously condemned noncircumcision. Jews who forsake the rite can expect neither heaven nor forgiveness (M. Pirke Aboth 3:12; B. Yoma 85b). They will be "destroyed and slain from the earth" (Jubilees 15; see also 2 Baruch 66:5). This vitriol, claims Hall (1988:81), was surely aimed at no hypothetical Jew!

Some of this censure may have responded to the Greek occupation of Palestine in the second century B.C.E. (Smith 1980:13). Greek authorities brutally suppressed Judaism. They put "to death the women who had their children circumcised, and their families and those who circumcised them; and they hung the infants from their mothers' necks" (1 Maccabees 1:60–64) or "hurled them down headlong from the wall" (2 Maccabees 6:10). Jews today know well this martyrology and the Maccabean resistance, as memorialized by the festival of Hanukkah.

Less well known is the fact that the Maccabean revolt was not aimed solely at Greeks. Texts from late antiquity, including Josephus's *Jewish Antiquities* (12:253–56) and *War of the Jews* (1:34), report that some Israelites cut a "covenant" with the Greeks, agreeing even to epispasm and uncircumcision. The resistance "struck down" these Jewish "sinners," "rescued the law," and "forcibly circumcised all the uncircumcised boys . . . of Israel" (1 Maccabees 2:44–48). Circumcision divided Jew from Greek but also Jew from Jew (see also Smith 1980:13–14; Weitzman 1999). Were the noncircumcising Jews progressive reformers or vile apostates? Were the Maccabeans conservative fanatics or pious heroes? No longer did circumcision split the penis to define covenantal unity. Now the rite rent the body politic of Judaism into a clear moral uncertainty.

Josephus also reports that the Maccabeans, also known as the Hasmoneans, forcefully circumcised and converted the Idumaeans and Itureans (*Jewish Antiquities* 13:257–58, 314–19). The Jews did likewise to a Roman general (*War of the Jews* 2:449). But here, too, historical reality is murky. The Idumaeans in other ancient sources, such as Strabo's *Geography* (16.2.34), voluntarily converted (Weitzman 1999:39–44). Additionally, Weitzman (1999) understands the "forced circumcision" *not* as a conversion to Judaism but as a common branding of war captives that, moreover, incorporated non-Jewish laborers and mercenaries into the Jewish state. The "forced circumcision" served political, not religious, aims. To this, I add the possibility that any enactment of circumcision by ancient Jews that was *not* linked to the covenant would have undermined the religious importance of the rite. Once again we see that the premier "sign" of monotheism engendered no monolithic meanings.

When Mesopotamian royalty converted to Judaism, tells Josephus, the Queen counseled her son, Izates, against circumcision lest the people find it "strange and foreign," and refuse "to be ruled over by a Jew" (*Jewish Antiquities* 20:38–48). A Jewish merchant, moreover, advised the prince that God would forgive his foreskin. But another Jew scolded Izates, and the prince underwent the rite. Does this tale suggest that circumcision is sometimes optional (Collins 1985) or always necessary (Nolland 1981:193)? Here, again, the singular rite of Judaism admits to no single meaning.

Josephus drew on the Idumean incident when rewriting the tale of Esther to include another forced circumcision of Gentiles by Jews (*Jewish Antiquities* 11:284–85; Weitzman 1999). The same revision occurs in the third-century Greek translation of the Hebrew Bible, called the Septuagint. Some contemporary opponents of medical circumcision, as I criticize in a later chapter, naively cite these sources as proof of Jewish treachery (e.g., Aldeeb Abu-Sahlieh 2001:52–53). But these historical fictions do not point to historical reality. Rather, they express a moral debate over circumcision from within Judaism. The same is true for many aspects of the circumcision ceremony and liturgy, as I now show.

Fathers, Sons, and Mothers

Orthodox men generally shun childbirth (Matzner-Bekerman 1984; Holtzberg 1999:9). But circumcision is a father's responsibility (B. Kiddushin 29a). Should he neglect this "cardinal" duty of fatherhood, as the Zohar (ii:174b) calls it, then the local rabbis or community traditionally performed the rite—even against the father's wishes (HM 1:2). As a last resort, the boy himself sees to his own circumcision as an adult. Of course, these contingencies arise only through paternal delinquency. First and foremost, circumcision is enacted by fathers onto sons.

Most Jewish fathers, however, lack the necessary skills, tools, and esoteric knowledge, never mind the nerve. So the task falls to a ritual specialist, the *mohel*, whom the father appoints as his agent. The father may even hand the *mohel* the knife (Krohn 1985:98). Despite the rise of the *mohel* as a formal institution, though, circumcision remains an act of fatherhood.

The mother's presence during the rite is optional. Some communities exclude the mother lest her postpartum impurity defile male participants (Chill 1979:297; Dobrinsky 1980:54). Some Jewish women did historically serve as *mohels* (Klein 1998:318 n. 45). Still, the rabbis marginalized women's participation (Hoffman 1996:chap. 10). Women were deemed irrelevant to the rite, or contrary to its aims.

Circumcision sacralizes the father–son relationship. The rite also confounds it.[9] The *mohel* is no simple functionary but a figure who alleviates the psychodynamic complexities of a rite that requires fathers to cut their sons. Even Maimonides seemed to recognize this predicament when offering three reasons for the occurrence of circumcision during infancy (Stern 1993:141–42). First, adults would outright refuse. Second, infants experience little pain since their foreskins are "soft" and their undeveloped minds incapable of anticipating anguish. Third, since parental attachment increases with time, a later date for the ceremony might result in "the abandonment of circumcision because of the father's love and affection" for his son. Maimonides thus admits to what I have repeatedly argued: the existence of considerable Jewish anxiety over circumcision.

Mohels and Meat

Jewish communities often lacked the financial resources to support different religious specialists. Consequently, the *mohel* frequently doubled as the ritual slaughterer or *shochet* (Bloch 1980:10; Bauer 1993:167; see also Berman 1941). But there is more to the relationship between meat and *mohels* than economics and demography. In Talmudic astrology, a man born under the sign of Mars will become "a shedder of blood . . . a surgeon, a thief, a slaughterer, or a circumciser" (B. Shabbath 156a). The rabbis in this passage connected circumcision to healing but also to theft and butchering.

During the Sinai migration, says midrash (ER 19:5), many Israelites refused recircumcision by Joshua and were thus barred from the Passover feast. But when Moses prepared the paschal lamb, the aroma of Paradise so whetted their appetites that the stubborn Israelites readily submitted to the knife. The same midrash likens the Passover feast to a regal banquet.[10] "Unless the invited guests show my seal," decrees the king, referring to circumcision, "none can enter."

Jewish ceremonies typically include a festive meal (*seudath mitzvah*). Circumcision is no exception (B. Taanith 27a; B. Ketubot 8a; B. Shabbath 130a; J. D. Bleich 2001b).[11] Some rabbis traced the circumcision meal to Isaac's weaning feast (Genesis 21) and the consumption of biblical sacrifices. In

North Africa, a refusal to dine at the rite was downright insulting (Ohel 1973:68–70). Everywhere, guest should suppress their joy on account of the infant's pain.[12] Rabbi Hania recognized this predicament (T-Y Exodus 8:1; TL 4.7). A father, despite seeing his son's blood, "spends his money to celebrate the occasion." The preparation of kosher food resembles circumcision. Like many Jewish strictures, these obligations entail themes of cutting and separation (Bilu 2000:38). Jewish dietary rules arise from Deuteronomy 14 and especially Leviticus 11. Broadly speaking, the biblical worldview assigns a paradigmatic animal to each topographic zone created by God in Genesis 1. Cattle walk the land on cloven hoofs, eat plants, and chew their cud. Scaley fish swim the seas. Seed-eating birds fly the sky. With few exceptions, as Douglas (1966) argued famously, the Torah prohibits the consumption of animals that violate these norms, including pigs, camels, snakes, predators, and shellfish.

The Torah also declares, "You shall not boil a kid in its mother's milk" (Exodus 23:19; 34:26; Deuteronomy 14:21). Jews interpret this edict as forbidding mixtures of meat and dairy. Anthropologists may see a veiled expression of a mother–son incest taboo. But the intent remains the same, namely, to prevent disorder by separating categories (see chapter 1). Taboo animals and meals, like menstruating women, as well as rabbinic foreskins, are "unclean" or "polluting." (So is a postpartum mother, whom a nineteenthcentury text forbids from preparing her son's circumcision repast lest her pollution defile the other diners.[13]) Edible animals, like circumcised men, symbolize the holiness of cosmic distinctions.

The rabbinic dietary code, known as *kashrut* (from "fit" and "proper"), expands the biblical guidelines with rules for slaughter, inspection, and processing.[14] Disease and internal blemishes exclude an animal (B. Chullin 42a–59b). The butcher performs the slaughter with a quick slice across the throat, using a long single-edged blade. Ideally, death is immediate and painless. The butcher, too, must remove all blood from the meat (Genesis 9:4).[15] These culinary concerns with cutting, knives, blood, and bodily wholeness resemble the rite that symbolically koshers boys. The swift, deadly slice of the butcher's blade purges most of the animal's blood. But kosher meat must undergo further processing to ensure this removal. Typically, the meat is washed, soaked in water, salted, and washed again. The cutting and bathing that transform animals into edible meat parallel the circumcision and ritual immersion that transform male proselytes into Jews.

Ancient Israelites forged covenants of circumcision but also covenants of salt (Leviticus 2:13; Numbers 18:19; 2 Chronicles 13:5). Biblical salt was purifying (2 Kings 2:19–22). As a white preservative, salt symbolically resembles semen and thus evokes the enduring male fecundity attributed to circumcision (see also Delaney 1991:146). Jewish lore expressly attributed magical fertility to salt (Pollack 1971:105; Dobrinsky 1980:471; Patai 1983d:388–90; B. Shabbat 128b).[16] Newborns in ancient Israel and the Middle East were salted to promote health and vitality (Granqvist 1947:98; Morgenstern 1973:chap. 2; Patai 1983b; Brauer 1993:157; Ezekiel 16:4; B. Shabbat 129b). If this sprinkling magically removed the blood of birth, then it resembled circumcision and the koshering of meat (Archer 1990:39–40). In all these contexts, salt recalls several themes of relevance to circumcision, including male potency, permanence, and purity.

Even Jewish comics connect meat and circumcision. I offer two examples, including a joke:

Question: If a doctor carries a black bag and a plumber carries a toolbox, what does a *mohel* carry?
Answer: A Bris-kit!

My second example comes from an October 1993 episode of the television sitcom *Seinfeld*, titled "The Bris." A bumbling *mohel* mutters, "I coulda been a kosher butcher like my brother. The money's good. . . . And, cows have no families. You make a mistake with a cow, you move on with your life."

These puns may offend readers who see popular Jewish humor as a form of self-denigration whereby assimilated Jews mock their devout coreligionists. Historically, in fact, anti-Semitic fantasies readily connected Jewish circumcision to butchery, torture, and murder, as in the case of Jack the Ripper (Gilman 1991a; see also Efron 2001:206–22). An opponent of circumcision (Zindler 1990) sneered about "kosher cuts" in an issue of *The American Atheist*.

It hardly needs saying that my point is *not* to inflame or justify anti-Jewish rhetoric. Rather, I seek to identify moments of ambivalence toward circumcision from within Judaism. Jewish circumcision jokes may evidence the internalization of anti-Semitism. Or, as I prefer it, these jokes express longstanding but largely unstated Jewish ambivalence toward the rite.

The Knife

God told the prophet Joshua to prepare "flint," "stone," or "*sharp*" knives for the recircumcision of the Israelites (Joshua 5). Consequently, sharpness emerged in rabbinic culture as the primary quality of a *mohel*'s blade (*izmail*, or *mohel-messer* in Yiddish). The rabbis dismissed any significance to Zipporah's use of a stone knife in Exodus 4 since that rite occurred under duress (YD 264:15). The *mohel* must also use a metal blade. Butchering knives, we saw, conform to similar standards. In fact, the rabbis often spoke about these two knives together (GR 56:6). The circumcision knife in Kurdistan may even have slaughtered poultry (Brauer 1993:167). Yet a *mohel*'s blade is shorter (two to three inches) than a butcher's knife.

Unlike a butcher's blade, too, no rule prohibits nicks and imperfections on the *mohel*'s knife. Yet circumcision knives are sharpened on both edges to prevent injury to the infant should the *mohel* inadvertently try to sever the foreskin with a blunt edge. This feature also ensures a swift procedure since the *mohel* need not fumble to orient his blade. At least one *mohel* brings his knives to a kosher butcher for whetting (Romberg 1982:48). Both blades are honed to avoid pain.

The *mohel*'s skill with his knife is legendary in Jewish lore. It is also the stuff of comedy, as in this joke that widely circulates the Internet:

> Once upon a time a powerful Emperor of the Rising Sun advertised for a new Chief Samurai. After a year, only three men applied for the job: a Japanese Samurai, a Chinese Samurai, and a Jewish Samurai. "Demonstrate your skills!" commanded the Emperor.
>
> The Japanese samurai stepped forward, opened a tiny box and released a fly. Whoosh went his sword, and the fly dropped dead to the floor, neatly cut in two pieces. "Impressive," said the Emperor.
>
> Then the Chinese Samurai showed his skill. He smiled confidently, stepped forward, and opened a tiny box, releasing a fly. Whoosh, whoosh went his sword. The fly dropped dead on the floor in four neat pieces. "Now that is very impressive," nodded the Emperor.
>
> Finally, the Emperor looked to the Jewish Samurai. The Jewish Samurai opened a tiny box, and out popped a fly. He drew his sword. Whoosh, whoosh, whoosh, whoosh, whoosh. A gust of wind filled the room. But the fly was still alive and buzzing around. The Emperor, obviously disappointed, asked, "After all that, why is the fly not dead?" "Dead, schmed," replied the Jewish Samurai. "Dead is easy. Circumcision . . . now THAT takes skill!"

The punch line in another version is "Circumcision's not supposed to kill!" Is the association of the *mohel*'s knife with a deadly sword as far-fetched as it seems? Let us again return to the rabbis.

Orthodox Jews find scriptural justification for the double-edged circumcision blade in Psalm 149:6, "with paeans to God in their throats and two-edged swords in their hands" (Romberg 1982:46; Krohn 1985:80). But no religious discussion of circumcision seems willing to consider the full passage of Psalm 149, which stresses the violent "punishment" of God's enemies. The double-edged circumcision knife thus cuts two ways, protecting Jewish boys while slaying the ungodly.

Similar aggression surfaces in a midrash about the angel who guards Eden with a "fiery ever-turning sword." The rabbis understood this flaming saber as an allusion to hellfire, which circumcision averted, as well as to Joshua's circumcision knives or "swords" (GR 21:9). Here, again, the double-edged blade of the covenant engenders double-edged meaning.

Another midrash comments on the same symbolism (Ginzberg 1909–1938:VI:251 n. 42; Krohn 1985:80; Ginsburg 1998:219). How could David, asked the rabbis, a mere youth, fling a pebble through Goliath's massive armored helmet? The headpiece intentionally split, they reasoned, so the stone could strike the giant's forehead. To reward metal for this honorable deed, God requires *mohels* to split the penis with metal knives.[17] During the circumcision ceremony, the *mohel* declares invalid any circumcision performed by a "man who is fearful and fainthearted." This allusion to bravery derives from Deuteronomy 20:5–9, which details exemptions for military duty. Perhaps the martial ethos evoked by the *mohel's* declaration responded at some point in European history to increasing hostility from Christianity. Or perhaps this avowal expressed rabbinic unease over a rite that seemed irreducibly violent.

From Violence to Birth

The person who cradles the infant during circumcision is called the *sandek*, an honor generally extended to men. A sixteenth-century rabbi judged it poor taste for women to glimpse the boy's penis (Chill 1979:299). But perhaps another reason explains this male role.

The term *sandek* derives from a Greek word for the Christian godfather, who lifts the child from the baptismal font (Hoffman 1996:200–203). Since baptism cleanses infants from the sin of parental intercourse and the impurity of birth, only spiritual parents or godparents can rightly sponsor the ceremony. Baptism is a clear rite of rebirth in which, traditionally, men do the rebirthing.

The *sandek* is often likened to the ancient priests who presented offerings to God (Cohen 1984:41; Krohn 1985:67; Hoffman 1996:207). The circumcision liturgy repeatedly equates the boy's blood with sacrifice. Adult men, in other words, cut infant boys to confront their transgressions. The child represents parental misdeeds. The Belzer Rebbe, a nineteenth-century Hasidic rabbi, offered a slightly different view (Krohn 1985:151). Fathers accept their own circumcision by spilling the blood of their children.

Unlike the Christian godparent, the *sandek* accepts no religious duties on behalf of the child. But like baptism, the Jewish boy's position atop the *sandek*'s knees, sometimes resting on a pillow, symbolizes male rebirth. The rabbis tied similar poses to death (B. Kiddushin 72a–b), breast-feeding (B. Megilah 13b), and sexuality (B. Yevamoth 77a). Biblical culture assigned this position to birth, adoption, and paternal blessings (Genesis 30:3; 48:8–12; 50:23). Traditionally, the *sandek* also draped his prayer shawl over the boy's forehead. This gesture, too, alludes to birth, which, as I discussed earlier, the rabbis timed at the appearance of the infant's forehead. Drawing together these themes of sacrifice and parturition, I suggest that the *sandek* symbolically kills the infant boy's feminine identity in order to rebirth him into masculinity.

The circumcision ceremony makes numerous references to marriage, thus recalling the "bloody bridegroom" incident in Exodus and traditional greetings of birth in the Middle East (chapter 5). Draping a prayer shawl over the infant resembles birth, as I just claimed, but also a biblical act of betrothal (Ruth 2:12). The liturgy often mentions the future marriage of the boy. During the rite, ultra-Orthodox Jews call him "bridegroom" (Bilu 2000:58 n. 7). The boy's garments may resemble wedding garb (Rabinowitz 1972:190; Ohel 1973:67; Gutmann 1987:pl. Ivb; B. Shabbath 133b). When the *mohel* mentions "three acts," he evokes the three stages of the circumcision procedure, which I detail shortly, as well as a biblical husband's three obligations to provide his wife with food, clothing, and "conjugal rights" (Exodus 21:10–11; Krohn 1985:155). Because these matrimonial idioms are enacted during a largely all-male ritual, they flirt with homoerotic taboo and symbolically set circumcision against the institution of heterosexual marriage that the covenant seemingly upholds.

In the thirteenth century, Rabbi Samson ben Tzadok denounced the custom of allowing women to hold infants during circumcision (Hoffman 1996:196–97; Baumgarten 2003:119–20). Not only were women distracting men's thoughts, but they were "snatching away the commandment from the men." But not for long. Mothers started to pass their sons to the *sandek* through the synagogue doorway or a special portal that possibly derived from church baptismal doors (Gaster 1980:62; Gutmann 1983a:131). They also handed their infants to male and female intermediaries, called respectively *ba'al brit* and *ba'alat brit* (Hoffman 1996:chap. 11). The latter role eventually declined, and longer lying-in periods made mothers simply incapable of attending a son's circumcision (Baumgarten 2003). Women were never for-mally or entirely excluded from circumcision. But motherhood was pushed to the periphery.

Today, the infant is typically passed from the mother to a woman called *kvatterin*, who hands the child to a man (*kvatter*). In turn, he presents the boy to the *sandek*. Couples wishing to conceive often serve in these roles to magically promote fertility. Yet pregnant women in some traditions should decline to serve as *kvatterin* lest the shock of the rite harm the gestating child (Holtzberg 1999:12)—a child who may shortly undergo his own circumci-sion.

The marginalization of motherhood during circumcision allowed male religious leaders to continue to maintain their ritual prerogatives. But these historical developments also lend support to a thesis I have repeatedly advanced, namely, that circumcision presents men as the gender primarily responsible for reproducing the community.

The Bloody Cloth

Earlier generations of European or Ashkenazic Jews staged circumcision in the synagogue, not private homes. Attendance was a *mitzvah*, or "pious deed." Yet Jews hesitated to announce these ceremonies publicly lest they attract hostile Church and civil authorities, who often banned the rite or recorded its occurrence for conscription and tax rolls (Davidovitch 1974:117 n. 6). Accordingly, Jewish communities contrived subtle invitations, in-cluding aromatic spices, special cakes, and lit candles (Trachtenberg 1939:171–72; Pollack 1971:18; Chill 1979:298; Bloch 1980:11; Patai 1983a:293; B. Sanhedrin 32b). One such declaration was the bloody cloth.

Medieval Jews advertised circumcision by draping fabric over the syna-gogue doorway (YD 265:5). Sometimes they dangled the soiled towel on which the *mohel* wiped his bloody hands (Gross 1995; Goldin 1996:169). North African Jews displayed colored scarves (Klein 1998:220). They also exhibited red dresses, recalled Shlomo Gean regarding an oral history project on Libyan Jews. He traced this practice to Spain, where, after a ban on cir-cumcision, Jews exhibited red laundry to announce the rite (http://sunsite .berkeley.edu/JewsofLibya). A single theme underlies these customs: the pub-lic display of blood.

A thirteenth-century manuscript likens the display of the *mohel*'s gory cloth to the sacrificial blood smeared on Israelite doorways in ancient Egypt (Gross 1995). The bloody towel also symbolized the infant's ritual death and rebirth (see also Ohel 1973:67; Pollock 1973:300). But I prefer to see these circumcision banners as mirroring the bloody sheets that once confirmed a bride's virginity in North Africa, the Middle East, and the Mediterranean.

Admittedly, these nuptial trophies are not normally associated with Jews. Nonetheless, blood was an important indicator of bridal purity and virginity in biblical and rabbinic cultures (Deuteronomy 22:15; B. Kutuboth; Dobrinsky 1980:128). In early modern Italy, Jewish communities recorded the names of girls who successfully passed this hymenal test (Adelman 1991:144–45). It seems reasonable to see the display of the *mohel's* bloody cloth as similar proof of a successful, hopefully fertile genital penetration. For cross-cultural corroboration, note that the removal of the foreskin during Muslim circumcision often parallels the bride's marital defloration (Bouhdiba 1985:182–86; Delaney 1991:86; Mehta 1996:220). The bloody towel, I am suggesting, allowed European Jews to transform an authorized symbol into a subversive announcement about the perseverance of the covenant and rabbinic manhood against Christian hegemony. At the same time, the towel further communicated the gendered instability of Jewish masculinity.

Genital Glances

Legend tells that King David once exclaimed in a bathhouse, "Woe is me that I stand naked without any precepts about me!" But the king quickly realized that circumcision always clothes men in a garment of holiness and religious obligation. Like the cabinet that houses the Torah scrolls, remarked the Zohar (ii:214b), circumcision "contains" man.

David found comfort in the sight of his circumcised penis. But the naked truth of circumcision is more complex. The covenantal rite perilously tacks between concealment and exposure, between public and intimate, and between morality and taboo.

The rabbis denounced Jews who tried to hide their circumcision. Yet they also forbid men from exposing the penis during prayer (chapter 2; Stern 1994:230–31). Devotional etiquette requires the separation of the contemplative upper body, or heart, from the less restrained genitals (Epstein 1948:chap. 2; Eilberg-Schwartz 1994:208–22). Ironically, the act of circumcision exposes the penis to God, men, and prayer. Its genital location, moreover, seems to disrupt as much as it sustains the ideal of subordinating desire to reason.

One sage boasted of never having glanced at his own penis (B. Shabbath 118b). The mystics forbid men from staring at "the sign of the covenant . . . because this is emblematic of the Righteous One" (Zohar iii:84a). Rabbinic

culture generally banned men from touching their genitals and strongly censored masturbation for its nonprocreative intent (B. Shabbath 41a; B. Niddah 13a, 43a). One who violates this edict "should make an endeavor to be
Sandek, i.e., that children be circumcised on his knees" (KSA 151:7). Of
course, the *sandek* enables another man to manipulate a child's penis. Sometimes the *mohel*, as I discuss shortly, cauterizes the wound with his mouth.
Righteous Jews, declares the Talmud, "cling to the covenant of Abraham"
(B. Kethuboth 8b). While this image recalls biblical oath taking (chapter 4),
it also, like many aspects of the circumcision ritual, violates rabbinic modesty.[18] In multiple ways, I am arguing, the circumcision ritual verges on taboo
since rabbinic authorities denounced public nudity, genital caressing, and
homoeroticism.

Liturgical Ambiguities

As Maimonides seemingly recognized, there is no simple solution to the tension between circumcised exposure and concealment. The ceremonial liturgy
proves no less dissonant. After the initial greetings and blessings, the *mohel*
recites several biblical verses. One possibility is Numbers 25:10–12, where
God rewards Phinehas for impaling an Israelite man and his illicit lover
(chapter 4). Jews often view circumcision as a celebration of parental love
that joyfully welcomes boys into a family, community, and tradition (see
chapter 10). But the invocation of Phinehas's rage transforms circumcision
into an aggressive threat of blood and pain (cf. Schachter 1986). Misplace
your covenantal penis and suffer a circumcision that cuts off your life, not
just your foreskin!

A frequent liturgical refrain during the circumcision ceremony is, "Even
as this child has entered into the covenant, so may he enter into the Torah,
the nuptial canopy, and into good deeds." This way, the circumcision liturgy
pins the central institutions of Judaism—marriage, scriptural study, and
piety—onto male ritual (Hoffman 1996:82–83). But the circumcision liturgy
also decenters this patriarchy through a curiously double-voiced blessing.

The blessing begins by praising God who, among other things, "set a statute in *his flesh*, and sealed [stamped] his descendants with the sign of the holy
covenant." This statement plainly refers to the mark of circumcision in the
male body and so celebrates masculine privilege. Yet the idiom "his flesh"
can also designate a close relative, including a man's *wife* (B. Baba Bathra
111b; Krohn 1985:129). From this angle, the circumcision blessing alludes
to uterine fertility. A similar tension over the gender of fertility arises during

grace after the circumcision meal, when men *and* women praise God for "thy covenant which thou hast sealed in our flesh."

The same blessing asks God to reward circumcision by delivering the child "from the pit" or "destruction." This phrase alludes to hell and therefore construes circumcision as a type of magical protection (Flusser and Safrai 1980; Wolfson 1987a:80 n. 7). More important, the phrase evokes Zipporah and so transforms circumcision into a female rite, thus placing the covenant yet again in the hands of woman.

Later in the ceremony, the *mohel* asks God to "preserve this child to his father and to his mother," adding, "Let thy father and thy mother rejoice, She who bore you will exult" (Proverbs 23:25). The rabbis identified the "father" and "mother" here not as the boy's birth parents, as we might expect, but as God and Israel (Krohn 1985:132). The phrase "*she who bore you*" also refers to men since "he who teaches the son of his neighbor the Torah . . . [is] as if he had begotten him" (B. Sanhedrin 19b). Once again, the circumcision liturgy feminizes men, this time giving voice to a maternal masculinity.

German Jews sing a medieval poem during the circumcision "grace after meals" (*birkat hamazon*) that communicates a similar symbolism. The poem includes the sentence, "A woman may circumcise but a gentile may not, for only the circumcised may circumcise." This statement refers to a complex Talmudic debate concerning the eligibility to perform circumcision (B. Avodah Zarah 26b–27a; Krohn 1985:164). On the one hand, women are prohibited since the covenant was given to Abraham, not Sarah. On the other hand, since the rabbis often classified *all* Israelites as the "circumcised" (chapter 1), woman can legitimately perform the rite. The weight of rabbinic opinion excluded women. Nonetheless, the medieval poem calls into question this orthodoxy, providing yet another example of how the circumcision liturgy challenges paternal prerogative by reluctantly acknowledging the primacy of women and mothers.

Punishment or Reward?

Jews traditionally reserve a chair at circumcision ceremonies for the prophet Elijah, who, among other privileges, will herald the messianic era (PRE 19, 29). Historically, this throne partly responded to the rise of Christian messianism after the Crusades (Hoffman 1996:248–49 n. 35). Within the narrower context of circumcision, Elijah's Chair offers the infant—really, his parents—magical protection from evil and demons (Dobrinsky 1980:64–

65). In modern Israel, Jews of Indian ancestry perform circumcision in Israel at Elijah's tomb (Isenberg 1988:231 n. 15). Syrian Jews place money on a "tray of Elijah" for charity (Sutton 1979:60).[19] Today, Elijah is best known for magically sipping wine from a special goblet during the Passover feast, or *seder*. The prophet once quaffed a similar drink during circumcision (Hoffman 1996:248–49 n. 35). Despite the emotional and ceremonial importance of Elijah, the presence of this "groom of the bloods of circumcision" is paradoxical.

Prooftext for Elijah's attendance at circumcision occurs in 1 Kings, where the prophet flees to a cave. "Why are you here?" asks God. "I am moved by zeal for the Lord," replies Elijah. The Israelites "have forsaken Your covenant . . . and they are out to take my life." For some rabbis, God *rewarded* Elijah for his zealotry, granting him a special seat at every circumcision (PRE 29). For others, Elijah's presence at the rite is divine *punishment* for slandering the Israelites who do, despite his claim to the contrary, perform circumcision (Zohar I:93a, 209a–b; Krohn 1985:77–78). Elijah, then, like so many other elements of the rite, casts into doubt any official morality.

Wallowing in Blood

The *mohel* not only severs the child's foreskin. He also names the boy. The rabbis justified this custom with reference to Abram's name change in Genesis 17. To anthropologists, ritual naming often symbolizes rebirth. The circumcision liturgy supports this interpretation through the symbolism of blood.

During the naming portion of the ceremony, the *mohel* twice utters a phrase spoken by God in the prophetic literature: "Then I passed by you and saw you wallowing in your blood, and I said to you: In your blood, [you shall] live. And I said to you: In your blood, live" (Ezekiel 16:6). The rabbis intended the ceremonial invocation of this blood to refer to the sacrifice and circumcision that preceded the biblical exodus from Egypt (ER 17:3; 19:12; PRE 29; Hoffman 1996:chap. 6). Male blood rebirths boys, just as it once rebirthed the Israelites into freedom.

The full Ezekiel passage, however, resists this simple morality. The episode concerns the plight of a young girl who personifies Israel. As a newborn, she is abandoned by heathen nations—umbilicus uncut, body bloodied from birth—to die in the wilderness. Yet God saw the child and said compassionately, "In your blood, live." What I want to highlight, though, is not what the circumcision liturgy includes but what it omits.

The infant Israel matures until her "breasts became firm." Then, narrates God, "You were still naked and bare when I passed by you [again] and saw that your time for love had arrived. So I spread My robe over you"—a biblical gesture of erotic espousal, we have seen—"and covered your nakedness, and I entered into a covenant with you." God bathes and anoints Israel, yet she plays the harlot, and suffers violent punishment by God in language that frankly resembles a sexual assault (Ezekiel 16:42). These themes of divine incest, phallic retribution, and rape, however much unstated during the cir-cumcision liturgy, are not so easily dismissed or eclipsed by covenantal morality.

Traditionally, the circumcision liturgy is spoken by men to men. But the ceremonial version of the bloody Ezekiel incident includes feminine pro-nouns and verbs. Boyarin (1992:495–96) and Eilberg-Schwartz (1994:173) see this linguistic revision as a type of couvade that transforms male ritual blood into female menstrual blood. Since rabbinic circumcision removes a blemish, continues Boyarin, the Ezekiel passage during the ceremony con-figures men as beautiful women destined for God's pleasure. I agree. Never-theless, I am surprised at how quickly scholars pass over the violent imagery in the original text—violence that is surely known by many attendees at circumcision, including the *mohel*. Perhaps the best we can say about the role of this passage during the ceremony is that it expresses a broad ambivalence concerning the relationship between masculinity and women.

The Three Stages of Circumcision

The rabbis devised three stages to the circumcision rite (*brit milah*), called *milah, periah*, and *metzitzah* (YD 264:3; HM 2:2). *Milah* refers to the excision of the foreskin to expose the glans and corona. The *mohel* typically tugs the prepuce with his thumb and index finger and slides the foreskin into a nar-row slit on a metal barrier, or "shield" (*mogen*), to protect the glans from the knife. Then he slices it off.

The second stage of the rite, *periah*, requires the *mohel* to remove the underlying mucous membrane that covers the corona. The function of *periah* is to fully uncover the glans (YD 264:3; B. Shabbath 137b). Traditionally, the *mohel* tears or cuts the membrane with a sharpened fingernail (Romberg 1982:41). This gesture inspired a fascinating corpus of folklore. If the *mohel* uses two fingernails, for example, the boy grows "stupid" (Zimmels 1997:163). A mystical *mohel* may glimpse a flash of "fiery letters" on the penis as he peels away the membrane (Goldberger 1991:242–43). The color of the letters foretells the child's fate.

The third stage of the circumcision procedure is called *metzitzah*, or "sucking." The *mohel* briefly extracts blood from the child's wound, traditionally using his mouth. He then expectorates the blood into a goblet from which, as I discuss shortly, the boy and his parents sip.

Today, various mechanical devices assist circumcision. Hospitals often employ a Gomco clamp, developed in the 1930s by a physician-*mohel* (Weiss 1962b:36; Grossman 1982). Orthodox Jews shun this tool since it intentionally halts the flow of blood, thus negating a central theme of the rite (Romberg 1982:59). In the 1950s, another *mohel*, Harry Bronstein, redesigned the traditional circumcision "shield" into the Mogen clamp. Bronstein sought to balance Jewish law, which bans modern clamps, and hospital regulations, which often ban *mohels*. Yet the Mogen clamp proved no more acceptable to Orthodox Jews since it removes the foreskin and mucous membrane in the same motion, thereby conflating two separate stages of the rite. Other modern utensils similarly violate one or another point of religious law. Many Orthodox Jews, too, fear that medical innovations might transform a holy ritual into a secular procedure (Matzner-Bekerman 1984:53; Holtzberg 1999:16).

While the Torah mandates the removal of the foreskin (*milah*), it offers no procedural guidelines and fails to mention "uncovering" (*periah*) or "sucking" (*metzitzah*). The latter two stages were codified in the Mishnah (Shabbat 19:3) and Talmud (B. Shabbath 133b). Still, rabbis both classic and modern discerned biblical allusions to "uncovering," as when God commanded a *second* circumcision in Joshua 4 or imposed a "statute *and* an ordinance" in Exodus 15 (B. Yevamoth 71b; NR 11:3; Zohar i:93b; Zohar ii:40a, 60b, 125b; Hirsch 1988:82–83).

Scholars generally contend that the biblical rite required the Israelites, like the Egyptians, merely to snip the tip of the foreskin. Later, the rabbis designed a more extreme procedure in response to assimilated Jews who resorted to epispasm (Hall 1988:74; Rubin 2003).[20] Not surprisingly, contemporary opponents of circumcision strongly endorse this view in order to undermine traditionalist claims that the rite is divine, not human (e.g., Bertschinger 1991). I will say more on this debate in a later chapter. Now, I want to turn to the third and final stage of the ceremony.

Sucking the Wound

After the *mohel* removes the foreskin, as I just mentioned, he draws blood from the boy's penis in a hemostatic gesture called *metzitzah*, or "sucking." The Talmud first mentions *metzitzah* but fails to specify a precise method.

Prior to the 1880s, though, the *mohel* directly applied his mouth to the wound. Otherwise, the *mohel* committed a "transgression" (YD 264:3; B. Shabbath 133b; Goldberger 1991:chap. 4). The rabbis offered many justifications for oral *metzitzah* (see Goldberger 1991:91–98). Numerically, for example, the word "circumcision" (*milah*) equaled the sum of the final letters of Numbers 23:24, "he shall drink the blood of the wounded [slain]." According to the chief rabbi of sixteenth-century Egypt, the mouth of a *mohel* who performed oral *metzitzah* resists decay after death and infestation by worms.

With the rise of medical science and Reform Judaism in the latter nineteenth century, oral *metzitzah* became enormously controversial (Katz 1998a; Judd 2003). Civil authorities in Europe, as I show in chapter 9, and physicians on both sides of the Atlantic criticized oral *metzitzah* for the spread of syphilis and other diseases. Assimilated and reformist Jews, embracing the modernist ideals of progress and rationality, spurned the practice as anachronistic, repugnant, and unhygienic.

Today, oral *metzitzah* persists only among the ultratraditional Orthodox (e.g., Goldberger 1991; cf. Shields 1972). Many Jews reject the practice, opting instead for indirect suction through a glass pipette or the use of a sponge, even while endorsing a medical rationale for the procedure. *Metzitzah* both halts the bleeding and draws blood to prevent infection. The Reform and Conservative branches of modern Judaism further prohibit oral *metzitzah* out of concern for the transmission of HIV (see Cohen 1989). Some traditionalists scoff at this alarm. They stress the chastity of Orthodox Jews, the disinfectant properties of saliva and alcohol (the *mohel*, we will see, swishes in his mouth the blood with wine), and the medical expertise of God (Goldberger 1991; Holtzberg 1999:17). Later, I return to the role of oral *metzitzah* in the clash between tradition and modernity. Now, I discuss how traditional *metzitzah* imbues circumcision with taboo and transgression.

Consider the *mohel's* gory hands and mouth, an impression vividly recalled by the sixteenth-century essayist Michel de Montaigne (1957:944–46). So bloody are the *mohel's* lips that someone else often needs to recite the subsequent benedictions (Goldberger 1991:86–89). In effect, the *mohel* becomes the very demon from which the rite he enacts offers protection.

In midrash, we have seen, foreskins appeared in consequence of the erotic transgression in Eden. Since Adam and Eve sinned by touching and eating the forbidden fruit, reasoned an eighteenth-century Moroccan rabbi, the *mohel* likewise uses his hands and mouth to remove the foreskin (Goldberger 1991:89–90). But *metzitzah* is no less transgressive than the taboo snack in Eden. The homoerotic tones of the gesture contravene the heterosexual and procreative thrust of the covenant (see also Zimmerman 1951:11; Malev 1966:514–15). Several *mohels* remark on the ease of performing the rite when the infant's penis is stimulated to an erection (Snowman 1904:25). Yet rabbinic law generally forbids men to glance at or kiss genitalia (KSA 150:5; Boyarin 1993:chap. 4). Insofar as the *mohel* acts as the father's agent, moreover, *metzitzah* appears incestuous. The gesture also resembles ritualized, intergenerational homosexuality in Melanesia (Herdt 1981) by harnessing homoeroticism to heterosexual and cultural reproduction.

Metzitzah hints at the swallowing of blood, not just semen. Of course, the Hebrew Bible categorically prohibits the consumption of blood, a practice reserved for God (Ezekiel 44:7) and witches (1 Samuel 14:33; 28:8). Nonetheless, some rabbis validated oral *metzitzah* with reference to Numbers 23:24, where Israel, likened to a predatory lion, "Rests not till it has feasted on prey, And drunk the blood of the slain."

Metzitzah also resembles a jarring event in the life of Ezekiel. Overcome by a vision of God's "loins," the prophet falls to his face. God orders him to arise, then commands, "Open your mouth and eat what I am giving you . . . eat this scroll. . . . Mortal, feed your stomach and fill your belly with this scroll that I give you" (Ezekiel 2:8–3:3). "I ate it," says Ezekiel, "and it tasted as sweet as honey." Later, God resumes this phallo-oral debasement by telling the prophet to eat cake baked on human excrement (Ezekiel 4:12). Although many scholars discuss the relationship between the Ezekiel passage and circumcision (e.g., Goldberg 1987:114; Marcus 1996:54–56), they tend surprisingly to disregard the sexually aggressive imagery.

Metzitzah is no ordinary ritual procedure. Its meaning expands well beyond hygiene. *Metzitzah* usurps God's diet, resembles witchcraft, violates sexual norms, and transforms covenantal morality into carnivorous animality. This gesture irreducibly violates the very codes of conduct and worship that circumcision and Judaism otherwise represent.

A Sip of Blood

Medieval Jews dunked the severed foreskin in a bowl of spiced water during circumcision, then washed their hands and faces in the bloody liquid (Trachtenberg 1939). Sometimes the infant's blood directly dripped into a basin of perfumed water for adolescent boys to rinse their hands, faces, and mouths (Hoffman 1996:103–5). In addition to evoking the ancient temple sacrifices, argues Hoffman, these ablutions expand the ritual focus beyond the child to encompass the entire community in covenantal renewal.

During the annual Passover *seder*, Jews spill drops of red wine to somberly recall the spilt blood of the Egyptians. Wine also symbolizes blood during the circumcision ceremony (Goldberger 1991:chap. 4; Hoffman 1996). The *mohel* raises a goblet and recites the standard blessing over wine (*kiddush*).[21] But no sip immediately follows. Why the peculiar delay, which threatens to waste a ritual utterance of God's name? Because, answers Hoffman (1996:91), the wine is blessed as wine but quaffed as blood.

The first person to sip during the circumcision ceremony is the infant. After the *mohel* performs *metzitzah*, he traditionally spits the child's blood into a goblet of wine or sloshes the blood and wine in his mouth and expectorates into a cup. Then the *mohel* dips his finger and gives the child a taste.[22] The boy's parents next take a sip, followed by the *mohel*. In colonial America, a father counseled his son to "dip your little finger into the cup or glass you spit yᵉ blood & drop a little into yᵉ child's mouth" (Zimmerman 1954–1955). Today, most Jews sip only wine. But they once drank blood.

The original symbolism of the circumcision nip will likely offend modern sensibilities. Today, circumcision wine is drunk as wine, not blood. It is often said to sweeten divine judgment or to alleviate the child's pain (Goldberger 1991:98). But, frankly speaking, these modern glosses merely try to sweeten a rite that was originally intended to be painfully unpalatable. The infant, to repeat, once sipped his own blood. Moreover, while Reform Judaism permits the use of anesthesia during circumcision, traditionalists refuse since God allegedly rewarded Abraham for the pain (see Landes and Robbin 1990; J. D. Bleich 2000:54–55). The use of anesthesia, in this view, "is like sealing a covenant with a stone, which does not feel anything, and not with a human being" (Matzner-Bekerman 1984:53). All evidence points to the fact that the infant traditionally sipped no wine for comfort.

Sipping the circumcision wine as wine rather than blood also dilutes the symbolic potency of the rite. The Torah, to repeat, firmly prohibits the consumption of blood, one of the premier laws incumbent on all of humanity and not just Jews. Yet the paramount ritual remembrance of the covenant, with all its promise of progeny, requires participants to violate this decree by drinking a child's "life force." To abandon this complex morality, regardless of whether or not one endorses it, is to deny the ceremony the very power that has enabled it to endure.

Classic male initiation rites typically purge novices of maternal blood so they can grow into adult men. Initiates often ingest masculine substances and foods to assist this transformation. Jewish circumcision adheres to a similar pattern. Ideally, the infant drinks when the *mohel* chants, "In your blood, live" (Hoffman 1996:91–92).[23] Then he receives his Hebrew name. The boy loses female blood, or the blood of birth, then gains male blood and a new name.

Similarly, we must position the communal cup of circumcision wine against the polluting blood of menstruation and childbirth. In fact, a sip of circumcision blood symbolically assures the mother of a speedy postpartum recovery (Krohn 1985:135). In accordance with a widespread folk world-view, the father sips his son's blood to magically replenish his own vital fluids (Chyet and Mirsky 1990). Needless to say, no rite in Judaism offers partici-pants a drink of menstrual blood—no rite, that is, unless the blood is con-cocted by men, as during the biblical purification from corpses (chapter 5). No ritual drink, too, follows the birth of daughters. Only the delivery of a son requires parents to drink to their health and to wash away the impurity of birth with a cup of masculine blood.

Umbilical Chords Cut and Connected

Circumcision, I mentioned in chapter 4, allows men to mirror or complete the cutting of the infant's umbilical chord (see also Pollock 1973:300). A folk rite among Eastern European Jews, one also connected to circumcision, allows men to do just the opposite. They reattach the umbilicus, thereby tethering boys to a divine mother under male control.

Jews handle the parchment Torah scroll as a regal woman. She is dressed in finery, bedecked with gold and silver ornaments, and cloistered in an ornamented cabinet. When the Torah is removed from seclusion during prayer, her audience arises. If she tumbles, they fast. She is publicly undressed for chanting before an adoring, traditionally male audience. No human hands, only a pointer, caress her parchment skin.

For centuries, Western European Jews circumcised boys atop white linen, just after morning prayers in the synagogue. The cloth was torn into strips and sewn into a long band called a *wimpel* in Yiddish or a *mappah* in Hebrew (Weber, Friedlander, and Armbruster 1997). The boy's mother and other female kin—in some places, virgins and brides (Gutmann 1983b:168)—ornamented the *wimpel* with inscriptions and iconography that represented the ideal life of a male Jew. These designs included an astrological sign and the liturgical phrase "may he grow up to a life of Torah, marriage, and good deeds." Some years later, the boy would formally offer his *wimpel* to the syna-gogue as a gift to wrap a Torah scroll. Then the *wimpel* was stored until the boy's bar mitzvah, when it again swaddled the Torah.

The *wimpel* binds the fate of Jewish boys to the Torah (Kirshenblatt-

Gimblett 1982). The binder, too, portrays circumcision as a rite that secures or contains the Law. In my view, the *wimpel* also enables men to retether boys to a divine mother whose ability to nourish the Jewish people is contingent on male ritual. During circumcision, men culturally sever a natural umbilicus that joined mother and son. Later, men use a remnant of this rite as a cultural umbilicus to fuse the boy to the Torah and male fellowship. Together, circumcision and the *wimpel* eclipse mothering and assert the identity of men as nourishers and life-givers.

Only a small segment of the *wimpel* actually enwraps the Torah. The rest of the sash is coiled and tucked between the two scrolls. It is not difficult to see here an image of men inserting a young boy's phallus into the folds of the female Torah. This custom, like circumcision, represents reproduction as well as intimacy between man and God. Ironically, this imagery also violates rabbinic law, which forbids intercourse in the same room as the Torah.

In legend, a Roman general taunted the great Rabbi Akiva, asking, "If God so desired circumcision, why are boys born foreskinned?" Akiva replied by equating the rite with the cutting of newborn umbilical cords by mothers (TL 4.7). Humanity's task, he meant, is to refine God's creations. But Rabbi Akiva's response had another level of meaning. He likened men during circumcision to mothers. The *wimpel* also feminizes men. In so doing, the *wimpel* sustains and threatens the masculine ideology of circumcision.

Eating the Foreskin

The rabbis loathed the foreskin as an impediment to male fecundity. The folk had a different view. They saw the prepuce as enhancing female fertility. European synagogues once auctioned the foreskin, reports Aurand (1939:46), "which is generally purchased by a new married Man for his Wife to carry about her in a Box, believing it to promote Fruitfulness of the Womb." In some Jewish North African and Sephardic communities, barren women swallowed foreskins, sometimes dipped in honey, to promote pregnancy and the birth of sons (Patai 1983a:290, 293, 297, 1983b:358–59).[24] The "bleeding foreskin" was also plunked in a raw egg and guzzled (Brauer 1942:17–38; Ohel 1973:67, 69–70). So convincing was this cure for barrenness, reports Ohel, that a Moslem offered a Jew one hundred francs to steal the foreskin for his own wife!

Less dramatic gestures also attest to the magical ability of circumcision to encourage conception. Jews carried the boy between his mother and the *mohel*, drank water from a glass placed beneath Elijah's Chair, sipped the circumcision wine, glanced at the *mohel's* knife, and commissioned the carving of Elijah's Chair (Dobrinsky 1980:74; Patai 1983b:358; Klein 1998:223). The rabbis neither promoted nor protested these customs. But eating the foreskin they could not abide (Patai 1983b:258–59, 413; Zimmels 1997:163, 246 n. 71). Officially, the prepuce was vile. But the folk—and particularly women—resisted this orthodoxy.

Did Jewish women eat foreskins because they were attracted to the power of taboo or beholden to folkloristic beliefs that subtly contested the rabbis and covenantal patriarchy? Regardless, circumcision was too important to be left in the hands of the authorities.

Throughout this chapter, I argued that various aspects of the traditional circumcision ceremony speak to contrary meanings that uphold and undermine the dominant meanings of Jewish culture and the covenant. The enduring power of circumcision arises precisely from this resistance to any singular vision or script of meaning. Both in biblical cultures, as I showed in earlier chapters, and in Jewish traditions, circumcision simultaneously challenged and championed its own moral vision.

Symbolically, there is ample evidence from biblical texts, rabbinic legends, liturgy, and ritual gestures to state with some certainty that Jews viewed circumcision with marked ambivalence—an ambivalence, I hope it is now clear, that imbued the ceremony with a profound degree of awe. But for all this ambivalence, the rite was still framed by a sense of moral purpose. By contrast, Christianity discerned no ethical virtue in circumcision. The rite offered only a threat to hegemony. It is to that far darker vision that I now turn.

Notes

1. English sources on the circumcision ceremony include Chill (1979), Cohen (1984), Krohn (1985), Levy (1990), Hoffman (1996), Kunin (1998), and the photographs in Lieberman (1997). Translated rabbinic texts include YD, HM, and the Talmud; I provide full citations in the Abbreviations.

2. Rather than combine the masculine and feminine plurals (*mohelim* and *mohelot*) into something awkward, such as *mohelim/ot*, I simply use the Anglicized word *mohels*.

3. Medieval rabbis counted 613 male sinews and organs. Circumcision thus created bodily wholeness and piously corroborated the bawdy adage that a man equals his penis.

4. Unless otherwise noted, I focus in this chapter on Orthodox Judaism. Conservative and especially Reform Judaism relax many regulations.

5. For historical instances of delayed circumcision due to the unavailability of a *mohel*, see Brauer (1993:167) and Marcus (1951:79–82, 175).

6. Ken Katz, "Surrogate mother in Denver Helps Israelis Have Twins: A Humanitarian Story with *Halachic* Implications," Intermountain Jewish News, April 6, 2001, reprinted online at www.denvermohel.com/Articles/ArticlesAndPress.htm.

7. See Responsa 28 in *Current Reform Responsa*, edited by Solomon B. Freehof (Cincinnati: Hebrew Union College Press, 1969).

8. *The Minor Tractates of the Talmud*, vol. 2, translated by A. Cohen (London: Soncino Press, 1965), 603–13.

9. Crapanzano (1981:27) keenly analyzes father–son tension in the Moroccan Muslim rite.

10. For Jewish and Muslim skits that burlesque circumcision, see Crapanzano (1981:29), Brauer (1993:290–92), and Delaney (1991:141).

11. The spoof *Martha Stuart's Better Than You at Entertaining* (T. Connor and J. Downey New York: HarperPerennial, 1996]) mocks the circumcision meal with cocktail wieners suggestively arranged with pairs of Swedish meatballs and calamari tips in red sauce.

12. In deference to this anguish, the circumcision liturgy omits the standard blessing of gratitude (*shehecheyanu*). But to celebrate the occasion, the liturgy forgoes standard elegies (*Taḥanun*). Sephardic rites may also include a musical procession.

13. Question 521, in *Reasons for Jewish Customs and Traditions (Taamei HaMinhagim)*, Rabbi Abraham Isaac Sperlling, translated by Abraham Matts (New York: Bloch). (Orig. Hebrew 1890)

14. For the circumvention of kosher rules by American Jews who enjoy Chinese food, see Tuchman and Levine (1993).

15. Jews also refrain from eating the sciatic nerve (chapter 4) and much of the hindquarters.

16. Psychoanalytic readers may see phallic imagery when God transformed Lot's wife into a pillar of salt (Jones 1912; Zeligs 1974:27).

17. That the decapitation of Goliath, the "uncircumcised one" (1 Samuel 17:36), reminded the rabbis of circumcision provides further support for my analysis in chapter 6.

18. Recognizing this predicament, Maimonides (HM 3:5) ruled that, during an adult's circumcision, the penis should remain covered for the blessings.

19. For other charitable auctions and gifts at circumcision, see Ohel (1973:68–71), Dobrinsky (1980:65), and Brauer (1993:165).

20. Stern (1994:66 n. 121) is one of the few modern scholars who disagrees with this argument, finding no comparable effort "to curb apostasy" by enhancing the rigor of any other commandment.

21. Sephardic Jews also bless scents, such as lemon and rose water, in partial reference to the midrashic hill of putrefying foreskins that so pleased God (Dobrinsky 1980:65; chapter 4).

22. Some *mohels* spit the mixture onto the ground (Goldberger 1991:95) or poured it

before the cabinet of Torah scrolls (Zimmels 1997:163). The folk once infuriated the rabbis by inking magical charms with circumcision blood (Zimmels 1997:163).

23. While offering the child a sip, the *mohel* may curve his fingers to form a Hebrew name of God in a gesture of supplication.

24. Sephardic remedies for "fright" (*espantu*), called *mumia*, contained dried foreskins (Lévy and Zumwalt 2002:142). For Australian Aboriginal and Muslim parallels, see Róheim (1945:68–69) and Kennedy (1970:176–77).

CHAPTER EIGHT

Circumcision, Anti-Semitism, and Christ's Foreskin

Ironically, it is Christianity and not Judaism that indelibly etched circumcision on the Jewish body and fostered a preoccupation with the prepuce. But circumcision for Christianity is no mark of membership in the covenantal community. It is, instead, a moral and physical mar that threatens the very existence of Christianity.

Circumcision is a contentious topic throughout the New Testament, especially in the letters of Paul. Christ's foreskin was the object of medieval devotion. Nearly all anti-Semitic canards in European history, moreover, from blood libels and coin clippings to Shylock's "pound of flesh," evidence a pervasive dread of circumcision. In this chapter, I survey diverse aspects of European history to demonstrate the pervasiveness of this alarm.

Crucifixion as Circumcision

The Gospels (Matthew, Mark, Luke, and John), composed in Greek during the latter third of the first century, more or less present parallel biographies of Christ. Many of these legends reflect the rituals of early Judaism and, sometimes through violation, long-standing themes that date to ancient Israel.

For example, Christ underwent an eighth-day circumcision (Luke 1:59; 2:21). He healed a hemorrhaging or menstruating woman (Matthew 9:20; Mark 5:25–29) and offered the apostles a taste of his flesh and blood at the Last Supper (Matthew 26:26–29; John 6:22–59; John 2:52–66; Mark 14:22–25). During the Crucifixion, a Roman soldier lanced Christ's torso (John

19:34). Sawyer (1995) correctly interprets the resulting stream of blood and water as a male rendition of menstruation, birth, and lactation that seeks to beget a new world—a world, we will see, largely devoid of Jews.

Early Christianity paralleled the nailing of Christ's body on the Cross to birth a new covenant with the bodily rite that symbolized membership into the older Jewish covenant. More than that, the early Christians understood crucifixion to culminate and replace circumcision (Galatians 5:11; 24; Borgen 1982:40–41; Ferguson 1988). Only through pain and suffering does Christ's crucifixion offer humanity the hope of atonement (Romans 3:25; Ephesians 1:7; 1 John 1:7; 1 Peter 1:18–19). The covenantal "sign" thus shifts from a minor stab on an infant's penis to bloody torture and agonizing death. By destroying the entire body and not just the foreskin, the Crucifixion signaled the end of Judaism and a new theological beginning. A crude joke builds on this parallel. Question: What's the difference between crucifixion and circumcision? Answer: In crucifixion, they throw out the whole Jew.[1]

The early church fathers, no less than modern theologians (Ashby 1995; Allen 1996), saw premonitions of Christ and the Crucifixion in the many references to circumcision in the Hebrew Bible (e.g., Augustine, *Tractates on the Gospel of John* 30:5; Justin Martyr, *Dialogue with Trypho* 114). For example, the Israelites, wrote Origen, initially circumcised with knives of iron as befitting the hardness of the Jewish heart (*Homilies on Joshua* 1:7). Later, Joshua performed the "second" circumcision with soft stone, thus foreshadowing true circumcision through faith in Christ.

Why, then, was Christ circumcised? The Venerable Bede, an eighth-century Benedictine monk, offered an answer in his homily "On the Feast Day of the Lord's Circumcision." Christ's circumcision demonstrated his Abrahamic lineage and showed the value of obedience (Steinberg 1983: 51–53). But Christ's death and resurrection, to repeat, obviated any further performance of the rite.

Crucifixion allowed a son to transcend the human world of his birth and join the divine realm of men. Like circumcision, then, the Crucifixion marginalized women by linking men to the eternal realm of God. After the Resurrection, in fact, Jesus appeared to Mary Magdalene yet forbid her to "hold on to me, because I have not yet ascended to the Father" (John 20:16–17). Here, as in circumcision, the presence of women imperils men's religious obligations.

The Gospels of Matthew and Luke characterize Jesus' mother, Mary, as a sexual virgin but also, initially, a possible adulterer (1 Matthew 1:18–19).

Over the next few centuries, official misogyny reshaped another Mary—Mary Magdalene—into an equally contrary woman. Despite meriting an encounter with Christ after the Resurrection, Mary Magdalene was nonetheless identified as the anonymous sinner mentioned in Luke (7:36–50) and other indecorous Marys (e.g., John 8:1–11; 12:1–8). That Christ came to occupy a position between two sexually ambiguous women with the same name, I contend, expresses the same relationship between men and motherhood dramatized by circumcision. The two Marys, cued to Christ's birth and death, also parallel the relationship between Christ's two cuts of circumcision and crucifixion.

Like circumcision, the Crucifixion represents oedipal tension between fathers and sons (see also Dundes 1980; Cronbach 1931–1932:639; Carroll 1992:67). The Gospels largely ignore Jesus' human father, emphasizing instead a close mother–son relationship and the efforts of the Son to usurp the divine Father's authority. As in all oedipal conflicts, the son triumphs. Christ ascends to the heavenly throne. Once there, however, he merges with God and so becomes his own father (Dundes 1980:260). By combining covenantal morality with sexual taboo, Christ resembles the circumcised penis.

God the Father punishes his Son by nailing the boy to a giant phallus (Dundes 1980). The Cross symbolizes death yet eternal life. Similarly, circumcision feints with a castrative cut but unleashes progeny. Both Christ's crucifixion and Jewish circumcision feminize young men by penetrating them with another man's phallus—either the *mohel's* knife or the soldier's lance. Both rites resemble male initiation (Dundes 1980) in using blood and pain to separate a boy from his mother, then to join him to a gender-exclusive fellowship. The life and death of Christ, I am suggesting, represents a grand elaboration of the very Jewish rite he supposedly replaced.

Paul and Circumcision

The penis was a key sign of ethnicity in the ancient Mediterranean. Jews were circumcised; Gentiles were not. But a first-century Jew, one who initially opposed Christ but then converted during an ecstatic experience on the road to Damascus (Acts 9), cast the legitimacy of this distinction into ceaseless and impassioned contention. Toward unifying humanity in Christ, Saul of Tarsus, renamed Paul, sought to erase all bodily signs of religious distinctiveness. The fate of the new covenant, never mind the survival of Judaism, hung on the foreskin.

Despite the universal outlook of monotheism, the Mosaic covenant was bestowed onto one people and one gender. Paul's critique of early Judaism, argues Boyarin (1994:52–53), resulted from this tension between universalism and exclusion. At the same time, Paul espoused Hellenistic dualism in which the nonmaterial essences of reality prevail over the material, bodily world. Paul never questioned the authenticity of the Hebrew Bible as a divine revelation given to the Jews. Rather, Paul *allegorized* the Jewish people and the Torah as an outer, fleshy facade for an inner, spiritual reality accessible only through faith in Christ (Boyarin 1994; Lupton 1999). Bodily circumcision, like the old Mosaic code, once privileged the Jews. But Christ's crucifixion and resurrection nullified this ontology by revealing it as a "veil" for the truth (2 Corinthians 3:14). Christ alone offered salvation.

Paul phrased his mission to unite humanity in Christ almost exclusively in terms of erasing Jewish distinctiveness (Boyarin 1994:152). Consequently, he critiqued those practices that most obviously symbolized Jewish identity, namely, the dietary prohibitions, Sabbath restrictions, and especially circumcision. Only by renouncing flesh and embracing the Spirit of Christ could Jews attain salvation. But then they are no longer Jews. They are Christians. Paul's inclusive moral system, Boyarin recognizes, universalized a particular worldview that admitted of no significant Jewish practices.

Did Paul dismiss circumcision to ease conversion? Unlikely. Ancient devotees would hardly have flinched at the removal of a mere foreskin. Neither the early church nor the rabbis regarded circumcision as a serious bar to conversion. Rather, Paul offered three main arguments against circumcision. First, Abraham "received the sign of circumcision as a seal of the righteousness that he had by faith while he was still *un*circumcised" (Romans 4:9–12; Galatians 3:6–9).[2] Circumcision was therefore posterior to faith. Second, Paul rephrased Hellenistic dualism such that spiritual things are superior to physical things (Colossians 3:11–14). Faith trumps ritual. Third, Paul echoed the prophetic literature of the Hebrew Bible (e.g., Jeremiah 9:24–25) to assert that "true circumcision" referred not to the physical removal of the penile foreskin but to ethical conduct, so-called circumcision of the heart (Philippines 3:3).[3]

At first blush, Paul offers a program of religious reform that any reasonable Jew, then or now, would seemingly endorse. Circumcision "is indeed of value if you obey the law; but if you break the law, your circumcision has become uncircumcision" (Romans 2:25). Paul censored Jews (and early Christians) who viewed circumcision as a boast of piety (Ephesians 2:8–9). He pushed for greater connection between everyday ethics and Jewish rituals (Borgen

1982). And Paul rebuffed Jews who await salvation solely on the basis of genealogy and ritual competence, what he called "works," rather than ethical conduct (Boyarin 1994:87–95). But Paul goes much further than simple reform.

A "person is not a Jew who is one outwardly, nor is true circumcision something external and physical," Paul wrote (Romans 2:28–29). "Rather, a person is a Jew who is one inwardly, and real circumcision is a matter of the heart—it is spiritual and not literal." No traditional Jewish authority would countenance this heresy, for, however much circumcision represents ethical conduct, God still demands the physical procedure. Many Jewish thinkers, like Paul, allegorized circumcision, including Philo of Alexandria and Maimonides (see Borgen 1982; Boyarin 1993; Stern 1993; Barclay 1998). But they also, unlike Paul, fiercely defended the physical procedure as a legitimate and distinctive mark of Jewish identity and devotion. For Paul, Jewish circumcision is false because it is bodily and bound to the Mosaic Law. Christian circumcision is true because it is ethical and Christ centered. In Paul's theology, those who cut a fleshy covenant are "cut off" (ekpipto) from salvation. Indeed, the true Jew, wrote Paul, the Jew who really upholds the Law, is the Jew who abandons all Jewish practices and professes faith in Christ (Romans 3:31). The true Jew, in other words, is no Jew at all. Moreover, Paul never spoke about Jews who were circumcised and ethical. His critique of Judaism often amounted to caricature.

On the surface, Paul dismissed differences between the "circumcised" (peritome) and the "foreskinned" (akroboustia) as superficial and irrelevant (1 Corinthians 7:18–19). Ethics mattered, not phalloi. In actuality, though, Paul's theology favored the foreskinned since crucifixion destroyed Christ's ethnic or Jewish body—a circumcised body—in order to birth a new, universal, uncircumcised body defined as pure Spirit (Boyarin 1994:117).[4] This way, Boyarin (1994:156) argues convincingly, Paul established Jewish "difference" as the primary threat to Christian hegemony. Indeed, Paul grouped circumcision with other debased "works of the flesh," such as fornication, idolatry, witchcraft, and drunkenness (Galatians 5). Paul also associated circumcision with dogs, "evil workers," mutilation, and castration (Galatians 5:12; Philippians 3:2–4).[5] Ever since, the Jew's circumcised penis stands against the global mission of Christianity.

The Mosaic Law, conceded Paul, once served its rightful purpose. It curtailed "transgressions" and disciplined the unrighteous in a world without Christ (Galatians 3:19–25; 1 Timothy 1:8–11). Likewise, circumcision symbolized the entrustment of the Jews with "the oracles of God" (Romans 3:1–2). At the same time, circumcision and other rites enslaved the Jews in bodily practices until their eventual liberation in Christ (Galatians 4:1–7). In the final analysis, Paul sought to excise circumcision from Christianity in order to circumcise all flesh from truthful human experience. The Jew in this worldview is simply wrong.

Not surprisingly, Paul advocated chastity (1 Corinthians 7:1–9). He begrudgingly accepted marriage as a necessary evil to curb the sin of fornication, which, at best, leads to death and decay. Only spiritual reproduction promises eternal life (Romans 7:1–6). This, after all, was the true message of God's first command in Genesis. In multiple ways, writes Boyarin (1993:57), Paul's theology threatened the "corporeal integrity of the Jewish people."

Following Paul, the church fathers such as Augustine and Chrysostom derided Judaism as a carnal religion. But the real obsession with sexuality was their own. Christianity enthusiastically embraced renunciation (Brown 1988). The gnostic Gospel of Philip (82:26–29) viewed Jewish circumcision as teaching "that it is proper to destroy the flesh."[6] Taking this lesson to heart, Origen severed his own genitals! Indeed, the rolls of Catholic saints include more than three-score eunuchs. At least one Christian sect, the Skoptsy of Russia, still practiced male and female emasculation until the 1930s (Engelstein 1999). Jews cut the penis, but the religion of uncircumcision assailed sexuality.

The rabbis never responded to Paul by name. But they did seemingly answer his foreskinned polemics (Wolfson 1987b:194, 1998:226–28; Boyarin 1992:492–93, 1994:127–28; Hoffman 1996:113–15). With literary and historical license, we can follow Hoenig (1963) and imagine a conversation between Paul and the classic rabbis:

Paul: "Circumcision is nothing" (Acts 15:24).
Rabbis: "Great is circumcision" (M. Nedarim 3:11; B. Shabbath 137b).
Paul: A "new creation" exists in Christ (Galatians 6:15).
Rabbis: Heaven and earth exist through circumcision (see chapter 1).
Paul: Abraham was righteous before circumcision.
Rabbis: Abraham became "whole" after circumcision (see chapter 4).
Paul: One becomes "complete" in Christ (Colossians 2:10–11).
Rabbis: Circumcision allows men to unite with God, attaining "the summit of perfection" (Zohar i:88b–89a).
Paul: Faith in Christ supercedes "works."

Rabbis: Circumcision fulfills all the commandments in the Torah and ideally leads to a life of "good works" (see Hoffman 1996:122).
Paul: Circumcision is mutilation, suitable only for dogs.
Rabbis: "Whosoever eateth with an uncircumcised person is as though he
were eating flesh of abomination" or "with a dog" (PRE 29; GR 11:3).

This fictitious debate, I stress, is pure fabrication despite the authenticity of
the individual statements. But it captures the historical importance of circumcision in the self-definition of Judaism and Christianity.

Boyarin (1997a) suggests that rabbinic endorsements of circumcision
react *against* Christianity rather than affirm what, *in its own terms*, Judaism
really is. To some degree, this is true. But it is also somewhat irrelevant since,
as I am arguing, the merit of foreskinlessness eventually emerged as a defining
difference between Jew and Christian.

Neither Male Nor Female?

Baptism in the Gospels is confessional (Matthew 3:13; Mark 1:4–5; Luke
3:3). For Paul, baptism crucifies "our old self" with Christ so "the body of sin
might be destroyed" to birth pure Spirit (Romans 6:3–9). Ever since, Christian thinkers such as Augustine, Ambrose, and Caesarius construe baptism
as a better spiritual replacement for fleshy circumcision (Ferguson 1988:489–
97). In this view, the Jews correctly tried to curtail lust by removing the foreskin. But the penile referent of the rite entrapped them within the very sinful
carnality they tried to excise. Only baptism and Christ's crucifixion offer
humanity a wholly valid cleansing.[7]

Paul famously phrased baptism as dissolving the distinctions between Jew
and Greek, slave and free, circumcision and uncircumcision, and male and
female (Galatians 3:27–29; Colossians 3:11; 1 Corinthians 7:19). But any
apparent egalitarianism fades before Paul's strident affirmations of male dominance (1 Corinthians 11:3–10; 14:34–35; 1 Timothy 2:9–15; see also
Boyarin 1994:chap. 8). Moreover, Paul *never* mentioned an obvious criticism
of circumcision: the rite confers the covenant *only* onto men.

However, three Christian thinkers in late antiquity did critique Judaism
for the noncircumcision of women, even while they themselves marginalized
women from their own theology (Cohen 1997). That women are not circumcised, wrote Justin Martyr in "Dialogue with Trypho the Jew" (23), separates
the rite from righteousness. Cyprian, the mid-third-century bishop of Car-
thage, contrasted the uselessness of circumcision for women with the univer-

sality of baptism (*Ad Quirinum*). Two centuries later, a fictitious debate of uncertain authorship, "Concerning the Dispute between the Church and Synagogue," elaborated on this point. The absence of circumcision implies that Jewish women lack salvation and full Jewish identity. How can Jews punish women for adultery, moreover, when their only sin is to fondle the sign of the covenant?

Of course, baptism also denies women covenantal equality (see Bloch and Guggenheim 1981). By washing away the fleshy sinfulness of biological birth, baptism diminishes uterine motherhood and emphasizes instead the rebirthing powers of a Heavenly Father. Insofar as both circumcision and baptism privilege men, the rites are similar. But while Judaism admits women into the community, Christianity reserves membership and salvation solely for the baptized. In this regard, emphasizes Cohen (1997), circumcision and baptism are dissimilar.

Later church thinkers also pondered the exclusion of women from circumcision (see Thompson 1995). Saint Thomas Aquinas argued that, as a penalty for Original Sin, only men required circumcision since fathers and not mothers provide the "active generation" of conception.[8] For Luther, the female equivalent of circumcision was the pain of childbirth. Never, however, did the church fathers criticize Jews for excluding women from the covenantal rite. Perhaps, surmises Cohen (1997), they recognized that Christianity offers women no greater equality.

Indeed, John Mirk opined in a fourteenth-century sermon that God gave circumcision to men because women lack sufficient ability to purify themselves of lust (Smith 1995). Conversely, Margaret Fell, seeking to convert Jewish women to Quakerism in the seventeenth century, proposed that women, lacking a penis, are less swayed by fleshy desires than men and so more apt to become "circumcised in the heart" (Jowitt 1999:163–64). As a bonus, ex-Jewesses would carry no ambiguous mark.

Christianity abandoned circumcision neither to celebrate the body nor to promote a world of gendered equality. Rather, Christianity abandoned circumcision to render Judaism null and void. But this effort at ethnic erasure did not equally, as I now show, erase the allure of Christ's own circumcision.

The Holy Prepuce

In the fourteenth century, Catherine of Siena scrawled a note to Christ, saying, "You espouse our souls to you with the ring of your flesh" (Bynum 1987:377 n. 35). In "letter after letter," summarizes Bynum (1987:174–75),

Catherine affirmed that "we do not marry Christ with gold or silver but with the ring of Christ's foreskin, given in the Circumcision and accompanied by pain and the shedding of blood." Alphonsus Salmeron, a sixteenth-century Jesuit, concurred. "In this mystery of circumcision," he stated in *Commentarii in Evangelicam Historiam et in Acta Apostolorum*, "Jesus sends his brides . . . the fleshen ring of the most holy prepuce" (Bryk 1934:305–6). Christ's nuptial foreskin wedded medieval women to his fleshy suffering on the Cross (Bynum 1987:178).[9] But this wedding also bespeaks a somewhat taboo erotic encounter, not unlike circumcision, another penile rite that unites humanity—men, at least—with God.

Renaissance artists often pictured Christ's tumescent penis. Steinberg (1983) sees these erections as symbolizing chastity, masculine power, redemption from lust, and triumph over death by pointing to resurrection. Since Christ's circumcision ended all circumcisions, his erect penis stands as a moral exemplar for humanity—much like the circumcised penis in rabbinic Judaism, albeit to opposite ends.

Bynum (1986) disagrees with Steinberg and prefers instead to interpret Christ's circumcised penis as one of his many bloody wounds, including circumcision and crucifixion ordeals, that medieval culture associated with menstruation and motherhood. Christ was often imagined as a lactating mother (Bynum 1982, 1986, 1987; Mollenkott 1983). As Guerric, the twelfth-century abbot of Igny wrote, "The Holy Spirit was sent from heaven like milk poured out from Christ's own breasts" (after 1 Peter 2:2–3). Jesus' lactation arose partly from the long-standing belief, found even in Aristotle's *History of Animals* (7:3), that menstrual blood transforms during pregnancy into breast milk (Bynum 1982:132–33).[10] His own blood was therefore seen as nurturing. Kabbalah also linked breast and penis (chapter 4). But whereas the Jewish mystics, notes Wolfson (1995:217 n. 121), masculinized breastfeeding into the circumcised penis, the penis of Christ was transformed into a mother's breast.

Christ himself displayed uterine sentiments. He likened the Crucifixion and Resurrection to birth (John 16:21–22). Emulating Adam, who begat Eve, Christ birthed the church from his crucifixion wounds (Bynum 1986:97). These idioms of male birth and breast-feeding recall circumcision. They blur gender to express male envy of motherhood and allowed Christian men an intimate union with God that did not seemingly compromise their manhood.

Medieval men adored the Virgin. Women coupled with Christ through experiences that ranged from kisses to orgasm (Bynum 1982:161–62,

1987:chap. 5).[11] Devotion climaxed during communion, when the faithful ate Christ's body in Eucharistic ecstasy (Bynum 1987:chap. 2). They also sipped wine as blood, transforming a forbidden act into a male form of nourishment. Christ's body, then, like the Holy Phallus, symbolized the same masculine androgyny as the circumcised Jewish penis.

The Gospels, as I mentioned, frame Christ's life between two bloody wounds, circumcision and crucifixion. Christ willingly submitted to both ordeals (Steinberg 1983:51). The Roman lance doubles as the Jewish knife—so much so, shows Steinberg (1983:169–71), that Renaissance artists depicted the blood from Christ's wound as unnaturally flowing to his groin.

The Gospels of Mark (16:9), Luke (24:1), and John (20:1) timed Christ's resurrection to the first day of the week. To subsequent church thinkers such as Augustine and Thomas Aquinas, this timing implied that the Savior arose on the day following the Sabbath. Since the Sabbath was the seventh day, Resurrection occurred on the *eighth* day, thereby culminating circumcision. A sermon by Franciscus Cardulus in 1493, *Oratio de circumcisione* (Steinberg 1968:58), brilliantly interpreted Christ's final words on the cross, "It is finished" (John 14:30), as referring to circumcision!

Renaissance sermons preached on January 1, the traditional Feast of the Circumcision, repeatedly connected Christ's circumcision to the Passion and Resurrection (Steinberg 1983:61–64).[12] A poem by Robert Herrick, "To His Saviour. The New Yeers Gift," did likewise. "That little prettie bleeding part, Of Foreskin send to me: And Ile returne a bleeding Heart, For New-yeers gift to thee." The pain and blood of circumcision, argues Steinberg (1983), inflicted on an innocent child, even more powerfully attested to Christ's humanity than his crucifixion.

European painters frequently pictured Christ's circumcision ceremony, including Rembrandt, Fogg, Titian, Zurbaran, Mantegna, Parmigianino, Tura, Garofalo, and Signorelli. (Reproductions are often sold on eBay.) A subtle iconography represented the rite not as a Jewish practice but as Christian theology (J. Greenstein 1992:chap 6). Poets were no less enthralled, including Richard Cranshaw, Christopher Harvey, John Milton, and the anonymous author of the fourteenth-century composition "Sir Gawain and the Green Knight."

No other aspect of Christ's life so plainly expressed the Savior's Jewishness as his circumcision. But this recognition was reluctant and scornful. Augustine called circumcision a "mark of infamy" (*Reply to Faustus the Manichaean*, bk. 19). The rite lacked "reason," wrote Lactantius, "because, if God wishes it, He would have formed men thus from the beginning, not having the foreskin" (*The Divine Institutes*, bk. 4:17). Several late medieval painters sought to debase Judaism by depicting Christ's circumciser as a hideous woman (Abramson and Hannon 2003:106–9). Some Renaissance artists, seemingly unable to reconcile the Jewishness of Christ's circumcision with Christianity, simply cast his penis out of sight, often covering it with Mary's hand (Steinberg 1983:167). Sometimes they showed Christ *with* a foreskin. Either way, the Savior would appear neither marred nor diminished by Judaism.[13]

Christ's circumcision took "away from the Jews an excuse for not receiving Him," wrote Thomas Aquinas in *Summa Theologica* (3, Question 37). Only through sheer "obstinacy," exclaimed Chrysostom, do Jews retain circumcision and refuse Christ ("Discourses Against Judaizing Christians" 2:1–2). One would be hard pressed to find a more scathing indictment of bodily circumcision and the Jews in general than Martin Luther's notorious 1543 essay "On the Jews and Their Lies."[14] Luther calls the Jews obstinate, arrogant, liars, blind, disobedient, "full of malice, greed, envy, hatred toward one another, pride, usury, conceit," the vilest whore, and an evil slut. The synagogue is "a den of devils." Here are some reflections on circumcision:

> Therefore it is not a clever and ingenious, but a clumsy, foolish, and stupid lie when the Jews boast of their circumcision before God, presuming that God should regard them graciously for that reason, though they should certainly know from Scripture that they are not the only race circumcised in compliance with God's decree, and that they cannot on that account be God's special people.

> And still they brazenly strut before God, lie and boast about being God's only people by reason of their physical circumcision, unmindful of the circumcision of the heart.

> Subsequently, after they have scourged, crucified, spat upon, blasphemed, and cursed God in his word, as Isaiah 8 prophesies, they pretentiously trot out their circumcision and other vain, blasphemous, invented, and meaningless works.

Speaking to the Jews," wrote Luther, "is much the same as preaching the gospel to a sow." Circumcision, declared Origen in his "Homilies on Luke" (5:2), is "an empty sign, a mute deed."

Perhaps the Jewish mystics responded to this vitriol by noting that since "circumcision" and "word" are Hebrew homophones (chapter 6), only Jews incarnate God's word (Wolfson 1998). But rabbinic exegesis was no match for patristic nastiness. Origen's "On the Circumcision of Abraham" described the Jewish rite as "unseemly, detestable, disgusting." The faithful probably agreed.

But the faithful nonetheless remained captivated by the Savior's foreskin and penis. The Eucharist fulfills Christ's command to "Take, eat; this is my body" (Matthew 26:26)—or, as Shell (1997:346) puts it, "Eat me!" Some medieval women *and* men experienced pregnancy symptoms after ingesting the Host, thus emulating the miraculous conception of Christ in Mary (Bynum 1987). In this respect, the medieval Eucharist resembled divine fellatio (Carroll 1991), an oral insemination that recalls the scroll forced by God down Ezekiel's throat—a scroll evoked during the circumcision ceremony (chapter 7). The tone of this interpretation might displease some readers. But it is firmly anchored to medieval devotion.

Indeed, consider the striking vision of Agnes Blannbekin, a Viennese lay sister immortalized in an anonymous fourteenth-century biography, on January 1, the feast day of Christ's circumcision:

> Crying and with compassion, she began to think about the foreskin of Christ . . . And behold, soon she felt with the greatest sweetness on her tongue a little piece of skin alike the skin in an egg, which she swallowed. After she had swallowed it, she again felt the little skin on her tongue with sweetness as before, and again she swallowed it. And this happened to her about a hundred times . . . And so great was the sweetness of tasting that little skin that she felt in all [her] limbs and parts of the limbs a sweet transformation.[15]

In Italy, Christ's foreskin was called *carne vera sancta* (Bentley 1985:141), what Shell (1997) translates as "true and holy meat."[16] Even Christ encouraged this interpretation, saying, "Labor not for the meat which perisheth, but for that meat which endureth unto everlasting life, which the Son of man shall give unto you" (John 6:27). Kabbalah, too, we have seen, described the mystical union between man and God in strikingly erotic terms. But while Jewish men encountered God's circumcised penis, Christians tasted the Son's foreskin.

The Preputial Relic

Medieval fascination with Christ's foreskin extended to its fate after the resurrection. Did it arise, or remain behind? There was no simple answer.

An earthbound prepuce would confirm Christ as "the spouse of our humanity" (Bynum 1987:175). Likewise, a foreskinless resurrection, argued

Carvajo in *Oratio in die circumcisionis*, would finally show the Jews "the brother whom they had not received" (Steinberg 1983:135). Yet if Christ *did* arise circumcised, shuddered Guibert of Nogent in the twelfth century, then we all might suffer an incomplete resurrection (Bynum 1990:243). Equally horrible was the idea that any part of Christ's body remained on earth to endure putrefaction (Bynum 1991:77–78). A preputial restoration, writes Steinberg (1983:85–86, 167), would also signify victory over death.

The possibility that Christ ascended to heaven with an intact foreskin also averted a fascinating question. If Christ's foreskin remained on earth after the resurrection, then where was it? The Eucharist was a prime candidate. As an earthly materialization of Christ's body, the wafer eaten during communion could reasonably symbolize Christ's phallic remnant. Indeed, medieval paintings of Christ's circumcision sometimes represented the rite as a variant of Eucharistic devotion (J. Greenstein 1992:168–69). But the faithful yearned for something less symbolic. Many churches rose to the occasion. They boasted possession of Christ's severed foreskin (Remondino 1891:chap. 7; Saintyves 1912:169–84; Bryk 1934:23–28; Bentley 1985:138–42; Shell 1997).[17] The details of these fantasies, however convoluted, are worth summarizing.

In The Golden Legend (*Aurea Legenda*), a vast collection of hagiographies (lives of the saints) compiled by Jacobus de Voragine in 1275, an angel presents Christ's foreskin to Charlemagne. The king "solemnly enshrined it at Aix-la-Chapelle, in the church of Our Lady." From there, the foreskin traveled to the Church of Saint John Lateran in Rome.[18] "At the end of the fourteenth century," writes Sumption (1975:46), "the Swedish visionary St. Bridget enjoyed a revelation in which the Virgin assured her" of its authenticity. In 1527, a German soldier filched the prepuce during the sack of Rome, then confessed on his deathbed. The papacy initiated a search. Magdalena de Strozzi located the sealed container, which emitted a pleasant aroma. When she held it aloft, her hands stiffened like stone (Remondino 1891:chap. 7; Saintyves 1912:77; Bentley 1985:139). Only "a young girl of great sweetness" could open the box. Thieves later filched a piece of the relic. In consequence, they encountered a tempest so fierce that they feared their last hour. Today, the whereabouts of this foreskin are unknown.

The fictitious, anonymous fourteenth-century work *Mandeville's Travels* tells a different legend (chap. 12). King Charles the Bald takes the Charlemagne prepuce to Paris, then to Peyters, Chartres, and finally to the French Abbey of Charroux in 788 (Saintyves 1912:179; Bentley 1985:139).[19] This foreskin renewed fertility and eased birth. Its worship merited a papal indulgence—an honor that might instead have been granted, as per Sumption (1975:46), to the Holy Prepuce at Boulogne. At any rate, the Charroux foreskin was lost during the Huguenot destruction in the 1560s and rediscovered in 1856 (Saintyves 1912:180). A new church was dedicated to the foreskin in 1862. Alas, this prepuce also disappeared.

The Benedictine abbey at Coulombs, in the diocese of Chartres, housed another claimant to the Holy Foreskin. Henry V allegedly borrowed this relic to assist his wife, Catherine of Valois, during the birth of their child in 1421. When Henry presented the foreskin to Sainte-Chapelle in Paris for safekeeping during war, King Louis XI took a bow. Eventually, the relic was returned to Coulombs. It vanished in the nineteenth century.

The Italian parish of Calcata displayed another Holy Prepuce. By the late nineteenth century, though, the Vatican's patience with these phallic trophies had worn thin. In 1900, Rome threatened to excommunicate anyone who spoke about the Calcata foreskin (Bentley 1985:141–42). It was purloined in 1983.

The Holy Prepuce also surfaced in a church near Antwerp and at the Cathedral of Puy in Velay and elsewhere. A common test for foreskinned authenticity, reports Collin de Plancy in his early nineteenth century *Dictionnaire critique des reliques et des images miraculeuses*, was taste (Shell 1997:347). A physician, supervised by a priest, sampled the skin for the flavor of genuine holiness. The taster was called a *croque-prépuce*, or "foreskin cruncher."

Further candidates for the Holy Prepuce are listed in Alfons Viktor Mueller's book *Die "hochheilige" Vorhaut Christi im Kult und in der Theologie der Papstkirche*, published in Berlin in 1907. Mueller, a Dominican monk, registers foreskins at Metz, Hildensheim, Bruegge, Besancon, and elsewhere, many of which were earlier mentioned on page 13 of Henry Foulis's 1677 treatise *The history of Romish treasons and usurpations*.

G. W. Foote and J. M. Wheeler, two "earnest Freethinkers," mention additional foreskins in their 1887 book *Crimes of Christianity*. They also refer to an 1761 English volume, *Authentic memoirs concerning the Portuguese Inquisition*, which tells on page 166,

> the real Santo Prepucio was kept at Rome, and fell, among other things, into the hands of some soldiers, when the Duke of Bourbon's army plundered that city; that it would not suffer itself to be touched by such profane wretches; upon which, one, more penetrating than the rest, beginning to suspect the truth, sent for a pure virgin, in order to make trial of its virtue, when it readily expanded. This precious relic seems to have been lost, amidst the confusion, but was soon replaced . . .

Foote and Wheeler (1887:94) additionally mention *De Praeputio Domini Nostri Jesu Christi Diatriba*, a seventeenth-century text by Leo Allatius (properly named Leone Allacci), then custodian of the Vatican Library. Allatius, report Foote and Wheeler, claims that Christ's foreskin "ascended, like Jesus himself, and expanded into one of the rings of Saturn."

That the Holy Prepuce proved so prolific might bedevil modern science but not Catholic dogma. As Paulinus explained in the fifth century (Letter 31), the multiplicity of Holy Foreskins mirrored the miraculous ability of Christ's body to endlessly multiply as the Eucharist (Shell 1997:349). But not all clerics concurred.

Across Europe, the faithful could admire a bewildering variety of relics, including Christ's cradle, Last Supper cup, crucifixion nails, and the pots that held the water he turned into wine. Calvin mocked this fraudulent "madness" and the gullibility of the faithful in his 1543 essay "An Admonition Showing the Advantages Which Christendom Might Derive from an Inventory on Relics." Here is what he said about the Holy Prepuce:

> Luke relates that the Lord was circumcised, but it is nowhere said that the skin was preserved for relics. All ancient histories are silent respecting it, and for the space of five hundred years this subject was not once broached in the Christian Church. Where was it lying hid all the time, and how did it so suddenly burst into notice? Moreover, how came it to travel so far as Charrox? But as a proof of its genuineness, they say that some drops of blood fell from it. . . . It is plainly a mere absurdity . . . what shall we say of the prepuce which is shown at Rome, in the church of Joannes Lateranensis? As it is certain there was only one, it cannot possibly be both at Rome and Charrox.

The allure of this relic persists even today. In 1997, the London television program *Without Walls* broadcast an account of a British journalist who traveled to Italy in search of the Holy Prepuce. An Internet parody in 2000 called "The Second Coming Project" reported the cloning of Christ from various body parts, including his foreskin. And in 1998, Madeline Schwartzman released the film *Aphrodisiac*, a wonderful fantasy about the arrival of the Holy Prepuce in the most unholy of modern cities, New York.

The Jewish Load

It is not enough to view circumcision through the lens of early Christianity. We must also turn to Greek and Roman authors. Many ethnic groups practiced circumcision in late antiquity. Aristophenes mocked the foreskinless Egyptians, Phoenicians, and "vile barbarians" (*Birds* line 505; *Platus* line 265). The ancient penis alone failed definitively to identify Jew and Gentile (Cohen 1997). Still, for "Greek and Latin writers," notes Stern (1974–1984:II:443–44 n. 14), "the Jews were the circumcised *par excellence*."

Circumcision violated Hellenistic standards of foreskinned beauty (Schäfer 1997:103–5)—standards, I add, extolled today by opponents of the procedure (Hodges 2001). Roman satire was scathing (see also Stern 1974–1984; Signer 1990; L. Feldman 1993). Petronius mentions a Jewish slave in the *Satyricon* whose perfection is marred only by snoring and circumcision. (An exaggerated nose compensates for the Jew's diminished penis!) Martial's bawdy *Epigrams* scoffed at the Jew's circumcised penis—a penis that was also shunned as enormous, lecherous, and aggressively homosexual (Cohen 1996:62–63; Schäfer 1997:101–2). For the Greeks and Romans, circumcision unleashed the Jew's hypermasculine sexuality.

An infamously ribald epigram by Martial (35) mentions a slave who, in Cohen's (1996:60) translation, "has a Jewish load under his bare skin (*Iudaeum nuda sub cute pondus habet*)." Cohen (1996:62–63) identifies this "load" or "weight" as circumcision itself, which became financially burdensome after Rome enacted a Jewish tax (*fiscus Judaicus*).[20] An elderly man was even stripped before "a very crowded court, to see whether he was circumcised" (Stern 1974–1984:III:128; Smallwood 1976:376). The Spanish Inquisition used similar disrobings to identify crypto-Jews (Conversos) and crypto-Muslims who, despite coerced conversion to Catholicism, secretly retained their religious traditions (Vincent 1992:81; Shapiro 1996:32). The Nazis, too, fatally undressed suspected Jewish men. Even today, reports Kakar (1996:126), during religious riots in India, men strip potential foes to distinguish circumcised Muslims from foreskinned Hindus. The wrong penis can be fatal.

Let us return to Martial's epigram. In some Latin versions, the "Jewish load" is not "under his bare skin" but "under *no* skin," thus referring to the grotesque size and carnality of the Jew's circumcised penis (Cohen 1996:64; Schäfer 1997:100). Sallustius Neoplatonicus connected circumcision to cannibalism and incest (*De Deis et Mundo* 9:5). Most imaginatively, Pseudo-Acro claimed that circumcision originated with a medical slip by Moses' physician (*Scholia on Horace* 1.9.70; L. Feldman 1993:158). To prevent the appearance of phallic inferiority, Moses imposed the rite on all Jews!

Despite this unflattering rhetoric, most scholars do not see any systematic or widespread anti-Judaism in late antiquity (Gager 1983; L. Feldman 1993).

Ancient authors praised Jewish wisdom, courage, temperance, and justice (L. Feldman 1993:chaps. 6–8). Still, they *always* denounced circumcision.

The anonymous authors of *Historiae Augustae*, writing in the late fourth century, attributed a Jewish revolt against Rome in 132–135, called the bar Kokhba rebellion, to a ban on circumcision enacted by the emperor Hadrian.[21] But while the edict did precede rebellion, it specified "genital mutilation," not circumcision (Stern 1974–1984:III:620–21; Smallwood 1976; Rabello 1995; Schäfer 1997:103–5). The prohibition was part of a broad campaign to "civilize" ethnic groups by outlawing or legislating castration. The rabbis reviled Hadrian. He crushed the Jewish revolt, destroyed Jerusalem, and renamed the city Aelia Capitolina. Yet Hadrian opposed neither Judaism nor circumcision.

Indeed, Abusch (2003) argues that Jewish circumcision did not even exist as a legal category in Roman law until Hadrian's successor, Antoninus Pius, emended the ban to permit Jews "to circumcise" (Modestin, *Digest* 48.8.11; see also Linder 1987:99–102; B. Yoma 53b; 84a–b; B. Me'il 17a–b). For non-Jews, the ban remained in force. Violators "suffer[ed] the punishment of the castrator."

Pervasive anti-Judaism emerged *only* with the rise of Christianity. Much of this loathing was based on the Gospels. Judas Iscariot, whom Matthew (27:9) connects to Israel, betrays Christ for thirty pieces of silver (Matthew 26:14–16, 47–50; Mark 14:10–11, 43–46; Luke 22:47–48). Jews are particularly odious in the Gospel of John. The Pauline Letters are often no better (e.g., 1 Thessalonians 2:14–16). The early church fathers were worse. For John Chrysostom, Jews were dogs, thieves, keepers of taverns, and Christ killers (*Eight Homilies Against the Jews*). The reason for this increasing bitterness is the subject of much debate (see Gager 1983). But one theme remains constant from the pagan Greeks and Latins through Paul and the early church fathers: contempt for circumcision.

The idea that circumcision insulted God became official policy throughout the Western world when the emperor Constantine converted to Christianity in 312. Periodic renewals of Hadrian's ban were now aimed explicitly at Jews and circumcision. In 415, Judaism was denied its former status as a *religio* and dismissed as *superstitio* (Smallwood 1976:545). Legislation labeled circumcision a "mark of infamy" (Linder 1987:267–72). The 438 revision of Hadrian's ban denied administrative positions to the "blindly senseless" Jews lest they exercise authority over Christians. The 535 revision converted synagogues into churches. Intermarriage was banned. Whole towns of Jews were forcibly converted. Circumcision remained as odious as it was to the Roman satirists. But satire now yielded to theological hatred.

Menstruating Jewish Men

After the hegemonic rise of Christianity, the Jewish penis shifted gender. Whereas the Roman poets, we just saw, ridiculed the circumcised penis as excessively masculine, it now became contemptuously feminine. Yet it retained its dangerous qualities.

In seventeenth-century Spain, King Phillip III appointed Juan de Quiñones de Benavente to the position of magistrate (*alcalde*) over the Escorial. Among Quiñones de Benavente's many duties was the apprehension of Judaizers for the Inquisition. The Catholic Church long feared these secretive heretics since 1492, when Spain offered Jews and Moors a choice between baptism or expulsion. Quiñones de Benavente eventually composed a treatise on Judaism (Yerushalmi 1971:126–31). His thesis? Jewish men menstruated.

In earlier chapters, I situated biblical and Jewish circumcision in a cultural schema of manhood that was partly modeled after female fertility. Simply put, circumcision emulated menstruation. Yet, despite its many paradoxes, this cast of manhood was *legitimately* male. Christianity also understood Jewish circumcision as feminizing and menstrual. But in this context, the rite attested to the *illegitimacy* of Jewish masculinity.

Christian theologians such as Justin Martyr often viewed circumcision as a mark of divine punishment for rejecting the Savior (*Dialogue with Trypho* 16). Medieval Europeans employed the same logic to associate Jews with excessive blood (Johnson 1998; Beusterien 1999). These beliefs were biblically rooted. When Pilate washed his hands of Christ's blood during Jesus' trial, a Jewish mob screamed, "His blood be on us and on our children" (Matthew 27:24–25). Judas, after betraying Christ, swelled and burst so "all his bowels gushed out" (Acts 1:18–20). This condition was later understood as a bloody anus (Johnson 1998). To medieval Christians, Jews would continue to suffer these miseries as long as they spurned Christ.

Because Jews demanded the blood of Christ, wrote the thirteenth-century anatomist Thomas de Cantimpré in *Miraculorum et exemplorum memorabilium sui temporis libri duo*, they suffer their own bloody "defect." By "this inconvenient flow the impious progeny are incurably afflicted, until such time as the sinner, repenting, acknowledges the blood of Christ and is healed" (Johnson 1998:288; D. Katz 1999). The Jewish lifestyle also supposedly contributed to a surfeit of blood. Here is a thirteenth-century text, *Omnes homines*:

Because the Jews (*Judei*) are not in work or motion nor in converse with men, and also because they are in great fear because we avenge the passion of Christ our redeemer—all things produce coldness and impede digestion. For this reason much melancholic blood is generated in them, which is expelled or purged in them at the menstrual time.

The Latin word *Judei*, notes Biller (1992:198), refers to *all* Jews, regardless of gender, and *not* specifically women. Cecco d'Ascoli, a fourteenth-century Italian astrologer, is more direct (Biller 1992:198). "After the death of Christ, all Jewish men, like women, suffer menstruation."

Medieval Europeans—Jew and Christian alike—were awash in bloody beliefs and rites (Trachtenberg 1939:6–7; Zimmels 1997; D. Katz 1999). Menstrual blood was feared as a symbol of death yet drizzled into medicinal remedies and love magic. Through the prevailing one-sex model of gender (Laqueur 1990), in which female was the anatomical inversion of male, neither menstruation nor lactation was categorically confined to women. Even Christ and the rabbis, we have seen, subscribed to this androgyny, which partly accounted for male bloodletting, or phlebotomy (D. Katz 1999). The flow of blood seemed particularly strong in Portugal, home to bullfighting and the self-flagellating *disciplinantes de sangre* (Yerushalmi 1971). Everywhere, of course, the faithful drank Christ's blood during communion.

In this bloody milieu, Jews were charged with savagely violating Christian images, icons, and the Host, the very body of Christ, which Jews allegedly stabbed, slashed, hammered, pierced, sliced, whipped, boiled, burned, and stomped (Trachtenberg 1943; Zafran 1973). In most cases, the Host supposedly bled. Meanwhile, Christians themselves snatched the Host and icons for magic (Trachtenberg 1943:115). Nary a wayside crucifix, reported a sixteenth-century theologian, remained intact! Why "*these* images failed to bleed," comments Trachtenberg (1943:121), "is no doubt beside the point." Medieval Christians, so it seems, punished Jews for their own unorthodoxy.

Given the pervasiveness of blood in European culture and accusations of Host desecration, "why was it not equally plausible," asks Yerushalmi (1971:127), "that Jewish males should bleed in punishment?" After all, observed Quiñones de Benavente, the Old Testament God often disciplined the unrighteous with bodily ordeals, including hemorrhoids (1 Samuel 5–6). In addition to unnatural menstruation, Jews were also befouled with rectal conditions, skin ailments, bloodstains, birth deformities, blindness, and large noses (Yerushalmi 1971:131–33).[22] The Jews, too, emitted a fetid stench (*foetor judaicus*), cleansed only by the waters of baptism. This ungodly aroma perhaps arose from a stereotypical fondness for "filthy lucre." Indeed, the fecal connotations of money also explain the common slur "dirty Jew" (Dundes 1997). Medieval Jews were even depicted in the act of eating swine excrement and suckling from sows (Trachtenberg 1943). Like the foul devil with whom they consorted (John 8:44; Revelation 2:9; 3:9), Jews sprouted horns and tail. Many of these unholy excrescences and blights, I propose, pointed to another of the Jew's bodily disfigurements: his circumcision.

Popular tales of the Apocalypse also featured Jewish circumcision. In the tenth century, Adso of Montier-en-Der composed a widely enjoyed "Letter on the Origin and Time of the Antichrist" (Rhoads and Lupton 1999). The Archfiend, born to the Jews of Babylon, "will slay all the Christians he cannot convert to his case," then "circumcise himself and pretend that he is the son of Almighty God." In a fourth-century version of this tale by Sulpicius Severus, the Antichrist will "by law impose circumcision on all" (Second Dialogue 14). Christ always triumphs. But until then, the Jew seeks to mar the body of Christendom just as his own body is marred for refusing Christ.

Blood Libel and Circumcision

Medieval Jews were not content merely to desecrate the Host to mock the Crucifixion. They also supposedly tortured, murdered, and drank the blood of Christian boys. But it was the Jew who actually suffered through the resulting trials, executions, and massacres. The medieval blood libel even fueled the expulsion of the Jews from England in the thirteenth century. This canard, I will show, is a twisted rendition of circumcision.

The first formal allegation of Jewish ritual murder dates to the discovery of a boy's corpse near Norwich, England, in 1144. A decade later, the youth's death apotheosized into the martyrdom of William of Norwich, who now died cruelly during a mock crucifixion staged by Jews to honor Passover or dishonor Easter (Jacobs 1893:19–21; Roth 1964:9). Similar accusations soon followed. By the 1150s, tales of ritual murder regularly included forced circumcision. In 1168, for example, a boy named Harold was reputedly abducted and fatally tortured by "the Jews of all England coming together as if to circumcise" (Jacobs 1893:45–47). English ballads and legends memorialize the idea of ritual murder. In Chaucer's "The Prioress Tale," for a famous example, a Jew slashes the throat of an innocent child who sings devotional songs to the Virgin. Chaucer specifically mentions "young Hugh of Lincoln," perhaps the most infamous instance of blood libel, "slain also by cursed

Jews." Long after Edward I expelled Jews from England in 1290, tales of blood libel provided the only image of Judaism in a land emptied of Jews.

Samuel Purchas, the English clergyman and world historian, elaborately described the "Iewish crime" in *Purchase His Pilgrimage* (1626:1152–53). Around Easter, Jews would abduct and circumcise a Christian boy, then "crucife him out of their divellish malice to Christ." One boy, miraculously rescued, told how the Jews played a game of hide-and-seek with his severed prepuce. To conceal their crime, they restored his foreskin!

Purchas's account of the "Jewish crime" recurs with slight variation on pages 96 to 101 of D'Blossiers Tovey's *Anglia Judaica: Or, the History and Antiquities of the Jews in England* (1738). Here, the Bishop of Norwich "condemn'd four of the Criminal to be drawn at a Horse's Tail, and hang'd."[23] Tovey (1738:65) also reports that "one Bonefand a Jew of Bedfor was indicted, not for circumcising, but totaly cutting off the Privy member of one Richard." Finally, Tovey (1738:149) attributes Henry III's effort to convert the Jews of England to a priest besotted with a Jewish women whose parents assented to the marriage only on condition of circumcision. For Tovey, the circumcising Jew subverted Christianity and emasculated England.

Purchas and Tovey based their accounts of the "Jewish crime" on the famous chronicles of medieval England by Matthew Paris, a thirteenth-century monk. Paris's 1236–1259 *Chronica Majora*[24] thrice mentions a forced circumcision by the Jews of Norwich, each time with a different date, each time magnifying the alleged circumcision into ritual murder (Menache 1997).[25] In 1244, reports Paris, Jews inscribed a Hebrew phrase into their victim's flesh (*English History* 2:21–22; Roth 1964:55–56; Menache 1997:148). Typically, the guilty party was collective: *all* the Jews of England. Typically, too, the victim was canonized.

Initially, it was said, Jews sought Christian blood to magically ease their bodily afflictions from the betrayal of Christ. Over time, though, they used this blood for other nefarious purposes—to color the pale cheeks of their daughters, to mix into a Passover dish, to anoint their dead in case Christ really is the messiah, and so forth (Trachtenberg 1943). But the Jews make "a miserable mistake," wrote Thomas Calvert, a Yorkshire minister in his 1648 pamphlet "The Blessed Jew of Marocco: Or, A Blackmoor Made White." The Jews "shed Christian blood by murder, rather than to seek Christs blood by faith."

Hungarian Jews supposedly enhanced fertility by strangling Christian virgins with the strands of phylacteries, then smearing the blood on their children's genitals (Trachtenberg 1943:151). This accusation of ritual murder, I suggest, transforms circumcision, a rite that promotes progeny by cutting a young Jew's penis, into a fatal assault by Jews onto youthful Gentile genitals. The Spanish blood libel also suggests anxiety about Jewish circumcision, especially in regard to the secret conversion of Christian and Muslim slaves (Baer 1992:II:11, 48, 361). Fernando de la Plaza, reports Baer (1992:II:290), a fifteenth-century Franciscan, boasted of gathering one hundred Christian foreskins wickedly snipped by Jews.[26] Jews during the Spanish Inquisition "confessed" to healing circumcision with Christian blood (Trachtenberg 1943:149–50). A popular drama in seventeenth-century Germany, the *Endingen Judenspiel*, commemorated one such fictional event from 1470 (Trachtenberg 1943:150–51). The Jews, wrote Antonio Bonfini, the court historian to King Mathias Corvinus of Hungary, believed that "the blood of a Christian was a good remedy for the alleviation of the wound of circumcision" (D. Katz 1999:454). The *mohel* who cuts a Jewish boy's penis has now expanded grotesquely into a wide-ranging fear that all Jews seek to cut the lifeblood from Christianity. Indeed, Calvin's exposé of relics, which I discussed earlier, mentions an "impious knife" used by a Jew to stab the Communion wafer. The "Parisans regard [it] with greater veneration than the host itself."

European artists widely depicted the "Jewish crime." In a fifteenth-century woodcut depicting the Jewish murder of Simon of Trent, an elderly and bearded man named Moses cuts the boy's penis. Blood drips into a dish. In another fifteenth-century image of the same ritual murder, where the Jews wear pig badges, the victim again clearly suffers the slicing away of the tip of his penis. In both instances, the fatal circumcision occupies the center of the illustration.[27] From whence did these fantasies arise?

During communion, the faithful ritually kill and sip the blood of a young Jewish man, namely, Christ. Through "projective inversion," argues Dundes (1991b), Christians displace their guilt over this deicide by accusing Jews of murdering and drinking the blood of young Christian boys. Another source for the idea of ritual murder was prosaic ethnocentrism inflamed by the specific image of the Jew as a Christ killer. I now suggest that various aspects of Jewish ceremonial life, when viewed through a lens tinted by anti-Semitism, also fueled the blood libel.

Earlier, I discussed the importance of knives and blood in rabbinic circumcision and kosher butchery. To a medieval merchant or peasant, the fate of kosher animals also perhaps awaited infant boys.

Additionally, two moments in the circumcision ceremony likely inflamed a populace already committed to the reality of Jewish ritual murder. First,

Jews *do* sip real or symbolic blood, accompanied, moreover, by a liturgical affirmation of healing (chapter 7). After the rise of Christianity, in fact, Jews muted the bloody symbolism of ritual wine in reaction to the Eucharist (Hoffman 1996:90). So fearful were some Jews of the blood libel in the sixteenth and seventeenth centuries that they ceased drinking red wine altogether during the Passover *seder* (Gross 1995:173–74). This wine, we have seen, partly symbolizes the blood of Egyptian firstborns (chapter 7). Similarly, the rabbis frequently equated the bloods of circumcision and the paschal sacrifice (chapter 5). Regardless of what these symbols meant to medieval Jews, they perhaps signified something more sinister to Christians.

The second moment during the circumcision ceremony that possibly contributed to accusations of ritual murder was when the *mohel* sucked the infant's wound and expectorated the blood into a goblet. To the uneducated folk of medieval Europe, this gesture conceivably appeared murderous, even cannibalistic. Finally, recall the image of a medieval Jewish father carrying his son, enwrapped in a prayer shawl, to the boy's initiation into religious education (chapter 6). To non-Jews, this procession could have conjured abduction.

Three circumcision objects also perchance pointed to ritual murder. The *mohel* sometimes draped a bloody towel above the synagogue doorway (chapter 7). Gross (1995) proposes that this custom disappeared after the thirteenth century in response to the blood libel. The *mohel*, too, placed the severed foreskin in a small bowl. Paintings of Christ's circumcision often included this vessel. In depictions of ritual murder, though, the same bowl captures the Christian victim's blood (Zafran 1973:60–61). Finally, circumcision requires a knife. This instrument is conspicuously displayed in portraits of Christ's circumcision and, not surprisingly, ritual murder.

The tragic fate of some Jewish communities after Pope Urban II called for the First Crusade in 1096 also contributed to charges of ritual murder. Christian mobs swept across the Rhineland, forcing Jewish communities into baptism or massacre. Many Jews opted for self-inflicted martyrdom. They slew their own children, then themselves. These suicides were phrased as enactments of the ancient Temple sacrifices (Marcus 1996:100–101). To maintain biblical purity, Jews of the Rhineland preferred their own blades to Christian swords. The Chronicle of Solomon bar Simson, a Jewish account of the massacre at Mainz, alludes in various ways to circumcision. It refers to the murderous Christian mob as "the uncircumcised" and tells that two Jewish daughters sharpened their knife "so that it would have no notch," then offered their throats to their mother. In the Chronicle of Rabbi Eliezer bar

Nathan, a father pronounces the benediction for ritual slaughter over his son.[28]

Christian fears of ritual murder also found support in the Hebrew Bible, especially the sacrifice of Isaac (Zafran 1973:chap. 2). If the Jews killed Christ and cut down their own children, why would they not also slice, circumcise, and murder Christians?

Let me be clear that I am *not* suggesting that Jews themselves directly contributed to the blood libel. I am *not* blaming the victims. Rather, I am simply proposing that aspects of Jewish ritual could appear to suggest ritual murder when viewed through a non-Jewish lens of ignorance and bigotry. Ethnocentrism, then or now, has few limits.

The Shakespearian Prick

Popular views of circumcision and menstruating Jewish men color even the plays of Shakespeare. "If you prick us," asks Shylock famously in *The Merchant of Venice*, "do we not bleed?" The Jewish moneylender's rhetorical question seemingly affirmed the oneness of humanity. Jew and Christian are ultimately the same. But Shylock lied. To Shakespeare's audience, Jews *were* different.

First, Jewish men menstruated, a medieval belief still current in Elizabethan England. If you prick Jews, they bleed. But if you don't prick them, they also bleed, men and women alike! Second, the Jewish body was marked by circumcision. Shakespeare wrote *The Merchant of Venice* in 1597. By then, the word "prick" had become a vulgar term for the penis (D. Katz 1999:460–61). Shylock's prick was pricked. Third, "pricks" also referred to Hebrew vowel points and cantillation marks, thus tying Shylock's tongue, like that of Moses, to his penis. Shylock's appeal to universal brotherhood ironically excluded male Jews by invoking a prick that is thrice pricked through circumcision, male menstruation, and scriptural chanting.

In the play, Shylock usuriously loans 300 ducats to an honest Christian merchant, Antonio. When Shylock's daughter later flees with Antonio, the moneylender cries, "My daughter! O my ducats! . . . A sealed bag, two sealed bags of ducats. Of double ducats. . . . And jewels, two stones, two rich and precious stones." Shylock laments the loss of his purse, a word that also meant scrotum, which held two stones, or the euphemistic "family jewels" (Shell 1997:350). One of Christ's own foreskins was sealed in a gilded case called the Purse Reliquary of the Circumcision (Gauthier 1986:17–19 and ill. 3). When Shylock hopes to "catch" Antonio "on the hip," moreover, he invokes Jacob's wrestling wound (chapter 4), itself a metaphoric circumcision.

The most notorious allusion to circumcision in *The Merchant of Venice* occurs when Shylock menacingly demands, should Antonio default on the loan, "an equal pound, Of your fair flesh, to be cut off and taken, In what part of your body pleaseth me" (act 1, scene 3). By threatening to slice Antonio's "flesh," a biblical term for the penis, Shylock evokes the fearful image of the Jewish circumciser. Pay the Jew, or become one! By later targeting not Antonio's groin but his breast (act 2, scene 1), Shylock mocks Saint Paul's metaphoric "circumcision of the heart" (Shapiro 1996:121–22).[29] Ironically, the true emasculator was the Christian state (Shapiro 1996:122). Felons were often hung, then castrated.

Shapiro's masterful *Shakespeare and the Jews* (1996) furnishes crucial background to *The Merchant of Venice*. Shylock impersonates long-standing English anxiety over Jews and circumcision. In Alexander Silvayn's *The Orator*, translated from French into English in 1596, a Jew threatens to absolve a debt by severing a Christian's "privy members," which "would altogether weigh a just pound." Gregorio Leti included a similar incident in his 1680 revision of *The Life of Pope Sixtus the Fifth*. More noteworthy is the frontispiece of Thomas Coryate's account of his European travels, *Coryate's Crudities* (1611), during which time he failed to convert Venetian Jewry to Christianity. The illustration depicts Coryate fleeing a knife-wielding Jew.[30] Despite widespread horror at circumcision, notes Shapiro, many Englishmen relished the opportunity to witness the rite (see also Frojmovic 2003). In the end, of course, Shylock takes no flesh. The Jew converts to Christianity. Once again, recognizes Shapiro (1996:13), the waters of baptism cleanse the blood of circumcision.

Circumcision also surfaces in Shakespeare's tragedy *Othello*, named for a Moorish convert to Christianity. Othello recalls how he "took by th'throat the circumcised dog, And smote him" (act 5, scene 2). This foreskinless cur was a Muslim, not a Jew, "a malignant and turbaned Turk" who "Beat a Venetian [read Christian] and traduced the state." Yet the canine imagery derives from the letters of Paul.[31] When Othello dies by his own sword, Lupton (1997:84) sees a literal "circumcision of the heart" since it was Othello's besmirched penis, not his dark skin, that ultimately excluded him from Christian Europe.[32]

"We are villains both," says the Jew named Barabas to his Muslim confidant in Christopher Marlowe's play *The Jew of Malta* (1588–1590). "Both circumcised, we hate Christians both" (act 2, scene 3). Earlier in the scene,

Barabas sneers about "swine-eating Christians, Unchosen nation, never circumcis'd." The message is clear: Jew and Muslim unite in circumcision
against Christianity.

Circumcising Coins

Derisive references to Jewish circumcision permeate European literature.
Examples include *Tristram Shandy* (bk. 5, chap. 28), Rabelais's *Five Books of
the Lives, Heroic Deeds and Sayings of Gargantua and His Son Pantagruel* (bk.
3, chap. 18), Voltaire's *Candide* (chap. 8), Walter Scott's *Ivanhoe*, George
Elliot's *Daniel Deronda* (Carpenter 1988), Joyce's *Ulysses* (Derrida 1992),
Hogarth's *A Harlot's Progress*, and the poetry of Ezra Pound (Gilman
1995:74), Thomas Browne (Saunders 2000), and Robert Burns.[33] English
writers ridiculed Jews as "the circumcised Sons of Eve" and the "fore-skinne
clippers" (Wolper 1982:29; Felsenstein 1995:146). They identified the whole
Jewish people, men *and* women, by a deviant penis. Jews also displayed an
inferior intellect by reading the biblical command to circumcise literally. By
contrast, Christians interpreted Scripture through sophisticated literary
devices such as allegory and pun (Ellis 1995:66). The marred Jewish penis
thus pointed to an equally inferior mind.

The viciousness of foreskinned wit peaked in England during the 1753
debate over the Jewish Naturalization Act. This legislation applied only to a
handful of foreign-born Jews (Felsenstein 1995:188). Nonetheless, the "Jew
Bill" unleashed a spate of parodies that ridiculed the Jews as cunning, blasphemous, disloyal, and promiscuous (Wolper 1982; Felsenstein 1995; Shapiro 1996:chap. 7; Dresser 1998). Opponents of the "Jew Bill" especially
targeted circumcision, reviving, in many cases, the medieval blood libel.[34]
Here is one ditty from the *London Evening Post*:

> When mighty Roast Pork was the Englishman's Food,
> It ennobled our Veins and enriched our Blood.
> And a Jew's Dish of Foreskins was not understood.
> Then Britons be wise at the critical Pinch,
> And in such a Cause be not Cowards and Flinch,
> But the best of your Property guard ev'ry Inch.[35]

What the Jews truly wanted was not citizenship but the emasculation of
England.

In the early eighteenth century, Alexander Pope wrote a pamphlet, A

Strange but True Relation How Edmund Curll, of Fleet street, Stationer, Out of an extraordinary Desire of Lucre, went into Change Alley, and was converted from the Christian Religion by certain Eminent Jews: And how he was circumcis'd and initiated into their Mysteries.[36] Unfortunately, "the unmanly Ceremonial" castrated poor Curll. The "barbarous and cruel Jews" cast him out, wanting for pennies and penis.

The inflammatory rhetoric surrounding the "Jew Bill" similarly linked circumcision to lucre—and, not surprisingly, to Shylock. In *The Christian's New Warning Piece: or, A Full and True Account of the Circumcision of Sir E.T. Bart,* an ambitious young Briton, eyeing a seat in Parliament, foolishly courts wealthy Jews. The "Enemies of Christianity" agree to lend support in exchange for a foreskin and assistance in transforming England into "New Jerusalem." But the prepuce disappears, and the "barbarous and merciless Jews" revoke the contract. Sir E.T. becomes another victim to circumcised greed and treachery.

Cartoons opposing the "Circumcision Bill" lampooned the Jews as butchers brandishing knives and razors.[37] Opponents of the act often invoked the circumcision episode of Genesis 34—neglecting, of course, to mention Dinah's rape. This rhetorical move, dating to the third-century "Testaments of the Twelve Patriarchs," casts circumcision as massacre.[38] When the "Jew Bill" was repealed in 1753, one editorial cartoon gleefully depicted a circumcision knife (Felsenstein 1995:213). The blade is broken.

Circumcision was not the only cut associated with English Jews. Matthew Paris's 1247 *Chronica majora* reported on "coins being clipped by circumcised people and infidel Jews who, because of the heavy royal taxes, were reduced as beggars"[39] (see also *English History* 2:340–41). Numerous English Jews in the thirteenth century were tried, convicted, and killed for clipping coins. This fiduciary outrage, along with the blood libel, contributed to the 1290 expulsion. A relentless tirade against readmission by William Prynne in 1656, *A Short Demurrer to the Jewes,* reminds readers of Jewish coin clipping as well as "blasphemies, apostasies . . . circumcising and crucifying Christian children . . . extortion, brokage, usury, frauds, unconscionable Jewish cutthroat dealing, and discrepancy of manners from the English." A similar caricature later appeared visually in a 1912 issue of the patently anti-Semitic periodical *Kikeriki! Vienna Humoristic People's Paper (Kikeriki! Wiener humoristisches Volksblatt).* The cartoon depicts a disheveled and bearded Jew, complete with long earlocks and enormously exaggerated nose and lips, snipping the corner from a coin.[40] The title of the cartoon is "The Circumcision."

A poem in a 1753 anthology, *A Collection of the Best Pieces and Verse*

Against the Naturalization of the Jews, includes "In brave Edward's days they were caught in a gin, For clipping our coin, now to ad sins to sin, As they've got all our pelf, they'd be clipping our skin" (Shapiro 1996:210). *Joe Miller's Jests; or, the Wits Vade-Mecum*, a hugely successful 1739 anthology that underwent some twenty editions, is more to the point:

> What is to clip a thing but to pare it round? And what is paring round called in scripture, but circumcision? And who . . . dares practise circumcision, but one that has actually renounced the Christian-Religion, and is a Jew, a most obstinate and perverse Jew in his heart? (Felsenstein 1995:140)

Even after the fear of coin clipping subsided, writes Dresser (1998:76), the clipped Jews continued to snip away at the English body politic, only now through the more skillful means of political bribery.[41]

In broad strokes, my argument in this chapter was singular and simple: the image of the knife-wielding Jew, intent on emasculating Christian bodies and nations, is a time-honored European tradition. This hoary image, moreover, has influenced nearly all significant anti-Jewish canards in European history. It extends back through medieval culture to the early church fathers, the Letters of Paul, and even the ancient Greeks and Romans. Throughout this diverse history, one element remains stable: fear of the circumcised, circumcising Jew.

The rise of the Enlightenment did little to dampen the ideology of dangerous Jewish deformity (Gilman 1991d, 1993a; Efron 2001). Medieval tails, horns, and odor yielded to epilepsy, plague, long noses, thick lips, warts, swarthy or pale complexions, and crooked feet. The Jew, too, as a fidgety coward and an oversexed masturbator, suffered a perverse psyche. Like gypsies, homosexuals, criminals, blacks, and the insane, Jews stooped before the erect ideals of white, Christian, European manhood. Despite these new attributes, the Jew's deformed penis remained the definitive sign of his bodily, moral, and intellectual impairments. All Jewish differences ultimately pointed to a diminished penis.

The relationship between circumcision and European history seems best encapsulated by a Hebrew folktale from Galicia (Klein 1998:214–15). A Gentile girl, employed by a priest, accuses a wealthy Jew of fathering her son. She sues for child support, and wins. As the court sentences the Jew to prison, his lawyer unsheathes a knife. "If the child is truly a Jew, then he must be circumcised. Place him on the table, and I'll do it right now!" Terrified, the girl burst into tears, falls at the feet of the priest, and prays, "Do you want your child to become a Jew and be circumcised?" The Jew is acquitted.

Notes

1. On eBay, an evangelical minister offered a self-published sermon provocatively titled *Jesus Christ: The Foreskin of Humanity*.

2. During the circumcision ceremony, the *mohel* refers to a prenatal consecration that responded to, or perhaps influenced, early Christianity; compare Hoenig (1963) and Hoffman (1996:116–21) with Flusser and Safrai (1980).

3. That one cannot literally circumcise ears, lips, and heart was proof to Origen that all forms of circumcision are allegorical (*Commentary on the Epistle to the Romans* 2:13:24–25).

4. Paul circumcised one disciple, Timothy, presumably to appeal to a local Jewish population (Acts 16:1–3).

5. Elliott (2003) sees Paul's criticism of circumcision in Galatians as ultimately directed at the self-castrating rites of Cybele and Attis in Anatolia.

6. From James M. Robinson, ed., *The Nag Hammadi Library*, rev. ed. (San Francisco: HarperCollins, 1990).

7. For circumcision and baptism, see Vermes (1958), Neusner (1970), Flusser and Safrai (1980), and Hoffman (1996). An anonymous Jewish text from the late thirteenth century draws on Ezekiel 16:6 and Zechariah 9:11 to uphold salvation through the blood of circumcision, not the water of baptism (Berger 1996:92).

8. Since men are more lustful than women, argued Philo, and derive greater sexual pleasure, only they require circumcision. The rite also constrains male pride lest fathers attribute new life to themselves and not God.

9. Since medieval culture feminized fleshiness, Christ's foreskin was female (Bynum 1987:178), much like the biblical prepuce (chapter 4).

10. Medieval female mystics displayed bloody stigmata and practiced bodily mortifications that, like Christ's wounds upon the Cross, evoked the maternal breast (Bynum 1987:273; Carroll 1987). Christ's milk was seminal in the second-century Odes of Solomon (Engelbrecht 1999).

11. Medieval female ascetics renounced sexuality and food, surviving only by ingesting the Host (Bynum 1987). They also dined on lice, leprous bathwater, and pus. These transformations of the putrid into the pure recall rabbinic tales of rotting yet fragrant foreskins.

12. In 1970, Pope VI changed this feast day to the Solemnity of Mary.

13. A somewhat lighthearted debate arose during the 1970s in the *Journal of the American Medical Association* over the foreskinned state of Michelangelo's *David*!

14. Excerpted from Martin H. Bertram, "On The Jews and Their Lies," in *Luther's Works*, vol. 47 (Philadelphia: Fortress Press, 1971).

15. See *Agnes Blannbekin, Viennese Beguine: Life and Revelations*, translated by Ulrike Wiethaus (Cambridge: D.S. Brewer, 2002), chapter 37.

16. Novatian, a third-century Roman Presbyter, argued against the Jewish dietary laws by equating Christ with "true, and holy, and pure" meat ("On the Jewish Meats" 5).

17. In a fifth-century composition titled the "First Gospel of the Infancy of Jesus Christ," an old Hebrew woman preserves Christ's foreskin in an alabaster box of spikenard oil. "Mary the sinner" anointed Christ's head and feet with this oil, then wiped it off with her hair.

18. See *The Golden Legend of Jacobus de Voragine*, translated from the Latin by Granger Ryan and Helmut Ripperger (New York: Arno Press, 1969), 82.

19. See *Mandeville's Travels*, edited by M. C. Seymour (Oxford: Clarendon Press, 1967), chapter 11, 61, lines 10–14, and 239 n. 61/11.

20. The 1432 Synod of Castilian Jews also taxed circumcision, as well as other Jewish practices, to fund religious education (Baer 1992:II:261).

21. A famous rabbinic story tells about the circumcised conversion to Judaism by Hadrian's nephew (T-Y Exodus 6:5).

22. In 1673, Isaac Fernando Cardoso defended circumcision against these accusations in *Las excelencias delos Hebreos*. The rite remedied the sin of Adam and Eve and protected against the very ailments that supposedly afflicted Jews (Yerushalmi 1971:409, 434–35).

23. Astonishingly, a book on circumcision by a medical historian asks, "Was there any basis for Purchas's tale? Certainly there are indications of bizarre practices" (Gollaher 2000:40). But all Gollaher offers in the way of "indications" is Tovey's retelling of Purchas!

24. See J. A. Giles, *Matthew Paris's English History*, 3 vols. (London: Henry G. Bohn, 1852). Shapiro (1996:111) discusses other English references to the "Jewish crime" in the sixteenth and seventeenth centuries.

25. Paris's accounts of the forced circumcision at Norwich were echoed in the 1240 *Chronica Buriensis* (see *The Chronicle of Bury St. Edmunds 1212–1301*, by Antonia Gransden [London: Nelson, 1964], 10).

26. The Spanish Inquisition obsessed about Converso circumcisions, which sometimes occurred, despite the penalty of torture (Yerushalmi 1971:37–38; Baer 1992:II). Circumcision was a common topic for collections of bawdy Converso poems called Cancioneros (Yovel 1998).

27. The first image is from a facsimile of Hartmann Schedel's *Nuremburg Chronicle* or *Buch der Chroniken*, printed by Anton Koberger in 1493, now held at Kenyon College. It is widely depicted on the Internet (e.g., www.flholocaustmuseum.org/history_wing/anti semitism/crusades.cfm). For the second illustration, see Arthur M. Hind, *Early Italian Engraving: A Critical Catalogue with Complete Reproduction of All The Prints Described* (London, 1938–1948), plate 74, and Zafran (1973).

28. For both chronicles, see *The Jews and The Crusaders: The Hebrew Chronicles of the First and Second Crusades*, translated and edited by Shlomo Eidelberg (Madison: University of Wisconsin Press, 1977).

29. Two other penile puns in *The Merchant of Venice*: penniless Antonio refers to himself as a "tainted wether of the flock," or a castrated ram, and Shylock's Jewish financier is named Tubal, pronounced "two-balls" (Shapiro 1996:122; Shell 1997:351).

30. I am at a loss to explain how any scholar, such as Robert Darby, can cite Shapiro and still fail to mention anti-Semitism when surveying Christian opposition to circumcision (www.historyofcircumcision.net). One can only assume that, for opponents of circumcision today, Shylock remains no fiction. It is hoped that Darby's book on circumcision in Britain will prove more judicious (Darby 2005).

31. Robert Dabore's 1612 play *A Christian Turn'd Turke* also taunted Muslim circumcision. A forged eleventh-century letter, allegedly sent from the Byzantine emperor to Robert of Flanders, claimed that Muslims brutally circumcised Christian boys over baptismal fonts (Joranson 1950:813).

32. An undated postcard from eBay portrays a Victorian-era circumcision, accompanied by a line from Hamlet: "There's a Divinity that shapes our ends." Interestingly, the same exact connection was made by J. Jackson Clarke in "A Lecture on Circumcision," *The Polyclinic* 9 (1905):76–78.

33. For Hemingway's *The Sun Also Rises*, see Goldman (1984).

34. Across the Channel, the antireligious fervor of the Reign of Terror and the Thermidorian Reaction also censored Jewish circumcision (Helfand 1984:365).

35. Unless otherwise noted, all excerpts in this section derive from Wolper (1982).

36. *The Prose Works of Alexander Pope*, vol. 1, edited by N. Ault (Oxford: Basil Blackwell, 1936) 317–22.

37. Believing himself underpaid by his Jewish publisher, Beethoven allegedly commented on the brevity of Opus 135, "If [he] sends circumcised ducats he shall have a circumcised quartet"!

38. William Colbett, editor of the Federalist newspapers in New York City and Philadelphia, wrote that Democrats, in alliance with the Jews, wanted to circumcise Christians (Marcus 1989:527).

39. See *Chronicles of Matthew Paris: Monastic Life in the Thirteenth Century*, translated by Richard Vaughan (New York: St. Martins Press, 1984).

40. For a reprint of the cartoon, and an English translation, see Morton Irving Seiden, *The Paradox of Hate: A Study in Ritual Murder* (South Brunswick: Thomas Toseloff, 1967).

41. Circumcision to a nineteenth-century German pamphleteer suggested a way to save the "welfare of the nation:" castration, "we're only talking here about a couple more snips" (Geller 1997:185–86 n. 20).

CHAPTER NINE

Circumcision Contentions in Contemporary Judaism

n William Tenn's science fiction story, "On Venus, Have We Got a Rabbi," the future Interstellar Zionist Congress debates the essential definition of ewishness.[1] The issue was prompted by the descendants of a group of Jews from Paramus, New Jersey, who long ago traveled to the fourth planet of the tar Rigel. They physically assimilated with the local creatures. Yet they continue to assert a Jewish identity, even circumcising "a very little bit from the tip of their shortest tentacle."

For many Jews, declares Hoffman (1996:11), ritual circumcision (*brit milah*) is the "one eternal verity" of Jewish culture. Refusal "borders on heresy." As the founder of the nontheistic Humanistic Judaism movement writes, "To announce to your fellow-Jews that you intend to remain a ham-eating atheist is far less traumatic than to declare that you intend to leave your son uncircumcised" (Wine 1998:4). Many Jews agree with the seventeenth-century philosopher Baruch Spinoza, who declared circumcision in his *Theological Political Treatise* "so important . . . that it alone would preserve the nation forever." But many Jews also disagree with Spinoza. Today, as I now review, circumcision once again rents the Jewish community in bitter dispute.

Citizenship and Circumcision

In 1814, the Congress of Vienna convened to regulate the affairs of post-Napoleonic Europe. On the agenda was the status of European Jews, who increasingly demanded legal equality. But the Congress refused to grant Jews the full "rights of citizenship," settling instead for lesser "civil rights" (Philipson 1931:108). Still, this declaration set in motion a process that, despite bitter strife and anti-Jewish rioting, led to emancipation for European Jewry by the end of the century.

Yet citizenship and circumcision often seemed antithetical. For many Europeans, circumcision exemplified Judaism's stubborn resistance to modernity. Assimilated and reformist Jews concurred. Not only did this tribal rite separate Jews from their fellow citizens, but traditional circumcision methods, especially *metzitzah*, or "sucking," violated modern standards of hygiene, aesthetics, and ethics. Particularly troubling were increasing reports of circumcision fatalities due to unsanitary procedures and unscrupulous *mohels*. The practice warranted abandonment or, at the very least, modification.

When Henry Levien excoriated ritual circumcision in the *Medical Record* for 1894 as "an act of cruelty and barbarism," he advocated not abolition but merely regulation.[2] Not only did many Jewish physicians advocate for the cessation or modification of oral *metzitzah*, but they also pleaded for the replacement by surgical instruments of the *mohel's* sharpened fingernail (Gilman 1993a:60; Katz 1998a:364; Efron 2001:225–27; Judd 2003). By thus synthesizing tradition and modernity, circumcision would no longer challenge the Enlightenment ideals of rationality, science, and progressive morality. Rather, a modernized version of circumcision would finally cut the Jew into European society.

Traditional Jews fumed at their reformist coreligionists, especially on the issue of oral *metzitzah* (Katz 1998a). For one, circumcision *should* cut off Jews from the wider society. For another, appeals to rationality and modern hygiene undermined the authority of God and the rabbis. Even today, as I noted in the previous chapter, some advocates of oral *metzitzah* (e.g., Goldberger 1991) scoff at critics who boast greater medical knowledge than the Almighty.[3]

Circumcision was bitterly attacked in Paolo Mantegazza's influential study of human sexuality in the 1880s. In *The Sexual Relations of Mankind*, Mantegazza railed against masturbation, lesbianism, sodomy, homosexuality, and especially male circumcision (1935:98–99). The Jewish rite "is a sanguinary protest against universal brotherhood." Until Jews forsake this "odious brand . . . you cannot pretend to be our equal." The intelligentsia widely endorsed the view of circumcision as a token of Jewish separatism and barbarism (Gilman 1995:79–80). Like prostitution, another Jewish scourge, *metzitzah* attested to the Jew's inherent sexual deviance—an abnormality said to pose a serious danger to society through the spread of syphilis (Taylor 1873; Gilman 1993a:60–69; Judd 2003). The Jew can join humanity only when he sculpts his body, erotic desires, and psyche into the Euro-Christian norm—when he forsakes, in other words, circumcision.

Reluctant Admiration

Ironically, circumcision also sustained the very modern ideals it so often seemed to violate. In 1710, an anonymous physician and cleric published *Onania; Or, the Heinous Sin of Self-Pollution, and All Its Frightful Consequences, in both Sexes, Considered, with Spiritual and Physical Advice to those, who have already injar'd themselves by this abominable Practice. And reasonable Admonition to the Youth of the Nation (of both Sexes) and those whose Tuition they are under, whether Parents, Guardians, Masters, or Mistresses.* Self-pollution, asserted the author, spawned gonorrhea, watery seed, distemper, fainting, fits, impotence, consumption, incontinence, promiscuity, and death. Masturbation assaulted mind, body, nation, and "Christian Purity."

Far more influential was Simon-Andre Tissot's 1766 book *Onanism: Or, A Treatise upon the Disorders Produced by Masturbation: Or, the Dangerous Effect of Secret and Excessive Venery,* revised in 1775. Masturbation now led to melancholy, catalpsy, epilepsy, imbecility, and the fatal decay of the nervous system. Within a few decades, Victorian Americans and Britons linked masturbation to a host of psychological, moral, and physiological maladies, including alcoholism, asthma, gout, headaches, spinal curvature, polio, phimosis, and chronic ear infection. By disrupting the economy of vital male fluids, writes Laqueur (1990:228–29), masturbation prevented men from erecting the moral pillars of society, namely, work, marriage, and reproduction. As a solitary vice, moreover, onanism shockingly violated the Aristotlean dictum that man is a social animal.

The reigning nineteenth-century theory of disease, called "reflex nervous theory" or "reflex neurosis," attributed illness to disturbances in the equilibrium of the nervous system, especially at sensitive bodily sites such as the genitals. This paradigm explains the first consequential medical circumcision. In 1870, Dr. Lewis A. Sayre, puzzled by a boy's partial paralysis and overall ill health, prepared to administer a diagnostic electric current to test the leg reflexes (Sayre 1870). "Oh, doctor!," cautioned the nurse, "be very careful—don't touch his pee-pee—it's very sore." Sayre then noticed an infected foreskin and performed an unanticipated circumcision. The boy gained his health and mobility, which Sayre attributed to the circumcised "quieting [of] his nervous system." Thereafter, Sayre tirelessly championed medical circumcision and eventually assumed the presidency of the American Medical Association.

By the 1880s, physicians on both sides of the Atlantic promoted the routine circumcision of boys as a broad hygienic measure and a specific prophylaxis against syphilis (Crossland 1891; Wolbarst 1914; see also Gollaher 2000). One proponent (Ricketts 1894) even fashioned himself after the biblical David, who brought 200 non-Jewish foreskins to Saul! The allure of circumcision was as much moral as medical. Jews, noted S. G. A. Brown (1896–1897), rarely "figure in silly crimes, police or divorce courts." Many advocates of medical circumcision were stirred by evangelical sentiments (Darby 2001). For them, the benefit of the procedure was that it would create not more Jews but less sinful Christians.[4]

Perhaps the strongest endorsement of routine circumcision was Remondino's *History of Circumcision from the Earliest Times to the Present. Moral and Physical Reasons for its Performance, with a History of Eunuchism, Hermaphrodism, Etc., and of the Different Operations Practiced Upon the Prepuce* (1891). Here, circumcision protects against tuberculosis, syphilis, gonorrhea, phimosis, nocturnal enuresis, dysuria, penile cancer, feeblemindedness, nervous ailments, impotence, and, of course, masturbation. The foreskinless enjoyed longer lives, fewer doctor bills, and an "euthanasian death."

Circumcision quickly emerged as a bodily mark of modernity. The procedure, too, helped legitimate the new medical professions and eased parental anxieties over the emerging concepts of childhood purity and teenage sexuality (Hare 1962; Neuman 1975; Paige 1978; Hall 1992; Gollaher 2000). Circumcision also contributed to the rise of the "therapeutic state," which phrases social control through ideologies of health (Szasz 1996). In Britain, moreover, circumcision offered "moral restraint" to a middle-class seeking to define itself against the "debauched aristocracy and the degenerate working classes" (Moscucci 1996:64). Last, circumcision in America befit the ideal of the "self-made man" by promising to subordinate youthful lust to productive labor.

American reformers, armed with moral righteousness and the newly established germ theory of disease, targeted not just foreskins but all bodily sources of illness, stench, and filth. The rise of medical circumcision corresponded with the widespread appearance of underarm deodorants (first patented in 1888 as "Mum"), public health programs, physical education, sanitary measures aimed at tidying and Americanizing uncouth immigrants, and, as always, Christian revivalism. Even cold breakfast cereals debuted. Sylvester Graham, Harvey Kellogg, and C. W. Post—foreskin foes all—

championed a diet of unrefined, coarse, and natural foods instead of hot, lust-ful, spicy fare.[5] The prepuce was merely the tip of a body politic that required a thoroughgoing cleansing.

Several medical studies in America and England concluded that, among urban immigrants, Jews seemed uniquely healthy. Why? Circumcision was a leading explanation. The "superior cleanliness of the Hebrew penis," in Hutchinson's (1890) words, supposedly reduced Jewish rates of death, still-births, insanity, illness, idiocy, and syphilis (Gollaher 2000:93–106). But there was no consensus on the issue, even among Jewish physicians. Never-theless, critics of circumcision, such as Gollaher (2000:93) and especially Fleiss and Hodges (2002), repeat an old falsehood (e.g., Thompson 1920) and blame Jews for the medicalization of the procedure.[6] But the evidence, as I now show in a brief digression, tells otherwise.

Not surprisingly, most authors who endorsed (or opposed, for that matter) circumcision in the late nineteenth and early twentieth centuries failed to report their religious or ethnic affiliations. Consequently, we can determine the prevalence of Jews in this literature only through the inexact methodol-ogy of trying to identify Jewish-sounding surnames. And so I did, surveying the bibliographies of anticircumcision essays as well as the online version of the *Index-Catalogue of the Library of the Surgeon General's Office* at the National Library of Medicine (www.indexcat.nlm.nih.gov). Of 212 journal articles (and a few books) that promoted circumcision between the years 1855 and 1937, representing 192 authors, I discerned fifty Jewish-sounding surnames—a mere 25% of the procircumcision voice. Some Jewish physi-cians *did* actively promote medical circumcision. But to shape the medicali-zation of circumcision into a distinctly *Jewish* effort or to emphasize the *Jewish* identity of circumcision advocates is misleading.

Physicians who understood circumcision to confer some advantage to the Jews disputed the mechanism (Gilman 1993a, 1993c; Darby 2001). Did the foreskin attract disease? Did circumcision contribute to Jewish reproductive segregation, resulting in a uniquely beneficial heredity? Or did circumcision enclose the Jews in high standard of morality? Underlying these questions, stresses Gilman, was the time-honored view of the Jewish body as differ-ent—a difference now worthy of emulation rather than ridicule.

Given the pervasiveness of Victorian anti-Semitism, the promotion of cir-cumcision posed something of a problem. Non-Jewish surgeons who prac-ticed the medical procedure often denounced the Jewish rite, especially *metzitzah*, lest they appear to endorse an ancient ritual or, worse, emulate the Jews. Either tact would undermine the authority of the new medical professions (Gollaher 2000:94). It would also imply the inferiority of Christianity to Judaism.

One solution to this problem was to appeal to Old Testament authority and biblical morality rather than Jewish custom. Another was to admire the dogged resilience of the Jews—proof enough of a salutary benefit to circumcision and other, often stereotypical Jewish practices, such as temperance and chastity (Hyam 1990:77–78; Moscucci 1996:65; Efron 2001:chap 4). Advocates of circumcision also linked the procedure to Christianity, erasing entirely its Jewishness. In 1899, for example, a newspaper article in the *Los Gatos Mail* encouraged the American colonization of the Philippines, saying, "There is no dilly-dallying with these uncircumcised, uncivilized, unthankful and treacherous cutthroats; the sooner soldiers are sent there in sufficient numbers to finish up the business, the better it will be for Christianity and human progress" (Miller 1982:75). The mar of Jewishness, when contrasted with the "uncivilized," now identified the superior morality of Christianity!

"Playing the Jew"

Fin de siècle notions of circumcision touched on more than just science and barbarism, especially in German-speaking countries. While Europeans typically distinguished between "Jew" and "Jewess," the default gender was male. In Richard Andree's 1881 book *Zur Volkskunde der Juden*, the Yiddish phrase "to make into a Jew" (*jüdischen*) meant "to circumcise" (Gilman 1995:74).[7] Gilman (1995:79) also reports a lavatory graffito, "Ihr ohne Vorhaut, Seid nicht vorlaut," or "You without a foreskin, shouldn't be too pushy." Normative Judaism denoted a diminished phallus.

So diminished was the Jewish penis that the clitoris in Vienna was called the "Jew" (Gilman 1993b:38–39). Female masturbation was "playing the Jew." Likewise, a German word for the Jewish penis, *Schmock*, resembles *Schmuckkasten*, or female genitals (Gilman 1991b:87–88). The connection between *metzitzah* and prostitution, writes Gilman (1993a:66), also feminized the Jew.[8] The Jew's shortened, female penis shaped other bodily fantasies, such as the elongated Jewish nose (Gilman 1994:387–88) and the Jew's menstrual nosebleeds (Geller 1993:58–63). This feminization, Geller observes, partly arose from the simultaneous efforts by both women and Jews to enter German politics. The foreskinless threatened foreskinned hegemony.

The association of circumcision with emasculation and feminization subtly influenced Freud (Geller 1993, 1999; Gilman 1991b, 1993a).[9] When Freud theorized female identity and sexuality as the absence of a penis, he expressed typical European misogyny. But Freud's theories also evidence the internalization of anti-Semitism in a society that valorized the foreskinned phallus as a symbol of normality. Freud transferred to women the penile diminishment popularly associated with Jewish men that resulted in Jewish marginalization (Roith 1987:85–86). Additionally, Freud's notion of castration anxiety universalized to all males the Jew's circumcised disability (Boyarin 1997b:232–39).[10] But while most men overcome castration anxiety, Freud implied, women are not so lucky. Unwittingly, Freud did to women what Europeans did to Jews: deny them admission to a phallocentric society.

Zionism, too, like Freud, both accepted and resisted the stereotype of the feminized male Jew. In the early twentieth century, Max Nordau famously promoted "muscle Jewry." He implored Jews to revisit a "glorious past" by shaping their feeble bodies through physical exercise into strong, muscular, manly physiques—into, that is, Zionist heroes who would finally best Gentile adversaries. But while Nordau accepted the popular view of the emasculated Jew, he did not attribute this emasculation to circumcision. Just the opposite, as he wrote in a 1900 issue of Die Jüdische Turnzeitung,

Our new muscle Jews [Muskeljuden] have not yet regained the heroism of their fore-fathers . . . to take part in battles and compete with the trained Hellenic athletes and strong northern barbarians. But morally speaking, we are better off today than yesterday, for the old Jewish circus performers were ashamed of their Judaism and sought, by way of a surgical pinch, to hide the sign of their religious affiliation . . . while today, the members of Bar Kochba [an allusion to the second-century rebellion against Rome] proudly and freely proclaim their Jewishness. (translation by Presner 2003:283)

Here, circumcision points not to emasculation but, when coupled to body-building, to Zionist heroism. "The organ of Jewish virility," writes Presner (2003:283), "evokes national pride."

The Circumcision Reformation

Religious reforms, sustained by the Enlightenment precepts of secular knowledge, progress, and individualism, swept through European Jewish communities in the mid-nineteenth century. In Frankfurt, a group of lay Jews organized the Society of the Friends of Reform in 1842. After several years of deliberation, the Society established Reform Judaism (Philipson 1931; Boxman 1986). Key pillars of tradition were rejected, including the dietary rules, the invariance of the Mosaic Law, and the yearning to return to Palestine. Indeed, Jews should now regard their country of birth or residence as their home. In other words, the Jew should strive to become a citizen and not just a Jew. Most controversially, the Society affirmed the *optional* status of circumcision. No longer would the rite unequivocally define the Jew. But the final declaration of the Society omitted this reform. The issue was too contentious.

In 1844, Samuel Holdheim, a leader of the reform movement and the rabbi of Frankfurt, argued against the compulsory status of circumcision in a pamphlet titled "Über die Beschneidung zunächst in religiös-dogmatischer Beziehung," or "Circumcision, Viewed Religiously and Dogmatically" (Boxman 1986:44–48; Katz 1998b:345). Holdheim appealed to Talmudic authority to assert that birth, not ritual, conferred Jewish identity (B. Hulin 4; B. Avodah Zarah 27a). He also appealed to logic. If the neglect of no other biblical command was said to annul Jewishness, then why circumcision? The martyrs perished for defending the dietary rules as much as circumcision, yet rarely are nonkosher Jews tossed from the community or accused of profaning the dead! Finally, Holdheim appealed to the great hallmark of the modern era: the "individual's freedom of conscience."

Holdheim never advocated the abandonment of circumcision. Other Jews did so. Joseph Johlson's 1843 pamphlet sought to replace circumcision with a symbolic ceremony for boys *and* girls. So radical was this proposal that Johlson wrote under a pseudonym (Katz 1998b:342). Rather, Holdheim aimed only to divest circumcision of its singular importance in determining male Jewishness.[11] He also wanted to diminish rabbinic authority. Both reforms meant to tailor Judaism to the norms of the modern state.

In the mid-nineteenth century, circumcision was a legal and not merely religious issue. Several European states, including Prussia and Austria, mandated the registration of a child's religious identity (Gilman 1993a:60, 1995:82). But Jews, as Judd (2003) shows, suddenly spoke with divided voices on how to define Jewishness. In Germany, some Jewish fathers refused at midcentury to circumcise their sons. But they still requested a Jewish identity for the child (Katz 1998b; Judd 2003). Would rabbis comply? Was a child neither circumcised nor baptized a legal Jew or a legal Christian? Were foreskinned boys born to Jewish parents full Jews, partial Jews, or non-Jews? If circumcision no longer determined male Jewishness, what did?

In America, circumcision never determined legal status or citizenship as in Europe. But the debate was no less acrimonious. A 1891 pamphlet published by the Memphis *Jewish Spectator* descried circumcision as a "barbarous excrescence" (Boxman 1986:15–17). In response, the Cincinnati *Israelite* published a letter declaring "the siege engine" of secular reasoning "too ridiculously small to batter down the giant tower which withstood all attacks these 3,000 years."

As Jewish reformers pushed circumcision to the religious periphery, assimilated Jews increasingly performed the rite not to renew the covenant but simply to avoid attention by civil authorities or mockery by fellow Jews. Mid-century circumcision invitations often phrased the ceremony as a social event (Katz 1998b:323–24). Reformers, too, supported efforts by the state to bring the rite into regulatory supervision. In 1818, Prussia required certification of a *mohel*'s "good character." Shortly thereafter, the Jewish community of Berlin insisted on a medical presence at circumcision, as did the Frankfurt sanitary bureau in 1843, which also started to appoint *mohels* (Remondino 1891:157; Hyman 1987; Katz 1998a, 1998b; Efron 2001:chap. 6). A decade later, France required state authorization of both *mohels* and kosher butchers and banned oral *metzitzah* entirely, specifying instead the use of a sponge dipped in wine and water.[12]

The medicalization of circumcision, as I noted earlier, allowed Jews to harness science to the modernization of Judaism. They could now defend a religion so often derided as savage. Some Jews advocated the abolishment of the rite. But many Jewish physicians lauded circumcision against those they derisively called "Jews of the enlightened (?) school" (Moses 1871:374) and "progressive Hebrew physicians imbued with the spirit of Listerism" (Hochlerner 1894). The "old Mosaic rite," boasted Hirschfeld (1858), "receives a confirmation, perhaps stronger and more binding upon our age than that in which the Legislator lived." Circumcision, wrote Remondino (1891), enhanced the "faculty for the enjoyment of life that the Hebrew enjoys in contrast to his uncircumcised brethren." The Jew could finally claim to join a wider humanity since, as Efron (2001:223) puts it, "there was nothing particularistic about the desire for good health."

Nowhere was the goal of modernizing Judaism more evident than in the official creed of Reform Judaism, which gelled through a series of international conferences, beginning in the 1840s. The movement built on the short-lived Society of the Friends of Reform and continued to challenge many of the foundational precepts of traditional Judaism, including the beliefs in heaven, hell, and bodily resurrection (Philipson 1931:275–76). The Pittsburgh Platform of 1885 proclaimed Judaism "a progressive religion, ever striving to be in accord with the postulates of reason." Reform Judaism

instituted novel practices, such as vernacular prayer, girls' religious education, and, for men, uncapped worship.

Circumcision remained at the forefront of controversy. In 1846, the Bres-
lau Conference banned direct oral *metzitzah* for Reform Jews and adopted a
series of medical reforms.[13] Yet these developments addressed only the performance of circumcision, not its religious status. By the end of the century,
though, Reform Judaism was clear: circumcision was optional. The rite was
valued, even encouraged. But it no longer defined a male Jew. Birth alone
sufficed to establish full Jewish status—or, in the case of converts, a personal
declaration of faith following a course of study.[14] The rite now signaled the
quintessential moral condition of modernity: individual choice.

Some rabbis, fearing embarrassment, tried to confine the dispute over circumcision to the Jewish community. But not the elderly rabbi of Frankfurt,
Solomon Abraham Trier, who appealed to the city senate in the 1840s to
rescind legislation that construed circumcision as optional for Jews. By now,
most German localities regulated the procedure through civil sanitary codes,
as did many Jewish communities through their own regulations (Philipson
1931:183; Judd 2003:151). Ironically, Trier sought support from the same
secular authorities who undermined rabbinic authority. But to no avail. Trier
had better success with his colleagues, who resoundingly endorsed the rite in
an 1894 volume, *Rabbinical Responses on Circumcision* (see Katz 1998b:327–
36). They threatened the reformist "apostates" with economic ostracism,
exclusion from cemeteries, and excommunication.

Reform Judaism, I stress again, never abandoned circumcision. In fact, the
Augsburg synod of 1871 declared "the supreme importance of circumcision
in Judaism." Rather, the movement sought only to challenge the compulsory
status of the rite. Indeed, the reformers abandoned nearly *all* major tenets of
traditional Judaism *except* circumcision (Hoffman 1996:9). Why? There seem
to be two answers: sentiment and syncretism.

Since circumcision is a long-standing tradition of deep significance to
many Jews, Reform Judaism affirmed the meaningfulness of the rite while
denying its obligatory status. Additionally, the medicalization of circumcision allowed Jews, then and now, to fuse tradition with modernity (Boxman
1986:179–85; Greenbaum 1999). Circumcision, too, I suggest, lent expression to a muted sense of ethnic pride. For centuries, Jews suffered Christian
calls to abandon circumcision. Now Jews could return to favor. Against a
rising tide of anti-Semitism in the late nineteenth century, Jews could defend
circumcision as a harbinger of science (Efron 2001:chap. 6). By linking the
rite with reduced concupiscence and syphilis, moreover, Jews could invert

a time-honored slur (Efron 2001:229). It was not the foreskinless Jew who threatened society and morality but the foreskinned Christian.

Contemporary Jewish Opposition to Ritual Circumcision

The bitter controversy over Jewish circumcision waned after the opening decades of the twentieth century. The issue periodically flared, but most twentieth-century Jews, to argue from silence, seemed either content with the rite or muted their resentment. After the Holocaust, moreover, called the Shoah in Hebrew, many Jews viewed the performance of brit milah as a powerful declaration of Jewish survival.

After several decades of quiescence, Jewish debates over circumcision gained momentum in the 1980s. By the mid-1990s, circumcision again split the Jewish community in bitter dispute. The controversy received extensive coverage in special issues of Conservative Judaism (1990, vol. 42, no. 4) and Moment magazine (February 1992) and during an August 1998 segment of All Things Considered on National Public Radio. It was—and remains—a fairly common topic in newspapers.

Actually, Jewish novelists had long expressed a profound uncertainty about circumcision and the meaning of Jewish identity. Prominent examples include Salomo Friedlaender's The Operated Goy (1922),[15] I. J. Singer's The Family Carnovsky (1943), Arthur Koestler's Thieves in the Night (1946), Bernard Malamud's The Assistant (1957), I. B. Singer's Yentl (1978), Primo Levy's The Periodic Table (1984), Philip Roth's Counterlife (1986), and Dan Jacobson's The God-fearer (1992). The topic seems especially salient in contemporary German fiction (Gilman 1993a, 1995; relatedly, Kovács and Vajda 2003).

Recent films, too, feature circumcision episodes, most notably Europa, Europa (1990; see Lungstrum 1998) but also A Price Above Rubies (1998), Dad on the Run (2000), My Wife Is an Actress (2001), and, earlier, Woody Allen's Annie Hall (1977).[16] In the United States, circumcision plots appeared on many television dramas and sitcoms, including M*A*S*H*, Saturday Night Live, thirtysomething, Cheers, Will & Grace, Dharma & Greg, L.A. Law, St. Elsewhere, South Park, and, as I discussed in chapter 7, Seinfeld.[17]

Today, ambivalence toward the rite is far more explicit. Several short films rethink brit milah or outright advocate uncircumcision, including Keren Markuze's *The 8th Day*, Victor Schonfeld's *It's a Boy*, Nurith Aviv's *Circumcision*, and, on a more lighthearted note, David Bezmozgis's *L.A. Mohel*.

More significantly, Jews over the past decade have published scores, if not hundreds, of essays pro and especially con. Perhaps best known is *Questioning Circumcision: A Jewish Perspective*, a book by Ronald Goldman (1998), the executive director of the Jewish Circumcision Resource Center (http://jewishcircumcision.org). The Alternative Bris Support Group, organized by Helen Bryce in northern California, disseminates an impressive packet of readings. Included are moving letters from anguished parents who questioned the rite yet received only incredulous hostility from their family, an ethnocentric column from *Playboy* magazine, and whimsical verse from a lesbian juggler performance artist titled "Circumcision: A Poem to be Recited while Juggling Three Big Knives." As in the late nineteenth century, the Jewish penis is again exposed to public debate.

Despite the increasing importance of this debate to contemporary Jews, scholars of Judaism enigmatically neglect the issue (but see Hoffman 1996:209–20; Glick 2004; and, of course, the work of Gilman). My task in the rest of this chapter is to redress this omission by critically analyzing Jewish opposition to ritual circumcision (*brit milah*). Frankly, I take no sides in this debate. Critique is not endorsement. Nonetheless, I strive to expose unsettling themes, assumptions, and implications—and I do so with no less a critical eye than I cast in the previous chapter at non-Jewish images of the rite.

The Neurotic Jew

Numerous organizations working to eradicate medical circumcision, as I detail in chapter 10, attribute severe social, sexual, and psychological consequences to the rite. These afflictions include post-traumatic stress disorder, low self-esteem, rage, fear, feelings of betrayal, sexual dysfunction, depression, teenage suicide, alcoholism, theft, hatred, and violence toward women. Jews today levy the same allegations against *brit milah*.

For example, the rite constitutes a form of psychotherapeutic wounding. Jewish men circumcise their sons as "a way of repeating the trauma of their own circumcision . . . we tend to act out our repressed feelings on those who are weaker" (Goldman 1998, 2004). Circumcising Jews are either reviled as religious fundamentalists or pitied as the victims of a "culturally conditioned terror" (Goodman 1999b; see also Sandel 1996). Circumcision, continues

Goodman, is "compulsive behavior on the part of people who at some level do want to stop." The Jew is both victim and perpetrator.

Many opponents of circumcision see the procedure as encoding the boy's brain for sadomasochism and anxiety. The rite, too, irreparably disrupts the mother–infant bond (see chapter 10). In consequence, circumcised men are chronically distrustful of intimate relationships. This explains, writes Goldman (1998), why Judaism construes circumcision as "a desire for God's protection." Since Jewish men "received no protection when they were circumcised as infants," they look to God to recapture the lost parental nurture they never enjoyed as an infant. The rite is the source of Jewish distress—and its false cure.

From Foreskins to Mother Jokes

In April 1997, Francine Klagsbrun defended traditional *brit milah* in her monthly column in *Moment* magazine. The subsequent issue contained angry rebuttals.[18] Many Jewish men, claimed the founder of Healing Our Wounds, are "extremely angry" about the loss of their foreskin. To Klagsbrun's contention that circumcision entails only momentary pain, one writer responded, "I'm sure she would find it distasteful if I tried to state that having a mastectomy is no big deal."[19] Opponents of male circumcision often allege discrimination against men. Most Westerners, as I discuss in the next chapter, including Jews, readily denounce the genital mutilation of women in Africa. Yet they tolerate, even celebrate, the same barbarism on their own sons! In this view, men are doubly abused, first by circumcision, then by denial of their pain.

Circumcision harms men, but also mothers. In Miriam Pollack's (1995) essay, "Circumcision: A Jewish Feminist Perspective," the rite impairs the boy's brain, hinders his capacity for sexual pleasure, ruptures the mother–son bond, and contributes to "fears of intimacy and commitment which plague our male–female relations." Pollack also addresses specifically Jewish concerns. She rightly calls attention to the ritual erasure of motherhood during traditional *brit milah* (see also Glanzberg-Krainin 2003). But in so doing, Pollack endorses a view of history long discredited by scholars. She attributes circumcision to a "god worshiping, patriarchal, dominance and violence-based culture" that destroyed a "magnificent, highly developed and peaceful" noncircumcising, goddess-worshipping, matrilineal, and egalitarian society.

Many Jews argue that circumcision causes the unique expression and viciousness of Jewish misogyny. The rite, for example, explains the prominence of jokes about Jewish women—specifically, the stereotypical Jewish American mother and her daughter, the Jewish American princess.

Question: Why are Jewish men circumcised?
Answer: Because Jewish women won't touch anything that isn't 20 percent off.[20]

But circumcision, proposes Goldman (1998:61–64), goes far beyond sexist humor. It also explains the "serious problem" of Jewish domestic violence.[21] "It may be," proposes Goldman, "that, from the infant's perspective, while he is having his penis cut, he is experiencing a betrayal by his mother." In turn, "Jewish male anger toward and distrust of women may arouse a similar response in women."

Judaism, asserts Goodman (1997), forces mothers "to violate all their maternal instincts which urge them to cherish and protect the child; if they do not, they will be cast out of their tribe, spiritual exiles." Jewish mothers are torn between loyalty to their children and loyalty to their tradition (Goodman 1999a:23–24). A good mother cannot be a good Jew—and a good Jew cannot be good mother.

The Holocaust

A powerful leitmotif in the contemporary debate over brit milah is the Holocaust, or Shoah. In a letter to the editor of the Northern California Jewish Bulletin (May 31, 1985), the son of survivors explains that, despite his parents' decision to forgo the rite out of concern for future persecutions, he feels no less Jewish. Only Nazis, writes Karsenty (1988), identify Jews from the penis. To "give up the milla (surgery) does not necessarily mean rejecting a brit (covenant)." Uncircumcision grants no posthumous victory to Hitler.

The Holocaust assumes a different tone when circumcision itself is viewed as a type of terror. Many critics of the rite draw inspiration from the work of the popular Swiss psychiatrist Alice Miller. In books such as For Your Own Good: Hidden Cruelty in Child-Rearing and the Roots of Violence (1983) and Banished Knowledge: Facing Childhood Injuries (1990), Miller connects the normalization of childhood violence to, among other things, the acceptance and appeal of brutal political regimes such as fascism and National Socialism. Children who suffer violence, in other words, grow into violent adults.

Writing in The American Atheist, Marilyn Milos and Norman Cohen

(1999) support their opposition to circumcision with reference to Miller's thesis. They specifically mention the connection between brutal child raising and Nazism. This rhetorical strategy implies that circumcision is the moral equivalent of the Holocaust, only this time perpetrated by Jews onto Jews.

Pollack (1997) also parallels circumcision and the Holocaust. She invokes Elie Weisel, then denounces the martyrology of circumcision in which "it was more important to irreversibly mark and mutilate our Jewish sons, making them easy targets for oppressors" than to "risk their survival, perhaps at the price of assimilation, with an intact body." At best, circumcision wounds Jews. At worst, it transforms the covenant from a promise of life into certain death. For proponents of circumcision, the rite memorializes Jewish tragedy. For opponents, it is a Jewish tragedy.

Foreskinned Judaism as neo-Pauline Christianity

Many Jews who oppose circumcision celebrate the "natural" wholeness of the child, thus espousing a "naturalistic orientation" akin to New Age sensibilities (Tabory and Erez 2003:167–68). They also, I suggest, approach the Hellenistic outlook of Paul and early Christianity. Since humanity was created perfectly "in the image of God," writes Goodman (1999a:24), circumcision "is a form of blasphemy." Asks Moss (1991), embracing a particular cultural view of nature, "What about the concern that circumcision involves the surgical alteration of a perfectly natural God-given part of the body?"

Jews today, Goldman (1998) stresses, inconsistently abide by the Torah. Not only does circumcision violate the biblical ban on cutting the human body, but Jews who persist with the rite shun other biblical laws, such as animal sacrifice. Jewish critics of circumcision, echoing Paul, chastise those who "boast" of their Jewishness on the basis of circumcision while neglecting most other religious precepts and beliefs. Today, imply critics, circumcising Jews emphasize "works," invoking Paul yet again, over "faith." Rather, stresses Goodman (1997), Jews should circumcise their allegorical hearts, not their literal foreskins. This way, Jews can greet all newborns with a rite that, as Goodman (1999a) writes elsewhere, is "truly welcoming and truly purely symbolic."

Contemporary Jews, writes Moss (1991), stress empty ritual obligations over true spirituality and faith. Their rites, to paraphrase Goodman, are not "truly purely symbolic." This criticism of circumcision, too, like the "faith" versus "works" polarity, resembles an early Christian portrayal—some would say caricature—of Judaism. The rabbis, Moss reminds us, emphasized the importance of linking ritual performance to genuine commitment. To Jews lacking orthodox convictions, Moss continues, circumcision is tantamount to an empty gesture. Worse, the rite resemble idolatry, thus biblically punishable by the same "cutting off" penalty as its neglect! In effect, circumcision critics strive to reshape Judaism into a form of Pauline Christianity—without, of course, Christ.

Ironically, Jewish advocates of circumcision occasionally summon Paul to the defense of the rite. In the 1980s, Helen Latner championed universal circumcision in *The Jewish Week* to prevent future persecution on the basis of a distinctive Jewish body (Wallerstein 1983:45). If Paul advocated foreskinned globalism, Latner globalized the foreskinless.

Persecution from Within

Circumcision for Goldman (1998) is doubly deficient. First, the rite fails to ensure the survival of Judaism against assimilation, much as circumcision supporters would have us believe. Second, it fails to distinctively mark the Jewish body since most American boys are now foreskinless. At the same time, it cuts many Jews *off* from Judaism.

So shaken was a Jewish physician after reading Goldman's book *Circumcision: The Hidden Trauma* (1997) that he experienced several months of "intense anxiety and mourning for my lost foreskin. . . . Raging anger and uncontrolled sobbing were daily occurrences" (Reiss 2004). Another Jewish man, writing on the popular Internet site In Memory of the Sexually Mutilated Child, reports a similar reaction after reading Bigelow's *The Joy of Uncircumcising!* (1998), a book I discuss in chapter 10. He "curled up in a fetal position . . . and cried and grieved" (www.sexuallymutilatedchild.org/levitt). Then woe yielded to rage:

> I denounce Judaism . . . as sick, perverted and immoral. . . . I fantasize about revenge on the mohel who circumcised me. . . . One of the main reasons I'm active in the intact baby movement is to vent my rage in a positive way and not end up in prison. I've put a MOHEL = MENGELE sign across the back of my car.

This type of fury is especially common in the movement to ban medical circumcision. In the next chapter, I link this anger over the lost foreskin to other modern "losses" in contemporary society. For now, I want only to illustrate what circumcision opponents identify as two uniquely Jewish aspects of this rage.

In the 1992–1993 newsletter of the Walking Stick Foundation (dedicated to the "aboriginal wisdom of Judaism [and] . . . earth-honoring traditions"), Joshua Susskind asserts that most Jews are "either angry at the *goyim*, angry at our religion, or angry at their parents." This wrath springs not from "our collective history of oppression" but from "personal histories of betrayal . . . by our parents to the *mohel*." Most Jews wrongly project this anger onto Gentiles. The circumcising Jew, in this view, is his own worst enemy—and for that, apparently, Jews can thank their parents, not the *goyim* they so often blame for their historical woes.

Earlier, I mentioned the oft-repeated claim that since oppressed persons unconsciously victimize others, circumcised Jews cut Jewish infants. The rite is a form of self-persecution, if not self-hatred. By the same logic, claims Rothenberg (1989), Jews oppress the working classes, and Israel oppresses Arabs. Only by retaining his foreskin can the brutalized, brutalizing Jew halt this cycle of terror.

Rabbinic Validation?

Many opponents of *brit milah* look to biblical texts for validation. For example, Goldman (1998) finds support in the failure of Moses to circumcise his own son (Exodus 4:25). He also honors the foreskinned generation that fled Egyptian enslavement (Joshua 5:5). Of course, proponents of the rite could easily respond that the Hebrew Bible plainly censors both foreskinned lapses. God almost kills Moses for neglecting the rite, then orders a mass circumcision of the Israelites prior to entering the Promised Land. Neither case necessarily sustains an uncircumcised Judaism.

Jewish "intactivists," too, tend to reproach Dinah's brothers for the circumcision massacre in Genesis 34. Yet they often fail to mention Dinah's rape (e.g., Romberg 1985:34). This omission, one could argue, undermines the moral force of the argument and recalls the medieval canard of Jewish vengeance.

Contemporary Jews who judge circumcision a violation of a child's inherent rights also seek support from rabbinic texts. Goodman (1999a:24–25, 1999b) highlights Talmudic passages that subordinate ritual practices to health concerns (B. Hulin 10a). The pain of the rite, says Goldman (1998:59), violates Hillel's famous dictum that "What is hateful to you, do not do to your neighbor" (B. Shabbath 31a). Would Hillel agree? Probably not. He strongly endorsed the rite. Moreover, since circumcision necessarily entails distress, the rabbis accepted the pain as "part of the divine *desiderátum*" (J. D. Bleich 2000:59–60). The classic rabbis, too, we have seen, attributed heroic merit to Abraham's stoicism during his own elderly rite.

Still, the rabbinic houses of Hillel and Shamai did argue over the precise role of circumcision during conversion and when determining the eligibility of religious duties (chapter 4). This dispute, as well as rabbinic references to "the uncircumcised," might reasonably appeal to contemporary opponents of the rite. Oddly, they neglect them.

An enduring question about Abraham might also support a diversity of opinions about circumcision from within Judaism. In rabbinic culture, Abraham's exemplary moral status partly arose from his eager and voluntary adherence to *all* the commandments in the Torah. Why, then, did Abraham wait so long to undergo circumcision—and why did he require divine prodding? A famous nineteenth-century Hungarian rabbi, Abraham Samuel Benjamin Wolf Schreiber, offered an answer (Krohn 1985:82). Since the pain and blood of circumcision potentially violate the Torah, Abraham hesitated. Of course, this commentary underscores the fact that circumcision does *not* violate the Torah, at least to Rabbi Schreiber. Nonetheless, Abraham's hesitation gave pause to the rabbis. It still does today.

Circumcision without Cutting

Many Jews today devise alternative rites to welcome newborns—boys *and* girls—into the covenantal community. These bloodless celebrations, often called Brit Shalom, assume many forms. They may repeat the traditional circumcision liturgy while omitting the actual cutting or focus solely on naming the child (Goldman 1998:95–108). Other ceremonies strive for greater creativity—say, a "covenant wrapping" that encloses the infant in a prayer shawl (Wechterman 2003). Alternative liturgies often praise the "natural" perfection of the child and stress parental unwillingness to inflict harm.

Several alternative welcoming rites recall the halting of Abraham's knife above Isaac (e.g., www.cirp.org/pages/cultural/bris_shalom.html). The real test of Abraham, declares a "Covenant of Wholeness" ceremony,

> was not whether Abraham would blindly obey God but if he would use his innate moral sense and tell God: "NO! It is WRONG to maim innocent babies just so I could have a piece of land." "NO! It is wrong to murder even on your command." Abraham failed these tests and we have been living with his failure ever since.

The rabbi officiating at the rite then responds,

> We are gathered together today, in the last year of a century which has given us profound and unprecedented insight into our humanity. . . . But this century has also given us the Holocaust, a bloodletting of unprecedented proportion. Given both the insight and the brutality of our century, we are inevitably led to conclude that there must be no more bloodshed in God's name. We continue where Abraham left off: We shall do the child no harm. (www.nocirc.org/religion/Naming_ceremony.php)

The nontheistic Society for Humanistic Judaism goes even further: it omits from its covenant rites all references to God.[22]

Many covenant ceremonies expressly lend voice to the values of modern liberalism. Nearly all Jewish parents who forgo circumcision emphasize, like the late nineteenth-century reformers, the importance of personal choice in religious belief and practice (see also Tabory and Erez 2003:168–69). One covenant rite, involving candles and an "eerie but lovely call to the prophet Elijah," reflected, as the mother said, "*our* wishes for our son," not the dictates of tradition or God (Hills 1987). Participants planted a plum tree atop the boy's placenta, then voiced the hope that its fruit will fill his "little belly" and, mirroring a traditional aspiration, its branches support his marriage canopy. *The Oakland Tribune*[23] reported on the ritual circumcision of a fig!

The ritual planting of saplings in lieu of circumcision, however much it violates rabbinic sensibilities, nonetheless builds on Talmudic precedent (B. Gittin 57a). The fruitful imagery, too, conforms to biblical idioms (chapter 4).[24] It also, somewhat ironically, recalls the folkloristic burial of foreskins. Klein (1998:231) ties the popularity of tree-planting covenant rites to the establishment of the state of Israel. Few traditionalists, to repeat, would endorse these innovations. Yet many liberal Jews would equally reject the inclusion of overtly nationalistic or Zionist tones.

Jews who favor nontraditional newborn rites tend to condemn conventional Judaism for its patriarchy and primitivism. The religion neglects the birth of girls yet greets boys with brutal pain. By design, many recent covenant rites rebuff this doubled sexism by celebrating equally the birth of boys and girls through a rite that, like the planting of trees, forgoes any physical distress. Eilberg-Schwartz (1995), writing in the liberal Jewish monthly *Tikkun*, counseled parents and especially fathers to embrace a nurturing rather than aggressive deity and to welcome children through an act of care, not wounding. Parents, he suggested, should feed their infants.

Several years later, *Tikkun* published another covenant rite that rejected, as it said, the traditional "pound of flesh." However violent the world, declared Kimmel (2001), his own son "would enter it without violence done to him . . . he would not bleed by our hand." Instead, the Kimmels welcomed their child with a traditional Middle Eastern gesture of greeting: they washed his feet. This rite intentionally sought to evoke Abraham's hospitality toward the strangers who foretold the birth of Isaac (see also Moss 1992:23). But it also conjures Jesus and baptism (see also Raul-Friedman 1992:33). Orthodox Jews such as Judith Bleich (1983) find another objection. According to some classic rabbis, Abraham offered to wash the strangers' feet not as a gesture of welcome but, rather, to ensure that, as potential idolaters, they did not pollute his tent. Hardly a fitting gesture, in Bleich's view, to welcome a new Jew!

Recent covenant rites also tend to express an earnest self-righteousness. Hence, Goldman (1998:73) boasts that noncircumcising parents "gain the freedom, power, and self-respect that comes to those who act in conformance with their own convictions." Similarly, Tabory and Erez (2003:171) show that noncircumcising Israelis tend to profess a superior sense of genuine spirituality.[25]

Traditionalists criticize recent covenant rites as "transparently conceived" (Granatstein 1975; Kletenik 1998; Gordis 1998). For many Jews, circumcision derives its authority and emotional intensity from an aura of mystery and antiquity, from symbolic complexity that resists simplification, and from a muted sense of history and ideology. By contrast, noncircumcising covenant rites tend overtly—some might say honestly—to acknowledge their own contrivance and political motivations.

Female Rites and Rights

Traditional Jews tend to maintain that, since God commanded Abraham to perform circumcision, the honor of performing *brit milah* generally excludes women. But Jews aspiring to an egalitarian covenant defy this segregation or sexism. The well-known *Second Jewish Catalog* advocates full participation by women in the rite (Strassfeld and Strassfeld 1976:24–37). The Reform and Conservative branches of modern Judaism certify men *and* women as *mohels*.[26] Women, suggests one Reform rabbi, can best relate to anxious mothers.[27] Haberman (2003) gains inspiration from Zipporah in Exodus 4 and the intimate centrality of blood in women's experience.

Not all Jewish feminists, however, endorse female *mohels* (properly called *mohelot*), albeit for reasons that differ from Orthodox critics. Trachtman and

Blustain (1999), writing in the feminist Jewish magazine *Lilith*, wonder if *mohelot* will further distance men from birth and pregnancy and fuel the image of the "castrating mother." They also tell of hearing a snide comment from a male relative, "Would you trust your son's penis to a feminist?" A subsequent letter to the editor of *Lilith* offered a more basic challenge to *mohelot*: why must women seek validity by defining themselves as men? But if there is merit to my argument that circumcision represents a male rendition of female fertility, then *mohelot* are not so much emulating men as "taking back" their originary uterine capacities.

Egalitarian Jews, as I mentioned earlier, often create covenant rites to celebrate the birth of their daughters. Recent sources of inspiration include *Jewish and Female: Choices and Changes in Our Lives Today* (Schneider 1984), *A Breath of Life: Feminism in the American Jewish Community* (Fishman 1993), *Celebrating Your New Jewish Daughter: Creating Jewish Ways to Welcome Baby Girls* (Cohen 2001), and Plaskow's (1979) essay "Bringing a Daughter into the Covenant," in *Womanspirit Rising: A Feminist Reader in Religion* (see also Klein 1998:228–30). These ceremonies tend, more so than noncircumcising rites for boys, to refer to biblical passages, rabbinic texts, and traditional themes to avoid the appearance of artifice and to establish historical continuity. They often borrow motifs from the traditional naming rites for girls that were practiced by Jews outside the European, or Ashkenazic, tradition, such as the Sephardic *zeved habat* naming ceremony or Las Fadas ("The Fairies"), a rite that either invoked or warned away spirits (see Dobrinsky 1980; Cohen 2002). Despite these historical connections, modern welcoming rites for girls typically celebrate or at least evidence the influence of Western feminism.

In the *Second Jewish Catalog*, girls' rites frequently invoke biblical heroines and prophetesses. One ceremony drizzles wine on a parchment inscription of the girl's name, recalling the covenantal significance of circumcision blood. Another suggests that parents sew a girl's swaddling cloth into Torah ornaments, much like a boy's *wimpel* or Torah binder (chapter 7). In *The Jewish Woman: New Perspectives*, Leifer and Leifer (1976) write about dipping a baby girl in a small ritual bath (*mikvah*) to symbolize female fertility—a gesture that one Orthodox critic rejects for, among other things, its resemblance to Christian baptism (J. Bleich 1983). Even a recent children's book about *brit milah* that never actually describes the procedure challenges phallocentrism by focusing on the elder sister's feelings. To alleviate her anxiety, the story parallels the circumcision with her own *Simchat Bat* welcoming rite.[28]

Rabbi Sandy Sasso (1973), the first woman ordained by the Reconstructionist Rabbinical College, devised a rite called *b'rit b'not Israel* to consecrate a girl's first Sabbath. The ceremony also formalizes the child's Hebrew name. Sasso focused her ritual innovation on the Sabbath since Jewish traditions link the Sabbath, like circumcision, to covenantal perpetuity. A revised version of the rite appeared in a 1991 compilation, *A Ceremonial Sampler: New Rites, Celebrations, and Observances of Jewish Women* (Levine 1991), a collection that also includes ceremonies for pregnancy, birth, weaning, hysterectomy, first menstruation, and vegetarianism.[29] Levy (1990:14) offers a *dam berit*, or "blood covenant" rite, that is cued to a newborn girl's small vaginal flow. Other ceremonies emphasize the girl's future menstruation.

Perhaps the most scandalous suggestion for a girl's covenant rite literally mirrors circumcision. The ceremony ruptures the infant's hymen. It opens the "girl's generative area so that her seed, also, can be directly and symbolically dedicated to God" (Gendler 1974).[30] The author of this rite wanted, in part, to respond to couvade, that is, the message of male circumcision that Jewish mothers merely "raise the children that have been *begotten* by the men." Gendler concedes "shock, dismay, anxiety and disapproval." But she rejects any suggestion that ritual hymenotomy parallels "cruel and painful" clitoral excision. As an added bonus, Gendler's hymenal rite would frustrate a traditional prerogative of patriarchy: future husbands could no longer test their brides for virginity.

The "beauty" of new celebrations for daughters, writes Cohen (2002) in an essay from *United Synagogue Review*, is precisely their newness. They lack, unlike *brit milah*, any fixed liturgy, and so they reflect the personality and religious commitments of the family, not the dictates of tradition. "Loved ones," writes Cohen (2002), "read passages from the Psalms or Song of Songs, or from Shakespeare, Abraham Johsua Heschel, or the lyrics of the Grateful Dead—if that's what they find meaningful." Of course, it is precisely this level of innovation—the emphasis on personal spirituality, we might say, rather than communal tradition—that many Orthodox or Conservative Jews find so distasteful. "Liturgical creativity," cautions Judith Bleich (1983), "requires vigilance . . . to avoid the pitfalls of alien concepts and foreign traditions."

What Risks for Judaism?

Since late antiquity, we have seen, Jews have defended ritual circumcision against Greco-Roman satire, Christianity, anti-Semitism, civil authorities, the merely curious, and even other Jews. The rabbis promoted the rite in terms of faith, bodily and moral perfection, divine intimacy, erotic restraint, mystical secrets, and sacrifice. Today, circumcising Jews reiterate these themes when justifying the rite against their noncircumcising coreligionists. They also address more recent concerns.

Organizations opposing circumcision, as I elaborate in the next chapter, maintain an extensive presence in cyberspace. The Internet is no less appealing to Jewish proponents, especially *mohels* (e.g., www.mohel.net, www.calla mohel.com, www.brismilah.org, www.brismilah.com, and www.imohel .com). A group called Advocating Circumcision Today hosts several Internet domains, including www.act-now.org, www.its-a-boy.org, www.mohel.com, and www.milah.net. The Berit Mila Program of Reform Judaism offers an elaborate website (www.beritmila.org), including links to the occasional online newsletter of the National Organization of American Mohalim/ot.

Some proponents of Jewish circumcision advance medical arguments (Kunin and Miller 1992; Schoen 1997; Silver 2005). But Orthodox Jews often resist this tact to preserve the covenantal significance—that is, the theology—of the rite. Indeed, Novak (1982) derides a medical rationale as "counter-covenantal." Jewish law generally forbids *mohels* from circumcising non-Jews. This rule serves to underscore the religious intent of *brit milah*. Nonetheless, some *mohels* perform strictly medical or secular procedures to enhance the status of the rite, much to the consternation of more devout practitioners (e.g., Sokobin 1976; Romberg 1982:26–27). Schur (1971) believes that *mohels* who medicalize *brit milah* in the hopes of preserving the tradition might unwittingly contribute to its demise should the medical community eventually reject the procedure.

Most supporters of *brit milah* look to religion and emotion for justification (e.g., Klagsbrun 1997). In *Moment* magazine, Roth (1992) dismissed the common criticism that the rite pertains to primitive notions of fertility and patriarchy. Once, maybe. But these archaic themes are unknown to most Jews today and so largely irrelevant. Rather, the rite sanctifies Jewish tradition and the community, consecrates a Jewish parent's obligations, and hallows the life of a new Jew. The ceremony, too, celebrates hard-won religious freedom and acknowledges "the weight of history."

Many Jews, Roth (1992) continues, no matter how assimilated and secular, abide by the belief that "Jews died to circumcise their sons because circumcision ensures our physical survival." Raul-Freidman (1992) concurs: the six million victims of the Holocaust "kept the covenant: they kept the faith." Opponents of the rite reject this sentiment as coercive and, in regard to stemming assimilation, simply incorrect. Nonetheless, the post-Holocaust view of *brit milah* as a triumph over Nazism imbues the rite with deep significance to many Jews.

Not surprisingly, most Jews who support religious circumcision reject the charge that the rite amounts to little more than a painful mutilation, lacking, as Moss (1990) sees it, "transcendent meaning." This accusation, contends Landes and Robbin (1990), merely repeats Greco-Roman and early Christian bigotry. Only Jews ignorant of Judaism, in this view, look on circumcision as meaningless. Yet, frankly speaking, superficiality extends to both sides. As Glick (2004) shows, many Jewish endorsements of circumcision lack serious consideration of rabbinic texts, especially the violent imagery surrounding the rite.

Landes and Robbin (1990) also see *brit milah* as creating communal solidarity, defining the sexual and marital boundaries of the community, and, most intriguingly, reducing the incidence of Jewish rape. Circumcision is "a protest against this natural propensity of men," a rite that "affirms the value of sexuality through restraint," and "a sign of the Law that seeks to set both women and men free from all bondage." Here, proponents identify an egalitarian message in the very ceremony that dissidents view as quintessentially sexist.

To opponents of circumcision, as I noted earlier, the rite cuts an unbridgeable psychological chasm between mother and son. To the contrary, writes Kletenik (1998), "maternal bonds are only strengthened as a mother guides her children through the inevitably painful events in life," including circumcision. Similarly, Landes and Robbin (1990) understand the ceremony to enclose an infant within a community and historical tradition. Both Neusner (1987), a conservative scholar of Judaism, and Emmanuel Levinas (Cohen 1998:70), a philosopher of post-Holocaust ethics, understand the value of circumcision as expanding birth from a private, intimate, and biological affair into a public event that renews the community and affirms the individual Jew's communal obligations. The rite also enmeshes parents and child in a network of enduring social ties. In effect, the rite resists the very individualism that opponents endorse.

Ritual circumcision, say critics, rests on the assumption that children are the mere property of their parents who can do to them as they wish. To proponents, the rite does just the opposite: it transforms children from property into an ethical obligation (Gordis 1998). Indeed, the rite induces anxiety precisely to force Jews to contemplate the extent of their devotion and identity. It is the horror of the ritual, says a *Boston Globe* columnist on beliefnet .com, that accounts for its potency (Cahners n.d.). "When we draw our infant's blood—something that strips the gears of our parental instincts—we too are showing our commitment—as well as our entitlement to God's promises." Anything more commonplace, anything less grisly, and we "forgot that we were closing a deal with the Almighty." What risks, imply many advocates of *brit milah*, are you willing to take for your faith and tradition?

Sublime Pain

Some Jews, we have seen, denounce ritual circumcision as an unjustifiable infliction of agony onto a helpless infant in violation of Jewish ethics and basic human rights. Many advocates of the rite also admit to the pain, but they seek to harness it to moral purposes. The pain expresses "tough love" (Kletenik 1998) or leads to personal growth. As Rabbi Arthur Waskow (1989), a major figure in the Jewish Renewal movement, understands it, the rite intensely binds together father and son as in birth. The father becomes "motherly" by "nurturing the cycle of the generations," and his newly circumcised son appears "vulnerable" and "open," hence "womanly." Far from representing a ruthless patriarchy, says Rabbi Waskow, the pain of circumcision transforms Jewish men into mothers who nourish the community.

Rabbi David Zaslow (2003) offers a similar view. He understands circumcision as a spiritual bonding between fathers and sons that emulates, moreover, menstruation. The rite creates "male love and compassion" when fathers "cry for their sons and for all the pain their sons will experience in their lives." This redemptive anguish, Zaslow continues—and *brit milah* in general—exists well beyond everyday notions of what is rational, moral, and immoral. The rite is irreducibly spiritual. By implication, the very effort to think about the rite logically, whether to endorse or to criticize it, denies the ceremony its defining quality.

Fathers who circumcise their own sons seem especially compelled to address the issue of pain. Kozberg (1984) describes *brit milah* as "a gesture of love" whereby the child experiences "a basic tenet of the community: for the Jew, the transcendence of one's humanness in order to be more fully human will be sometimes—perhaps often—painful" (see also Maller 1992). To another circumcising father, the intense anxiety provoked by the rite effected an intimate, almost mystical union between himself and his son (Meyer 1992). It was this sense of oneness that eased the father's "deep feelings of nervousness at that awesome time" when he looked into his son's eyes, "trusting and serene," and performed the rite.

In a moving essay in *The New York Times Magazine*, Hammerman (1994) also embraced the anguish of circumcision. The father channels his "natural anger and jealously" (see also Herzbrun 1991:8). "No parent," continues Hammerman,

> should be denied this experience, even vicariously, of inflicting upon his child a ritualized blow so intense as to make both shake and recoil, but so controlled that no damage is really done, so that this might be the worst the child will ever know from his parent's hand. For it is from the parent's hand that Abraham's knife dangles, every moment of every day.

Here, the very pain that speaks against the rite to some Jews is precisely what transforms to other Jews a perfunctory procedure into a religious experience of sublime meaning.

Circumcision Chic

Ironically, at a time of mounting pressure by Jews and others to abandon circumcision, *brit milah* often takes on a fashionable quality. In December 1996, *The New York Times Magazine* hailed Dr. Fred R. Kogen, "The Mohel of the Moment," for his Hollywood celebrity status. Kogen's website (www .ebris.com) boasts the circumcision of a biker boy in the Mojave Desert amid T-shirts and beer. *Los Angels Magazine* titled him "Best of L.A." for 1999. Instead of "grey beard, black hat and long coat," Kogen dons Armani-looking suits and drives a Lexus. Undoubtedly, Kogen is the first *mohel* honored by *Cosmopolitan* as "Bachelor of the Month."

In 1999, *The New Yorker* lauded its own celebrity *mohel*, Philip L. Sherman, in "The Talk of the Town." Catering to affluent Westchester and Long Island, Sherman totes beeper, cell phone, and Polo cologne. As befitting a *mohel* whose websites are www.emoil.com and www.emohel.com, Sherman stuffs his circumcision tools in an Eddie Bauer computer bag. He even performed a circumcision in an Internet café. *Esquire* magazine also joined the chic circumcision *shtick*, featuring its own *mohel* in 1981, one who collects sports cars and vintage motorcycles.

Circumcision is equally appealing to many Jews who shun lavish materialism, such as the Jewish Renewal movement (Schachter-Shalomi 1983:98–106) and some variants of New Age Judaism. The website for Kodesh (www.kodesh.org), a Jewish self-actualization organization that fuses pop notions of Eastern mysticism with Kabbalah, describes circumcision as the "ancient art of Jewish spiritual surgery (truly 'holystic' medicine)."

The Politics of Foreskinless Identity

Opponents of circumcision rarely phrase their stance as a cultural preference rooted in a particular historical outlook. To do so would suggest that circumcision and uncircumcision are in some sense morally equivalent. Rather, critics naturalize their cultural preference through appeal to the universal truths of nature, rationality, progress, human rights, and individualism.

But all "subject positions" on circumcision are equally political and equally situated in culture and history. (I recognize that circumcising Jews who anchor the rite to a timeless God rather than "culture and history" will also find my claims here rather objectionable.) By way of an illustration, I turn to a vitriolic response to the Jewish anticircumcision movement published in *Commentary* magazine by the noted conservative scholar Jon Levenson (2000). Levenson rightly criticizes the sloppy scholarship of many circumcision critics (he specifically targets Gollaher and Goldman) in regard to Jewish history and rabbinic texts. More important, Levenson sees circumcision as resisting the romantic tradition that venerates "natural man and his raw instincts." The rite, too, destabilizes Western notions of personhood that valorize personal choice, egocentric desire, and the transcendent individual.

Levenson's defense of circumcision also excoriates "contemporary liberal culture" for promoting the "interchangeability of sexual roles" and eroding the "traditional virtues of sacrifice, discipline, and obedience" as well as "the sanctity of marriage." To the common refrain that circumcision reduces erotic pleasure, Levenson scolds liberalism for elevating sexuality above all other concerns.[31] Frankly, I find Levenson's polemic excessive. But it exemplifies my point that debates over circumcision only marginally concern the penis and focus instead on clashing worldviews concerning ethics, personhood, and the politics of identity.

Compared to Levenson, Boyarin and Boyarin (1995) affirm radical rather than conservative politics. But they still agree that circumcision challenges dominant Euro-Christian notions of nature, perfection, mutilation, and personhood. The very existence of circumcised Jewish (and Muslim) "Others" have long threatened the hegemony of foreskinned European Christianity. For Boyarin and Boyarin, circumcision celebrates the legitimacy of ethnic differences.[32] To the extent that the rite defines the Jew as a native to "tradition" rather than "place," circumcision also represents a diasporic alternative to nationalism. Finally, *brit milah* opposes the pervasive American ideal of the "self-made man." Instead of individuals privately choosing their ethnic identities from a dehistoricized marketplace of "self-invention," circumcision publicly marks the Jew as a self given in history.

Of course, when viewed as an act of free choice, as liberal nonreligious Jews tend to see it, circumcision reproduces traditional Jewish difference through the very "marketplace of ethnicity" that, from another angle, the rite resists. Simply put, both the performance and the refusal of brit milah represent a diversity of opinions concerning the politics of identity.

Ironically, circumcision poses far more dilemmas for Reform Judaism than for Orthodoxy precisely because the Reform movement embraces individualism and self-identification (Ellenson 1990; Finley 1990:183–84). In 1983, the Central Conference of American Rabbis, the official organization of Reform Judaism in the United States, formally defined a Jew as any person born to a Jewish parent—mother or father—who also publicly declares a Jewish identity. Orthodox Judaism descried the transformation of Jewish identity from birth into a voluntary association. Subsequently, reports Ellenson (1990:776), a Reform mohel refused to circumcise a boy whose Jewish mother professed belief in Jesus Christ. An Orthodox mohel did so instead!

A Different Hegemony

In Israel, the official prominence of Orthodox Judaism cuts a different relationship between circumcision and the state. Prior to a 2001 ruling by the Israeli Supreme Court, hospitals could legally advertise only the circumcision services of mohels approved by the Chief Rabbinate and the Ministry of Religious Affairs. The official penis was an Orthodox penis.

The Israel Religious Action Center (www.irac.org) filed suit on behalf of an organization of physicians, called Milah Tovah, who perform secular circumcisions. Milah Tovah appeals to parents who "dislike" the Orthodox rite (www.milatova.co.il). They advertise better sanitary conditions, no prayers or metzitzah, and, unlike Orthodox mohels who lack medical credentials, the administration of anesthesia.

Another Israeli circumcision controversy pertains to the dead. One strand of rabbinic thought links the messianic resurrection of men to circumcision (e.g., B. Sanhedrin 110b). As a result, some Jews perform abbreviated graveside rites for the uncircumcised (Romberg 1982:chap. 18).[33] Not all rabbis endorsed these circumcisions (Lieberman 1974b:266–67). Reform Judaism opposes the custom. But in Israel, state and military authorities formally sanction the Orthodox circumcision of deceased Jews, typically émigrés, without consent from the deceased or his kin.[34] Orthodox rabbis see these impromptu rites as acts of ultimate kindness. To critics, they are grotesque violations of basic civil rights.

Israel automatically grants citizenship to all Jews, circumcised or not. Posthumous circumcisions undermine that identity, as does, writes Siegel (1998:68), a common question asked of émigrés, Are you circumcised? In both cases, the foreskin that was initially irrelevant for the determination of Jewish identity suddenly threatens Jewishness. In the diaspora, argue Boyarin and Boyarin (1995), circumcision resists hegemonic demands by the state on its citizenry. In Israel, the rite sustains that hegemony.

Counterphallocentrism

Traditionally, Euro-Christian men won the hearts of angelic women through feats of martial honor. Alternatively, men forsook the sword and sexuality for a life of cloistered study and worship. Either way, legitimate manhood excluded the possibility of a tender, nurturing heterosexuality.

Classic Judaism knew neither battle-hardened knighthood nor monastic renunciation. Until the rise of militant Zionism, the ideal Jewish man was the passive, studious, and gentle scholar, called the *Yeshiva-Bokhur*, and his secular brother, the *mentsh* (Boyarin 1997b:68–69; but see Rosenberg 2001). Viewed from the perspective of Christianity and European culture, Jewish men were nonmen. They were wimps, unable to live up to the chivalric ideal of Christianity—and obviously barred from the monastery. If one needed any proof, then a quick glance at the castrated Jewish penis would suffice. But from within Jewish culture, circumcision and humility were traits of genuine heterosexual and procreative masculinity.

Jewish women traditionally filled public roles that European culture normally assigned to men. They conducted business, economically supported their spouses, and interacted with government officials. Jewish men stayed indoors, avoided commerce and conflict, and performed housework. But however much Jewish men appeared to act like non-Jewish women, stresses Boyarin (1997b:81), they still succeeded at the two endeavors the broader culture valued as quintessentially male: attracting women and siring sons.

Rabbinic culture inverted Euro-Christian norms but still favored men. It was, says Boyarin (1997b:153), a "kindler, gentler" patriarchy. Circumcision marked and partly sustained this hierarchy. Nonetheless, argues Boyarin (1997b), circumcision was *not* castrative because masculinity was *not* defined in terms of phallic aggression. Circumcision snipped the foreskin rather than a symbol of male privilege. In this framework, numerous jokes about circumcision that play with the theme of castration anxiety miss the point.

Question: What do you call an uncircumcised Jew?
Answer: A woman.
Question: What do you call the useless skin at the end of the penis?
Answer: A man.
Question: What's the difference between circumcision and divorce?
Answer: In divorce, you get rid of the whole schmuck!

Theses jokes are wrong or misguided because, as Boyarin would argue, they construe circumcision as phallic and castrative rather than "counterphallic." In traditional Judaism, circumcision appropriated for men desirable qualities normally associated with women. Yet for all his apparent feminization, the circumcised Jew never renounced heterosexuality, marriage, and reproduction. Indeed, Jewish women found his femininity alluring. In this sense, circumcision destabalizes Jewish and non-Jewish masculinities while nonetheless preserving a strict masculine norm.

The feminine inflection of Jewish manhood, in this view, only seems humorous and deviant when judged against hegemonic cultural norms. Then the Jew and his "clip-tip" or "half-dick" fail to measure up.[35]

Despite this, many Jews today see circumcision as a mark of ambivalent or lesser manhood. Jackie Mason, after the cancellation of his 1989 television sitcom Chicken Soup, commented to the effect that "well, at least Americans now know what a Jew looks like." To this, Richard Merkin replied in the February 1991 issue of Gentleman's Quarterly, "If Jackie Mason is even remotely like a typical Jew, then I'm in the market for a used foreskin in a medium—um, make that a medium large." Anxiety over Jewish bodily difference, writes Gilman (1991c:29), translates into a fantasy about an enlarged, more powerful, non-Jewish phallus.

Jewish ambivalence toward circumcision is nicely captured by a popular joke with many variants. The joke also responds to the idea of castrated circumcised difference, albeit ironically:

A Jewish fabric salesman, on his last day before retirement, was complaining to the buyer from Bloomingdale's that he had never been able to make a single sale to the store. "Please give me just one order," he pleaded. "I've been trying to sell to Bloomingdale's for years, yet you always refuse, and now, well, now that I'm about to retire, whaddya say?" "Ok, ok," says the buyer. "Send me enough fabric to reach from the tip of your nose to the tip of your penis." The next day a huge truck rolls up to Bloomingdale's and begins to unload 8,000 miles of fabric. The enraged buyer screams to the ribbon salesman over the phone, "What the hell's going on?" The salesman replies, "I was circumcised in Minsk!"

How does the Jew respond to the mockery of the Jewish body—elongated nose and diminished penis? With his superior wit and phallus.

For two millennia, Europeans have looked on circumcision as the key symbol of the Jew's uncertain role in society. Beginning in the late nineteenth century, I showed, Jews did likewise. They, too, viewed circumcision as a sign their own ambivalent position in Western civilization—a sign to be defended, revised, or altogether abandoned. At the same time, Jews increasingly viewed circumcision as a sign of an essential uncertainty about the very meaning of Jewishness.

A confluence of historical developments in the nineteenth century pushed circumcision to the forefront of contestation. The rite did or did not admit Jews as full modern citizens into European civilization. The rite did or did not represent modern standards of progress, science, hygiene, and rationality. The Jew remained sexually, physiologically, and mentally unique. But the status of this uniqueness shifted. To many, the Jew remained a pariah. To others, he was suddenly worthy of emulation. Jews themselves shared these differing stances. The community effectively split on the role of circumcision to cut the Jew into or out of European society. Indeed, this type of ambivalence, I would argue, is one of the defining features of modern, assimilated Judaism.

In the second half of the chapter, I surveyed contemporary opposition to brit milah within the Jewish community—as well as, to a lesser degree, its defense. It is not the opposition per se that is so often problematic, I implied, but rather its rhetorical excesses. I am not speaking about debates over the politics of identity or the role of the irrational in formulating modern religious ritual. I am not speaking about different views on how to confront the issue of pain. Rather, I refer to recurrent assertions that the Jew is both the victim and the perpetrator of his own circumcised wound; that circumcision is the source, and false cure, of distinctly Jewish neuroses; and that circumcision enacts a style of brutal childraising that also fueled Nazism. Again and again, Jews today censure the rite with tones and assumptions that revive an almost medieval anti-Judaism.

In the logic of many circumcision opponents, Jewish women consent to circumcision—but only in revenge for Jewish men who despise women for allowing the rite. In earlier chapters, I extensively analyzed the gendered dimensions of circumcision in biblical and rabbinic cultures. In one avenue of interpretation, I argued that circumcision scripts manhood against—yet in terms of—motherhood. In Judaism, circumcision *does* sustain male privi-

lege. But circumcision does *not* singularly cause modern misogyny. To critique the rite as a symbol of male privilege, I say as the Jewish father of a
daughter, *is* valid. But to construe the rite as a central source of misogyny
among contemporary Jews is to commit what the great philosopher Alfred
North Whitehead dubbed the "fallacy of misplaced concreteness." Indeed,
most feminist scholars of Judaism, such as Prell (1999), explain popular
images of Jewish women (and men) not in reference to circumcision or any
other ritual for that matter. Rather, they anchor these sexist images to
broader tensions that arose, at least in America, during the complex process
of assimilation in the early twentieth century.

Some Jewish proponents of circumcision believe the rite to create a *docile*
form of manhood. Opponents of the rite utterly reject this argument. Yet
they subscribe to the very same logic when asserting that circumcision creates a *hostile* Jew. Clearly, the adult imagination about circumcision is far
more powerful—to opponent and proponent alike—than the infant's experience of the rite.

Circumcision critics, I maintain, frequently resemble Paul when mobilizing an apparent contradiction between ritual and belief (Paul's "faith" versus
"works") to push for a Judaism devoid of circumcision. These arguments are
persuasive. But they confuse rabbinic Judaism with ancient Israel and thus
neglect 1,500 years of rabbinic thought. When opponents do consider rabbinic texts and interpretations, however superficially, they simply dismiss
them as, in Goldman's (1998:69) words, a "rationalization" for enacting
"repressed feelings on those who are weaker." Thus formulated, the entirety
of rabbinic scholarship is cast aside as a psychological delusion. Luther, the
sixteenth-century author of "The Jews and Their Lies," would be pleased.

Many Jewish critics of circumcision essentialize the rite by attributing
validity *only* to premodern orthodoxy—the very orthodoxy they reject. This
tact refuses to validate the full spectrum of meanings contemporary Jews
bring to circumcision, including diffuse commitments to ethnicity, tradition,
and family (see also Schur 1971). It only allows for sanctimonious accusations of hypocrisy, that is, the assertion that Jews who circumcise yet decline
Orthodox belief are insincere or false Jews. Modern meanings that circumcising Jews attribute to the rite diverge absolutely from rabbinic traditions. The
rabbis would likely have dismissed them. But it seems tendentious to conclude that they are wanting for genuine spirituality or valid significance. The
early Church Fathers ridiculed circumcision as a false, "mute sign." Circumcision foes, I am suggesting, often seem to agree.

Critics of *brit milah* also resemble Paul when they denounce their non-

Orthodox yet circumcising coreligionists for trapping themselves in meaningless bodily rites. But Judaism, we have seen, is a corporeal religion, marked and enacted through bodily practices. It is not a religion defined solely on the basis of belief, sentiment, faith, or the "heart." It requires embodiment. A disembodied, noncircumcising Judaism, however much its sensibilities resonate with American liberalism, runs the risk of resembling Pauline Christianity without Christ.

Often, we saw, Jewish opponents of circumcision reproduce stereotypes of the damaged Jewish psyche. But they also offer an equally stereotyped solution: utilize the superior Jewish brain (Gilman 1996).[36] "Jews are some of the smartest people in the world," we read at www.jewsagainstcircumcision.org. "We are 1/3rd of 1% of the population, yet we hold 33% of Nobel prizes. We are smart enough to understand that mutilating a little boys' [sic] penis is not an acceptable practice in modern times." In one way or another, the Jew's penis points to his brain—a brain either crazed or brilliant.

Portrayals of the Jews as uniquely deranged and blemished, intent on harming children and women, never mind themselves, in order futilely to escape their bodily and psychic impairments are nothing new. Any medieval peasant would recognize them. What is new, I contend, is the incorporation of these images into Judaism by Jews who still wish to assert a Jewish identity. It is now the Jew, not the Christian, who often fears the knife-wielding Jew.

Most Jews who oppose circumcision in America, I think it fair to say, tend to reside on the liberal side of the social and political spectrum. Jewish adherents, we have seen, seemingly offer a greater representation of American political and lifestyle ideologies, ranging from New Age to conservative Orthodox. The rite has assimilated to Judaism much of American culture.[37] Conversely, the multiplicity of voices supporting circumcision evidences the full assimilation of Judaism into American society.

Yet circumcision remains, I believe, the preeminent symbol of the Jew's ambivalent role in society—especially to Jews. No longer does the rite commemorate the covenant. It now memorializes a plurality of perspectives on the relationship between tradition and modernity, distinctiveness and assimilation, individualism and community, Judaism as a singular theology and an ethnic plurality.

Spinoza was wrong. The evidence presented in this chapter speaks loudly to the argument that circumcision will *not* preserve the Jewish community. The resistance to circumcision—like the adherence to the rite—admits of great anguish but little compromise. Instead, I believe, circumcision will continue to foment Jewish debates over what exactly Judaism is—namely, a community united in its divisions, set apart from itself as much as it is cut into and off the wider culture.

Notes

1. Published in Jack Dann, ed., *Wandering Stars: An Anthology of Jewish Fantasy and Science Fiction* (New York: Harper & Row, 1974).

2. The Ohio state legislature tried to ban ritual circumcision in the 1880s but balked over constitutional concerns (Gollaher 2000:94–95).

3. In 2005, the Rabbinical Council of America, a governing body of Orthodox Judaism, ruled that suction through a sterile tube fully satisfied the obligation of oral *metzitzah* (www.rabbis.org/news/030105.cfm). The chief rabbi of Israel declared likewise in 2002 after oral *metzitzah* transmitted several cases of neonatal genital herpes (Gesundheit 2004).

4. For female circumcision in America and Britain, see Sheehan (1981) and Moscucci (1996).

5. The study of food, morality, and masturbation in nineteenth-century America is now something of a cottage industry and includes a terrific essay on the Internet titled "Porn Flakes." Kellogg's 1891 magnum opus *Plain Facts for Old And Young: Embracing the Natural History of Hygiene of Organic Life* is now available online (http://etext.lib.virginia.edu/toc/modeng/public/KelPlai.html). Incidentally, Kellogg partly penned the book during his honeymoon in lieu of more erotic pursuits.

6. Gollaher's (2000) error is magnified by the fact that his system for citing rabbinic texts is so plainly wrong that one questions whether he read them.

7. Even Jewish women sometimes assimilated circumcision into their identity (Geller 1997).

8. It also construed Judaism as an inherently diseased religion (Gilman 1993a). Why, asked Emanuel Rosenbaum in *Meziza: Ist sie religiös geboten? Wirkt sie heilend oder schädlich?* (1913), did public health officials focus on Jewish ritual but *not* aseptic hospital procedures (Efron 2001:23)? If saliva transmitted syphilis, why the concern with sanitizing *metzitzah* but not restaurant tableware?

9. The most notorious Jewish statement on the male Jew's femininity was Otto Weininger's *Sex and Character* (1906), originally published in German in 1903.

10. Freud also, along with Wilhelm Fliess, tried to escape racial stereotyping by arguing that all men and not just Jews experienced nosebleeds as part of physiological periodicity (Gilman 1987:304).

11. On a different front, nineteenth-century scholars eroded circumcision of its Jewish authenticity by stressing the Egyptian origins of the rite (Katz 1998b:324–25).

12. In 1916, the newly created Board of Milah in New York City, in cooperation with the Department of Health, also prohibited direct oral *metzitzah* (Wallerstein 1980:159).

13. For the published documents from the Reform conferences, see volumes 1 to 3 of the *Year Book of the Central Conference of American Rabbis* and Philipson (1931).

14. Traditionally, circumcised male converts give up two drops of blood. But there is some Talmudic debate on this issue (B. Shabbath 135a).

15. Friedlaender wrote the book, under the pseudonym Mynona, in response to Oskar Panizza's *The Operated Jew* (1893).

16. An anticircumcision website actually monitors representations of circumcision in film and on television (www.circumstitions.com).

17. Often, Jewish critics object to the caricature of Judaism (e.g., Pearl and Pearl 1999), while opponents of circumcision protest the lack of censure (www.circumstitions.com/TVSitcoms.html).

18. The letters are reprinted at www.jewishcircumcision.org/klagsbrun.htm.

19. What (1995) powerfully discusses her son's circumcision after she endured a double mastectomy.

20. A postcard style dating to the early twentieth century (I purchased one on eBay) and often copyrighted by Samuel Goldring shows a young boy lying on bed between a matronly woman (his mother?) and a stereotypically razor-brandishing *mohel*. The upper caption reads in Hebrew, *mazel tov*, or "best wishes." The lower caption says, "Abie gets his first 10% cut."

21. For a different, I would say more insightful, analysis of so-called JAP jokes, see Dundes (1985), Prell (1992, 2000), and Biale (1997:chap. 9).

22. See the summer 1988 issue of *Humanistic Judaism* (vol. 16, no. 3), "Becoming Parents."

23. Yasmin Anwar, "Ceremony Raises Tempest among Jews," *Oakland Tribune*. My clipping of the article was furnished by Helen Bryce of the Alternative Bris Support Group. Unfortunately, I am unable to locate the date of the article.

24. Floral idioms also occur in Bader's (1999: 29): *Haikus for Jews: For You, a Little Wisdom*: "Looking for pink buds/to prune back/the *mohel* tends/his flower garden."

25. For the Israeli anticircumcision movement, see www.kahal.org and Zoossmann-Diskin and Blustein (1999).

26. Orthodox Jews once scolded Reform Jewry for abandoning *brit milah*. Even today, Orthodox *mohels* may refuse to circumcise Reform Jews (Boxman 1986:90–91). Consequently, Reform Judaism in the 1980s developed its own certification program for physician-*mohels* (see Boxman 1986:87–102; Barth 1990). Again, Orthodox resistance ensued only now, writes Boxman, for the effort by Reform Jews to reclaim the rite! For *mohels* in Conservative Judaism, see Grodin and Schoenberg (1988).

27. Mike Weiss, "A Women's Touch," *Atlanta Jewish Times*, June 8, 2001 (www.atljewishtimes.com/archives/2001/060801cs.htm).

28. S. Wilkowski, *Baby's Bris*, illustrations by J. Friedman (Rockville, Md.: Kar-Ben Copies, 1999).

29. In the same spirit, Frymer-Kensky (1995) offers meditations on menstrual blood, women's bodies, and birth in *Motherprayer: The Pregnant Woman's Spiritual Companion*.

30. E. M. Broner included a similar rite in her 1978 novel *A Weave of Women*. For male

circumcision as paralleling the perforation of a girl's hymen to unseal procreative power, see Knight (2001).

31. Among several letters to the editor in the June 2000 issue of *Commentary*, Gollaher speaks of libel, another writer warns of class-action legal suits against *mohels*, and a third affirms his uncircumcised son's Jewishness "because his mother and I are Jewish, because we teach him Jewish values, and because his grandparents died in Auschwitz."

32. The circumcised Jew, wrote Derrida (1986a:46), "exhibits his castration as an erection that defies the other."

33. Diasporic Jews may sprinkle dust from Israel on the deceased's forehead, eyes, heart, navel, and circumcision.

34. A Hasidic group called Friends of Refugees of Eastern Europe (www.russianjewry .com) sponsors the circumcision of Soviet-Russian émigrés partly to challenge Christian missionaries.

35. The feminizing, emasculating, homosexual connotations of Jewish circumcision were prominent in "Whoopee," a 1929 Wild West Ziegfeld extravaganza (Most 1999).

36. For an earlier psychoanalytic expression of this theme, see Glenn (1960).

37. The ceremony even offers opportunities for online entrepreneurship, as in the "Bris Bag," described as "all the mohel-approved items you need for a bris milah in a beautiful diaper bag, saving you time, money and the hassle of putting it all together" (www.brisbag.com).

CHAPTER TEN

Old Whine in New Foreskins: Anti-Judaism in the Contemporary Debate over Medical Circumcision

Throughout this book, I often eluded to a growing controversy over routine medical circumcision in contemporary Western societies, especially in the United States. I want now to analyze the portrayal of the Jew in this debate. To frame my discussion, I begin with several voices from two prominent anticircumcision sources: the Internet site www.sexuallymutilatedchild.org and Ronald Goldman's pioneering 1997 book *Circumcision: The Hidden Trauma*:

> When I think about what my parents let happen to me, I want to take a razor and slit their throats.

> Words cannot describe the rage I feel toward the pervert who did this to me.

> It taught me how to hate.

These comments typify the declarations of rage that permeate the growing movement to eradicate male circumcision.

Often, this fury turns to the Jew. George C. Denniston, a physician affiliated with the Department of Family Medicine at the University of Washington, the founder of the organization Doctors Against Circumcision (D.O.C.), and a leading figure in the movement speaks eloquently to this issue:

Lest I be accused of being anti-Semitic by presenting these facts, let me say that I can conceive of nothing more likely to promote prejudice than the recognition that Moslem and Jewish physicians are making several hundred dollars for each Christian infant they mutilate. (Denniston 1994)

The reference to Moslems, however, is somewhat gratuitous. For, as we will see, almost all the key opponents of medical circumcision, as well as Muslim critics of the Islamic rite, ultimately blame the Jews.

"Genital Integrity"

Once established in the early twentieth century as an integral part of hospital birth, male circumcision hardly merited a pause. The rationale for the procedure was no longer anchored to masturbation, sexual excess, and "nervous energy." But it remained connected to hygiene. Physicians increasingly saw medical circumcision (what I will abbreviate as MC) as a prophylactic against urinary tract infections, various complications of the foreskin, and penile cancer.

The procedure declined dramatically in Britain after the creation of the National Health Service in 1948. Since English physicians failed to agree on the medical benefits of MC, if any, the procedure was excluded from automatic coverage. The United States, of course, never developed a national health plan, so there was little incentive to formulate a singular policy on MC. Consequently, the medical procedure persisted—for better or worse. For several decades, American physicians and health care associations promoted MC. Most medical organizations such as the American Pediatrics Association now acknowledge *some* health benefits to MC. Yet they recently ceased to endorse its routine occurrence. It remains, like *brit milah* to Reform Jews, a matter of personal choice. Approximately 60 percent of all newborn American boys are circumcised after birth.

Today, the idea and practice of routine MC elicits impassioned, sometimes furious moral, medical, and religious debate. In this chapter, I read the anti-circumcision movement as a forum for expressing deep anxieties over almost everything but the foreskin—anxieties about masculinity, motherhood, sexuality, the medicalization of birth, state power, *and* the insidious influence of the Jews.

The Internet is the main venue for the current debate over medical circumcision. In the previous chapter, I mentioned cyberspace advocates of the

Jewish rite. Many proponents of the medical procedure also maintain websites, including the following:

CIRCLIST (www.circlist.com)
CIRCUMCISIONINFO.com (http://circumcisioninfo.com)
International Circumcision Reference Center (www.circinfo.com)
Circumcision Online News (www.geocities.com/HotSprings/2754)
www.circumcision.net
Circumcision Agency (www.circumcision-agency.com)

Three physicians active in the promotion of medical circumcision also host extensive websites: Gerald N. Weiss's Circumcision Information (www.users .dircon.co.uk/~vernon/G_Weiss), Brian Morris's Benefits of Circumcision (www.circinfo.net), and Edgar J. Schoen's Circumcision: A Lifetime of Medical Benefits (www.medicirc.org).[1] Yet cyberspace advocates of MC pale before the number and stridency of anticircumcision websites.

Indeed, the number of anticircumcision activist groups may surprise some readers. They include the following:

CIRP (Circumcision Information Resource Pages; www.cirp.org)
NOCIRC (National Organization of Circumcision Resources; www.no circ.org)
NOHARMM (National Organization to Halt the Abuse and Routine Mutilation of Males; www.noharmm.org)
MUSIC (Musicians United to Stop Involuntary Circumcision; www .musiciansunited.org)
Mothers Against Circumcision (www.mothersagainstcirc.org)
S.I.C. Society (Stop Infant Circumcision Society; www.stopinfantcircum cision.org)
Nurses for the Rights of the Child (http://nurses.cirp.org)
ARC (Attorneys for the Rights of the Child; www.arclaw.org)
In Memory of the Sexually Mutilated Child (www.sexuallymutilated child.org)
International Coalition for Genital Integrity (www.icgi.org)
The Intactivism Pages (www.circumstitions.com), which includes "A Gallery of Famous Intact Men"
NotJustSkin (www.notjustskin.org, affiliated with NOCIRC)
Students for Genital Integrity (www.studentsforgenitalintegrity.org)
Foreskin (www.foreskin.org)

Some of these groups have formal status with the United Nations as nongovernmental organizations (Svoboda 2004). NOCIRC has sponsored eight international symposia on "Circumcision, Sexual Mutilations, and Genital Integrity." Kluwer Academic Publishers has released four of the proceedings: *Sexual Mutilations: A Human Tragedy* (1997), *Male and Female Circumcision: Medical, Legal, and Ethical Considerations in Pediatric Practice* (1999), *Understanding Circumcision: A Multi-Disciplinary Approach to a Multi-Dimensional Problem* (2001), and *Flesh and Blood: Perspectives on the Problem of Circumcision in Contemporary Society* (2004). "Intactivists" gather every April in Washington, D.C., for "Genital Integrity Week" to petition Congress. Therapists, counseling centers, and support groups address the "trauma" of circumcision.[2]

In order fully to understand the specific images of the Jew in the debate over male circumcision, it is necessary first to sketch a relevant context. With this in mind, I now review the major objections to the medical procedure.

Foreskinned Wholeness

Critics claim that MC acutely disrupts patterns of infant sleeping, crying, nursing, and the mother–child bond more generally. The procedure, too, induces long-term mental and physiological harm. The pain of circumcision is likened to torture, resulting in shock, semicoma, and even infant depression and post-traumatic stress disorder.[3] Goldman (1997:132) claims that circumcised boys cover their penises during diaper changing because they "fear further damage to their genitals and may not trust their caretaker."[4] The procedure is even alleged to cause SIDS, or sudden infant death syndrome (Carter 1979:27; Romberg 1985:298–99; Denniston 1994; deMause 1995). "If circumcision is comparable to rape," asks Goldman (1997:172), "how do we know that SIDS is not, at least in some cases, infant suicide?"

Circumcised men, we are told, report a wide range of emotional dysfunctions (Goldman 1997, 1998; Rhinehart 1999; Hammond 1999). They experience rage, hate, fear, betrayal, shame, distrust, victimization, powerlessness, withdrawal, low self-esteem, and emotional numbing. Foreskinless men feel mutilated, abused, alienated, robbed, diminished, and raped. They envy intact men, obsess about penis size, and suffer poor relationships and sexual anxieties. They are promiscuous, violent toward women, and abusive of alcohol and drugs.

The "profound trauma" of circumcision, states Denniston (1994), "keeps men from getting in touch . . . with their feelings—a deficiency that women are constantly accusing them of." By expending "immense reservoirs of psychic energy" to repress their wounds, the circumcised are unable to engage in "sensitive, creative works" (Baker 1996). Additionally, writes Hammond (1997:128–29), many circumcised men refuse counseling because of a "well-founded" mistrust of doctors. To make matters worse, society refuses to validate these traumas—much like, says Bigelow (1998:92), collective denials of slavery and rape.

Ample cross-cultural data attest to the psychological trauma of ritualized *adolescent* circumcision (e.g., Cansever 1965; Öztürk 1973). There is no controversy on this point.[5] What does seem open to challenge (or at least debate) is the effort by circumcision critics such as Goldman (1997:133) to extrapolate from these studies in order to posit a direct *causal* relationship between severe adult distress and a properly performed neonatal circumcision. An alternative view would assume that adults project their own emotional unease with the procedure onto the circumcised infant (see also Romirowsky 1990). It is clear that many American men today publicly write their anxieties, tragedies, and autobiographies into their foreskinned absences. Indeed, the psychological, social, and sexual damages attributed to circumcision resemble the quintessential woes of contemporary society. What is less clear is whether the lost foreskin causes or symbolizes this modern alienation.

Why Men Squirm

Many opponents of MC allege that adult men can recover the memory of their own infancy circumcision (e.g., Baker 1996; Goodman 1997; Denniston 1998). They do so through psychotherapeutic regression that taps into "motor memories" (Schmaltz 1991:23), "mind-body" memories (Zoske 1998), or what Goldman (1997:9) calls a "very deep feeling-experiential-body level that relies on its own kind of knowing." These memories, Goldman continues, explain why adult men squirm when discussing circumcision.

After recovering these memories, one man felt guilty from his inability to protect his infant self from the circumcision (Breeding 1991). Other men, claims Rhinehart (1999), may experience "the feel of sharp metallic instruments cutting into one's flesh . . . the sense of being overpowered by big people, being alone and helpless, feelings of terror." A Jewish man conjured "a bunch of evil, leering monsters who are going to devour me. . . . I had something they wanted and they took it from me" (Romberg 1985:305–16).

A similar sentiment is conveyed by a postcard I purchased on eBay. It depicts a young, naked, innocent-looking boy, standing in the corner of a room, covering his genitals, beneath the words "Who Me??" Before the child stands a much larger, bespeckled man with a long black coat and a cap. With one hand, the man beckons the child. With the other, he holds a large pair of shears behind his back.

In a NOHARMM Progress Report titled "My Story of Ritual Abuse," another Jewish man attributes to his circumcision a recurring childhood nightmare of a "long bearded goat"—the *mohel*—eating its way through the bedroom wall to bite his flesh (http://noharmm.org/mystory.htm). This particular rite also explains the victim's anger, genital insecurity, and hostility to Judaism as well as his aversion to alcohol since the *mohel*'s wine-soaked gauze failed to calm him during the circumcision.

I do not want to question the legitimacy of these analyses beyond suggesting that they raise reasonable questions about diagnosis, treatment, efficacy, and, again, the source of the anguish. I turn instead to less evident issues. First, the classic rabbis, we have seen, linked Jewish circumcision to various types of bodily, collective, and masculine memories. How ironic that similar themes should now arise to critique the rite.

Second, many critics of MC draw their data, theories, and authority from the discourse of Western biomedicine and science. That the procedure is medically unwarranted does not, in their view, invalidate medicine. But other opponents of MC critique the entirety of Western science. They extend the idea of recoverable "body memories" to birth, gestation, conception, even a person's separate existence as sperm and egg![6] The opposition to MC in this view joins a broader critique of the Enlightenment. In so doing, New Age critics of the procedure ironically resemble traditional Jews who endorse the rite, although, to be sure, neither group would likely appreciate the parallel.

The New Epispasm

Many men who bemoan their circumcision now turn to foreskin restoration. For assistance, aspiring restorers can turn to Bigelow's (1998) compendium *The Joy of Uncircumcising!* as well as the National Organization of Restoring Men, or Norm (www.norm.org), formerly known as RECAP, and Brothers United for Future Foreskins, or BUFF. Typically, the skin from the penis shaft is stretched over the glans, then taped or tied to a lead fishing weight, steel ball, weighted cone, or infant bottle nipple (see also Gilman 1997; Gollaher

2000:chap. 7). The restoration process last from a few months to several years.

Among several commercial devices that assist foreskin restoration are the P.U.D. (Penile Uncircumcising Device), Foreballs, and, at the high end of the market (about $400), the VacuTrac (www.foreskinrestoration.info). As an added bonus, the latter device also promises, like so many e-mail solicitations, to increase length. Other preputial extenders include Tug Ahoy (www .tugahoy.com), ForeSkin Natural Restorer (www.4restore.com), and Your-Skin Restoration Cone (www.tlctugger.com) as well as surgical techniques (Brandes and McAninch 1999). There is even a lubricating undergarment foreskin substitute called ManHood (www.manhood.mb.ca). Instead of circumcising boys to resemble their fathers, exclaim Ritter and Denniston (1996), adult men should restore their foreskins to resemble their intact sons.

Foreskin restoration, says Warren (1999:308), "is a journey from saying *I am a victim* to being able to say *I was a victim.*" Bigelow (1998:120) equates modern restorers with the courageous Hellenistic Jews who practiced epispasm. Foreskin restoration allegedly "improves body image, improves self-esteem, dispels feelings of victimization, and empowers men to make choices about their own sexuality" (Hodges and Warner 1995). Reintact men report feeling virile, confident, proud, whole, natural, sexy, normal, and healed (Griffiths 1999). To many men, so it seems, a renewed foreskin conquers the ailments typically assigned to modern society.

Jewish Nazis

Why, if circumcision is so horrible, does it persist? In answering this question, opponents of the procedure appeal not to religion, tradition, sentiment, or medicine but instead to denial and repetition-compulsion. That is, cut men deny their psychological pain while nonetheless unconsciously reliving their circumcised trauma by sadistically cutting infants (Miller 1990:139–40; Sandel 1996). As Baker (1997:179–80) writes, "Those who have had technocratic perinatal flesh-wounding rituals imprinted on them in hospital neonatal wards, often become compelled to reenact these rituals on their own children." What's more, writes Denniston (1999:221), the "anxiety-ridden circumcised father . . . is so disturbed by his newborn son's intact penis that he insists that it be surgically altered." One hardly needs to point out the implications of these statements for Jews and Judaism.

But lest the implications seem vague, let me cite from J. M. Foley's (1966) book *The Practice of Circumcision: A Reevaluation*, also excerpted in the July

1966 issue of *Fact Magazine* as "The Unkindest Cut of All." Circumcised men, tells Foley, envy yet despise their neighbor's foreskin. They also view their own circumcision as "a stigma of inferiority." To overcome this self-hatred, "Jew, Moor, and Turk forced circumcision on servants, slaves, and whole nations of conquered people," including, in this scenario, Christians. Supporters of circumcision include "homosexuals," Foley continues, who seek to overcome their fear of castration by cutting others, and "anti-Semitic Jews, ashamed of their mark and eager to make it universal." Foley's book receives widespread endorsement.

Critics of circumcision often evoke the Spanish Inquisition, the Salem witch trials, and especially Nazism. Rhinehart (1999) equates pediatric "circumcisers" and *mohels* with concentration camp commanders: "they too had their rationalizations." Denniston (1999:397–98) likens circumcising physicians with Nazi scientists who affirmed the racial inferiority of Jews. In the *Cambridge Quarterly of Healthcare Ethics*, Denniston (1997a:90–92) also claims that medical circumcision is "a religious ritual, which has overflowed onto millions of innocent victims." "Hopefully," he adds after citing the Nuremberg Code on voluntary consent, "Jewish doctors, who so fervently want others to abide by this code, will give this plea their special consideration."[7] These statements communicate the message that, at some level, medical circumcision is the moral equivalence of the Holocaust, only this time perpetrated by Jews.

Circumcision and Male Violence

Many "intactivists" tie the high incidence of sexual assault and domestic violence in America to MC (Northrup 1994). Like rapists and spousal abusers, writes Goldman (1997:162–68), "circumcisers" impose their will on the bodies of others, then deny their victims' pain. Physicians who perform the procedure "suffer from some form of psychosexual sickness" (Price 1996:29).[8] James W. Prescott, a former official at the National Institutes of Health, understands circumcision to imprint "the brain for sado-masochistic behaviors" (1975; see also Fleiss 1997; Rhinehart 1999; Trachtenberg 1999:213). Again and again, we read that infant circumcision permanently codes the neurological architecture of the brain for deviant sexuality and excessive aggression. Here, as in the nineteenth-century stereotypes of the Jews, an altered penis points to a damaged psyche.

Critics also construe circumcision as child abuse (Miller 1990:139–40;

Goldman 1997:168–71). Like other forms of childhood neglect, the trauma of MC leads to depression and suicide but also to the following:

• Alcohol and drug addiction (to assuage psychological pain)
• Unprotected sex and teenage pregnancies (to overcompensate for poor self-esteem)
• Increased male competition (to offset a diminished phallus)[9]
• Divorce and men who refuse marriage (circumcised men are unable to tolerate the emotional stress of relationships)
• Needless surgery (cut men like to cut)
• Unwarranted episiotomies, hysterectomies, and mastectomies (to deny women the erotic pleasure circumcised men themselves lack)
• Antisocial behaviors such as hard-core pornography, loud rock music, and violent crime (to reenact the "excessive stimulation" and "subsequent numbing" of infant circumcision)
• Theft (to avenge the theft of the foreskin)

In turn, these psychological problems result in soaring medical expenses, rising insurance premiums, and higher taxes since the circumcised disproportionately require welfare, law enforcement, and prisons. I think it fair to say that, in the popular literature opposing the procedure, no aspect of body politic is safe from the cut of circumcision.

A Matriarchal Assault, or an Assault on Motherhood?

Intactivists generally view circumcision as a patriarchal assault on a mother's natural instincts to protect her newborn. Yet others, especially from within the men's movement, understand the procedure as a matriarchal emasculation of man's natural dominance.

Rosemary Romberg's book *Circumcision: The Painful Dilemma* (1985) illustrates powerfully the first view. One anguished mother tells how *brit milah* violently destroyed the beautiful, intimate rhythm she established with her son. The rite, too, forced her to cut off "a lot of feelings" and to repress her natural protective instinct (Romberg 1985:80–84). The child "was screaming and there was no doubt in his scream that he wanted mother . . . to come and protect him from this pain!!" Years later, she still feels "an element of detachment" toward her son. Moss (1990) similarly reports that, after her own son's circumcision, it took "weeks to develop what I would consider a maternal instinct . . . and months to feel I truly knew my child."

To explain how circumcision results in maternal detachment, Romberg (1985:288) looks to animal biology. The mother develops an "instinctive rejection reaction . . . similar to the way a mother animal is likely to kill or reject her infant if it is has been injured." Circumcision, in this view, emotionally harms mothers, who emotionally harm their sons.

In turn, circumcised men unconsciously blame mothers and women for their own psychological trauma, resulting in misogyny, sexual assault, and rape (Laibow 1991; Milos and Macris 1992; Price 1996:32; Goldman 1997:131). Indeed, Bigelow (1998:97) connects "the bound and gagged woman shrinking from a man with a knife" so often depicted on men's detective magazines and "the fact that most men in this country had a similar experience when they were babies." It is, says Baker (1996), "just like some bad Jewish-mother joke."

In an essay published in the *Journal of the American Medical Association*, Morgan (1965) attributed MC to "latent female antagonism toward the penis." As Newman (1991) declares in the magazine *Changing Men*, "For all of us who were cut when us and mother and world were still synonymous, the vagina dentata is a concrete reality." Carter (1979:27) attributed MC to "the neurotic, sexually frustrated woman who derives satisfaction from the mutilation of the male organ." Morgan titled his essay, which the anticircumcision movement often views as its pioneering document, "The Rape of the Phallus."

Circumcisers and Abortionists

When opponents of MC defend a man's right to control his body, they borrow rhetoric from the pro-choice movement. But as self-described "intactivists" who promote "genital integrity" rather than oppose something, they mirror the language of the pro-life movement (Gollaher 2000:174–76). Adversaries of abortion and circumcision both deploy gut-wrenching photos and films of screaming fetuses and infants. Both groups speak about innocent victims, ruthless physicians, lifelong psychological scarring, and potential complications. Both groups heckle their medical rivals as "abortionists" and "circumcisers." Both groups deplore a general decline in social morality. And both groups allege to represent the rights of vulnerable mothers who would otherwise suffer invasive exploitation by a ruthless, greedy medical industry.

A website titled Circumvent Circumcision (http://circumvent.org) endorses a group provocatively called the PLO, or Penis Liberation Organization. Taking a cue from the legal effort to pursue reparations for torture and slavery, Circumvent Circumcision advocates foreskin reparations. More chillingly, Circumvent Circumcision emulates the radical fringe of the anti-abortion movement and posts the names, addresses, telephone numbers, and state credential numbers of "circumcisers." It also links to another website, Circumciser Hall of Infamy, that lists several physicians and declares, "These doctors have sexually mutilated literally tens of thousands of innocent babies. The fact that these people are still alive and free to walk the streets is a disgusting commentary on how little value society has for its children." Readers are admonished to report these "child abusers" to the proper authorities.

Foreskinless Sexuality

Opponents of circumcision tie the procedure to three aspects of human sexuality: reduced pleasure, unnatural sexual practices, and homosexuality. First, MC is said to so mar penile sensitivity that intercourse becomes unenjoyable. "I don't have sex with anyone," reports one man at www.sexuallymutilated child.org/feelings.htm, "because I wouldn't want to have sex with anyone who would have sex with someone who was circumcised." Says another, "I have even gone so far as to use condoms, cut and placed in a tedious, time-consuming task on myself to simulate a foreskin."

The research director of a controversial organization, the Orgone Biophysical Research Center (www.orgonelab.org), argues that the true purpose of circumcision is to thwart sexual pleasure by impairing a child's "emotional fluidity and energy level" (DeMeo 1997:6). Prescott (1994) proposes that MC inhibits "the development of the neurointegrative brain" and thus prevents men from attaining "spiritual states of sexuality." Circumcision is strongly condemned by the Research Center for Multiple, Sexual Orgasms (www.actionlove.com) as well as what is touted humbly as "the most important book on sexuality ever written."[10] The issue for Bigelow (1998:24–26) is one of national pride: circumcision contributes to the reputation of American men as poor lovers!

Second, MC apparently so damages a man's central nervous system that he finds "normal" intercourse unsatisfactory. Consequently, the foreskinless pursue unnatural and deviant sexual practices such as fellatio, sodomy, and "prolonged periods of intense and excessive thrusting" (Hammond 1997:127; see also Laumann, Masi, and Zuckerman 2000; Cold and Taylor 1999; O'Hara and O'Hara 1999).[11] Foreskinless men also allegedly experience "problem-masturbation" (Foley 1966; see also Goldman 1997:120–21; Denniston 1998). In the late nineteenth century, circumcision aimed to curb masturbation. Now, circumcision promotes it.

Third, MC increases a man's likelihood of homosexuality (Carter 1979). "The only reason I'm gay," says a man at www.sexuallymutilatedchild.org, "is that I was circumcised when I was a baby. I feel deprived. It's only with an uncircumcised man that I can have a foreskin." Take away a man's prepuce, and you evidently take away his desire for women. Indeed, circumcision opponents not only tend to advocate a singular vision of normal sexuality, but they also reduce the entirety of erotic pleasure for men and women to the prepuce.

As the Foreskin Goes, So Goes the Man

An essay in M.E.N. Magazine traces the anticircumcision movement to an "awakening" during the 1980s "in the psyches of American men" (Hodges and Warner 1995). Men realized that they were "alienated" from their bodies through a mythology of genital filth that translated into "surgical reduction." Today, a "men's pro-choice movement" is "wrenching the stainless-steel scalpels from the hands of the circumcisers and beating them into silver spoons for our sons."

The men's movement is deeply committed to abolishing male circumcision. The procedure, writes Keen (1991:30–31) in his popular Fire in the Belly, defines masculinity through "wounding." The discarded foreskin, exclaims Farrell in The Myth of Male Power: Why Men Are the Disposable Sex, represents the "disposability" of modern men "as soldiers, workers, dads" (Farrell 1993:355). The amputated foreskin typifies the extraneous role of man in modern society.

The men's movement, too, often voices its opposition to MC with pop-Jungian terminology. Circumcision damages men at an "archetypal depth" (Zoske 1998:20) and severs them from eons of uncircumcised sacred and psychic symbols (Monick 1987). Long ago, the foreskinned phallus was revered as life giver, protector, and "symbol of masculine soul" (Zoske 1999:280–81). Today, the poor penis is mocked, cut, and degraded as "either a giver or receiver of pain." Apparently, circumcision is one of the causes of so-called "irritable male syndrome", recently propounded in the latest book by Jed Diamond, a key figure—books, tapes, workshops, television programs, lectures—in the men's health movement.

Newman (1991) hails the foreskinned erection as a symbol of love, "in which everyone, male and female, must reach out of themselves" to connect with the world. It "takes real existential courage," he continues, "to reach out for another person, to enter them, *to allow them to accept you or not.*" This is "the love we betray when we allow our male children to be circumcised." By cutting down the phallus, MC denies men and women the ability to attain the highest level of love and "existential courage."

The prepuce also represents the natural side of manhood (Bigelow 1998:113). Yet this masculine birthright is now clipped by feminism and soft civilization. Circumcision emasculates men by restraining or taming their innate, wild expansiveness (Regan 1996). To the men's movement, the retention of the foreskin often seems to promise a renewed penetration back into a glorious, mythic past of unfettered masculinity and, ultimately, male superiority.

A well-known joke about circumcision plays with many of the themes so important to the men's movement:

First woman: Did you hear that they stopped performing circumcision?
Second woman: No, why?
First woman: They discovered that they were throwing away the wrong part!

This joke illustrates three anxieties that subtend much of the opposition to MC within the men's movement: the fear of emasculation, an unease with the discarding of traditional gender roles, and a distrust of women.

Is Circumcision in a Child's Best Interests?

The legal aspects of Jewish circumcision or *brit milah* in the United States is a fascinating yet still-unwritten history. I think it fair to say that the rite is permissible by virtue of a general commitment to a vaguely defined sense of Judeo-Christian heritage coupled to legal ambiguity. No Jewish son in the United States has yet succeeded in suing (or perhaps even attempted to sue) his parents for *brit milah.* Yet several Jewish parents in the United States have successfully sued hospitals that ignored their preference for a religious circumcision and instead performed a medical procedure (Miller 1997–1998). Today, the rite remains a valid parental prerogative.

Some states require *mohels* to obtain limited licensure. Yet a New York court, reports Miller (1997–1998:170–71), ruled in *Zakhartchenko v. Weinberger* that a "religious ritual, such as circumcision, anciently practiced and reasonably conducted, is not subject to governmental restrictions so long as it" does not threaten the "peace or safety of this state." Yet the very same circumcision, when performed by a physician rather than a *mohel*, would constitute "the practice of medicine" and thus be subject to governmental oversight. In fact, this difference explains why insurance companies do not reimburse for ritual circumcision—and why, by implication, a *mohel* who performs circumcision on a non-Jewish boy might be liable for practicing medicine without a license.[12] The same logic suggests an ambiguous legal status for a circumcision performed by a *mohel* for Jewish parents who are nonreligious yet nonetheless request the rite as a token of Jewish ethnicity. Indeed, efforts by the courts to refrain from intervening in religious circumcision might someday require a legal definition of the "anciently practiced" standard never mind who is and is not a Jew.

More consequential for the *mohel* and Judaism are current efforts to ban all forms of infant circumcision through legislation and litigation. Lawyers routinely frame MC as child abuse (Price 1996; Richards 1996; cf. Freeman 1999; Benatar and Benatar 2003). The procedure allegedly violates the UN Convention on the Rights of the Child and the UN Convention Against Torture (Gatrad, Sheikh, and Jacks 2002). Legislation prohibiting MC currently circulates the U.S. Congress and the California state legislature (www .mgmbill.org). The issue has resulted in several court cases (www.arclaw.org; Llewellyn 2004). But in the absence of procedural negligence or the failure to obtain parental consent, no trial has reached a guilty verdict.

One legal objection to MC maintains that parental consent is legitimate *only* for interventions that *clearly* represent the child's best interests (Bhimji 2000:10–15). Since ritual and medical circumcisions fail to satisfy this criterion, the procedure should wait until the child himself can offer or refuse consent.

While the idea of legally empowering children might seem appealing, argue proponents of circumcision, such empowerment would not prove beneficial or moral in regard to immunizations, schooling, and other aspects of childraising. By attributing immense psychological, physiological, and sexual damages to circumcision, moreover, foes of the procedure imply that anyone who does consent to the rite thereby signals their own legal incompetence (Freeman 1999:76). Additionally, it seems naive to expect older children raised in devout Jewish or Muslim households to offer truly candid consent (Somerville 2000:chap. 8). Indeed, one could argue that delayed circumcision would entail greater, not less, parental coercion and emotional distress. Finally, the courts consistently refuse to codify the "best interests" of children, which are legally understood to be situational and flexible rather than absolute (Freeman 1999:75). These "best interests" include physical and financial concerns but also intellectual and spiritual considerations. In short, the matter of consent is hardly straightforward—for either proponents or opponents.

Another legal objection to MC in the United States begins with the right of the states to limit the exercise of religious belief, especially in regard to minors. Appeals to the First Amendment of the U.S. Constitution do not, for example, legally justify withholding medical treatment from children or tattooing minors. On this basis, claim opponents, the courts should also ban the circumcision of infants (Brigman 1984–1985; Van Howe et al. 1999; Bhimji 2000:7–10). The Constitution, in this view, protects a Jew's *belief* in the Abrahamic covenant but not the enactment of that belief as the removal of an infant's foreskin.

Many states specifically *exempt* Jewish circumcision from statutes that might otherwise prohibit the rite (Miller 1997–1998). From this angle, the law rests not on absolute moral values but on, as I stated previously, public acceptance of a collective heritage (Miller 2002). As many participants in the debate note, the law protects circumcision but not, for example, the incising of 666 on a child's forehead! Even Somerville (2000:chap. 8), who opposes medical circumcision, deems it ethical to permit the religious circumcision of infant boys for "those who believe they have a fundamental, absolute religious obligation" (see also Katz 1999). This qualification excludes parents whose religiosity permits a choice in the matter or who view the rite as a custom or tradition rather than an inviolable theological duty. But it does permit the procedure.

Another legal challenge to religious circumcision in the United States turns on the equal protection clause of the Fourteenth Amendment. In 1996, Congress passed the Federal Prohibition of Female Genital Mutilation Act (S.1030). Boys, argue opponents of MC, should rightly receive the same protection (Richards 1996; Van Howe et al. 1999; Bhimji 2000). At some level, this argument assumes that male and female genital alterations are analogous in procedure, physiological consequence, and social intent (Miller 1997–1998:186; McBride 2000:225). That MC is not illegal, say opponents, evidences a pervasive sexism in American culture—a sexism that harms men.

Does religious circumcision unjustly assign a body-altering identity onto a child who might someday prefer otherwise? Or would the denial of circumcision to a Jewish or Muslim child "undermine," as Freeman (1999) puts it, "that child's right to cultural heritage and identity"? Does the invasiveness of the procedure enable or hinder personal well-being? Legal opponents of the rite construe the individual as an autonomous, self-made agent, born whole or complete, who, as I discussed in the previous chapter, selects an identity as an adult from the marketplace of ethnicity. By contrast, proponents of Jewish circumcision see the rite as part of a tradition in which male children require a postpartum bodily refinement and where the community defines the person and specifies parental obligations. For them, parents have a legal right—and a moral obligation—to mark their sons. For opponents, only the child, not the parents, can make that decision.

An Iatrogenic Epidemic

Opponents of medical circumcision fiercely vilify physicians for their "fanatical" and "insatiable" support of the procedure (Morgan 1965; Briggs 1985:139; Seiden 1996). Denniston (1997) calls MC an "iatrogenic epidemic" that violates the Hippocratic Oath. Van Howe (1999c) accuses medical journals of allowing "zealots . . . free reign to present biased, one-sided, out-dated, inaccurate information." Of course, circumcision advocates state otherwise, claiming that major medical professions pander to extremism by refusing to endorse the procedure.

For years, advocates of MC tied the procedure to reduced rates of urinary tract infections and other medical conditions, such as penile and cervical cancer (Weiss and Harter 1998; Gollaher 2000:chap. 6; Schoen, Colby, and Ray 2000; Travis et al. 2002). So convinced was Ravich (1973:10) of the medical benefits from MC that he described the apostle Paul's opposition to the rite as "a frightful and needless loss of life in the millions."

Recently, the medical discourse on circumcision has shifted to AIDS. Growing evidence from southern and central Africa suggests that MC inhibits the spread of HIV and other sexually transmitted infections (Halperin and Bailey 1999; Bailey, Plummer, and Moses 2001; USAID/AIDSMark 2003).[13] Opponents of the rite vehemently disagree (Van Howe 1999b), even claiming that MC *causes* the spread of AIDS (Money 1989; Erickson 1994). Once again the circumcised penis is the site of hygienic marvels or horrors— this time on the body of Africans, not Jews. Yet the medical evidence seems increasingly compelling—and increasingly debated. The sheer volume of this debate is quite astounding. In April 2005, I performed a quick keyword search for "male circumcision" on PubMed, a massive online database of medical publications (www.ncbi.nlm.nih.gov/entrez/query.fcgi). In the past decade alone, there were 1,038 publications.

Enemies of God

Some opponents of circumcision avowedly frame their opposition through Christian theology. Typical examples from the Internet include "Circumcision and the Christian Parent" (www.noharmm.org/christianparent.htm), Christians for Wholeness (www.acts15.org), and Catholics Against Circumcision (www.catholicsagainstcircumcision.org). The Circumcision Information and Resource Pages (CIRP) contains links to several Christian arguments against circumcision (www.cirp.org/pages/cultural). One essay, "The Holy Bible, Circumcision, False Prophets, and Christian Parents," is hosted by The Creation Concept (www.sentex.net/~tcc/index.html), a website devoted to validating the biblical flood.

More important than Creationism is the reigning image of the Jew in many Christian anticircumcision arguments. To illustrate this image, I now examine two other online essays recommended by the Circumcision Information and Resource Pages. "What the Bible Really Says about Routine Infant Circumcision" (www.stopcirc.com/christian.html) asks,

> And what about those Jews who continue to cling to the Old Covenant and the shedding of their sons' blood? Are these . . . the people of God? . . . Not by any means. . . . Those who continue to sacrifice the flesh of their baby boys as part of the Old Covenant do so in rejection of Christ and His atoning sacrifice. . . . They are enemies of God.

Echoing Paul, this essay also dubs circumcision "the equivalent of a dog returning to its vomit."

Another essay endorsed by CIRP, "Circumcision and Christianity: A Call to Christian Action" (www.cirp.org/pages/cultural/lewis1), offers a comparable view of Judaism. "Jesus was crucified and killed by the mistaken, fearful, circumcising, sick and sickening, sexually mutilating religious culture of the Jews." Judaism, the website continues, "is fundamentally about justice, mercy, and walking humbly with God, not about unjustly, unmercifully, arrogantly chopping up babies' penises, sexually butchering and mutilating men for life." Another essay on the CIRP website, "Christianity and Circumcision: A Call to Christian Action," also claims that circumcising Jews are false Jews (www.cirp.org/pages/cultural/lewis1). The author calls circumcision an "ancient, destructive, mutilative Jewish myth" and an "ancient evil." Here, the circumcised Jew is an enemy not only of Christianity but also of his own religion.

In the published proceedings of the Fifth International Symposia on Circumcision, Sexual Mutilations, and Genital Integrity, Trachtenberg (1999) traces the American medical procedure to "unconscious fantasies" about a hygienic "chosen people." He also refers to MC as a "cultural mental regression" from Christianity to "the Hebrew commandments of the Old Testament." Many circumcision opponents strongly caution against anti-Semitism (Wallerstein 1983). Still, the knife-wielding Jew continues to threaten Christian bodies and minds. The vituperation cast at Judaism by critics of MC often speaks to far more than a medical procedure. It suggests an enduring hatred and fear of the Jew.

A Harmful Jewish Mistake

"We can be sure of at least *one* thing," writes Carter in *Routine Circumcision: The Tragic Myth* (1979), "CIRCUMCISION PAYS!" Since the medical procedure is so often tied to Jews, it comes as little surprise that the theme of money often arises in the anticircumcision movement (e.g., Goldman 1997:chap. 2; Van Howe 1997:115–16). Some readers may think I exaggerate this anti-Semitism. But the evidence, as I now show, suggests otherwise.

Carter's book was published and distributed in the United States by Noontide Press of Torrance, California (www.noontidepress.com). Noontide Press also sells the autobiography of David Duke, a former leader of the Ku Klux Klan turned politician who unabashedly trumpets white supremacy. (Duke authored *Jewish Supremacism: My Awakening on the Jewish Question*.) Noontide Press, too, offers an anniversary edition of *The Hoax of the Twentieth Century: The Case against the Presumed Extermination of European Jewry*, leaflets such as "A Look at the Powerful Jewish Lobby" and "Auschwitz: Myths and Facts," and works by the Holocaust-denying Institute for Historical Review. Carter's *Routine Circumcision: The Tragic Myth* is widely endorsed by White Pride organizations as well as mainstream groups opposing routine circumcision—groups that seem unable or unwilling to divorce themselves from Carter's more extreme comments and admirers.

Another widely promoted, authoritative book opposing circumcision is Lewis's *In the Name of Humanity*, a 1949 title from the Freethought Press. It was republished by The Book Tree, the same company that reissued *The Protocols of the Elders of Zion* (www.thebooktree.com).[14] *In the Name of Humanity* discusses Judaism with such phrases as "primitive savagery," "monstrous perversity," and "extreme religious fanaticism." The illustrations grotesquely caricature Jewish facial features. Lewis deemed it "almost impossible to believe that parents who love their children could stand by and see them so unmercifully tortured for a religious purpose"—that is, circumcised. "Don't *you* be guilty," Lewis continued (1949:113), "of acts which will hinder *your* child from developing into a normal, happy, human being." Otherwise, implies Lewis, your son will grow up as disfigured and miserable as a Jew. The Arabic translation of Lewis's book is titled *Circumcision Is a Harmful Jewish Mistake.*[15]

Earlier, I mentioned the work of Prescott (1975), who sees circumcision as permanently altering the brain. He also contends that the rite evidences a Judeo-Christian "war" between body and soul (1989). But any such conflict, we saw in a prior chapter, is properly attributed to Hellenism and not Judaism. This error, however, seems minor in comparison to Prescott's more extreme proposition that there is a "link between circumcision and the willingness to kill oneself or others for one's religious/national beliefs. . . . The willingness of many Muslim men to die or kill for their religious beliefs is well known" (1989). Muslims, Jews, and Christians all "carried their religions on the edge of the sword—the same sword that cuts the genitals of children (male and female): and which mutilates their souls."

The Anti-American Jew

"Anti-semitism comes easily to a circumcised Gentile." So speaks a voice on the "Feelings Too Violent to Describe" arena of the popular website www .sexuallymutilatedchild.org. Writes another,

> I recently saw the movie *Schindler's List*, and it struck me that these [circumcising physicians] are the same butchers who were murdering Jews in Nazi Germany. . . . They have now found their niche as contemporary doctors who circumcise.

Throughout European history, writes Gilman (1995:105), "the social category of the Jewish male consists exclusively of damaged and abused individuals, who themselves damage and abuse." This category endures in the contemporary opposition to medical circumcision.

To further evidence the pervasiveness of Jewish treachery—and I choose this word with care and precision—among those who oppose medical circumcision, I now turn to the book *What Your Doctor May Not Tell You about Circumcision: Untold Facts on America's Most Widely Performed—and Most Unnecessary—Surgery* (2002). This book is written by leading figures in the anticircumcision movement, Paul Fleiss and Frederick Hodges, and published by Warner Books, a subsidiary of AOL Time Warner, one of the largest global media and entertainment companies. The book is part of a health care series that addresses, among other conditions, breast cancer, menopause, colorectal cancer, and hypertension. The book, in other words, purports to offer sound, scientific, medical advice—"facts," as the subtitle declares.

The tone of the book is established in the introduction, where Jews, Muslims, and other "primitive" or "aboriginal" cultures are set against uncircumcising "civilizations" (xv). Circumcision, we learn later, "cuts off" an American boy "from the heritage of his ancestors" and the "civilized world." Indeed, the "great heroes of American political and popular history were all intact" (92), a declaration that plainly marginalizes the circumcised (read the Jews) from American culture.

Christianity, claim Fleiss and Hodges, wisely rejected circumcision as "an insult to the wisdom of God in designing the human body." Those who "condemned circumcision" were "enlightened holy men who worked hard to establish, spread, and safeguard Christianity" (99). So captivated are Fleiss and Hodges by the foreskinned heroism of early Christianity that they rather humorously celebrate Origen as one of the "great Church fathers" who rejected circumcision—failing to realize that, far from advocating genital integrity, Origen actually castrated himself!

Fleiss and Hodges applaud "forward-thinking" Jews who are "freeing Judaism from circumcision" (109). "We become model citizens who are worthy in the eyes of God when we lay down the tools of violence and protect" children (116). Not only does this statement repeat the time-honored view that Jews are divinely despised, but it also suggests that, along with Muslims, Jews can join civil society only by emulating Christianity. Actually, though, Fleiss and Hodges exculpate Muslims since they endorse a website that views circumcision as a Jewish intrusion into Islam (www.quran.org/khatne.htm). Ultimately, the Jew bears responsibility for this tragedy.

Circumcision, Fleiss and Hodges continue, is an "un-American" effort "to compromise our freedoms and subvert our culture" (190). They attribute the acceptance of the procedure to a medical McCarthyism that exploited the fear of communism and "mass paranoia about the need to conform" (133). Fleiss and Hodges cast proponents of circumcision as irrational, greedy extremists and charlatans.[16] Who are they? Mainly physicians with Jewish-sounding surnames—Jews, they write, who, when confronted with contrary evidence, devised the "unleashing [of] mass circumcision" to preserve their tribal ritual (128–29). In this book, the "untold facts" about circumcision almost always point to the Jews.

In an earlier essay that appeared online in *Fathering Magazine*, Hodges (1996a) wrote, "A handful of very vocal and very influential Jewish doctors devoted their lives to inventing medical rationalizations for circumcision." Why? Because the "forced circumcision of non-Jewish babies validated the circumcision of Jewish babies, gave these particular Jews a sense of security in their own practices, and gave them a gratifying sense of munificence towards others." But the Jewish plot failed. Instead, "it engendered a deep resentment among many non-Jews towards Jews." Hodges doubly denounces the Jews— first for seeking to justify their illegitimate religion by cutting non-Jewish babies and second for causing anti-Semitism.

A long-standing tactic used to discredit circumcision is to position Jews outside the Western tradition. In an interview in *Fathering Magazine*, Hodges (1996b) links circumcision to "authoritarian forces that imposed the dogma of desert religions on Westerners . . . by suppressing native Western values and attitudes towards children, and what they could not suppress they absorbed and claimed as their own innovation." Others in the anticircumcision movement mirror this xenophobia (e.g., Fleiss 1997; Fletcher 1999:269). "In an ideal world," continues Hodges,

> an American school system would . . . insure the ascendancy of native Western values. . . . Children would learn about May Day and Samhain first. Information about alien religious events such as ritual genital mutilation, child sacrifice, Rosh Hasanah, and Lent would be introduced later as part of anthropological surveys. Children would learn the names of Western deities first . . . Ahena, Gaia, Thor, Pan, Eros, Odin, Freya . . . before they learned how many enemy penises were cut off in the name of Jehovah. . . . A Western father would not only protect his child but ensure that the circumciser was locked up somewhere where he could never gain access to children.

In an ideal world, in other words, the Jew would cease to exist. He would be "locked up somewhere" or converted to "native Western values."

Thus framed, the Jew joins two other circumcisers who currently bedevil the civilized world: tribal Africans and Islamic terrorists (Gilman 1999). As one discussant in an anticircumcision Internet listserv (INTACT-L) remarked in May 2002, "It is a virtual certainty that 100% of the men who flew the planes into the World Trade Towers and the Pentagon were genitally mutilated for life as children." Whether he resides within Western society or outside it, the circumcising Semite threatens civilization.

Jewish Vengeance

A prominent moral and scholarly figure in the anticircumcision movement is Sami A. Aldeeb Abu-Sahlieh, often called Sami Aldeeb, a staff legal adviser at the Swiss Institute of Comparative Law and a self-identified Palestinian Christian. His book *Male and Female Circumcision among Jews, Christians and Muslims: Religious, Medical, Social and Legal Debate* (2001) represents a significant, thorough scholarly effort. It is particularly useful for English speakers interested in Muslim circumcision. The books aims "for justice, peace and reconciliation in a better world where human beings, from all the religions, can live together." Yet many of Aldeeb Abu-Sahlieh's claims about the Jews seem decidedly at odds with this aspiration. Let me offer just three examples.

First, Aldeeb Abu-Sahlieh contends that all references to circumcision in classical Islam were frankly "forged by Jews." Muslim opponents of the rite agree. Despite the many, often tragic differences between the West and Islam today, the anticircumcision movement offers one point of convergence: Jews are corrupting outsiders.

Second, the Jews, reports Aldeeb Abu-Sahlieh, also introduced female circumcision into the Islamic world. Indeed, the Jews themselves practice these rites. But they deny doing so because an acknowledgment would "admit women into the inner circle" of Judaism.[17]

Finally, Aldeeb Abu-Sahlieh blames the Jews for medical circumcision. The practice among Christians is actively promoted by Jewish physicians and Jewish scientists as well as "the media facilities they have to distribute information, and their access to financial means." What's more, American Jews exported circumcision to Germany in the 1950s "for revenge." Aldeeb Abu-Sahlieh also, in an earlier essay published in the journal *Medicine and Law* (1994), describes the circumcision of Christians in the United States as "premeditated action on the part of the Jewish medical community after the second World War . . . to make it more difficult to distinguish between Jews and non-Jews in the event of a future persecution of the Jews." The medicalization of circumcision, too, assists "Jewish proselytizing."[18]

The Arabic edition of Aldeeb Abu-Sahlieh's book, published by Riad El-Rayyes Books in Beirut, includes an introduction by Nawal el Saadawi, the celebrated Egyptian feminist, author, physician, and human rights advocate. An English translation is posted on at least three websites: the Female Genital Cutting Education and Networking Project (www.fgmnetwork.org/authors/samialdeeb/nawal.html), an organization subsumed under NOCIRC; Sami Aldeeb's home page (www.lpj.org/Nonviolence/Sami/Nawal.html); and el Saadawi's website (www.nawalsaadawi.net). It is precisely because el Saadawi has such acclaimed international prominence that her statements

about Jews in the introduction to Aldeeb Abu-Sahlieh's book are so troubling.

For example, El Saadawi speaks about "the secret relationship between
forcefully overtaking the land of Palestine and the cutting of boys' foreskins."
When Muslims endorse the rite, she continues, they unknowingly confirm
"that Israelism has crept into Islam." El Saadawi also conjures a secret conspiracy when she writes about the endorsement of male circumcision by "the
Jewish American general committee." She contends that male circumcision
is "not any different from old or new mass murders in the colonialist wars."
Finally, el Saadawi accuses Jews of evading their responsibility for the spread
of the practice by blaming the ancient Egyptians for its origin and then dis-
crediting Arabs with accusations of female circumcision.[19] Opponents of
male circumcision, whether religious or secular, Western or Arabic, Christian or Muslim, all seem ultimately to root their critique in a scathing indictment of Jewish deceit and hostility.

The debate over circumcision, to draw a phrase from Laqueur (1990:236),
is "a narrative of culture in anatomical disguise . . . language of biology gives
this tale its rhetorical authority but does not describe a deeper reality in
nerves and flesh." As Wolper (1982:33) concluded for the British uproar in
the late nineteenth century over the "Jew Bill," circumcision often evokes
broader fears about loss—losses that, frankly speaking, seem far less tangible
than the foreskin.

The sources of anxiety that color the current opposition to medical circumcision with rage are many—religious pluralism, sexuality, the roles of
men and women, violence, biomedicine, globalization, and autonomy, to
name just a few. To this list, we must also add the characteristically American
predilection to exaggerated self-declarations of woe, especially attributions
of psychological abuse and personal inadequacy, and ongoing debates over
parenting and childraising. I think it hardly an exaggeration to say that there
is little wrong with contemporary society that has not been attributed to
male circumcision.

"Given the horrendous proportions of child abuse," says Wine (1988:7),
himself an opponent of the procedure, "a little foreskin removal . . . hardly
deserves the hostility it receives." I agree. But I also want to suggest an explanation. Circumcision *is* an easily identifiable childhood event. It *is* painful.
It *does* results in the loss of bodily tissue. Hence, male circumcision readily
lends itself as a focal symbol for social and psychological problems that present neither clear-cut origins nor clear-cut solutions. At the same time, the
medicalization of circumcision in the West offer the illusion of someone to

blame: a time-honored enemy of civilization who cuts the flesh from the body and body politic, namely, the Jew.

To further evidence my contention that the opposition to MC often concerns other issues, consider briefly the matter of "foreskin harvesting." Fleiss and Hodges (2002:142) warn about physicians and hospitals that sell foreskins to private biomedical companies for transformation into insulin, reconstructive skin grafts, and dermis for pharmaceutical and cosmetic testing. They call this practice the "legalized plunder of our children's bodies." Foreskins, write Denniston, Hodges, and Milos (1999:vii–viii), "have now become the raw resources of the new economic epoch of biotechnology." This "commercial exploitation" of children by "transnational biotechnology corporations . . . is one of the most important issues ever to face humanity," as important, they write, as "human slavery."

This rhetorical hyperbole clearly seeks to promote public outcry against MC by evoking wider angst over globalization, technology, corporate greed, and waning individual autonomy. The specter of "foreskin harvesting," too, would seem related to contemporary unease over the increasing commodification of the body, most evident in the impassioned public debates over stem cells and cloning. If "transnational biotechnology corporations" today steal baby foreskins, who knows what they will seize tomorrow?

The humor columnist Dave Barry offers a shrewd insight into another dimension of foreskinless discontent. Normally, comments Barry in a 1991 column titled "The Unkindest Cut of All," middle-aged white guys are the persecutors.[20] Now, through the anticircumcision and foreskin restoration movements, the victimizer can assert his own identity as a victim. I similarly suggest that circumcision appeals to male rage because it seems to expose the great lie of feminism that men still possess phallic privilege and power. What better a symbol of male vulnerability than a penis bloodied by women and mothers?

Often, we have seen, opponents of male circumcision link the rite to female genital mutilation (FGM). Yet the visceral and public outcry against FGM, say many anthropologists and feminist scholars, however well intentioned, obscures the more widespread suffering by African women due to economic exploitation, famine, lack of basic health care, war, and international isolation—global processes in which, unlike in FGM, the West shares moral culpability (Gruenbaum 1996; Abusharaf 1998). No simple legislation, moreover, can possibly hope to alleviate these predicaments. Likewise, "intactivists" can be said to ignore the truly serious issues that beset children today. They focus on cut foreskins, not cut school budgets. So powerful is the image of an assaulted genital that the alleged "right" to some ideal of sexual pleasure gains ascendancy over all other measures of well-being.

Perhaps, then, Jews and Africans provide yet another example of a bar-baric Other against which the West can validate its own sense of moral pur-pose and superiority (see Lyons 1981; Gilman 1999; Gollaher 2000:chap. 8; Shweder 2000; Silverman 2004). Indeed, while Jewish advocates of circumci-sion reject the common parallel with FGM, both camps, pro and con, equally demonize Africans as barbaric. Often, the efforts to liberate African women from their cultural traditions often resembles the first-century exhortations of Paul, who sought to save Jews from their own bodily rites and false beliefs. I am not endorsing female genital mutilation or male circumcision. My com-ments are not "procircumcision" but "anti-anticircumcision." That is, I seek to critique rhetorical excesses and troublesome implications and to expose an enduring intolerance.

Many opponents of male circumcision, as I have noted, caution against anti-Semitism and even, however simplistically, wrestle with the moral implications of cultural diversity, ethnocentrism, and cultural criticism (e.g., Boyd 1998:88–96). Yet these calls for moral and religious pluralism are muted by the sheer quantity and din of more objectionable voices that repre-sent the Jew as a monstrous aberration of humanity. And these voices, I stress, emerge from the *center* of the anticircumcision movement, not a dis-credited fringe. Nowhere in this book did I focus on statements issued by the National Alliance, Stormfront, the Christian Separatist Church Society, and the Christian Defense League. I exclusively focused on mainstream figures, publications, and websites. I am not suggesting that all opponents of male circumcision vilify Jews and Judaism. But many do so. I think it fair to say that, in the everyday literature opposing male circumcision, a persistent anti-Judaism now passes as a matter-of-fact assessment of objective reality. And it passes largely unnoticed.

What, to invoke a recent book, is the "untold fact" about male circumci-sion? That the Jew continues to threaten civilization and American values. Once again, the Jew becomes a knife-wielding heretic intent on mutilating Christian bodies and virtue.

Notes

1. Schoen's procircumcision poems include "Ode to the Circumcised Male" (*Ameri-can Journal of Diseases in Childhood* 141 [1987]:128) and "Circumcision Revision" (*Journal of Urology* 146 [1990]:1619). Uncircumcision verse includes "Ode to My Husband's Miss-

ing Foreskin" (www.sexuallymutilatedchild.org/ode.htm) and "The Rape of the Cock: or, The Nerve-rending Story" (www.circumstitions.com/Rape.html).

2. At one point, a group called Uncut Entertainment aspired to produce a feature-length Hollywood film, but I am unable to find any further information, and their former Web address (www.uncutentertainment.net) now functions as a search engine for adult websites.

3. Some opponents fear that recent developments in anesthesia might simply make the procedure more acceptable (Moss 1990; Van Howe 1999a).

4. I do not deny the occurrence of valid complications (see www.cirp.org/library/complications). John Colapinto's 2001 book, As Nature Made Him: The Boy Who was Raised as a Girl (New York: HarperCollins), recounts the tragedy of a horribly botched circumcision.

5. Sometimes other events color circumcision experiences with disturbing memories (Ferenczi 1950; Kennedy 1986).

6. See the Association for Pre- and Perinatal Psychology and Health (www.birth psychology.com).

7. A book by another anthropologist—one who avowedly opposes the rite—praises the ethics of Denniston in the preface (Glick 2005). A comparison of my book with that of Glick will undoubtedly prove an interesting exercise. For a review of Glick, see Michaelson (2005).

8. For equally aggressive voices, see "Medical Fraud and the Criminal Assault of Boys" (http://med-fraud.org) and "Circumcision Anger: A Place to Vent Your Anger If You Feel You Need to Scream" (www.fathermag.com/circ/mail).

9. Baker (1996) declares fancifully that, since foreskins secrete cooperative phero-mones, circumcised men are unnaturally anxious, competitive, and domineering.

10. Kristen O'Hara, Sex as Nature Intended It: The Most Important Thing You Need to Know about Making Love but No One Could Tell You until Now, 2nd ed. (Hudson, Mass.: Turning Point, 2002), www.sexasnatureintendedit.com.

11. See also Zwang (1997), who elsewhere (1999) condemns circumcision in shock-ingly homophobic and anti-Semitic terms.

12. Some mohels carry liability insurance—yet some insurance companies restrict this coverage only to mohels who possess a medical license.

13. The foreskin, which is susceptible to minute scratches and tears, contains special-ized cells (e.g., Langerhans) that readily join with HIV and other pathogens.

14. The listing of this edition of The Protocols on www.barnesandnoble.com and www.amazon.com provoked considerable controversy since the dust-jacket promotion, which was reproduced on Amazon.com, said, "If the Protocols are real, we had better take a close look at international affairs around the world. We neither support nor deny this message. We are only providing access to those to want to read them." The publisher has since modified its stance, and Amazon has posted a special message about the book.

15. Al-khitan dalalah isra'iliyyah mu'dhiyah, Matabi' dar al-sha'b, translated by Hafni Nassif (Cairo, 1971). Cited by Sami A. Aldeeb Abu-Sahlieh, "Male and Female Circum-

cision: The Myth of Difference," www.lpj.org/Nonviolence/Sami/articles/eng-articles/ myth.htm.

16. Apropos of greed, I might mention that Fleiss is the father of Heidi Fleiss, the noted "Hollywood Madame." He received three years' probation and community service after pleading guilty to tax evasion and conspiracy.

17. In part, Aldeeb Abu-Sahlieh draws on the practice of female circumcision among Jews from Ethiopia, called Falashas or "Beta Israel." But this practice clearly pertains not to their "Jewishness," as Cohen (1997:564) puts it, but to their "Ethiopianness." Nonetheless, the Falashas are much beloved by Arabic opponents of male circumcision for proof that the Jews not only practice but originated female circumcision. From a very different perspective, Levin (2000) offers a terrific reading of ambivalence surrounding the association of black (Ethiopian) Jewishness with female circumcision in a Gloria Naylor novel, *Bailey's Café*.

18. A leading Jewish opponent of the rite, Miriam Pollack (1997:171), makes similar assertions.

19. The same themes occur in a 1999 Postmasters Fellowship thesis from American University in Cairo by Seham Abd el Salam, "Male Genital Mutilation (Circumcision): A Feminist Study of Muted Gender Issue," reproduced by NOHARMM (www.noharmm .org/muted.htm).

20. Reprinted in *Dave Barry Is Not Making This Up* (New York: Crown, 1994), 61. I was alerted to this passage by Gilman (1996:182).

Conclusion

Over the past eight years, innumerable friends and acquaintances have exclaimed, "You're writing a book about *what?*" After the usual banter over potential cover illustrations, they invariably asked, "So, what does circumcision *really* mean?" Frankly, I remain unsure. What I am certain, however, is that the rite in Judaism has endured—for better or worse—precisely because it has *no* single meaning. Rituals that communicate only unitary, transparent, or logical messages, devoid of deep emotions, are not very compelling. They rarely form significant cultural narratives, and they rarely invoke the impassioned debates that now surround the performance and neglect of circumcision.

If *brit milah* conveyed just one meaning, then neither the classic rabbis nor myself for that matter would have found it necessary to write about it. Indeed, the one overwhelming fact about Jewish circumcision is that its profound significance pertains to an equally profound irreducibility. The rite asserts, then denies, its own symbolism and morality. The import of circumcision has little to do with its plurality of meanings. By itself, this quality is rather uninteresting. Rather, circumcision engenders *contrary* meanings and then inscribes those meanings into the very flesh of Jews—Jewish boys, of course, not girls. This unfinalizability, I maintain, accounts for the centrality of *brit milah* in Jewish history.

All significant rituals have something in common: they resist interpretation. In the great biblical tale of architectural folly known as the Tower of Babel, Jacques Derrida (1991:3) playfully saw a metaphor for his brilliant yet perplexing theory of literary deconstruction. Like the fate of the legendary ziggurat, wrote Derrida, the search for a definitive textual meaning often arrives at "the irreducible multiplicity of tongues" and "the impossibility of

241

finality, of totalizing." Derrida's insight into the mythic, divinely trimmed tower also applies to circumcision.[1] In more ways than one, the rite "cuts off" its own meanings. Like the actual slice, the name of which the Oxford English Dictionary traces to the Latin term "to cut around" (circumcīdĕre), the messages of brit milah move in circles.

The philosopher David Levin illuminated another approach to the opacity of circumcision. At the conclusion of grace, notes Levin (1985:202–6), devout Jews thank God "for thy covenant, which thou has sealed into our flesh." This praise refers to the opening of the male body to receive the fleshy inscription of the covenant. More subtly, though, it also acknowledges our inability to open the rite to resolution or clarity. Despite the rabbinic ideal of uncovering the glans to signify the revelation of mystical secrets, the messages of brit milah remain sealed—sealed in flesh and sealed to everyday understandings. It is difficult, I am suggesting, to write about Jewish circumcision because the rite so often seems only to expose its own incomprehensibility.

It is also difficult to write about circumcision since any book-length study, such as my own, runs the risk of appearing to reduce Judaism to the penis, thus sustaining the very phallocentrism I aimed to critique. In Woody Allen's memorable 1977 film Annie Hall, the central character, a neurotic New Yorker named Alvie Singer, bemoans that "the failure of the country to get behind New York City is anti-Semitism. . . . I'm not discussing politics or economics. This is foreskin." One rarely looks to Woody Allen for moral counsel these days, but Alvie Singer had a point: the Jew is often defined by foreskinlessness.

Of course, foreskins and the lack thereof generally characterize only one-half of the Jewish people. To define the religion solely in penile terms, especially by Jews, is to shape Judaism into a caricature of itself and also, perhaps more seriously, to neglect entirely the role and experiences of women. Notwithstanding the focus of this book, it is not my wish to reduce Judaism to men and circumcision. In an ironic way, I argued, circumcision itself resists this possibility. The rite privileges masculinity, to be sure, but only so men can assume the role and fecundity of mothers.

Most studies of brit milah today—indeed, nearly all studies—either condemn or condone the rite. This is another reason why it is difficult to write about circumcision. If anything, there is far too much simple-mindedness and single-mindedness about the issue today. I judge this book a success if readers learned something new but also if they found their own moral position and symbolic commitments challenged.

In one old legend, a Jewish family willingly violates a royal edict against the preeminent Jewish rite. The local prefect reports the offense, and the Jewish family sets out for the palace to receive their punishment (Gaster 1934, story 192). Along the way, they stop at an inn. The Gentile hostess hears their woeful tale and offers to swap her own child so the king will spare the family. The Jews agree. When the monarch sees the child's foreskinned penis, he rebukes the astonished prefect, who assures the king that the boy was indeed circumcised. Yet the miraculous regrowth of the child's foreskin, the prefect concludes, surely shows that "the Jews have such a faithful God that when they pray to Him with their full heart, He does their will." So impressed was the king that he rescinded the ban. The two boys, circumcised and foreskinned, became lifelong friends and "great men."

Triumphant tales of this sort, where circumcision enables a rapprochement between Jew and non-Jew, are relatively rare in Jewish history and lore. More typically, circumcision leads to horrible death. For this reason, the rite today seems unique among all Jewish ceremonies for its ability to evoke unparalleled emotional passion. In medieval Europe, argues Goldin (1996:175–76), circumcision inverted everyday social reality by placing the normally marginalized Jews at the center of the community—albeit a community defined by God, not the monarch or Church. Yet circumcision also served as a script for the retelling of martyrdom: a father brings his son to a group of fellow Jews who recite prayers, after which the child receives not a circumcision but a fatal cutting at the hands of a Christian mob.

In the twentieth century, the rite became forever fused to the tragedy of the Holocaust. A mother, holding aloft her newborn son in a concentration camp, turns to another Jew and says, "Here, circumcise the child, for I want him to die as a proper Jew" (Yerushalmi 1989:II:164–65; see also Harlow 1990; Goldberger 1991:46–50). Indeed, martyrdom is precisely what distinguishes *brit milah* from mere circumcision, writes Lewis (1990). One does *not* suffer death to defend a minor medical procedure. But Jews *do* sacrifice their lives to preserve the covenant and *brit milah*. From this angle, any attempt to analyze the rite, such as my own, inevitably erodes its emotional significance. Like the Holocaust, *brit milah* lies *beyond* analysis, that is, *beyond* normal ways of thinking. It challenges the ordinary. Circumcision foes reject this argument. They see appeals to the sacred as masking the reality of unjustified terror. Supporters, however, believe the true tragedy of circumcision to be the commonplace effort to strip the rite of its numinous qualities, reducing it to a mere procedure. Is the rite amenable to reason, or is it, as Rabbi David Zaslow (2003) believes, "a covenant *above* reason"?

Actually, it is both. But one further reason why it is so difficult to write about circumcision is that, given the extreme politicization of the rite, it no longer seems possible to acknowledge—no, to accept—moral ambiguity and ambivalence.

Indeed, I avoided endorsing *any* consistent moral claims in this book to focus instead on unpacking the strife and dialogicality in and about the rite. But participants in the debate today largely refuse to countenance this complexity. For example, my own work was erroneously construed as "pro-circ" by a posting on the anticircumcision Internet listserv called INTACT-L (short for intact-list). "Who's this?" asked the participant. "Seems like procirc works in progress at DePauw University in Indiana. Any intactivists on campus?" The writer then listed several potential student organizations that might be enlisted to oppose my supposedly procircumcision work, including the Coalition for Women's Concerns, the Committee for Latino Concerns, the Defending the Children of America Project, the International Student Association, and the DePauw Christian Fellowship. Another interlocutor typed,

> If pro-circ Jews can broad-brush-accuse Intactivists of "anti-Semitism" every time one criticizes ritualized male genital mutilation, why can't Intactivists claim the reverse every time a Jewish writer publicly defends medicalized forced circumcision? What would we call such bigotry? Antigoyism; Antihumanism; Antichristianism; Semitic sexual oppression; Reverse anti-Semitism?

Wrote someone else, after contacting me by e-mail, "I wanted to let him know that we are watching VERY closely what he says. I hope it makes him VERY careful about WHAT he says and HOW he says it." I have tried to be careful. But I suspect that those who view the rite as either a repetition of tragedy or a repudiation of it will disagree.

What, then, *did* I say? My overall goal, to reiterate from the introduction, was to discern the contrary meanings of Jewish circumcision, the symbolic nuances that simultaneously argue both for and against the rite. This approach alone, I maintain, adequately captures what Bakhtin called the "contradictory, double-faced fullness of life"—that is, the ambiguities and ambivalences that make *brit milah* so powerful and so worthy of advocacy *and* condemnation.

Perhaps I can best summarize Jewish circumcision, at least in contemporary culture, by juxtaposing two popular images. The first image occurred on television in the early 1990s during an episode titled "Kaddish for Uncle

Manny" on the show *Northern Exposure*. In this episode, the star of the dramatic sitcom, a stereotypical Jewish doctor from New York City named Joel Fleishman, wishes to recite a customary remembrance prayer (*kaddish*) in honor of his recently deceased uncle. The Gentiles of Cicily, Alaska, where Fleishman begrudgingly fulfills a loan obligation from medical school, try to assist him in gathering a religious quorum (*minyan*). What, asks one character, does a Jew look like? With "the proliferation of circumcision," comments another Gentile, "the tip of the penis . . . is no longer a . . . yardstick" (Gilman 1996:189; Porush 1996:120). Here, amid the Jewish diminishment of American manhood, the circumcised Jew has finally assimilated and joined the rest of humanity.

The second image occurred in an advertisement placed in college newspapers across the United States in the late 1990s by Birthright Israel.[2] This program funds trips to Israel for marginally affiliated young Jews. Each advertisement featured two photographs. The upper photo parodied the travails of Jewish life, accompanied by the caption "Sometimes it's hard being Jewish." The lower photo featured a relaxed, laughing young man floating in the Dead Sea. Beneath it read, "Sometimes it isn't."

There were several versions of the advertisement. The lower image remained the same. But the photograph depicting "Sometimes it's hard being Jewish" varied. In one version, the struggle of Jewish identity was illustrated by an elderly, bearded *mohel* brandishing scissors above a wailing infant.

In the end, I hope to unsettle readers about Jewish circumcision, an unease that reflects my own struggles and commitments—an unease that is reluctant either to maintain or to abandon the rite. The extent to which ritual circumcision or *brit milah* engenders such intense, sometimes agonizing ambivalence shows its unique suitability for the predicament of the modern Jew.

Sometimes it's hard being Jewish. Sometimes it isn't.

Notes

1. In fact, Derrida was captivated by the rite, especially the mystical notion of inscribing memory in a bodily absence (see Derrida 1986a, 1986b; Bennington and Derrida 1993; Robbins 1995).

2. For a critical response to the ad, see Gary Rosenblatt, "A Matter of Taste—Birthright Ads Are Hard to Swallow," *The Jewish News Weekly of Northern California*, October 15, 1999, www.jewishsf.com/content/2-0-/module/displaystory/story_id/12283/edition_id/236/format/html/displaystory.html.

Bibliography

Note: In keeping with scholarly convention, I omit all honorific titles, such as Rabbi. Additionally, all Internet sites mentioned in the bibliography and throughout the book were verified as accessible in either June or December 2005.

Abramson, Henry, and Carrie Hannon. 2003. Depicting the Ambiguous Wound: Circumcision in Medieval Art. In *The Covenant of Circumcision: New Perspectives on an Ancient Jewish Rite*, edited by E. W. Mark, 98–113. Hanover, N.H.: Brandeis University Press.

Abusch, Ra'anan. 2003. Circumcision and Castration under Roman Law in the Early Empire. In *The Covenant of Circumcision: New Perspectives on an Ancient Jewish Rite*, edited by E. W. Mark, 75–86. Hanover, N.H.: Brandeis University Press.

Abusharaf, Rogaia Mustafa. 1998. Unmasking Tradition: A Sudanese Anthropologist Confronts Female "Circumcision" and Its Terrible Tenacity. *The Sciences* 38:22–28.

Adelman, Howard. 1991. Italian Jewish Women. In *Jewish Women in Historical Perspective*, edited by J. Baskin, 135–58. Detroit: Wayne State University Press.

Adler, Rachel. 1977a. A Mother in Israel: Aspects of the Mother Role in Jewish Myth. In *Beyond Androcentrism: New Essays on Women and Religion*, edited by Rita M. Gross, 237–55. Missoula, Mont.: Scholars Press.

———. 1977b. Mother, Myth, Magic. *Davka Magazine* 17:20–24.

Ahmadu, Fuambai. 2000. Rites and Wrongs: An Insider/Outsider Reflects on Power and Excision. In *Female "Circumcision" in Africa: Culture, Controversy, and Change*, edited by B. Shell-Duncan and Y. Hernlund, 283–312. Boulder, Colo.: Lynne Rienner.

Aldeeb Abu-Sahlieh, Sami A. 1994. To Mutilate in the Name of Jehovah or Allah: Legitimization of Male and Female Circumcision. *Medicine and Law* 13:575–622.

———. 2001. *Male and Female Circumcision among Jews, Christians and Muslims: Religious, Medical, Social and Legal Debate*. Warren Center, Pa.: Shangri-La Publications.

Alexander, T. Desmond. 1983. Genesis 22 and the Covenant of Circumcision. *Journal for the Study of the Old Testament* 25:17–22.

Allen, Ronald B. 1996. The "Bloody Bridegroom" in Exodus 4:24–26. *Bibliotheca Sacr* 153:259–69.

Alter, Robert. 1996. *Genesis: Translation and Commentary.* New York: Norton.

Altschul, Martin S. 1989. Cultural Bias and the Urinary Tract Infection (UTI) Circumc sion Controversy. *Truth Seeker.* July/August 1989, 43–45.

Ammar, Hamed. 1954. *Growing Up in an Egyptian Village.* London: Routledge and Kega Paul.

Anderson, Gary A. 1989. Celibacy or Consummation in the Garden? Reflections on Earl Jewish and Christian Interpretations of the Garden of Eden. *Harvard Theological Revie* 82:121–48.

Archer, Léonie J. 1990. Bound by Blood: Circumcision and Menstrual Taboo in Post Exilic Judaism. In *After Eve: Women, Theology and the Christian Tradition,* edited by J. M Soskice, 38–61. London: Marshall Pickering.

Armstrong, Karen. 1993. *A History of God: The 4,000-Year Quest of Judaism, Christianit and Islam.* New York: Ballantine.

Ashby, G. W. 1995. The Bloody Bridegroom: The Interpretation of Exodus 4:24–26 *Expository Times* 106:203–5.

Aurand, A. Monroe, Jr. 1939. *Little Known Facts About the Ritual of the Jews and the Esoteri Folklore of the Pennsylvania-Germans. An Impartial Examination into Everyday Beliefs an Practices of the Pennsylvania-Germans, Diligently Compared with an English Interpretatio of The Jewish Ritual: Or, The Religious Customs and Ceremonies of the Jews, Used in thei Publick Worship and Private Devotions, published in London in 1753.* Harrisburg, Pa., pri vate printing, Aurand Press. (A reprinting of the 1753 book)

Aycock, D. Alan. 1983. The Mark of Cain. In *Structuralist Interpretations of Biblical Myth* edited by E. Leach and D. A. Aycock, 120–27. Cambridge: Cambridge Universit Press.

Bader, David M. 1999. *Haikus for Jews: For You, a Little Wisdom.* New York: Harmon Books.

Baer, Yitzhak. 1992. *A History of the Jews in Christian Spain.* Vols. 1–2. Translated by Loui Schoffman. Updated 1959. Philadelphia: Jewish Publication Society. (Orig. Hebrew 1945)

Bailey, Robert C., F. A. Plummer, and S. Moses. 2001. Male Circumcision and HIV Pre vention: Current Knowledge and Future Research Directions. *Lancet Infectious Diseases* 1:223–31.

Bailey, Stephen. 2000. *Kashrut, Tefillin, Tzitzit: Studies in the Purpose and Meaning of Sym bolic Mitzvot Inspired by the Commentaries of Rabbi Samson Raphael Hirsch.* Northvale, N.J.: Jason Aronson.

Bakan, David. 1979. *And They Took Themselves Wives: The Emergence of Patriarchy in Western Civilization.* San Francisco: Harper & Row.

———. 1997. Freud, Maimonides, and Incest. In *Religion, Society, and Psychoanalysis: Readings in Contemporary Theory,* edited by J. L. Jacobs and D. Capps, 23–27. Boulder, Colo.: Westview Press.

Baker, Jeannine Parvati. 1996. Ending Circumcision: Where Sex and Violence First Meet. *Primal Renaissance: The Journal of Primal Psychology* 2(1). Reprinted online at www.primalspirit.com/parvati2_1.htm.

———. 1997. The Wound Reveals the Cure: A Utah Model for Ending the Cycle of Sexual Mutilation. In *Sexual Mutilations: A Human Tragedy*, edited by G. C. Denniston and M. F. Milos, 179–83. New York: Plenum.

Bakhtin, Mikhail. 1984. *Rabelais and His World.* Bloomington: Indiana University Press.

Bal, Mieke. 1985. Sexuality, Sin, and Sorrow: The Emergence of Female Character (A Reading of Genesis 1–3). In *The Female Body in Western Culture: Contemporary Perspectives*, edited by S. R. Suleiman, 317–38. Cambridge, Mass.: Harvard University Press.

———. 1987. Delilah Decomposed: Samson's Talking Cure and the Rhetoric of Subjectivity. In *Lethal Love: Feminist Literary Readings of Biblical Love Stories*, 37–67. Bloomington: Indiana University Press.

Baldensperger, P. J. 1894. Birth, Marriage, and Death among the Fellahin of Palestine. *Palestine Exploration Fund Quarterly Statement* 1894:127–44.

Barclay, John M. G. 1998. Paul and Philo on Circumcision: Romans 2.25–9 in Social and Cultural Context. *New Testament Studies* 44:536–56.

Barth, Lewis M. 1991. Circumcision and the Unity of God: A Comment on Stern. *S'Vara* 2(2):49–51.

———, ed. 1990. *Berit Milah in the Reform Context.* Secaucus, N.J.: Carol Publishing Group: Berit Milah Board of Reform Judaism.

Bassett, F. W. 1971. Noah's Nakedness and the Curse of Canaan: A Case of Incest? *Vetus Testamentum* 21:232–37.

Batto, Bernard F. 1992. *Slaying the Dragon: Mythmaking in The Biblical Tradition.* Louisville, Ky.: Westminster/John Knox Press.

Baumgarten, Elisheva. 2003. Circumcision and Baptism: The Development of a Jewish Ritual in Christian Europe. In *The Covenant of Circumcision: New Perspectives on an Ancient Jewish Rite*, edited by E. W. Mark, 114–27. Hanover, N.H.: Brandeis University Press.

Beidelman, T. O. 1964. Pig (Guluwe): An Essay on Ngulu Sexual Symbolism and Ceremony. *Southwestern Journal of Anthropology* 20:359–92.

Benatar, Michael, and David Benatar. 2003. Between Prophylaxis and Child Abuse: The Ethics of Neonatal Male Circumcision. *American Journal of Bioethics* 3(2):35–48.

Benchekrouon, Mohamed F. 1982. Quelques aspects psychologiques de la circoncision au Maghreb. *Psychologie Medicale* 14:1227–31.

Bennington, Geoffrey, and Jacques Derrida. 1993. *Jacques Derrida.* Translated by Geoffrey Bennington. Chicago: Chicago University Press. (Orig. French ed. 1991)

Bentley, James. 1985. *Restless Bones: The Story of Relics.* London: Constable.

Berg, Charles. 1951. *The Unconscious Significance of Hair.* London: George Allen & Unwin.

Berger, David. 1996. *The Jewish-Christian Debate in the High Middle Ages: A Critical Edition of the Nizzahon Vetus.* Northvale, N.J.: Jason Aronson.

Berman, Jeremiah J. 1941. *Shehitah: A Study in the Cultural and Social Life of the Jewish People*. New York: Bloch.

Bernat, David A. 2002. Circumcision and 'Orlah in the Priestly Torah. Unpublished Ph.D. Thesis, Near Eastern and Judaic Studies Department, Brandeis University.

Bertschinger, Julia. 1991. Circumcision Choices. *Midwifery Today* 17:22–23. Reprinted online at www.noharmm.org/choices.htm.

Bettelheim, Bruno. 1954. *Symbolic Wounds: Puberty Rites and the Envious Male*. Glencoe, Ill.: Free Press.

Beusterien, John L. 1999. Jewish Male Menstruation in Seventeenth-Century Spain. *Bulletin of the History of Medicine* 73:447–56.

Bhimji, Arif. 2000. Infant Male Circumcision: A Violation of the Canadian Charter of Rights and Freedoms. *Health Care Law* 2000. Available online at www.longwoods.com/hl/pdf/circum.pdf.

Biale, David. 1982. The God with Breasts: El Shaddai in the Bible. *History of Religions* 21:240–56.

———. 1997. *Eros and the Jews: From Biblical Israel to Contemporary America*. Berkeley: University of California Press.

Biale, Rachel. 1984. *Women and Jewish Law: An Exploration of Women's Issues in Halakhic Sources*. New York: Schocken Books.

Bigelow, Jim. 1998. *The Joy of Uncircumcising!* 2nd ed. Aptos, Calif.: Hourglass Book Publishing. (1st ed. 1992)

———. 1999. Evangelical Christianity in America and Its Relationship to Infant Male Circumcision. In *Male and Female Circumcision: Medical, Legal, and Ethical Considerations in Pediatric Practice*, edited by G. C. Denniston, F. M. Hodges, and M. F. Milos, 173–77. New York: Kluwer Academic/Plenum.

Biller, Peter. 1992. Views of Jews from Paris around 1300: Christian or "Scientific"? *Studies in Church History* 29:192–99.

Bilu, Yoram. 2000. Circumcision, the First Haircut and the Torah: Ritual and Male Identity among the Ultraorthodox Community of Contemporary Israel. In *Imagined Masculinities: Male Identity and Culture in the Modern Middle East*, edited by M. Ghoussoub and E. Sinclair-Webb, 33–63. London: Saqi Books.

Bird, Phyllis. A. 1981. "Male and Female He Created Them": Gen. 1:27b in the Context of the Priestly Account of Creation. *Harvard Theological Review* 74:129–59.

Blaschke, Andreas. 1998. *Beschneidung: Zeugnisse der Bibel und verwandter Texte*. Tübingen: Francke Verlag.

Bleich, J. David. 1982. Jaundice and Circumcision. *Tradition* 20:161–66.

———. 2000. Circumcision: The Current Controversy. *Tradition* 33:45–69.

———. 2001a. Circumcision of a Child Born Sine Concubito. *Tradition* 35:61–62.

———. 2001b. Fish or Meat at a Brit Milah Repast? *Tradition* 35:55–60.

Bleich, Judith. 1983. The Symbolism in Innovative Rituals. *Sh'ma* 14/264. Reprinted online at www.clal.org/e112.html.

Bloch, Abraham P. 1980. *The Biblical and Historical Background of Jewish Customs and Ceremonies*. New York: Ktav Publishing House.

Bloch, Maurice. 1986. *From Blessing to Violence: History and Ideology in the Circumcision Ritual of the Merina of Madagascar*. Cambridge: Cambridge University Press.

Bloch, Maurice, and S. Guggenheim. 1981. Compadrazgo, Baptism, and the Symbolism of Second Birth. *Man* 16:376–86.

Bloom, Harold, and David Rosenberg. 1990. *The Book of J*. Translated from the Hebrew by D. Rosenberg, interpreted by H. Bloom. New York: Grove Weidenfeld.

Boddy, Janice. 1982. Womb as Oasis: The Symbolic Context of Pharaonic Circumcision in Rural Northern Sudan. *American Ethnologist* 9:682–98.

Boon, James A. 1999. Of Foreskins: (Un)Circumcision, Religious Histories, Difficult Description (Montaigne/Remondino). In *Verging on Extra-Vagance: Anthropology, History, Religion, Literature, Arts . . . Showbiz*, 43–71. Princeton, N.J.: Princeton University Press.

Borgen, Peder. 1982. Paul Preaches Circumcision and Pleases Men. In *Paul and Paulinism: Essays in Honour of C. K. Barrett*, edited by M. D. Hooker and S. G. Wilson, 37–46. London: SPCK.

Bouhdiba, Abdelwahab. 1985. *Sexuality in Islam*. Translated by Alan Sheridan. London: Routledge and Kegan Paul. (Orig. 1975)

Boxman, Bradd H. 1986. *The Significance of Brit Milah in Reform Judaism*. Unpublished rabbinic ordination thesis. Hebrew Union College-Jewish Institute of Religion, Cincinnati.

Boyarin, Daniel. 1990. The Eye in the Torah: Ocular Desire in Midrashic Hermeneutic. *Critical Inquiry* 16:532–50.

———. 1992. "This We Know to Be the Carnal Israel": Circumcision and the Erotic Life of God and Israel. *Critical Inquiry* 18:474–502.

———. 1993. *Carnal Israel: Reading Sex in Talmudic Culture*. Berkeley: University of California Press.

———. 1994. *A Radical Jew: Paul and the Politics of Identity*. Berkeley: University of California Press.

———. 1996. Rabbinic Resistance to Male Domination: A Case Study in Talmudic Cultural Poetics. In *Interpreting Judaism in a Postmodern Age*, edited by S. Kepnes, 118–41. New York: New York University Press.

———. 1997a. Jewish Studies as Teratology: The Rabbis as Monsters. *Jewish Quarterly Review* 88:57–66.

———. 1997b. *Unheroic Conduct: The Rise of Heterosexuality and the Invention of the Jewish Man*. Berkeley: University of California Press.

———. 1999. What Does a Jew Want?; or, The Political Meaning of the Phallus. In *The Psychoanalysis of Race*, edited by C. Lane, 211–40. New York: Columbia University Press.

Boyarin, Jonathan, and Daniel Boyarin. 1995. Self-Exposure as Theory: The Double-

Mark of the Male Jew. In *Rhetorics of Self-Making*, edited by D. Battaglia, 16–42. Berkeley: University of California Press.

Boyd, Billy Ray. 1998. *Circumcision Exposed: Rethinking a Medical and Cultural Tradition.* Freedom, Calif.: The Crossing Press.

Brandes, S. B., and J. W. McAninch. 1999. Surgical Methods of Restoring the Prepuce: A Critical Review. *British Journal of Urology International* 83, suppl. 1, 109–13.

Braude, William G. 1968. *Pesikta Rabbati: Discourses for Feasts, Fasts, and Special Sabbaths.* 2 vols. New Haven, Conn.: Yale University Press.

Brauer, Erich. 1942. The Jews of Afghanistan: An Anthropological Report. *Jewish Social Studies* 4:121–38.

———. 1993. *The Jews of Kurdistan.* Completed and edited by Raphael Patai. Detroit: Wayne State University Press. (Orig. Hebrew 1947)

Brav, Aaron. 1908. The Evil Eye among the Hebrews. *Ophthalmology* 5:427–35. Reprinted in *The Evil Eye: A Casebook*, edited by A. Dundes. 1981. Madison: University of Wisconsin Press, 1984, 44–54.

Breasted, James Henry. 1962. *Ancient Records of Egypt: Historical Documents from the Earliest Times to the Persian Conquest, Collected, Edited, and Translated with Commentary.* Vol. 3. New York: Russell & Russell.

Breeding, John. 1991. The Unkindest Cut: Altering Male Genitalia. *Man!*, winter 1991, 25–26.

Briggs, Anne. 1985. *Circumcision: What Every Parent Should Know.* Earlysville, Va.: Birth and Parenting Publishing.

Brigman, William E. 1984–1985. Circumcision as Child Abuse: The Legal and Constitutional Issues. *Journal of Family Law* 23:337–57.

Brod, Harry. 1995. Of Mice and Supermen: Images of Jewish Masculinity. In *Gender and Judaism: The Transformation of Tradition*, edited by T. M. Rudavsky, 279–93. New York: New York University Press.

Broner, E. M. 1978. *A Weave of Women.* Bloomington: Indiana University Press.

Bronner, Leila Leah. 1993. From Veil to Wig: Jewish Women's Hair Covering. *Judaism* 42:465–77.

———. 1994. *From Eve to Esther: Rabbinic Reconstructions of Biblical Women.* Louisville, Ky.: Westminster/John Knox Press.

Brown, Peter. 1988. *The Body and Society: Men, Women, and Sexual Renunciation in Early Christianity.* New York: Columbia University Press.

Brown, S. G. A. 1896–1897. The Mosaic Rite of Circumcision: A Plea for Its Performance during Childhood. *Journal of the Orificial Society* 5:299–304.

Bryk, Felix. 1934. *Circumcision in Man and Woman: Its History, Psychology and Ethnology.* New York: American Ethnological Press. (Reprint, New York: AMS Press, 1974)

Buber, Martin. 1946. *Moses.* London: Horovitz.

Burton, Roger V. and John W. M. Whiting. 1961. The Absent Father and Cross-Sex Identity. *Merrill-Palmer Quarterly of Behavior and Development* 7:85–95.

Bynum, Carol Walker. 1982. *Jesus as Mother: Studies in the Spirituality of the High Middle Ages*. Berkeley: University of California Press.

——. 1986. The Body of Christ in the Later Middle Ages: A Reply to Leo Steinberg. *Renaissance Quarterly* 39:399–439. Reprinted in *Fragmentation and Redemption: Essays on Gender and the Human Body in Medieval Religion*, 79–117. New York: Zone Books, 1991.

——. 1987. *Holy Feast and Holy Fast: The Religious Significance of Food to Medieval Women*. Berkeley: University of California Press.

——. 1990. Material Continuity, Personal Survival and the Resurrection of the Body: A Scholastic Discussion in Its Medieval and Modern Contexts. *History of Religions* 30:51–82. Reprinted in *Fragmentation and Redemption: Essays on Gender and the Human Body in Medieval Religion*, 239–97. New York: Zone Books, 1991.

——. 1991. Bodily Miracles and the Resurrection of the Body in the High Middle Ages. In *Belief in History: Innovative Approaches to European and American Religion*, edited by T. Kselman, 68–106. Notre Dame, Ind.: University of Notre Dame Press.

Cahners, Nancy. N.d. To Get on This Team, You've Got to Make the Cut: Some Thoughts on Ritual Circumcision. Online at www.beliefnet.com/story/9/story_939.html.

Calvin, John. 1543. An Admonition Showing the Advantages Which Christendom Might Derive from an Inventory on Relics. In *Calvin's Tracts and Treatises*. Vol. 1. Translated by Henry Beveridge. Grand Rapids, Mich.: Wm. B. Eerdmans, 1958.

Canaan, T. 1929. Water and "The Water of Life" in Palestinian Superstition. *Journal of the Palestine Oriental Society* 9:57–69.

Cansever, Gocke. 1965. Psychological Effects of Circumcision. *British Journal of Psychology* 38:321–31.

Carmichael, Calum M. 1977. A Ceremonial Crux: Removing a Man's Sandal as a Female Gesture of Contempt. *Journal of Biblical Literature* 96:321–36.

——. 1997. *Law, Legend, and Incest in the Bible: Leviticus 18–20*. Ithaca, N.Y.: Cornell University Press.

Carpenter, Mary Wilson. 1988. "A Bit of Her Flesh": Circumcision and "The Significa-tion of the Phallus" in *Daniel Deronda*. *Genders* 1:1–23.

Carroll, Michael P. 1977. Leach, Genesis, and Structural Analysis: A Critical Evaluation. *American Ethnologist* 4:663–77.

——. 1987. Heaven-Sent Wounds: A Kleinian View of the Stigmata in the Catholic Mystical Tradition. *Journal of Psychoanalytic Anthropology* 10:17–38.

——. 1991. Ernest Jones on Holy Communion: Refurbishing an Early Psychoanalytic Insight. *Journal of Psychohistory* 18:307–15.

——. 1992. *The Cult of the Virgin Mary*. Princeton, N.J.: Princeton University Press.

Carter, Nicholas. 1979. *Routine Circumcision: The Tragic Myth*. London: Londinium Press.

Cassuto, U. 1967. *A Commentary on the Book of Exodus*. Translated by Israel Abrahams. Jerusalem: Magnes Press, The Hebrew University. (Orig. Hebrew 1951)

Chebel, Malek. 1992. *Histoire de la circoncision des origines à nos jours*. Paris: Balland.

Chill, Abraham. 1979. *The Minhagim: The Customs and Ceremonies of Judaism, Their Origins and Rationale*. New York: Sepher-Hermon Press.

Chyet, Stanley F., and Norman B. Mirsky. 1990. Reflections of Circumcision as Sacrifice. In *Berit Mila in the Reform Context*, edited by L. M. Barth, 59–68. Secaucus, N.J.: Caro Publishing Group: Berit Milah Board of Reform Judaism.

Cohen, Alfred S. 1989. Brit Milah and the Spector of AIDS. In *AIDS in Jewish Thought and Law*, edited by G. Freudenthal, 113–34. New York: Ktav.

Cohen, Debra Nussbaum. 2001. *Celebrating Your New Jewish Daughter: Creating Jewish Ways to Welcome Baby Girls*. Woodstock, Vt.: Jewish Lights Publishing.

———. 2002. Celebrating Our New Daughters. *United Synagogue Review*, Fall 2002. Reprinted online at www.uscj.org/Celebrating_Our_New_5904.html.

Cohen, Eugene J. 1984. *Guide to Ritual Circumcision and Redemption of the First-Born Son*. New York: Ktav.

Cohen, Richard A. 1998. Bris Mila, Desire and Levinas. *SHOFAR* 16(3):63–70.

Cohen, Shaye J. D. 1985. The Origins of the Matrilineal Principle in Rabbinic Law. *AJS Review* 10(1):19–54.

———. 1990. The Rabbinic Conversion Ceremony. *Journal of Jewish Studies* 41:177–203.

———. 1992. Purity and Piety: The Separation of Menstruants from the Sancta. In *Daughters of the King: Women and the Synagogue*, edited by S. Grossman and R. Haut, 103–15. Philadelphia: Jewish Publication Society.

———. 1996. Did Martial Have a Circumcised Jewish Slave? In *The Jews in the Hellenistic-Roman World: Studies in Memory of Menahem Stern*, edited by I. M. Gafni, A. Oppenheimer, and D. R. Schwartz, 59–66. Jerusalem: Zalman Shazar Center for Jewish History.

———. 1997. Why Aren't Jewish Women Circumcised? *Gender and Society* 9:560–78.

———. 2003. A Brief History of Jewish Circumcision Blood. In *The Covenant of Circumcision: New Perspectives on an Ancient Jewish Rite*, edited by E. W. Mark, 30–42. Hanover, N.H.: Brandeis University Press.

Cold, C. J. and J. R. Taylor. 1999. The Prepuce. *British Journal of Urology International* 83, Supplement 1:34–44.

Collins, John J. 1985. A Symbol of Otherness: Circumcision and Salvation in the First Century. In *"To See Ourselves as Others See Us": Christians, Jews, "Others" in Late Antiquity*, edited by J. Neusner and E. S. Frerichs, 163–86. Chico, Calif: Scholars Press.

Colman, Wendy. 1994. "The Scenes Themselves Which Lie at the Bottom of the Story": Julius, Circumcision, and the Castration Complex. *Psychoanalytic Review* 81:603–25.

Coppens, J. 1941. La Prétendue agression nocturne de Jahvé contre Moïse, Séphorah et leur fils, (Exod. IV, 24–26). *Ephemerides Theologicae Lovanienses* 18:68–73.

Crapanzano, Vincent. 1981. Rite of Return. *Psychoanalytic Study of Society* 9:15–36.

Cronbach, Abraham. 1931–1932. The Psychoanalytic Study of Judaism. *Hebrew Union College Annual* 8–9:605–740.

Crossland, Jefferson C. 1891. The Hygiene of Circumcision. *New York Medical Journal* 53:484–85.

Daly, C. D. 1950. The Psycho-Biological Origins of Circumcision. *International Journal of Psycho-Analysis* 31:217–36.

Dan, Joseph. 1980. Samael, Lilith, and the Concept of Evil in Early Kabbalah. *AJS Review* 5:17–40.

Darby, Robert. 2001. "Where Doctors Differ": The Debate on Circumcision as a Protection against Syphilis, 1855–1914. *Journal of the Society for the Social History of Medicine* 16:57–78.

———. 2005. *A Surgical Temptation: The Demonization of the Foreskin and the Rise of Circumcision in Britain*. Chicago: University of Chicago Press.

Davidovitch, David. 1974. A Rare Parokhet for the Circumcision Ceremony. *Museum Haaretz Bulletin* 15–16:112–18.

de Groot, Joh. 1943. The Story of the Bloody Husband (Exodus IV 24–26). *Oudtestamentische Studiën* 2:10–17.

de Heusch, Luc. 1985. *Sacrifice in Africa: A Structuralist Approach*. Bloomington: Indiana University Press.

Delaney, Carol. 1977. The Legacy of Abraham. In *Beyond Androcentrism: New Essays on Women and Religion*, edited by R. M. Gross, 217–36. Missoula, Mont.: Scholars Press.

———. 1988. Mortal Flow: Menstruation in Turkish Village Society. In *Blood Magic: The Anthropology of Menstruation*, edited by T. Buckley and A. Gottlieb, 75–93. Berkeley: University of California Press.

———. 1991. *The Seed and the Soil: Gender and Cosmology in Turkish Village Society*. Berkeley: University of California Press.

———. 1995. Untangling the Meanings of Hair in Turkish Society. In *Off with Her Head! The Denial of Women's Identity in Myth, Ritual, and Culture*, edited by H. Eilberg-Schwartz and W. Doniger, 53–75. Berkeley: University of California Press.

———. 1998. *Abraham on Trial: The Social Legacy of Biblical Myth*. Princeton, N.J.: Princeton University Press.

———. 2001. Cutting the Ties That Bind: The Sacrifice of Abraham and Patriarchal Kinship. In *Relative Values: Reconfiguring Kinship Studies*, edited by S. Franklin and S. McKinnon, 445–67. Durham, N.C.: Duke University Press.

DeMeo, James. 1997. The Geography of Male and Female Genital Mutilation. In *Sexual Mutilations: A Human Tragedy*, edited by G. C. Denniston and M. F. Milos, 1–15. New York: Plenum.

deMause, Llyod. 1992. The History of Child Assault. *Empathic Parenting* 15:26–42.

———. 1995. Restaging Early Traumas in War and Social Violence. Reprinted online at www.psychohistory.com/htm/eln04_trauma.html.

Denniston, George. 1994. An Epidemic of Circumcision. Paper presented at the Third International Symposium on Circumcision, University of Maryland, May 22–25, 1994. Available online at www.nocirc.org/symposia/third/denniston3.html.

———. 1997a. Circumcision: Ethical and Human Rights Impact Assessment. *Cambridge Quarterly of Healthcare Ethics* 6:89–92.

————. 1997b. Circumcision: An Iatrogenic Epidemic. In *Sexual Mutilations: A Human Tragedy*, edited by G. C. Denniston and M. F. Milos, 103–9. New York: Plenum.

————. 1998. Chat with Dr. George Denniston: A Case against Circumcision. Online interview. ABCNews, July 6, 1998. Available online at http://abcnews.go.com/sections/living/chats/circumcision.html.

————. 1999. Tyranny of the Victims: An Analysis of Circumcision Advocacy. In *Male and Female Circumcision: Medical, Legal, and Ethical Considerations in Pediatric Practice*, edited by G. C. Denniston, F. M. Hodges, and M. F. Milos, 221–40. New York: Kluwer Academic/Plenum.

Denniston, George, Frederick Mansfield Hodges, and Marilyn Fayre Milos. 1999. Preface. In *Male and Female Circumcision: Medical, Legal, and Ethical Considerations in Pediatric Practice*, v–ix. New York: Kluwer Academic/Plenum.

Derrida, Jacques. 1986a. *Glas*. Translated by John P. Leavey Jr. and Richard Rand. Lincoln: University of Nebraska Press. (Orig. French 1974)

————. 1986b. Shibboleth. Translated by Joshua Wilner. In *Midrash and Literature*, edited by G. H. Hartman and S. Budick, 307–47. New Haven, Conn.: Yale University Press.

————. 1991. Des Tours de Babel. *Semeia* 54:3–34.

————. 1992. Ulysses Gramophone: Hear Say Yes in Joyce. In *Jacques Derrida: Acts of Literature*, edited by D. Attridge, 253–309. New York: Routledge. (Orig. French 1987)

Dessing, Nathal M. 2001. *Rituals of Birth, Circumcision, Marriage, and Death among Muslims in the Netherlands*. Leuven: Peeters.

Deutsch, Nathaniel. 2002. Rabbi Nahman of Bratslav: The Zaddik as Androgyne. In *God's Voice from the Void: Old and New Studies in Bratslav Hasidism*, edited by S. Magid, 193–215. Albany: State University of New York Press.

Dobrinsky, Herbert C. 1980. *Selected Laws and Customs of Sephardic Jewry: A Teacher's Resource Manual on the Ritual Practices of the Syrian, Moroccan, Judeo-Spanish, and Spanish and Portuguese Communities in North America*. Vols. 1–2. D.Ed. diss., Yeshiva University.

Donaldson, Mara E. 1981. Kinship Theory in the Patriarchal Narratives: The Case of the Barren Wife. *Journal of the American Academy of Religion* 49:77–87.

Douglas, Mary. 1966. *Purity and Danger: An Analysis of the Concepts of Pollution and Taboo*. London: Routledge and Kegan Paul.

Dreifuss, Gustav. 1965. A Psychological Study of Circumcision in Judaism. *Journal of Analytical Psychology* 10:23–31.

Dresser, Madge. 1997. The Painful Rite: Jewish Circumcision in English Thought 1753–1945. *Jewish Quarterly* 44(Summer):15–17.

————. 1998. Minority Rites: The Strange History of Circumcision in English Thought. *Jewish Culture and History* 1:72–87.

Driver, G. R. 1959. Lilith. *Palestine Exploration Quarterly* 91:55–58.

Dundes, Alan. 1962. Earth-Diver: Creation of the Mythopoeic Male. *American Anthropologist* 64:1032–51.

————. 1976. A Psychoanalytic Study of the Bullroarer. *Man* (n.s.) 11:220–38.

————. 1980. The Hero Pattern and the Life of Jesus. In *Interpreting Folklore*, 223–61. (Orig. 1977)

————. 1983. Couvade in Genesis. In *Studies in Aggadah and Jewish Folklore*, edited by K. Ben-Ami and J. Dan, 35–53. Jerusalem: The Magnes Press. (Reprinted in Alan Dundes, *Parsing through Customs: Essays by a Freudian Folklorist*, 145–66. Madison: University of Wisconsin Press, 1987.)

————. 1985. The JAP and the JAM in American Jokelore. *Journal of American Folklore* 98:456–75.

————. 1988. The Flood as Male Creation. In *The Flood Myth*, 167–82. Berkeley: University of California Press. (Orig. 1986)

————. 1991a. The Apple-Shot: Interpreting the Legend of William Tell. *Western Folklore* 50:327–60.

————. 1991b. The Ritual Murder or Blood Libel Legend: A Study of Anti-Semitic Victimization through Projective Inversion. In *The Blood Libel Legend: A Casebook in Anti-Semitic Folklore*, 336–76. Madison: University of Wisconsin Press. (Orig. 1989)

————. 1992. Wet and Dry, the Evil Eye: An Essay in Indo-European and Semitic Worldview. In *The Evil Eye: A Casebook*, 257–312. Madison: University of Wisconsin Press.

————. 1997. Why Is the Jew "Dirty"? A Psychoanalytic Study of Anti-Semitic Folklore. In *From Game to War: And Other Psychoanalytic Essays on Folklore*, 92–119. Lexington: University Press of Kentucky.

————. 1999. *Holy Writ and Oral Lit: The Bible as Folklore*. Lanham, Md.: Rowman & Littlefield.

————. 2002. *The Shabbat Elevator and Other Sabbath Subterfuges: An Unorthodox Essay on Circumventing Custom and Jewish Character*. Lanham, Md.: Rowman & Littlefield.

Dunsmuir, W. D., and E. M. Gordon. 1999. The History of Circumcision. *British Journal of Urology International* 83(suppl. 1):1–12.

Eckstein, Jerome. 1957. The Incest Taboo: Maimonides, Freud and Reik. *Psychoanalysis* 5(3):3–15.

Efron, John M. 2001. *Medicine and the German Jews: A History*. New Haven, Conn.: Yale University Press.

Eilberg-Schwartz, Howard. 1990. *The Savage in Judaism: An Anthropology of Israelite Religion and Ancient Judaism*. Bloomington: Indiana University Press.

————. 1994. *God's Phallus, And Other Problems for Men and Monotheism*. Boston: Beacon.

————. 1995. A Masculine Critique of a Father God. *Tikkun* 10(5):58–62.

Ellenson, David. 1990. "Who Is a Jew"? Issues of Jewish Status and Identity and Their Relationship to the Nature of Judaism in the Modern World. In *Berit Milah in the Reform Context*, edited by L. M. Barth, 69–81. Secaucus, N.J.: Carol Publishing Group: Berit Milah Board of Reform Judaism.

Elliott, John H. 1991. The Evil Eye in the First Testament: The Ecology and Culture of a Pervasive Belief. In *The Bible and the Politics of Exegesis: Essays in Honor of Norman K.*

Gottwald on His Sixty-Fifth Birthday, edited by D. Jobling, P. L. Day, and G.T. Sheppard, 147–59. Cleveland: Pilgrim Press.

Elliott, Susan. 2003. *Cutting Too Close for Comfort: Paul's Letter to the Galatians in Its Anatolian Cultic Context*. London: T & T Clark.

Ellis, Jim. 1995. The Wit of Circumcision, the Circumcision of Wit. In *The Wit of Seventeenth-Century Poetry*, edited by C. J. Summers and T.-L. Pebworth, 62–77. Columbia: University of Missouri Press.

Engelbrecht, Edward. 1999. God's Milk: An Orthodox Confession of the Eucharist. *Journal of Early Christian Studies* 7:509–26.

Engelstein, Laura. 1999. *Castration and the Heavenly Kingdom: A Russian Folktale*. Ithaca, N.Y.: Cornell University Press.

Epstein, Louis M. 1948. *Sex Laws and Customs in Judaism*. New York: Ktav.

Erickson, John A. 1994. Does Male Circumcision Help Spread AIDS? *The Backlash!* Reprinted online at www.sexuallymutilatedchild.org/does-c.htm.

Eslinger, Lyle. 1981. The Case of an Immodest Lady Wrestler in Deuteronomy XXV 11–12. *Vetus Testamentum* 31:269–81.

Farrell, Warren. 1993. *The Myth of Male Power: Why Men Are the Disposable Sex*. New York: Simon & Schuster.

Feldman, Arthur A. 1944. Freud's "Moses and Monotheism" and the Three Stages of Israelitish Religion. *Psychoanalytic Review* 31:361–418.

Feldman, David M. 1975. *Marital Relations, Birth Control, and Abortion in Jewish Law*. New York: Schocken Books.

Feldman, Louis H. 1993. *Jew and Gentile in the Ancient World: Attitudes and Interactions from Alexander to Justinian*. Princeton, N.J.: Princeton University Press.

Feldman, S. S. 1955. The Sin of Reuben, First-Born Son of Jacob. *Psychoanalysis and the Social Sciences* 4:282–87.

Felsenstein, Frank. 1995. *Anti-Semitic Stereotypes: A Paradigm of Otherness in English Popular Culture, 1660–1830*. Baltimore: The Johns Hopkins University Press.

Fenichel, Otto. 1946. Elements of a Psychoanalytic Theory of Anti-Semitism. In *Anti-Semitism: A Social Disease*, edited by E. Simmel, 11–32. New York: International Universities Press.

Ferenczi, Sándor. 1926. On the Symbolism of the Head of Medusa. In *Further Contributions to the Theory and Technique of Psychoanalysis*, compiled by John Rickman, 360. London: Hogarth Press. (Orig. German 1923)

———. 1950. The Psychic Consequences of a "Castration" in Childhood. In *Further Contributions to the Theory and Technique of Psycho-Analysis*, compiled by John Rickman, 2244–49. London: Hogarth Press, 1950. (Orig. German 1916–1917)

Ferguson, Everett. 1988. Spiritual Circumcision in Early Christianity. *Scottish Journal of Theology* 41:485–97.

Fewell, Danna Nolan, and David M. Gunn. 1991. Tipping the Balance: Sternberg's Reader and the Rape of Dinah. *Journal of Biblical Literature* 110:193–211.

Fink, Lawrence H. 1993. The Incident at the Lodging House. *Jewish Bible Quarterly* 21:236–41.

Finkel, Joshua. 1974. The Case of the Repeated Circumcision in Josh. 5:2.7: An Historical and Comparative Study. *Annals of the Jewish Academy of Arts and Sciences*, edited by H. L. Silverman, 177–213. New York: MSS Information Corp.

Finley, Mordecai. 1990. Berit Milah Issues in Modern Orthodoxy and Reform Judaism. In *Berit Milah in the Reform Context*, edited by L. M. Barth, 177–92. Secaucus, N.J.: Carol Publishing Group: Berit Milah Board of Reform Judaism.

Firestone, Reuven. 1990. *Journeys in Holy Lands: The Evolution of the Abraham-Ishmael Legends in Islamic Exegesis.* Albany: State University of New York Press.

————. 1993. Prophethood, Marriageable Consanguinity, and Text: The Problem of Abraham and Sara's Kinship Relationship and the Response of Jewish and Islamic Exegesis. *Jewish Quarterly Review* 83:331–47.

Fishman, Sylvia Barack. 1993. *A Breath of Life: Feminism in the American Jewish Community.* New York: Free Press.

Fleishman, Joseph. 2001. On the Significance of a Name Change and Circumcision in Genesis 17. *Journal of the Ancient Near Eastern Society* 28:19–32.

Fleiss, Paul M. 1997. Where Is My Foreskin? The Case against Circumcision. MOTHERING: *The Magazine of Natural Family Living*, winter 1997, 36–45. Reprinted online at www.foreskin.org/fleiss.htm.

Fleiss, Paul M., and F. M. Hodges. 2002. *What Your Doctor May Not Tell You about Circumcision: Untold Facts on America's Most Widely Performed—and Most Unnecessary—Surgery.* New York: Warner Books.

Fletcher, Christopher R. 1999. Circumcision in America in 1998: Attitudes, Beliefs, and Charges of American Physicians. In *Male and Female Circumcision: Medical, Legal, and Ethical Considerations in Pediatric Practice*, edited by G. C. Denniston, F. M. Hodges, and M. F. Milos, 259–71. New York: Kluwer Academic/Plenum.

Flusser, David, and Shmuel Safrai. 1980. Who Sanctified the Beloved in the Womb? *Immanuel* 11:46–55. (Orig. Hebrew 1978. Translated by Robert Broidy)

Foley, John M. 1966. *The Practice of Circumcision: A Revaluation.* New York: Materia Medica.

Forster, Brenda. 1993. The Biblical 'Ōmēn and Evidence for the Nurturance of Children by Hebrew Males. *Judaism* 42:321–31.

Foote, G. W. and J. M. Wheeler. 1887. *Crimes of Christianity.* Vol. 1. London: Progressive Publishing Company.

Fox, Everett. 1995. *The Five Books of Moses: Genesis, Exodus, Leviticus, Numbers, and Deuteronomy: A New Translation with Introductions, Commentary, and Notes.* New York: Schocken Books.

Fox, Michael V. 1974. The Sign of the Covenant: Circumcision in the Light of the Priestly 'ôt Etiologies. *Revue Biblique* 81:557–96.

Frazer, Sir James George. 1904. The Origins of Circumcision. *The Independent Review* 4:204–18.

———. 1918. *Folk-Lore in the Old Testament: Studies in Comparative Religion and Law.* Vols. 1–3. London: Macmillan.

Freeman, M. D. A. 1999. A Child's Right to Circumcision. *British Journal of Urology International* 83(suppl. 1):74–78.

Freud, Sigmund. 1900. The Interpretation of Dreams. *Standard Edition* IV.

———. 1905. Three Essays on the Theory of Sexuality. *Standard Edition* VII.

———. 1909. Analysis of a Phobia in a Five-Year-Old Boy. *Standard Edition* X.

———. 1913. Totem and Taboo. *Standard Edition* XIII.

———. 1922. Medusa's Head. *Standard Edition* XVIII.

———. 1939. Moses and Monotheism. *Standard Edition* XXIII.

———. 1940. An Outline of Psychoanalysis. *Standard Edition* XXIII.

Friedman, Richard Elliot. 1987. *Who Wrote the Bible?* New York: Summit Books.

Frojmovic, Eva. 2003. Christian Travelers to the Circumcision: Early Modern Representations. In *The Covenant of Circumcision: New Perspectives on an Ancient Jewish Rite*, edited by E. W. Mark, 128–41. Hanover, N.H.: Brandeis University Press.

Frolov, Serge. 1996. The Hero as Bloody Bridegroom: On the Meaning and Origin of Exodus 4:26. *Biblica* 77:520–23.

Frymer-Kensky, Tikva. 1983. Pollution, Purification, and Purgation in Biblical Israel. In *The Word of the Lord Shall Go Forth: Essays in Honor of David Noel Freedman in Celebration of His Sixtieth Birthday*, edited by C. L. Meyers and M. O'Connor, 399–414. Winona Lake, Ind.: Eisenbrauns.

———. 1995. *Motherprayer: The Pregnant Woman's Spiritual Companion.* New York: Riverhead Books.

Gager, John G. 1983. *The Origins of Anti-Semitism: Attitudes toward Judaism in Pagan and Christian Antiquity.* New York: Oxford University Press.

Gairdner, Douglas. 1949. The Fate of the Foreskin. *British Medical Journal* 2:1433–37.

Gardiner, A. 1961. *Egypt of the Pharaohs.* Oxford: Clarendon Press.

Gaster, Moses. 1900. Two Thousand Years of a Charm against the Child-Stealing Witch. *Folk-Lore* 11:129–62.

———. 1924. *The Exempla of the Rabbis: Being a Collection of Exempla, Apologues and Tales Culled from Hebrew Manuscripts and Rare Hebrew Books.* Reprint, New York: Ktav, 1968.

———. 1934. *Ma'Aseh Book: Book of Jewish Tales and Legends Translated from the Judeo-German.* Philadelphia: Jewish Publication Society of America. (Translated from a 1602 compilation by Jacob ben Abraham of Mezeritch [Basel: Konrad Waldkirch])

Gaster, T. H. 1980. *The Holy and the Profane: The Evolution of Jewish Folkways.* Rev. ed. New York: William Morrow. (Orig. 1955)

Gatrad, A. R., A. Sheikh, and H. Jacks. 2002. Religious Circumcision and the Human Rights Act. *Archives of Disease in Childhood* 86(2):76–78.

Gauthier, Marie-Madeleine. 1986. *Highways of the Faith: Relics and Reliquaries from Jerusalem to Compostela.* Translated by J. A. Underwood. Secaucus, N.J.: Wellfleet Press.

Gelernter, David. 1988. Tsipporah's Bridegroom: A Biblical Breaking Point. *Orim: A Jewish Journal at Yale* 3:46–57.

Gell, A. F. 1971. Penis Sheathing and Ritual Status in a West Sepik Village. *Man* 6:165–81.

Geller, Jay. 1993. A Paleontological View of Freud's Study of Religion: Unearthing the *Leitfossil* Circumcision. *Modern Judaism* 13:49–70.

———. 1997. Circumcision and Jewish Women's Identity: Rahel Levin Barnhagen's Failed Assimilation. In *Judaism since Gender*, edited by M. Perskowitz and L. Levitt, 174–87. New York: Routledge.

———. 1999. The Godfather of Psychoanalysis: Circumcision, Antisemitism, Homosexuality, and Freud's "Fighting Jew." *Journal of the American Academy of Religion* 67:355–85.

Geller, Stephen A. 1982. The Struggle at the Jabbok: The Use of Enigma in a Biblical Narrative. *Journal of the Ancient Near Eastern Society* 14:37–60.

Gendler, Mary. 1974. Sarah's Seed: A New Ritual for Women. *Response* 24:65–75.

Gesundheit, Benjamin, et al. 2004. Neonatal Genital Herpes Simplex Virus Type 1 Infection after Jewish Ritual Circumcision: Modern Medicine and Religious Tradition. *Pediatrics* 114:259–63. Reprinted online at http://pediatrics.aappublications.org/cgi/content/full/114/2/e259.

Gilbert, Scott F., and Ziony Zevit. 2001. Congenital Human Baculum Deficiency: The Generative Bone of Genesis 2:21–23. *American Journal of Medical Genetics* 101:284–85.

Gilman, Sander L. 1987. The Struggle of Psychiatry with Psychoanalysis: Who Won? *Critical Inquiry* 13:293–313.

———. 1991a. The Jewish Murderer: Jack the Ripper, Race, and Gender. In *The Jew's Body*, 104–27. New York: Routledge.

———. 1991b. The Jewish Psyche: Freud, Dora, and the Idea of the Hysteric. In *The Jew's Body*, 60–103. New York: Routledge.

———. 1991c. The Jewish Voice. In *The Jew's Body*, 10–37. New York: Routledge.

———. 1991d. *The Jew's Body*. New York: Routledge.

———. 1993a. The Construction of the Male Jew. In *Freud, Race, and Gender*, 49–92. Princeton, N.J.: Princeton University Press.

———. 1993b. Freud and the Epistemology of Race. In *Freud, Race, and Gender*, 12–48. Princeton, N.J.: Princeton University Press.

———. 1993c. Mark Twain and the Diseases of the Jews. *American Literature* 65:95–115.

———. 1994. The Jewish Nose: Are Jews White? Or, the History of the Nose Job. In *The Other in Jewish Thought and History: Constructions of Jewish Culture and Identity*, edited by L. J. Silberstein and R. L. Cohn, 364–401. New York: New York University Press.

———. 1995. Representing Jewish Sexuality: The Damaged Body as the Image of the Damaged Soul. In *Jews in Today's German Culture*, 71–108. Bloomington: Indiana University Press.

———. 1996. *Smart Jews: The Construction of the Image of Jewish Superior Intelligence*. Lincoln: University of Nebraska Press.

―――. 1997. Decircumcision: The First Aesthetic Surgery. *Modern Judaism* 17:201–10.

―――. 1999. "Barbaric" Rituals? In *Is Multiculturalism Bad for Women? Susan Moller Okin with Respondents*, edited by J. Cohen, M. Howard, and M. C. Nussbaum, 53–58. Princeton, N.J.: Princeton University Press.

Ginsburg, Eliezer. 1998. *On the Eighth Day: Discourses on Bris Milah Drawn from the Weekly Sidra*. Brooklyn, N.Y.: Mesorah.

Ginsburg, Elliot K. 1989. *The Sabbath in the Classical Kabbalah*. Albany: State University of New York Press.

Ginzberg, Louis. 1909–1938. *The Legends of the Jews*. Vols. I–VII. Philadelphia: Jewish Publication Society.

Glanzberg-Krainin, Deborah. 2003. Noam's Bris. In *The Covenant of Circumcision: New Perspectives on an Ancient Jewish Rite*, edited by E. W. Mark, 197–200. Hanover, N.H.: Brandeis University Press.

Glenn, Jules. 1960. Circumcision and Anti-Semitism. *Psychoanalytic Quarterly* 29:395–99.

Glick, Leonard B. 2004. "Something Less Than Joyful": Jewish Americans and the Circumcision Dilemma. In *Flesh and Blood: Perspectives on the Problem of Circumcision in Contemporary Society*, edited by G. C. Denniston, F. M. Hodges and M. F. Milos, 143–46. New York: Kluwer Academic/Plenum.

―――. 2005. *Marked in Your Flesh: Circumcision from Ancient Judea to Modern America*. Oxford: Oxford University Press.

Gluckman, Max. 1949. The Role of the Sexes in Wiko Circumcision Ceremonies. In *Social Structure: Studies Presented to A. R. Radcliffe-Brown*, edited by M. Fortes, 145–67. Oxford: Clarendon.

Goldberg, Harvey E. 1987. Torah and Children: Some Symbolic Aspects of the Reproduction of Jews and Judaism. In *Judaism Viewed from Within and Without: Anthropological Studies*, edited by H. E. Goldberg, 107–30. Albany: State University of New York Press.

―――. 1996. Cambridge in the Land of Canaan: Descent, Alliance, Circumcision, and Instruction in the Bible. *Journal of the Ancient Near Eastern Society* 24:9–34.

Goldberg, Sylvie Anne. 1996. *Crossing the Jabbok: Illness and Death in Ashkenazi Judaism in Sixteenth- through Nineteenth-Century Prague*. Translated by Carol Cosman. Berkeley: University of California Press.

Goldberger, Yonason Binyomin (Jonathan Benjamin). 1991. *Sanctity and Science: Insights into the Practice of Milah and Metzitzah*, translated from the Hebrew and edited by Avrohom Marmorstein. New York: Feldheim.

Goldin, Simha. 1996. The Role of Ceremonies in the Socialization Process: The Case of Jewish Communities of Northern France and Germany in the Middle Ages. *Archives de sciences sociales des religions* 95:163–78.

Goldingay, John. 2000. The Significance of Circumcision. *Journal for the Study of the Old Testament* 88:3–18.

Goldman, Liela. 1984. Hemingway's *The Sun Also Rises*: Circumcision and Castration. *Midstream* 30(9):55–56.

Goldman, Ronald. 1997. *Circumcision: The Hidden Trauma*. Boston: Vanguard.

———. 1998. *Questioning Circumcision: A Jewish Perspective*. Boston: Vanguard.

———. 2004. The Growing Jewish Circumcision Debate: A Psychosocial Critique. In *Flesh and Blood: Perspectives on the Problem of Circumcision in Contemporary Society*, edited by G. C. Denniston, F. M. Hodges, and M. F. Milos, 171–94. New York: Kluwer Academic/Plenum.

Gollaher, David L. 2000. *Circumcision: A History of the World's Most Controversial Surgery*. New York: Basic Books.

Gooding, D. W. 1977. Traditions of Interpretation of the Circumcision at Gilgal. In *Proceedings of the Sixth World Congress of Jewish Studies*, vol. 1, edited by A. Shinan, 149–64. Jerusalem: World Union of Jewish Studies.

Goodman, Jenny. 1997. Challenging Circumcision: A Jewish Perspective. In *Sexual Mutilations: A Human Tragedy*, edited by G. C. Denniston and M. F. Milos, 175–78. New York: Plenum.

———. 1999a. Jewish Circumcision: An Alternative Perspective. *British Journal of Urology International* 83(suppl. 1):22–27.

———. 1999b. A Jewish Perspective on Circumcision. In *Male and Female Circumcision: Medical, Legal, and Ethical Considerations in Pediatric Practice*, edited by G. C. Denniston, F. M. Hodges, and M. F. Milos, 179–82. New York: Kluwer Academic/Plenum.

Gordis, Daniel H. 1998. The Power of Ritual. Response to Dr. Ronald Goldman's "Circumcision: A Source of Jewish Pain." *Jewish Spectator* 62(3):61–62.

Gottstein, Alon Goshen. 1994. The Body as Image of God in Rabbinic Literature. *Harvard Theological Review* 87:171–95.

Graber, Robert Bates. 1981. A Psychocultural Theory of Male Genital Mutilation. *Journal of Psychoanalytic Anthropology* 4:413–34.

Granatstein, Melvin. 1975. Why I Won't Rupture My Daughter's Hymen—Reflections on Mary Gendler's "New Ritual for Women." *Response* 26:105–17.

Granqvist, Hilma Natalia. 1947. *Birth and Childhood among the Arabs: Studies in a Muhammadan Village in Palestine*. Helsingfors: Soderstrom.

Graves, Robert and Raphael Patai. 1983. *Hebrew Myths: The Book of Genesis*. New York: Greenwich House.

Greenbaum, Dorothy F. 1999. Opinion: Say Yes to Circumcision. *Reform Judaism*, Winter 1999. Online at http://reformjudaismmag.net/1199dg.html. 103–104.

Greenstein, Edward L. 1984. Biblical Law. In *Back to the Sources: Reading the Classic Jewish Texts*, edited by B. W. Holtz, 83–103. New York: Summit.

Greenstein, Jack M. 1992. *Mantegna and Painting as Historical Narrative*. Chicago: University of Chicago Press.

Griffiths, Wayne. 1999. Current Practices in Foreskin Restoration: The State of Affairs in the United States, and Results of a Survey of Restoring Men. In *Male and Female Circumcision: Medical, Legal, and Ethical Considerations in Pediatric Practice*, edited by G. C. Denniston, F. M. Hodges, and M. F. Milos, 295–302. New York: Kluwer Academic/Plenum.

Grodin, Michael Alan, and Elliot Salo Schoenberg. 1988. A New Tradition: Conservative Mohalim. *Conservative Judaism* 40:59–72.

Gross, Abraham. 1995. The Blood Libel and the Blood of Circumcision: An Ashkenazic
Custom That Disappeared in the Middle Ages. *Jewish Quarterly Review* 86:171–74.

Grossman, Elliot A. 1982. *Circumcision: A Pictorial Atlas of Its History, Instrument Development and Operative Techniques.* Great Neck, N.Y.: Todd & Honeywell.

Gruber, Mayer I. 1989. Breast-Feeding Practices in Biblical Israel and in Old Babylonian
Mesopotamia. *Journal of the Ancient Near Eastern Society* 19:61–83.

Gruenbaum, Ellen. 1996. The Cultural Debate over Female Circumcision: The Sudanese
Are Arguing This One Out for Themselves. *Medical Anthropology Quarterly* 10:455–75.

Gruenwald, Ithamar. 1993. Midrash and the "Midrashic Condition": Preliminary Considerations. In *The Midrashic Imagination: Jewish Exegesis, Thought, and History*, edited by
M. Fishbane, 6–22. Albany: State University of New York Press.

Gunkel, H. 1902–1903. Über die Beschneidung im alten Testament. *Archiv für Papyrus-
forschung und Verwandte Gebiete (APF)* 13–21 (2:13–21)

Gutmann, Joseph. 1983a. *The Jewish Sanctuary.* Leiden: E. J. Brill.

———. 1983b. Die Mappe Schuletragen: An Unusual Judeo-German Custom. *Visible
Religion* 2:167–73.

———. 1987. *The Jewish Life Cycle.* Leiden: E. J. Brill.

Haberman, Bonna Devora. 2003. Foreskin Sacrifice: Zipporah's Ritual and the Bloody
Bridegroom. In *The Covenant of Circumcision: New Perspectives on an Ancient Jewish Rite*,
edited by E. W. Mark, 18–29. Hanover, N.H.: Brandeis University Press.

Hall, Lesley A. 1992. Forbidden by God, Despised by Men: Masturbation, Medical Warn-
ings, Moral Panic and Manhood in Great Britain, 1850–1950. *Journal of the History of
Sexuality* 2:365–87.

Hall, Robert G. 1988. Epispasm and the Dating of Ancient Jewish Writings. *Journal for
the Study of the Pseudepigrapha* 2:71–86.

Hallpike, C. R. 1969. Social Hair. *Man* (n.s.) 4:256–64.

Halperin, D. T., and R. C. Bailey. 1999. Male Circumcision and HIV Infection: 10 Years
and Counting. *Lancet* 354:1813–15.

Halperin, David J. 1995. The Hidden Made Manifest: Muslim Traditions and the "Latent
Content" of Biblical and Rabbinic Stories. In *Pomegranates and Golden Bells: Studies in
Biblical, Jewish and Near Eastern Ritual, Law, and Literature in Honor of Jacob Milgrom*,
edited by D. P. Wright, D. N. Freedman and A. Hurvitz, 581–94. Winona Lake, Ind.:
Eisenbrauns.

Hammerman, Joshua J. 1994. About Men: Birth Rite. *The New York Times Magazine*,
March 13, 28–29.

Hammond, Tim. 1997. Long-Term Consequences of Neonatal Circumcision: A Preliminary Poll of Circumcised Males. In *Sexual Mutilations: A Human Tragedy*, edited by
G. C. Denniston and M. F. Milos, 125–29. New York: Plenum.

———. 1999. A Preliminary Poll of Men Circumcised in Infancy or Childhood. *British
Journal of Urology International* 83(suppl. 1):85–92.

Hansen, William. 1995. Abraham and the Grateful Dead Man. In *Folklore Interpreted: Essays in Honor of Alan Dundes*, edited by R. Bendix and R. Lévy Zumwalt, 355–65. New York: Garland.

Hare, E. H. 1962. Masturbatory Insanity: The History of an Idea. *Journal of Mental Science* 108:1–25.

Harlow, Jules. 1990. The Liturgy of the Brit Milah Ceremony: Concretizing the Moment. *Conservative Judaism* 42:27–37.

Harrington, Charles. 1968. Sexual Differentiation in Socialization and Some Male Genital Mutilations. *American Anthropologist* 70:951–56.

Heald, Suzette. 1999. *Manhood and Morality: Sex, Violence and Ritual in Gisu Society*. London: Blackwell.

Helfand, Jonathan. 1984. A German *Mohel* in Revolutionary France. *Revue des Études Juives* 143:365–71.

Herdt, Gilbert H. 1981. *Guardians of the Flutes: Idioms of Masculinity*. New York: Columbia University Press.

Hershman, P. 1974. Hair, Sex and Dirt. *Man* (n.s.) 9:274–98.

Herzbrun, Michael B. 1991. Circumcision: The Pain of the Fathers. *CCAR Journal* 38:1–13.

Hills, Paula. 1987. A Nontraditional "Circumcision" Ceremony. *Mothering*, Summer 1987, 40–41.

Hirsch, Emil G. 1892. The Evil Eye. *Folk-lorist* 1:69–74.

Hirsch, Samson Raphael. 1988. Milah. In *Samson Raphael Hirsch: The Collected Writings*, vol. 3, 66–111. New York: Philipp Feldheim.

Hirschfeld, Joseph. 1858. The Jewish Circumcision before a Medical Tribunal. *American Medical Monthly* 9:272–75.

Hobson, Robert F. 1961. Psychological Aspects of Circumcision. *Journal of Analytical Psychology* 6:5–33.

Hochlerner, R. 1894. Circumcision—Do We Need Legislation for It? *Medical Record* 46:702.

Hodges, Frederick. 1996a. The Historical Role of Jews in the American Medical View of Circumcision. *Fathering Magazine*. Online at www.fathermag.com/htmlmodules/circ/xjews-circ.html (Note: This essay is no longer available; my copy was accessed on December 20, 1996)

———. 1996b. Interview. Classic Fathering vs. the Judeo-Christian Model. *Fathering Magazine*. Online at www.fathermag.com/interviews/hodges-interview.html.

———. 2001. The Ideal Prepuce in Ancient Greece and Rome: Male Genital Aesthetics and Their Relation to *Lipodermos*, Circumcision, Foreskin Restoration, and the *Kynodesme*. *Bulletin of the History of Medicine* 75:375–405.

Hodges, Frederick, and Jerry W. Warner. 1995. The Right to Our Own Bodies: The History of Male Circumcision in the U.S. *M.E.N. Magazine*. Reprinted online at www.cirp.org/library/history/hodges-warner.

Hoenig, Sidney B. 1963. Circumcision: The Covenant of Abraham. *Jewish Quarterly Review* 53:322–34.

Hoffman, Lawrence A. 1979. A Symbol of Salvation in the Passover Haggadah. *Worship* 53:519–37.

———. 1996. *Covenant of Blood: Circumcision and Gender in Rabbinic Judaism*. Chicago: University of Chicago Press.

Holtzberg, Rabbi Avraham Yeshaya. 1999. *Kovetz Minhagim: An Anthology of Chabad-Lubavitch Customs regarding Pregnancy, Childbirth, Circumcision, Redemption of the First-born, and the Birth of Girls*. Compiled by Rabbi Avraham Yeshaya Holtzberg from the writings of the Rebbeim of Lubavitch. Translated by Shimon Neubort. Brooklyn, N.Y.: "Kehot" Publication Society.

Horowitz, Elliott. 1989. The Eve of the Circumcision: A Chapter in the History of Jewish Nightlife. *Journal of Social History* 33:45–69.

Houtman, C. 1983. Exodus 4:24–26 and Its Interpretation. *Journal of Northwest Semitic Languages* 11:81–103.

Hughes, Diane Owen. 1986. Distinguishing Signs: Ear-Rings, Jews and Franciscan Rhetoric in the Italian Renaissance City. *Past and Present* 112:3–59.

Hutchinson, J. 1890. A Plea for Circumcision. *Archives of Surgery* 2:15.

Hyam, Ronald. 1990. *Empire and Sexuality: The British Experience*. Manchester: Manchester University Press.

Hyman, Israel G. 1987. The Halakhic Issues of Meẓiẓah. *Proceedings of the Association of Orthodox Jewish Scientists* 8–9:17–44.

Isaac, Erich. 1964. Circumcision as a Covenant Rite. *Anthropos* 59:454–56.

———. 1967. The Enigma of Circumcision. *Commentary* 43:51–55.

Isenberg, Shirley Berry. 1988. *India's Bene Israel: A Comprehensive Inquiry and Sourcebook*. Berkeley, Calif.: Judah L. Magnes Museum.

Jacobs, Joseph. 1893. *The Jews of Angevin England: Documents and Records from Latin and Hebrew Sources Printed and Manuscript for the First Time Collected and Translated*. London: David Nutt.

Jay, Nancy. 1992. *Throughout Your Generations Forever: Sacrifice, Religion, and Paternity*. Chicago: University of Chicago Press.

Johnson, Willis. 1998. The Myth of Jewish Male Menses. *Journal of Medieval History* 24:273–95.

Jones, Ernest. 1912. The Symbolic Significance of Salt in Folklore and Superstition. In *Essays in Applied Psycho-Analysis*. Vol. 2, 1951. Chapter 2, 22–109. London: Hogarth Press and Institute of Psycho-Analysis.

———. 1914. Madonna's Conception through the Ear. In *Essays in Applied Psycho-Analysis*, Vol. 2. 1951. Chapter 14, 266–357. London: Hogarth Press and Institute of Psycho-Analysis.

Joranson, Einar. 1950. The Problem of the Spurious Letter of Emperor Alexius to the Count of Flanders. *American Historical Review* 55:811–32.

Jowitt, Claire. 1999. "Inward" and "Outward" Jews: Margaret Fell, Circumcision, and Women's Preaching. *Reformation* 4:139–67.

Judd, Robin. 2003. Circumcision and Modern Jewish Life: A German Case Study, 1843–1914. In *The Covenant of Circumcision: New Perspectives on an Ancient Jewish Rite*, edited by E. W. Mark, 142–55. Hanover, N.H.: Brandeis University Press.

Kakar, Sudhir. 1996. *The Colors of Violence: Cultural Identities, Religion, and Conflict*. Chicago: University of Chicago Press.

Kalimi, Isaac. 2002. "He Was Born Circumcised": Some Midrashic Sources, Their Concept, Roots and Presumably Historical Context. *Zeitschrift für die Neutestamentliche Wissenschaft* 93(1–2):1–12.

Kaplan, Aryeh. 1995. *The Bahir*. Translation, Introduction, and Commentary. Northvale, N.J.: Jason Aronson.

———. 1997. *Sefer Yetzirah*. Rev. ed. Translated, with commentary, by Aryeh Kaplan. York Beach, Me.: Samuel Weiser.

Kaplan, Lawrence. 1981. "And the Lord Sought to Kill Him" (Exod 4:24): Yet Once Again. *Hebrew Annual Review* 5:65–74.

Karsenty, Nelly. 1988. A Mother Questions Brit Milla. *Humanistic Judaism* 16(3):14–21.

Kasher, Hannah. 1995. Maimonides' View of Circumcision as a Factor Uniting the Jewish and Muslim Communities. In *Medieval and Modern Perspectives on Muslim-Jewish Relations*, edited by R. L. Nettler, 103–8. Luxembourg: Harwood.

Katz, David S. 1999. Shylock's Gender: Jewish Male Menstruation in Early Modern England. *Review of English Studies* 50:440–62.

Katz, Ilan. 1999. Is Male Circumcision Morally Defensible? In *Moral Agendas for Children's Welfare*, edited by M. King, 90–104. London: Routledge.

Katz, Jacob. 1998a. The Controversy over the *Meẓiẓah*, the Unrestricted Execution of the Rite of Circumcision. In *Divine Law in Human Hands: Case Studies in Halakhic Flexibility*, 357–402. Jerusalem: Magnes Press.

———. 1998b. The Struggle over Preserving the Rite of Circumcision in the First Part of the Nineteenth Century. In *Divine Law in Human Hands: Case Studies in Halakhic Flexibility*, 320–56. Jerusalem: Magnes Press.

Keen, S. 1991. *Fire in the Belly*. New York: Bantam.

Kennedy, Hansi. 1986. Trauma in Childhood: Signs and Sequelae as Seen in the Analysis of an Adolescent. *The Psychoanalytic Study of the Child* 41:209–19.

Kennedy, John G. 1970. Circumcision and Excision in Egyptian Nubia. *Man* (n.s.) 5:175–91.

Kerkeslager, Allen. 1997. Maintaining a Jewish Identity in the Greek Gymnasium: A "Jewish Load." *Journal for the Study of Judaism* 28:12–33.

Kern, Stephen. 1975. The Prehistory of Freud's Theory of Castration Anxiety. *Psychoanalytic Review* 62:309–14.

Kim, Susan. 1999. Bloody Signs: Circumcision and Pregnancy in the Old English Judith. *Exemplaria* 11:285–307.

Kimelman, Reuven. 1998. The Seduction of Eve and Feminist Readings of the Garden of

Eden. *Women in Judaism: A Multidisciplinary Journal* 1(2). Online at www.utoronto.ca
wjudaism/journal/journal_index2.html.

Kimmel, Michael S. 2001. The Kindest Un-Cut. *Tikkun* 16(3):43–48. Reprinted online
at www.cirp.org/pages/cultural/kimmel1.   .

Kirshenblatt-Gimblett, Barbara. 1982. The Cut That Binds: The Western Ashkenazi
Torah Binder as Nexus between Circumcision and Torah. In *Celebration: Studies in Fes
tivity and Ritual*, edited by V. Turner, 136–46. Washington, D.C.: Smithsonian Institu
tion Press.

Kisch, Guido. 1942. The Yellow Badge in History. *Historia Judaica* 4:95–127.

Kister, M.J. 1994. ". . . And He Was Born Circumcised . . .": Some Notes on Circumcision
in Ḥadīth. *Oriens* 34:10–30.

Kitahara, Michio. 1974. Living Quarter Arrangements in Polygyny and Circumcision and
Segregation of Males at Puberty. *Ethnology* 13:401–13.

———. 1976. A Cross-Cultural Test of the Freudian Theory of Circumcision. *Interna
tional Journal of Psychoanalytic Psychotherapy* 5:535–46.

Klagsbrun, Francine. 1997. Circumcision May Resemble Female Genital Mutilation but
It Has Meaning for Jewish Uniqueness. *Moment* 22(2):22.

Klein, Michelle. 1998. *A Time to Be Born: Customs and Folklore of Jewish Birth*. Philadelphia: Jewish Publication Society.

Kletenik, Rivy Poupko. 1998. It's Brit Milah, Not Circumcision: Response to Dr. Ronald
Goldman's "Circumcision: A Source of Jewish Pain." *Jewish Spectator* 62(3):59.

Klingbeil, Gerald A. 1997. Ritual Time in Leviticus 8 with Special Reference to the
Seven Day Period in the Old Testament. *Zeitschrift für die alttestamentliche Wissenschaft*
109:500–13.

Knight, Mary. 2001. Curing Cut or Ritual Mutilation? Some Remarks on the Practice of
Female and Male Circumcision in Graeco-Roman Egypt. *Isis* 92:317–38.

Koren, Israel. 1999. Friedrich Weinreb's Commentary on the Two Tales of Creation in
Genesis. *Jewish Studies Quarterly* 6:71–112.

Kosmala, Hans. 1962. The "Bloody Husband." *Vetus Testamentum* 12:14–28.

Kovács, Éva, and Júlia Vada. 2003. Circumcision in Hungary after the Shoah. In *The Covenant of Circumcision: New Perspectives on an Ancient Jewish Rite*, edited by E. W. Mark,
176–87. Hanover, N.H.: Brandeis University Press.

Kozberg, Cary D. 1984. A Father Performs a Berit Milah. *Journal for Reform Judaism*
31:3–9.

Kraemer, David. 1996. The Problem with Foreskin: Circumcision, Gender, Impurity, and
Death. In *Reading the Rabbis: The Talmud as Literature*, 109–23. New York: Oxford University Press.

Krapf, E. E. 1955. Shylock and Antonio: A Psychoanalytic Study of Shakespeare and
Antisemitism. *Psychoanalytic Review* 42:113–30.

Krauss, Samuel. 1970. The Jewish Rite of Covering the Head. In *Beauty and Holiness:
Studies in Jewish Customs and Ceremonial Art*, edited by J. Gutmann, 420–67. New York:
Ktav. (Orig. 1955)

Kristeva, Julia. 1982. *Powers of Horror: An Essay on Abjection*. Translated by Leon S. Rou-
diez. New York: Columbia University Press. (Orig. French 1980)

Krohn, Paysach J. 1985. *Bris Milah: Circumcision—The Covenant of Abraham: A Compendium of Laws, Rituals, and Customs from Birth to Bris, Anthologized from Talmudic, and
Traditional Sources*. New York: Mesorah.

Kunin, Samuel A. 1998. *Circumcision: Its Place in Judaism, Past and Present*. Los Angeles:
Isaac Nathan Publishing.

Kunin S., and R. Miller. 1992. The Penis Becomes a Scapegoat [letter to the editor].
Moment, December, 75, 77.

Kunin, Seth D. 1994. The Death of Isaac: Structuralist Analysis of Genesis 22. *Journal for
the Study of the Old Testament* 64:57–81.

———. 1995. *The Logic of Incest: A Structuralist Analysis of Hebrew Mythology*. Sheffield:
Sheffield Academic Press.

———. 1996. The Bridegroom of Blood: A Structuralist Analysis. *Journal for the Study of
the Old Testament* 70:3–16.

La Barre, Weston. 1962. *They Shall Take Up Serpents: Psychology of the Southern Snake-
Handling Culture*. Minneapolis: University of Minnesota Press.

Lacan, Jacques. 1977. Signification of the Phallus. In *Écrits: A Selection*, 281–91. New
York: Norton.

Lachs, Samuel Tobias. 1965. Serpent Folklore in Rabbinic Literature. *Jewish Social Studies*
27:168–84.

Laibow, Rima. 1991. Circumcision and Its Relationship to Attachment Impairment. Syl-
labus of Abstracts. Second International Symposium on Circumcision, San Francisco,
April 30, 1991, 14.

Landes, Daniel, and Sheryl Robbin. 1990. Current Debate: Circumcision Decision.
Grateful Pain. *Tikkun* 5(5):72–74.

Lansky, Melvin R., and Benjamin Kilborne. 1991. Circumcision and Biblical Narrative.
Psychoanalytic Study of Society 16:249–64.

Laqueur, Thomas. 1990. *Making Sex: Body and Gender from the Greeks to Freud*. Cambridge, Mass.: Harvard University Press.

Laumann Edward O., Christopher M. Masi, and Ezra W. Zuckerman. 2000. Circumcision
in the United States: Prevalence, Prophylactic Effects, and Sexual Practice. In *Sex,
Love, and Health in America: Private Choices and Public Policies*, edited by E. O. Laumann
and R. T. Michael, 277–301. Chicago: University of Chicago Press.

Lauterbach, Jacob Z. 1970. Should One Cover the Head When Participating in Divine
Worship? In *Studies in Jewish Custom and Folklore*, 225–39. New York: KTAV Publishing.
(Orig. 1928)

Layard, John. 1942. *Stone Men of Malekula*. London: Chatto & Windus.

Leach, Edmund. 1962. Genesis as Myth. *Discovery* 23(5):30–35. (Reprinted in *Genesis as
Myth and Other Essays*, by E. Leach, 7–23. London: Cape, 1969)

———. 1983. Why Did Moses Have a Sister? In *Structuralist Interpretations of Biblical*

Myth, edited by E. Leach and D. A. Aycock, 33–36. Cambridge: Cambridge Universit
Press.

Lehane, Terry Hohn. 1996. Zipporah and the Passover. *Jewish Bible Quarterly* 24:46–49.

Leifer, Daniel I., and Myra Leifer. 1976. On the Birth of a Daughter. In *The Jewis
Woman: New Perspectives*, edited by E. Koltun, 21–30. New York: Schocken Books.

Levenson, Jon D. 1993. *The Death and Resurrection of the Beloved Son: The Transformatio
of Child Sacrifice in Judaism and Christianity*. New Haven, Conn.: Yale University Press.
———. 2000. The New Enemies of Circumcision. *Commentary* 109(3):29–36.

Levi, Primo. 1984. *The Periodic Table*. Translated by Raymond Rosenthal. New York
Schocken Books. (Orig. Italian 1975)

Levien, Henry. 1894. Circumcision—Dangers of Unclean Surgery. *Medical Recor
46:619–21.

Levin, David Michael. 1985. *The Body's Recollection of Being: Phenomenological Psycholog
and the Deconstruction of Nihilism*. London: Routledge and Kegan Paul.

Levin, Robe. 2000. Ill at Ease with Mariam, Gloria Naylor's Infibulated Jew. *In Holdin
Their Own: Perspectives on the Multi-Ethnic Literatures of the United States*, edited by C
Fischer-Hornung and J. Raphael-Hernandez, 51–65. Rubingen: Stauffenburg Verlag.

Levine, Amy-Jill. 1995. Sacrifice and Salvation: Otherness and Domestication in th
Book of Judith. In *A Feminist Companion to Esther, Judith and Susanna*, edited by A
Brenner, 208–23. Sheffield: Sheffield Academic Press. (Orig. 1992)

Levine, Elizabeth Resnick, ed. 1991. *A Ceremonies Sampler: New Rites, Celebrations, an
Observances of Jewish Women*. San Diego: Woman's Institute for Continuing Jewis
Education.

Lévi-Strauss, Claude. 1955. The Structural Study of Myth. *Journal of American Folklor
78:428–44.
———. 1976. The Story of Asdiwal. In *Structural Anthropology, Volume II*. Chicago: Uni
versity of Chicago Press. (Orig. French 1958–1959)
———. 1988. Exode sur *Exode*. *L'Homme* 28:13–23.

Lévy, Isaac Jack, and Rosemary Lévy Zumwalt. 2002. *Ritual Medical Lore of Sephardi
Women: Sweetening the Spirits, Healing the Sick*. Urbana: University of Illinois Press.

Levy, Ludwig. 1917–1919a. Ist das Kainszeichen die Beschneidung? Ein kritischer Beitra
zur Bibelexegese. *Imago* 5:290–93.
———. 1917–1919b. Sexualsymbolik in der Paradiesgeschichte. *Imago* 5:16–30.

Levy, Richard N. 1990. The Liturgy of Berit Milah. In *Berit Milah in the Reform Contex
edited by L. M. Barth, 3–15. Secaucus, N.J.: Carol Publishing Group: Berit Mila
Board of Reform Judaism.

Levy, Robert I. 1973. *Tahitians: Mind and Experience in the Society Islands*. Chicago: Uni
versity of Chicago Press.

Lewis, Albert L. 1990. A Charge to the Physician/Mohel. *Conservative Judaism* 42:10–11

Lewis, Bernard. 1984. *The Jews of Islam*. Princeton, N.J.: Princeton University Press.

Lewis, Joseph. 1949. *In the Name of Humanity*. New York: Freethought Press.

Lieb, Michael. 2000. "A Thousand Fore-Skins": Circumcision, Violence, and Selfhood in Milton. *Milton Studies* 38:198–219.

Lieberman, Dale. 1994. Bris Milah. *Kerem*, Winter, 35–53.

———. 1997. *Witness to the Covenant of Circumcision: Bris Milah.* Northvale, N.J.: Jason Aronson.

Lieberman, Saul. 1974a. On Sins and Their Punishment. In *Texts and Studies*, 29–56. New York: Ktav.

———. 1974b. Some Aspects of After Life in Early Rabbinic Literature. In *Texts and Studies*, 235–72. New York: Ktav.

———. 1994. *Greek in Jewish Palestine/Hellenism in Jewish Palestine.* With a new Introduction by Dov Zlotnick. New York: Jewish Theological Seminary of America.

Linder, Amnon. 1987. *The Jews in Roman Imperial Legislation. Edited with Introductions, Translations, and Commentary.* Detroit: Wayne State University Press. (Orig. Hebrew 1983)

Lipset, David M., and Eric Kline Silverman. 2005. The Moral and the Grotesque: The Maternal Body and the Dialogics of Culture in Two Sepik River Societies (Iatmul and Murik). *Journal of Ritual Studies.* 19:17–52.

Llewellyn, David. 2004. Penile Torts in the Courts. In *Flesh and Blood: Perspectives on the Problem of Circumcision in Contemporary Society,* edited by G. C. Denniston, F. M. Hodges, and M. F. Milos, 69–79. New York: Kluwer Academic/Plenum.

Loewenstein, Rudolph M. 1951. *Christians and Jews: A Psychoanalytic Study.* New York: International Universities Press.

Lungstrum, Janet. 1998. Foreskin Fetishism: Jewish Male Difference in *Europa, Europa.* *Screen* 39:53–66.

Lupton, Julia Reinhard. 1997. *Othello* Circumcised: Shakespeare and the Pauline Discourse of Nations. *Representations* 57:73–89.

———. 1999. *Ethnos* and Circumcision in the Pauline Tradition: A Psychoanalytic Exegesis. In *The Psychoanalysis of Race,* edited by C. Lane, 193–210. New York: Columbia University Press.

Lupton, Mary Jane. 1993. *Menstruation and Psychoanalysis.* Urbana: University of Illinois Press.

Luzbetak, Louis J. 1951. *Marriage and the Family in Caucasia: A Contribution to the Study of North Caucasian Ethnology and Customary Law.* Studia Instituti Anthropos, vol. 3. Vienna-Mödling: St. Gabriel's Mission Press.

Lynch, M. J., and J. P. Pryor. 1993. Uncircumcision: A One-Step Procedure. *British Journal of Urology* 72:257–58.

Lyons, Harriet. 1981. Anthropologists, Moralities, and Relativities: The Problem of Genital Mutilations. *Canadian Review of Sociology and Anthropology* 18:499–518.

Malev, Milton. 1966. The Jewish Orthodox Circumcision Ceremony. *Journal of the American Psychoanalytic Association* 14:510–17.

Maller, Allen S. 1992. Pain and Circumcision. *CCAR Journal* 39(2):70.

———. 1993. The Bridegroom of Blood. *Jewish Bible Quarterly* 21:94–98.

Mantegazza, Paolo. 1935. *The Sexual Relations of Mankind.* Translated by Samuel Putnam. New York: Eugenics Publishing. (Orig. Italian 1885)

Marcus, Ivan G. 1996. *Rituals of Childhood: Jewish Acculturation in Medieval Europe.* New Haven, Conn.: Yale University Press.

Marcus, Jacob Rader. 1951. *Early American Jewry: The Jews of New York, New England and Canada, 1649–1790.* Vol. 1. Philadelphia: Jewish Publication Society.

———. 1989. *United States Jewry, 1776–1985.* Vol. 1. Detroit: Wayne State University Press.

———. 1999. *The Jew in the Medieval World: A Source Book: 315–1791.* Rev. ed. Cincinnati: Hebrew Union College Press. (Orig. 1938)

Margalit, Natan. 1995. Hair in TaNaKh: The Symbolism of Gender and Control. *Journal of the Association of Graduates in Near Eastern Studies* 5:43–52.

Mark, Elizabeth Wyner. 2003. Wounds, Vows, Emanations: A Phallic Trope in the Patriarchal Narrative. In *The Covenant of Circumcision: New Perspectives on an Ancient Jewish Rite,* edited by E. W. Mark, 3–17. Hanover, N.H.: Brandeis University Press.

Marmorstein, Emile. 1954. The Veil in Judaism and Islam. *Journal of Jewish Studies* 5:1–11.

Matzner-Bekerman, Shoshana. 1984. *The Jewish Child: Halakhic Perspectives.* New York: Ktav.

McBride, James. 2000. "To Make Martyrs of Their Children:" "Female Genital Mutilation," Religious Legitimation, and the Constitution. In *God Forbid: Religion and Sex in American Public Life,* edited by K. M. Sands, 219–44. Oxford: Oxford University Press.

McEleney, Neil J. 1974. Conversion, Circumcision and the Law. *New Testament Studies* 20:319–41.

McNutt, Paula A. 1994. The Kenites, the Midianites, and the Rechabites as Marginal Mediators in Ancient Israel. *Semeia* 67:109–32.

Mead, Margaret. 1949. *Male and Female: A Study of the Sexes in a Changing World.* New York: Dell.

Meeks, Wayne A. 1973. The Image of the Androgyne: Some Uses of a Symbol in Early Christianity. *History of Religions* 13:165–208.

Mehta, Deepak. 1996. Circumcision, Body and Community. *Contributions to Indian Sociology* 30:215–43.

Meigs, Anna S. 1984. *Food, Sex, and Pollution: A New Guinea Religion.* New Brunswick, N.J.: Rutgers University Press.

Menache, Sophia. 1985. Faith, Myth, and Politics—The Stereotype of the Jews and Their Expulsion from England and France. *Jewish Quarterly Review* 75:351–74.

———. 1997. Matthew Paris's Attitudes toward Anglo-Jewry. *Journal of Medieval Studies* 23:139–62.

Meyer, David J. 1992. Doing It Myself. *Moment* 17(1):45.

Michaelson, Jay. 2005. A Little Off the Top: The Controversy about Circumcision. *Forward,* September 2. Online at www.forward.com/articles/3883.

Milgrom, Jacob. 1976. Rationale for Cultic Law: The Case of Impurity. *Semeia* 45:103–9.

Milgrom, Jo. 1993. Some Second Thoughts about Adam's First Wife. In *Genesis 1–3 in the History of Exegesis: Intrigue in the Garden*, edited by G. A. Robins, 225–53. Lewiston, N.Y.: Edwin Mellen Press.

Miller, Alice. 1990. *Banished Knowledge: Facing Childhood Injuries*. Translated from the German by Leila Vennewitz. New York: Doubleday. (Orig. German 1988)

———. 1983. *For Your Own Good: Hidden Cruelty in Child-Rearing and the Roots of Violence*. Translated from the German by Hildegarde Hannum and Hunter Hannum. New York: Farrar, Straus and Giroux. (Orig. German 1980)

Miller, J. Maxwell. 1972. In the "Image" and "Likeness" of God. *Journal of Biblical Literature* 91:289–304.

Miller, Jeffrey H. 1997–1998. The Unregulated Practice of Ritual Circumcision: Conflicts Between New York Case Law and Statutes and Jewish Ritual Law. *Medical Trial and Technique Quarterly* 44:155–88.

Miller, Jeffrey P. 2002. Circumcision: Cultural-Legal Analysis. *Virginia Journal of Social Policy and the Law* 9:497–585.

Miller, Stuart Creighton. 1982. *"Benevolent Assimilation": The American Conquest of the Philippines, 1899–1903*. New Haven, Conn.: Yale University Press.

Milos, Marilyn Fayre, and Donna Macris. 1992. Circumcision: A Medical or a Human Rights Issue. *Journal of Nurse-Midwifery* 37(suppl. 2):87S–96S. Reprinted online at www.cirp.org/library/ethics/milos-macris.

Milos, Marilyn Fayre and Norman Cohen. 1999. Victory to the Children: Ending Circumcision in the Next Century. *The American Atheist*, Summer issue. Online at www.americanatheist.org/smr99/T2/milos-cohen.html.

Mohl, Paul C., Russel Adams, Donald M. Greer, and Kathy A. Sheley. 1981. Prepuce Restoration Seekers: Psychiatric Aspects. *Archives of Sexual Behavior* 10:383–93.

Mollenkott, Virginia. 1983. *The Divine Feminine: The Biblical Imagery of God as Female*. New York: Crossroads.

Money, John. 1989. Circumcision: Power and Profit, 2420 B.C. to 1988 A.D. *Zeitschrift für Sexualforschung* 2:101–8. Reprinted online at www.noharmm.org/money.htm.

Monick, E. 1987. *Phallos: Sacred Images of the Masculine*. Toronto: Inner City Books.

Montagu, Ashley. 1974. *Coming Into Being among the Australian Aborigines: A Study of the Procreative Beliefs of the Native Tribes of Australia*. London: Routledge and Kegan Paul. (Revised and expanded from a 1937 ed.)

———. 1995. Mutilated Humanity. *The Humanist* 55(4):12–15.

Montaigne, Michel de. 1957. *Travel Journal*. In *The Complete Works of Montaigne: Essays, Travel Journal, Letters*. Newly translated by Donald M. Frame, 859–1039. Stanford, Calif.: Stanford University Press. (Orig. 1580–1581)

Montgomery, James A. 1913. *Aramaic Incantation Texts from Nippur*. Philadelphia: University of Pennsylvania Museum.

Moore, Sally Falk. 1964. Descent and Symbolic Filiation. *American Anthropologist* 66:1308–20.

Morgan, William Keith C. 1965. The Rape of the Phallus. *Journal of the American Medical Association* 193:123–24. Reprinted online at www.cirp.org/library/general/morgan.

Morgenstern, Julian. 1963. The "Bloody Bridegroom" (?) (Exod. 4:24–26) Once Again. *Hebrew Union College Annual* 34:35–70.

———. 1973. *Rites of Birth, Marriage, Death and Kindred Occasions among the Semites.* New York: Ktav. (Orig. 1966, Cincinnati: Hebrew Union College Press)

Moscucci, Ornella. 1996. Clitoridectomy, Circumcision, and the Politics of Sexual Pleasure in Mid-Victorian Britain. In *Sexualities in Victoria Britain*, edited by A. H. Miller and J. E. Adams, 60–78. Bloomington: Indiana University Press.

Moses, M. J. 1871. The Value of Circumcision as a Hygienic and Therapeutic Measure. *New York Medical Journal* 14:368–71.

Moss, Lisa Braver. 1990. Current Debate: Circumcision Decision. A Painful Case. *Tikkun* 5(5):70–72.

———. 1991. The Jewish Roots of Anti-Circumcision Arguments. Paper presented at the Second International Symposium on Circumcision, San Francisco, April 30–May 3. Online at http://nocirc.org/symposia/second/moss.html.

———. 1992. Circumcision: A Jewish Inquiry. *Midstream* 38(1):20–23.

Most, Andrea. 1999. "Big Chief Izzy Horowitz": Theatricality and Jewish Identity in the Wild West. *American Jewish History* 87:313–41.

Munroe, Robert L., and Ruth H. Munroe. 1973. Psychological Interpretation of Male Initiation Rites: The Case of Male Pregnancy Symptoms. *Ethos* 1:490–98.

Naidoff, Bruce D. 1978. A Man to Work the Soil: A New Interpretation of Genesis 2–3. *Journal for the Study of the Old Testament* 5:2–14.

Neuman, R. P. 1975. Masturbation, Madness, and the Modern Concepts of Childhood and Adolescence. *Journal of Social History* 8:1–27.

Neusner, Jacob. 1970. The Jewish-Christian Argument in Fourth-Century Iran: Aphrahat on Circumcision, the Sabbath, and the Dietary Laws. *Journal of Ecumenical Studies* 7:282–98.

———. 1987. The Rite of Circumcision: The "Others" Who Come to Celebrate. In *The Enchantments of Judaism: Rites of Transformation from Birth through Death*, chap. 3. New York: Basic Books.

Newman, R. 1991. Circumcision: The False Initiation. *Changing Men* 23:19–21.

Niditch, Susan. 1985. *Chaos to Cosmos: Studies in Biblical Patterns of Creation.* Chico, Calif.: Scholars Press.

———. 1996. *Oral World and Written Word: Ancient Israelite Literature.* Louisville, Ky.: Westminster/John Knox Press.

Nolland, John. 1981. Uncircumcised Proselytes? *Journal for the Study of Judaism* 12:173–94.

Nordau, Max. 1995. Jewry of Muscle. In *The Jew in the Modern World: A Documentary History*, 2nd ed., edited by P. Mendes-Flohr and J. Reinharz, 547–48. New York: Oxford University Press. (Orig. German 1903)

Northrup, Christiane. 1994. *Women's Bodies, Women's Wisdom: Creating Physical and Emotional Health and Healing.* New York: Bantam. Partly excerpted online at www.birthpsychology.com/birthscene/circ.html.

Novak, David. 1982. The Opposition to Circumcision. *Sh'ma* 12 (May 20). Online at www.clal.org/e83.html.

Nunberg, Herman. 1949. Circumcision and the Problems of Bisexuality. *International Journal of Psychoanalysis* 28:145–79.

Obeyesekere, Gananath. 1981. *Medusa's Hair: An Essay on Personal Symbols and Religious Experience*. Chicago: University of Chicago Press.

O'Hara, K., and J. O'Hara. 1999. The Effect of Male Circumcision on the Sexual Enjoyment of the Female Partner. *British Journal of Urology International* 83(suppl. 1):79–84.

Ohel, M. Y. 1973. The Circumcision Ceremony among Immigrants from Tripolitania in Israeli Village of Dalton. *Israel Annals of Psychiatry and Related Disciplines* 11(1):66–71.

Olivelle, Patrick. 1998. Hair and Society: Social Significance of Hair in South Asian Traditions. In *Hair: Its Power and Meaning in Asian Cultures*, edited by A. Hiltebeitel and B. D. Miller, 11–49. Albany: State University of New York Press.

Olyan, Saul M. 1998. What Do Shaving Rites Accomplish and What Do They Signal in Biblical Ritual Contexts? *Journal of Biblical Literature* 117:611–22.

Öztürk, Orhan M. 1973. Ritual Circumcision and Castration Anxiety. *Psychiatry* 36:49–60.

Paige, Karen Ericksen. 1978. The Ritual of Circumcision. *Human Nature* 18:40–48.

Paige, Karen Ericksen and Jeffery Paige. 1981. *The Politics of Reproductive Ritual*. Berkeley: University of California Press.

Pardes, Ilana. 1989. Beyond Genesis 3. *Hebrew University Studies in Literature and the Arts* 17:161–87. (Reprinted as chapter 3 in Pardes 1992a)

———. 1992a. *Countertraditions in the Bible: A Feminist Approach*. Cambridge, Mass.: Harvard University Press.

———. 1992b. Zipporah and the Struggle for Deliverance. In *Countertraditions in the Bible: A Feminist Approach*, 79–97. Cambridge, Mass.: Harvard University Press.

———. 2000. *The Biography of Ancient Israel: National Narratives in the Bible*. Berkeley: University of California Press.

Patai, Raphael. 1945. Jewish Folk-Cures of Barrenness: II. From the Animal Kingdom. *Folk-Lore* 56:208–18.

———. 1947. *Man and Temple: In Ancient Jewish Myth and Ritual*. London: Thomas Nelson and Sons.

———. 1959. *Sex and Family in the Bible and the Middle East*. Garden City, N.Y.: Doubleday.

———. 1967. *The Hebrew Goddess*. New York: KTAV Publishing.

———. 1983a. Collectanea. In *On Jewish Folklore*, 288–301. Detroit: Wayne State University Press. (The passages I cite were all originally published in Hebrew in 1942)

———. 1983b. Jewish Birth Customs. In *On Jewish Folklore*, 337–443. (The sections I cite were originally published in Hebrew between the 1940s and 1960s)

———. 1983c. *On Jewish Folklore*. Detroit: Wayne State University Press.

———. 1983d. Sephardi Folkore. In *On Jewish Folklore*, 279–87. (Orig. unabridged version 1960)

Paul, Robert A. 1985. David and Saul at En Gedi. *Raritan* 4:110–32.

———. 1990. Bettelheim's Contribution to Anthropology. *Psychoanalytic Study of Society* 15:311–34.

———. 1996. *Moses and Civilization: The Meaning behind Freud's Myth*. New Haven, Conn.: Yale University Press.

Pearl, Jonathan, and Judith Pearl. 1999. *The Chosen Image: Television's Portrayal of Jewish Themes and Characters*. Jefferson, N.C.: McFarland.

Peto, Andrew. 1960. The Development of Ethical Monotheism. *Psychoanalytic Study of Society* 1960:311–76.

Philipson, David. 1931. *The Reform Movement in Judaism*. New and rev. ed. New York: Macmillan.

Pippin, Tina, and George Aichele. 2000. The Cut That Confuses, Or: In the Penile Colony. In *Culture, Entertainment and the Bible*, edited by G. Aichele, 106–23. Sheffield: Sheffield Academic Press.

Plaskow, Judith. 1979. Bringing a Daughter into the Covenant. In *Womanspirit Rising: A Feminist Reader in Religion*, edited by C. P. Christ and J. Plaskow, 179–84. New York: Harper & Row.

Plaut, W. Gunther. 1955. The Origin of the Word "Yarmulke." *Hebrew Union College Annual* 26:567–70.

Pollack, Herman. 1971. *Jewish Folkways in Germanic Lands (1648–1806)*. Cambridge, Mass.: MIT Press.

Pollack, Miriam. 1995. Circumcision: A Jewish Feminist Perspective. In *Jewish Women Speak Out: Expanding the Boundaries of Psychology*, edited by K. Weiner and A. Moon, 171–87. Seattle: Canopy Press.

———. 1997. Redefining the Sacred. In *Sexual Mutilations: A Human Tragedy*, edited by G. C. Denniston and M. F. Milos, 163–73. New York: Plenum.

Pollock, George H. 1973. Jewish Circumcision: A Birth and Initiation Rite of Passage. *Israel Annals of Psychiatry and Related Disciplines* 11(4):297–300.

Porton, Gary G. 1994. *The Stranger within Your Gates: Converts and Conversion in Rabbinic Literature*. Chicago: University of Chicago Press.

Porush, David. 1996. "Jews Don't Hitch": Northern Exposure's Depiction of a Jew's Assimilation to the American Religion or Why the Tip of the Penis Is No Longer a Yardstick. In *Representations of Jews through the Ages*, edited by L. J. Greenspoon and B. F. Le Beau, 115–29. Omaha: Creighton University Press.

Prell, Riv-Ellen. 1992. Why Jewish Princesses Don't Sweat: Desire and Consumption in Postwar American Jewish Culture. In *People of the Body: Jews and Judaism from an Embodied Perspective*, edited by H. Eilberg-Schwartz, 329–59. Albany: State University of New York Press.

———. 1999. *Fighting to Become Americans: Assimilation and Trouble between Jewish Women and Jewish Men*. Boston: Beacon.

Prescott, James W. 1975. Body Pleasure and the Origins of Violence. *The Futurist*, April

1975, 64–74; *Bulletin of the Atomic Scientists*, November 1975, 10–20. Reprinted online at www.violence.de/prescott/bulletin/article.html.

———. 1989. Genital Pain vs. Genital Pleasure: Why the One and Not the Other? *The Truth Seeker* 1(3):14–21. Reprinted online at www.violence.de/prescott/truthseeker/genpl.html.

———. 1994. The Origins of Human Love and Violence. *Pre- and Perinatal Psychology Journal* 10(3):143–88. Reprinted online at www.violence.de/prescott/pppj/article.html.

Presner, Todd Samuel. 2003. "Clear Heads, Solid Stomach, and Hard Muscle": Max Nordau and the Aesthetics of Jewish Regeneration. *Modernism/Modernity* 10:269–96.

Prewitt, Terry J. 1990. *The Elusive Covenant: A Structural-Semiotic Reading of Genesis*. Bloomington: Indiana University Press.

Price, Christopher. 1996. Male Circumcision: A Legal Affront. Brief submitted to the Law Commission of England and Wales, reprinted at www.cirp.org/library/legal/price-uklc. (A shorter version appeared as Male Circumcision: An Ethical and Legal Affront, *Bulletin of Medical Ethics* 128[1997]:13–19)

Propp, William H. 1987. The Origins of Infant Circumcision in Israel. *Hebrew Annual Review* 11:355–70.

———. 1993. That Bloody Bridegroom (Exodus IV 24–6). *Vetus Testamentum* 43:495–518.

Purchas, Samuel. 1626. *Purchase His Pilgrimage*. London.

Raab, Scott. 2000. The Foreskin. *Esquire* 133(1):91.

Rabello, Alfredo Mordechai. 1995. The Ban on Circumcision as a Cause of Bar Kokhbah's Rebellion. *Israeli Law Review* 29:176–214.

Rabinowitz, L. 1972. *The Social Life of the Jews of Northern France in the XII–XIV Centuries as Reflected in the Rabbinical Literature of the Period*. 2nd ed. New York: Hermon Press.

Rappoport, Angelo S. 1928. *Myth and Legend in Ancient Israel*. Vols. 1–3. London: Gresham.

Rashkow, Ilona N. 1993. *The Phallacy of Genesis: A Feminist-Psychoanalytic Approach*. Louisville, Ky.: Westminster/John Knox Press.

———. 1997. Oedipus Wrecks: Moses and God's Rod. In *Reading Bibles, Writing Bodies: Identity and the Book*, edited by T. K. Beal and D. M. Gunn, 72–84. London: Routledge.

———. 2000. *Taboo or Not Taboo: Sexuality and Family in the Hebrew Bible*. Minneapolis: Fortress Press.

Raul-Friedman, Esther. 1992. A Rebuttal—Circumcision: A Jewish Legacy. *Midstream* 38(4):31–33.

Ravich, Abraham. 1973. *Preventing V.D. and Cancer by Circumcision*. New York: Philosophical Library.

Regan, Matthias. 1996. Leaping into Wilderness: The Landscapes of the Men's Movement. *Bad Subjects* 29(November). Online at http://eserver.org/BS/29/regan.html.

Reik, Theodor. 1915–1916. The Puberty Rites of Savages. In *Ritual: Psychoanalytic Studies*, 1946. New York: Farrar, Straus and Company.

———. 1917–1919. Das Kainszeichen: Ein psychoanalytischer Beitrag zur Bibelerklär-
ung. *Imago* 5:31–42.

———. 1951. *Dogma and Compulsion: Psychoanalytic Studies of Religion and Myths.* Translated by Bernard Miall. New York: International Universities Press. (Orig. German versions from a variety of essays and books)

———. 1959. *Mystery on the Mountain: The Drama of the Sinai Revelation.* New York:
Harper & Brothers.

———. 1960. *The Creation of Women: A Psychoanalytic Inquiry into the Myth of Eve.* New
York: McGraw-Hill.

Reinach. A.-J. 1908. La Lutte de Jahvé avec Jacob et avec Moïse et l'Origine de la Circoncision. *Revue des Etudes Ethnographiques et Sociologiques* 1:1–25.

Reis, Pamela Tamarkin. 1991. The Bridegroom of Blood: A New Reading. *Judaism*
40:324–31.

Reiss, Mark D. 2004. My Painful Journey: A Retired Physician's Acknowledgment of Circumcision Trauma Leads Him to Activism. In *Flesh and Blood: Perspectives on the Problem of Circumcision in Contemporary Society*, edited by G. C. Denniston, F. M. Hodges,
and M. F. Milos, 195–206. New York: Kluwer Academic/Plenum.

Remondino, P. C. 1891. *History of Circumcision from the Earliest Times to the Present. Moral
and Physical Reasons for its Performance, with a History of Eunuchism, Hermaphrodism,
Etc., and of the Different Operations Practice Upon the Prepuce.* Philadelphia: F. A. Davis.
Reprint, New York: AMS Press, 1974.

Rhinehart, John. 1999. Neonatal Circumcision Reconsidered. *Transactional Analysis Journal* 29(3):215–21.

Rhoads, Bonita, and Julia Reinhard Lupton. 1999. Circumcising the Antichrist: An
Ethno-Historical Fantasy. *Jouvert* 3(2). Online at http://social.chass.ncsu.edu/jouvert/
v3i12/rhoad.htm.

Richards, David. 1996. Male Circumcision: Medical or Ritual? *Journal of Law and Medicine*
3:371–76.

Ricketts, B. Merrill. 1894. Circumcision: The Last Fifty of a Series of Two Hundred Circumcisions. *New York Medical Journal* 59:431–32.

Ritter, Thomas J., and George C. Denniston. 1996. *Say No to Circumcision: 40 Compelling
Reasons.* Aptos, Calif.: Hourglass Book Publishing.

Robbins, Jill. 1995. Circumcising Confession: Derrida, Autobiography, Judaism. *Diacritics*
25:20–38.

Robinson, Bernard P. 1986. Zipporah to the Rescue: A Contextual Study of Exodus IV
24–6. *Vetus Testamentum* 36:447–61.

Róheim, Geza. 1939. The Covenant of Abraham. *International Journal of Psychoanalysis*
20:452–59.

———. 1940. The Garden of Eden. *Psychoanalytic Review* 27:1–26, 177–99.

———. 1942. Transition Rites. *Psychoanalytic Quarterly* 11:336–74.

———. 1945. *The Eternal Ones of the Dream: A Psychoanalytic Interpretation of Australian
Myth and Ritual.* New York: International Universities Press.

————. 1949. The Symbolism of Subincision. *American Imago* 6:321–28.

————. 1952. The Evil Eye. In *The Evil Eye: A Casebook*, edited by A. Dundes, 211–22. Madison: University of Wisconsin Press, 1984.

————. 1955. Some Aspects of Semitic Monotheism. *Psychoanalysis and the Social Sciences* 4:169–222.

Roith, Estelle. 1987. *The Riddle of Freud: Jewish Influences on His Theory of Female Sexuality*. London: Tavistock.

Romberg, Henry C. 1982. *Bris Milah: A Book about the Jewish Ritual of Circumcision*. New York: Feldheim.

Romberg, Rosemary. 1985. *Circumcision: The Painful Dilemma*. South Hadley, Mass.: Bergin & Garvey.

Romirowsky, Samuel. 1990. Psycho-Social Aspects of Brit Milah. *Conservative Judaism* 42:41–45.

Rosen, Leora N. 1988. Male Adolescent Initiation Rituals: Whiting's Hypothesis Revisited. *Psychoanalytic Study of Society* 12:135–55.

Rosenbaum, Emanuel. 1913. *Meziza: Ist sie religiös geboten? Wirkt sie Heilend oder Schädlich?* Frankfort am Main: Sänger & Friedberg.

Rosenberg, Warren. 2001. *Legacy of Rage: Jewish Masculinity, Violence, and Culture*. Amherst: University of Massachusetts Press.

Rosenzweig, E. M. 1940. Some Notes, Historical and Psychoanalytical, on the People of Israel and the Land of Israel with Special References to Deuteronomy. *American Imago* 1:50–64.

Roth, Cecil. 1964. *A History of the Jews in England*. 3rd ed. Oxford: Clarendon Press.

Roth, Joel. 1992. The Meaning for Today. *Moment* 17(1):41–44.

Rothenberg, Moshe. 1989. Being Rational about Circumcision and Jewish Observance. *M.E.N.* 4:22–23.

Rubenstein, Richard L. 1963. The Significance of Castration Anxiety in Rabbinic Mythology. *Psychoanalytic Review* 50:129–52.

Rubin, Jody P. 1980. Celsus' Decircumcision Operation. *Urology* 16:121–24.

Rubin, Nissan. 2003. *Brit Milah: A Study of Change in Custom*. In *The Covenant of Circumcision: New Perspectives on an Ancient Jewish Rite*, edited by E. W. Mark, 87–97. Hanover, N.H.: Brandeis University Press.

Saintyves, P. 1912. *Les Reliques et les Images Légendaires*. Paris: Mercuvre de France.

Sandel, Margaret. 1996. Brit Milah: An Inscription of Social Power. *The Reconstructionist* 61(2):49–58.

Sarna, Nahum M. 1991. *The JPS Torah Commentary: Exodus*. Philadelphia: Jewish Publication Society.

Sasso, Sandy Eisenberg. 1973. B'rit B'not Israel: Observations of Women and Reconstructionism. *Response* 18:101–5.

Sasson, Jack M. 1966. Circumcision in the Ancient Near East. *Journal of Biblical Literature* 85:473–76.

Satlow, Michael L. 1995. *Tasting the Dish: Rabbinic Rhetorics of Sexuality*. Atlanta: Scholars Press.

Saunders, Benjamin. 2000. Circumcising Donne: The 1633 *Poems* and Readerly Desire. *Journal of Medieval and Early Modern Studies* 30:375–99.

Sawyer, Deborah F. 1995. Water and Blood: Birthing Images in John's Gospel. In *Words Remembered, Texts Renewed: Essays in Honour of John F. A. Sawyer*, edited by J. Davies, G. Harvey, and W. G. E. Watson, 300–309. Sheffield: Sheffield Academic Press.

Sayre, Lewis A. 1870. Partial Paralysis from Reflect Irritation, Caused by Congenital Phimosis and Adherent Prepuce. *Transactions of the American Medical Association*, 3–9.

Schachter, Lifsa. 1986. Reflections on the Brit Milah Ceremony. *Conservative Judaism* 38:38–41.

Schachter-Shalomi, Zalman. 1983. *The First Step: A Guide for the New Jewish Spirit*. Toronto: Bantam.

Schäfer, Peter. 1997. *Judeophobia: Attitudes toward the Jews in the Ancient World*. Cambridge, Mass.: Harvard University Press.

Schauss, Hayyim. 1950. *The Lifetime of a Jew: Throughout the Ages of Jewish History*. New York: Union of American Hebrew Congregations.

Schiffman, Lawrence H. 1985. *Who Was a Jew? Rabbinic and Halakhic Perspectives on the Jewish-Christian Schism*. Hoboken, N.J.: Ktav.

Schlossmann, Howard H. 1966. Circumcision as Defense: A Study in Psychoanalysis and Religion. *Psychoanalytic Quarterly* 35:340–56.

Schmaltz, Art. 1991. Male Circumcision. *The Creative Woman* 11(1):21–24.

Schneider, Susan Weidman. 1984. *Jewish and Female: Choices and Changes in Our Lives Today*. New York: Simon & Schuster.

Schoen, Edgar J. 1997. On the Cutting Edge: The Circumcision Decision. *Moment* 22(5):44–46, 68–69.

Schoen, Edgar J., Christopher J. Colby, and Thomas Ray. 2000. Newborn Circumcision Decreases Incidence and Costs of Urinary Tract Infections during the First Year of Life. *Pediatrics* 105:789–93.

Schoenfeld, C. G. 1966. Psychoanalysis and Anti-Semitism. *Psychoanalytic Review* 53:24–37.

Scholem, Gershom G. 1961. *Major Trends in Jewish Mysticism*. Reprinted from 3rd rev. ed. New York: Schocken Books. (Orig. 1941)

———. 1965. *On the Kabbalah and Its Symbolism*. Translated by Ralph Manheim. New York: Schocken Books. (Orig. 1960)

Schur, Daniel. 1971. *Variance of Behavior Patterns towards Ritual Circumcision*. Master of divinity thesis, Ashland Theological Seminary. Available online at www.tachash.org/heights/thesis.html.

Schwartz, Howard. 1992. Mermaid and Siren: The Polar Roles of Lilith and Eve in Jewish Lore. *Sagarin Review* 2:105–16. (Reprinted in *Reimagining the Bible: The Storytelling of the Rabbis*, 56–67. New York: Oxford University Press, 1998)

Seiden, Melvin. 1996. The Wound and the Covenant. *The Humanist* 56(4):28–30.

Seligman, Paul. 1965. Some Notes on the Collective Significance of Circumcision and Allied Practices. *Journal of Analytical Psychology* 10:5–21.

Shapiro, James. 1996. *Shakespeare and the Jews.* New York: Columbia University Press.

Sheehan, Elizabeth. 1981. Victorian Clitoridectomy: Isaac Baker Brown and His Harmless Operative Procedure. *Medical Anthropology Newsletter* 12:9–15.

Shell, Marc. 1997. The Holy Foreskin; or, Money, Relics, and Judeo-Christianity. In *Jews and Other Differences: The New Jewish Cultural Studies,* edited by J. Boyarin and D. Boyarin, 345–59. Minneapolis: University of Minnesota Press.

Shields, Mary E. 1995. Circumcision of the Prostitute: Gender, Sexuality, and the Call to Repentance in Jeremiah 3:1–4:4. *Biblical Interpretation* 3:61–74.

Shields, Yehudi Pesach. 1972. The Making of Metzitzah. *Tradition* 13:36–48.

Shweder R. A. 2000. What about "Female Genital Mutilation"? And Why Understanding Culture Matters in the First Place. *Daedalus* 129:209–32.

Siegel, Dina. 1998. *The Great Immigration: Russian Jews in Israel.* New York: Berghahn.

Signer, Michael. 1990. To See Ourselves as Others See Us: Circumcision in Pagan Antiquity and the Christian Middle Ages. In *Berit Milah in the Reform Context,* edited by L. M. Barth, 113–27. Secaucus, N.J.: Carol Publishing Group: Berit Mila Board of Reform Judaism.

Silberman, Jeffrey. 1988. The Birth of a Jewish Child. *Humanistic Judaism* 16(3):2–3.

Silver, Samuel 2005. Life or Death? Circumcision, Herpes, and Aids. *Toward Tradition.* Online at www.towardtradition.org/article_life_or_death.htm.

Silverman, Eric Kline. 2001. *Masculinity, Motherhood, and Mockery: Psychoanalyzing Culture and the Iatmul Naven Rite in New Guinea.* Ann Arbor: University of Michigan Press.

———. 2003. The Cut of Wholeness: Psychoanalytic Interpretations of Biblical Circumcision. In *The Covenant of Circumcision: New Perspectives on an Ancient Jewish Rite,* edited by E. W. Mark, 43–57. Hanover, N.H.: University Press of New England/ Brandeis University Press.

———. 2004. Anthropology and Circumcision. *Annual Review of Anthropology* 33:419–45.

Smallwood, E. Mary. 1976. *The Jews under Roman Rule: From Pompey to Diocletian.* Leiden: E. J. Brill.

Smith, Henry Preserved. 1906. Ethnological Parallels to Exodus iv. 24–26. *Journal of Biblical Literature* 25:14–24.

Smith, Jennifer. 1995. Shaving, Circumcision, Blood and Sin: Gendering the Audience in John Mirk's Sermons. In *Venus and Mars: Engendering Love and War in Medieval and Early Modern Europe,* edited by A. Lynch and P. Maddern, 106–18 Perth: University of Western Australia Press.

Smith, Jonathan Z. 1980. Fences and Neighbors: Some Contours of Early Judaism. In *Approaches to Ancient Judaism: Volume II,* edited by W. S. Green, 1–25. Atlanta: Scholars Press.

Smith, S. H. 1990. "Heel" and "Thigh": The Concept of Sexuality in the Jacob-Esau Narratives. *Vetus Testamentum* 40:464–73.

Snowman, Jacob. 1904. *The Surgery of Ritual Circumcision*. London: Initiation Society. (3rd ed. reprinted 1962)

Sokobin, Alan M. 1976. A Belated Response to a Responsum on Circumcision. *CCAR Journal*, Autumn, 67–72.

Somerville, Margaret A. 2000. *The Ethical Canary: Science, Society, and the Human Spirit*. Toronto: Viking.

Sorke, Susan. 2002. Mothers of Israel: Why the Rabbis Adopted a Matrilineal Principle. *Women in Judaism* 3(1). Online at www.utoronto.ca/wjudaism/journal/journal_index1 .html.

Spiegel, Shalom. 1993. *The Last Trial: On the Legends and Lore of the Command to Abraham to Offer Isaac as Sacrifice: The Akedah*. Woodstock, Vt.: Jewish Lights. (Orig. Hebrew ed. 1950)

Spock, Benjamin. 1942. Notes on the Psychology of Circumcision, Masturbation and Enuresis. *Urological and Cutaneous Review*, 768–70.

Steinberg, Leo. 1983. The Sexuality of Christ in Renaissance Art and Modern Oblivion. *October* 25: 1–222. (Reprinted as *The Sexuality of Christ in Renaissance Art and in Modern Oblivion*. 2nd ed., revised and expanded, 3–216. New York: Pantheon, 1996)

Steinmetz, Devora. 1991. *From Father to Son: Kinship, Conflict, and Continuity in Genesis*. Louisville, Ky.: Westminster/John Knox Press.

Stern, David, and Mark Jay Mirsky. 1990. *Rabbinic Fantasies: Imaginative Narratives from Classical Hebrew Literature*. Philadelphia: Jewish Publication Society.

Stern, Josef. 1993. Maimonides on the Covenant of Circumcision and the Unity of God. In *The Midrashic Imagination: Jewish Exegesis, Thought, and History*, edited by M. Fishbane, 131–54. Albany: State University of New York Press.

Stern, Menahem. 1974–1984. *Greek and Latin Authors on Jews and Judaism*. Vols. 1–3. Edited with introductions, translations, and commentary. Jerusalem: Israel Academy of Sciences and Humanities.

Stern, Sacha. 1994. *Jewish Identity in Early Rabbinic Writings*. Leiden: E. J. Brill.

Stetkevych, Suzanne Pinckney. 1996. Sarah and the Hyena: Laughter, Menstruation, and the Genesis of a Double Entendre. *History of Religions* 36:13–41.

Strassfeld, Sharon, and Michael Strassfeld, eds. 1976. *The Second Jewish Catalog*. Philadelphia: Jewish Publication Society.

Straus, Raphael. 1942. The "Jewish Hat" as an Aspect of Social History. *Jewish Social Studies* 4:59–72.

Sumption, Jonathan. 1975. *Pilgrimage: An Image of Mediaeval Religion*. Totowa, N.J.: Rowman & Littlefield.

Susskind, Joshua. 1992–1993. A Discussion of Circumcision. *Pumbedissa* 1(5) (newsletter of the Walking Stick Foundation; online at www.walkingstick.org; no longer available; accessed sometime in 1993–1994)

Sutton, Joseph A. D. 1979. *Magic Carpet: Aleppo-in-Flatbush. The Story of a Unique Ethnic Jewish Community*. New York: Thayer-Jacoby.

Svoboda, J. Steven. 2004. Educating the United Nations about Circumcision. In *Flesh and*

Blood: Perspectives on the Problem of Circumcision in Contemporary Society, edited by G. C. Denniston, F. M. Hodges, and M. F. Milos, 89–108. New York: Kluwer Academic/ Plenum.

Szasz, Thomas. 1996. Routine Neonatal Circumcision: Symbol of the Birth of the Therapeutic State. *Journal of Medicine and Philosophy* 21:137–48.

Tabory, Ephraim, and Sharon Erez. 2003. Circumscribed Circumcision: The Motivations and Identities of Israeli Parents Who Choose Not to Circumcise Their Sons. In *The Covenant of Circumcision: New Perspectives on an Ancient Jewish Rite*, edited by E. W. Mark, 161–76. Hanover, N.H.: Brandeis University Press.

Taylor, R. W. 1873. On the Question of the Transmission of Syphilitic Contagion in the Rite of Circumcision. *New York Medical Journal* 18:561–82.

Teubal, Savina J. 1984. *Sarah the Priestess: The First Matriarch of Genesis.* Athens, Ohio: Swallow Press.

Thompson, G. S. 1920. Circumcision: A Barbarous and Unnecessary Mutilation. *British Medical Journal*, no. 1: 436–37.

Thompson, John Lee. 1995. "'So Ridiculous a Sign': Men, Women, and the Lessons of Circumcision in Sixteenth-Century Exegesis." *Archiv für Reformationgeschichte* 86:236–56.

Tovey, D'Blossiers. 1738. *Anglia Judaica: Or, the History and Antiquities of the Jews in England.* Oxford.

Trachtenberg, Joshua. 1939. *Jewish Magic and Superstition: A Study in Folk Religion.* New York: Behrman's Jewish Book House.

———. 1943. *The Devil and the Jews: The Medieval Conception of the Jew and Its Relation to Modern Antisemitism.* New Haven, Conn.: Yale University Press.

Trachtenberg, Moisés. 1999. Psychoanalysis of Circumcision. In *Male and Female Circumcision: Medical, Legal, and Ethical Considerations in Pediatric Practice*, edited by G. C. Denniston, F. M. Hodges, and M. F. Milos, 209–14. New York: Kluwer Academic/ Plenum.

Trachtman, Ilana, and Sarah Blustain. 1999. When the Mohel Is a Woman: Moving an Ancient Ritual into a New Era. *Lilith* 24(1):10–14.

Travis J. W., A. Bhimji, D. Harrison, X. Castellsagué, F. X. Bosch, and N. Muñoz. 2002. Male Circumcision, Penile Human Papillomavirus Infection, and Cervical Cancer. *New England Journal of Medicine* 347:1452–53.

Trawick, Margaret. 1990. *Notes on Love in a Tamil Family.* Berkeley: University of California Press.

Trible, Phyllis. 1978. *God and the Rhetoric of Sexuality.* Philadelphia: Fortress Press.

———. 1983. *Texts of Terror: Literary Feminist Readings of Biblical Narratives.* Philadelphia: Fortress Press.

Tuchman, Gaye, and Harry Gene Levine. 1993. New York Jews and Chinese Food: The Social Construction of an Ethnic Pattern. *Journal of Contemporary Ethnography* 22:382–407.

Tucker, John T. 1949. Initiation Ceremonies for Luimbi Boys. *Africa* 19:53–60.

Turner, Victor. 1962. Three Symbols of Passage in Ndembu Circumcision Ritual. In *Essays on the Ritual of Social Relations*, edited by M. Gluckman, 124–73. Manchester: Manchester University Press.

———. 1967. Mukanda: The Rite of Circumcision. In *The Forest of Symbols: Aspects of Ndembu Ritual*, 151–279. Ithaca, N.Y.: Cornell University Press.

Tuzin, Donald F. 1995. Art and Procreative Illusion in the Sepik: Comparing the Abelam and the Arapesh. *Oceania* 65:289–303.

Ulmer, Rivka. 1994. *The Evil Eye in the Bible and in Rabbinic Literature*. Hoboken, N.J.: Ktav.

USAID/AIDSMark. 2003. *Male Circumcision: Current Epidemiological and Field Evidence; Program and Policy Implications for HIV Prevention and Reproductive Health*. Conference Report. Washington, D.C.: USAID.

van der Toorn, Karel. 1995. The Significance of the Veil in the Ancient Near East. In *Pomegranates and Golden Bells: Studies in Biblical, Jewish and Near Eastern Ritual, Law, and Literature in Honor of Jacob Milgrom*, edited by D. P. Wright, D. N Freedman, and A. Hurvitz, 327–39. Winona Lake, Ind.: Eisenbrauns.

Van Gennep, Arnold. 1960. *Rites of Passage*. Translated by Monika B. Vizedom and Gabrielle L. Caffe. Chicago: University of Chicago Press. (Orig. French ed. 1909).

Van Howe, Robert S. 1997. Why Does Neonatal Circumcision Persist in the United States? In *Sexual Mutilations: A Human Tragedy*, edited by G. C. Denniston and M. F. Milos, 111–19. New York: Plenum.

———. 1999a. Anaesthesia for Circumcision: A Review of the Literature. In *Male and Female Circumcision: Medical, Legal, and Ethical Considerations in Pediatric Practice*, edited by G. C. Denniston, F. M. Hodges, and M. F. Milos, 67–97. New York: Kluwer Academic/Plenum.

———. 1999b. Neonatal Circumcision and HIV Infection. In *Male and Female Circumcision: Medical, Legal, and Ethical Considerations in Pediatric Practice*, edited by G. C. Denniston, F. M. Hodges, and M. F. Milos, 99–129. New York: Kluwer Academic/Plenum.

———. 1999c. Peer-Review Bias Regarding Circumcision in American Medical Publishing: Subverting the Dominant Paradigm. In *Male and Female Circumcision: Medical, Legal, and Ethical Considerations in Pediatric Practice*, edited by G. C. Denniston, F. M. Hodges, and M. F. Milos, 357–78. New York: Kluwer Academic/Plenum.

Van Howe, Robert S., J. S. Svoboda, J. G. Dwyer, and C. P. Price. 1999. Involuntary Circumcision: The Legal Issues. *British Journal of Urology International* 83(suppl. 1):63–73.

Vermes, G. 1958. Baptism and Jewish Exegesis: New Light from Ancient Sources. *New Testament Studies* 4:308–19.

———. 1973. Circumcision and Exodus IV 24–26. In *Scripture and Tradition: Haggadic Studies*. 2nd rev. ed. Leiden: E. J. Brill.

Viens, A. M. 2004. Value Judgment, Harm, and Religious Liberty. *Journal of Medical Ethics* 30:241–47.

Vincent, Bernard. 1992. The *Moriscos* and Circumcision. Translated by Susan Isabel

Stein. In *Culture and Control in Counter-Reformation Spain*, edited by A. J. Cruz and M. E Perry, 78–92. Minneapolis: University of Minnesota Press.

Wallerstein, E. 1980. *Circumcision: An American Health Fallacy*. New York: Springer.

———. 1983. Circumcision and Anti-Semitism: An Update. *Humanistic Judaism* 11:43–46.

Warning, Wilfried. 1999–2000. Terminological Patterns and Genesis 17. *Hebrew Union College Annual* 70–71:93–107.

———. 2001. Terminological Patterns and the Verb מול "Circumcise" in the Pentateuch. *Biblishe Notizen* 106:52–56.

Warren, John P. 1999. Foreskin Restoration (Circumcision Reversal). In *Male and Female Circumcision: Medical, Legal, and Ethical Considerations in Pediatric Practice*, edited by G. C. Denniston, F. M. Hodges, and M. F. Milos, 303–9. New York: Kluwer Academic/Plenum.

Waskow, Arthur. 1989. The Bible's Sleeping Beauty and Her Great-Granddaughters. *Tikkun* 4:39–41, 125–28.

Wasserfall, Rahel R., ed. 1999. *Women and Water: Menstruation in Jewish Life and Law*. Hanover, N.H.: Brandeis University Press.

Waszak, Stephen J. 1978. The Historic Significance of Circumcision. *Obstetrics and Gynecology* 51:499–501.

Weber, Annette, Evelyn Friedlander, and Fritz Armbruster, eds. 1997. *Mappot . . . Blessed Be Who Comes: The Band of Jewish Tradition*. Osnabrück: Secolo Verlag.

Wechterman, Elyse. 2003. A Plea for Inclusion. In *The Covenant of Circumcision: New Perspectives on an Ancient Jewish Rite*, edited by E. W. Mark, 188–93. Hanover, N.H.: Brandeis University Press.

Weems, Benita J. 1995. *Battered Love: Marriage, Sex, and Violence in the Hebrew Prophets*. Minneapolis: Fortress Press.

Weininger, Otto. 1906. *Sex and Character*. 6th ed. London: William Heinemann. (Orig. German 1903)

Weiss, Charles. 1962a. Ritual Circumcision: Comments on Current Practices in American Hospitals. *Clinical Pediatrics* 1(1):65–72.

———. 1962b. A Worldwide Survey of the Current Practice of *Milah* (Ritual Circumcision). *Jewish Social Studies* 24:30–48.

———. 1966. Motives for Male Circumcision among Preliterate and Literate Peoples. *Journal of Sex Research* 2:69–88.

Weiss, Gerald N., and Andrea W. Hartner. 1998. *Circumcision: Frankly Speaking*. Fort Collins, Colo.: Wiser Publications.

Weissler, Chava. 1989. "For Women and for Men Who Are Like Women": The Construction of Gender in Yiddish Devotional Literature. *Journal of Feminist Studies in Religion* 5(2):3–24.

———. 1992. Mizvot Built into the Body: Tkhines for Niddah, Pregnancy, and Childbirth. In *People of the Body: Jews and Judaism from an Embodied Perspective*, edited by H. Eilberg-Schwartz, 101–15. Albany: State University of New York Press.

Weitzman, Steven. 1999. Forced Circumcision and the Shifting Role of Gentiles in Hasmonean Ideology. *Harvard Theological Review* 92:37–59.

Wellhausen, Julius. 1957. *Prolegomena to the History of Ancient Israel*. New York: Meridian. (Originally *History of Israel*, vol. 1, 1878)

Wenham, Gordon J. 1983. Why Does Sexual Intercourse Defile (Lev 15 18)? *Zeitschrift für die alttestamentliche Wissenschaft* 95:432–34.

Westheimer, Ruth K., and Jonathan Mark 1995. *Heavenly Sex: Sexuality in the Jewish Tradition*. New York: New York University Press.

What, Leslie. 1995. What God Takes: Bris and Mastectomy. *Lilith* 20(3):22–24.

White, C. M. N. 1953. Notes on the Circumcision Rites of the Balovale Tribes. *African Studies* 12:41–56.

Whitekettle, Richard. 1996. Levitical Thought and the Female Reproductive Cycle: Wombs, Wellsprings, and the Primeval World. *Vetus Testamentum* 46:376–91.

Whiting, John W. M., Richard Kluckhohn, and Albert Anthony. 1958. The Function of Male Initiation Ceremonies at Puberty. In *Readings in Social Psychology*, 3rd ed., edited by E. E. Maccoby, T. M. Newcomb, and E. L. Hartley, 359–70. New York: Henry Holt.

Williams, A. J. 1977. The Relationship of Genesis 3 20 to the Serpent. *Zeitschrift für die alttestamentliche Wissenschaft* 89:357–74.

Wine, Sherwin T. 1988. Circumcision. *Humanistic Judaism* 6(2):4–8.

Wolbarst, Abraham L. 1914. Universal Circumcision as a Sanitary Measure. *Journal of the American Medical Association* 62:92–97.

Wold, Donald J. 1979. The *Kareth* Penalty in P: Rationale and Cases. In *Society of Biblical Literature 1979 Seminar Papers*, vol. 1, edited by P. J. Achtemeier, 1–45. Missoula, Mont.: Scholars Press for the Society of Biblical Literature.

Wolfson, Elliot R. 1987a. Circumcision and the Divine Name: A Study in the Transmission of Esoteric Doctrine. *Jewish Quarterly Review* 78:77–112.

———. 1987b. Circumcision, Vision of God, and Textual Interpretation: From Midrashic Trope to Mystical Symbol. *History of Religions* 27:189–215.

———. 1989. Female Imaging of the Torah: From Literary Metaphor to Religious Symbol. In *From Ancient Israel to Modern Judaism: Intellect in Quest of Understanding: Essays in Honor of Marvin Fox*, vol. 2, edited by J. Neusner, E. S. Frerichs, and N. M. Sarna, 271–307. Atlanta: Scholars Press.

———. 1994a. *Through a Speculum That Shines: Vision and Imagination in Medieval Jewish Mysticism*. Princeton, N.J.: Princeton University Press.

———. 1994b. Woman—The Feminine as Other in Theosophic Kabbalah: Some Philosophical Observations on the Divine Androgyne. In *The Other in Jewish Thought and History: Constructions of Jewish Culture and Identity*, edited by L. J. Silberstein and R. L. Cohn, 166–204. New York: New York University Press.

———. 1995. Crossing Gender Boundaries in Kabbalistic Ritual and Myth. In *Circle in the Square: Studies in the Use of Gender in Kabbalistic Symbolism*, 79–121. Albany: State University of New York Press.

———. 1998. Re/Membering the Covenant: Memory, Forgetfulness, and the Construction of History in the Zohar. In *Jewish History and Jewish Memory: Essays in Honor of Yosef Haim Yerushalmi*, edited by E. Carlebach, J. M. Efron, and David N. Myers, 214–46. Hanover, N.H.: Brandeis University Press.

———. 2002. The Cut That Binds: Time, Memory, and the Ascetic Impulse. In *God's Voice from the Void: Old and New Studies in Bratslav Hasidism*, edited by S. Magid, 103–55. Albany: State University of New York Press.

———. 2003. Circumcision, Secrecy, and the Veiling of the Veil: Phallomorphic Exposure and Kabbalistic Esotericism. In *The Covenant of Circumcision: New Perspectives on an Ancient Jewish Rite*, edited by E. W. Mark, 58–70. Hanover: Brandeis University Press.

Wolper, Roy S. 1982. Circumcision as Polemic in the Jew Bill of 1753: The Cutter Cut? *Eighteenth Century Life* 7:28–36.

———. 1983. *Pieces on the "Jew Bill" (1753)*. Augustan Reprint Society, Publication 217. Los Angeles: William Andrews Clark Memorial Library, University of California.

Wood, Charles T. 1981. The Doctor's Dilemma: Sin, Salvation, and the Menstrual Cycle in Medieval Thought. *Speculum* 56:710–27.

Worth, Pati. 1995. Beyond Harm: The Politics of Circumcision. *Man, Alive!* 8(3):6–7.

Yerushalmi, Shmuel. 1989. *The Book of Tehillim. Me'am Lo'ez.* 2 vols. Psalms I: chaps 1–32; Psalms II: chaps. 33–61. Translated by Zvi Faier. New York: Moznaim.

Yerushalmi, Yosef Hayim. 1971. *From Spanish Court to Italian Ghetto: Isaac Cardoso: A Study in Seventeenth-Century Marranism and Jewish Apologetics.* New York: Columbia University Press.

Yovel, Yirmiyahu. 1998. Converso Dualities in the First Generation: The *Cancioneros*. *Jewish Social Studies* 4:1–28.

Zaborowski, Sigismond. 1897. La circoncision chez les Juifs et au Soudan. *Sociétié d'anthropologie de Paris* 8:164–81.

Zafran, Eric M. 1973. *The Iconography of Antisemitism: A Study of the Representation of the Jews in the Visual Arts of Europe 1400–1600.* Ph.D. diss., New York University.

Zaslow, David. 2003. A Covenant above Reason. In *The Covenant of Circumcision: New Perspectives on an Ancient Jewish Rite*, edited by E. W. Mark, 194–96. Hanover, N.H.: Brandeis University Press.

Zeligs, Dorothy F. 1961. Abraham and the Covenant of the Pieces: A Study in Ambivalence. *American Imago* 18:173–86.

———. 1974. Abraham, a Study in Fatherhood. In *Psychoanalysis and the Bible: A Study in Depth of Seven Leaders*, 1–34. New York: Bloch.

———. 1983. Why Did Moses Strike the Rock? A Psychoanalytic Study. In *Fields of Offerings: Studies in Honor of Raphael Patai*, edited by V. D. Sanua, 311–27. Rutherford, N.J.: Fairleigh Dickinson University Press. (Reprinted as chap. 13 in 1986)

———. 1986. *Moses: A Psychodynamic Study.* New York: Human Sciences Press.

Zimmels, H. Jacob. 1997. *Magicians, Theologians, and Doctors: Studies in Folk Medicine and Folklore as Reflected in the Rabbinical Responsa.* Northvale, N.J.: Jason Aronson. (Orig. 1952)

Zimmermann, Frank. 1951. Origin and Significance of the Jewish Rite of Circumcision. *Psychoanalytic Review* 38(2):103–12.

———. 1954–1955. A Letter and Memorandum on Ritual Circumcision, 1772. *Publication of the American Jewish Historical Society* 44(1–4):58–63.

Zindler, Frank R. 1990. Circumcision: The Stone Age in the Steel Age. *The American Atheist*, February 1990, 34–40.

Zirkle, Conway. 1936. Animals Impregnated by the Wind. *Isis* 25:95–130.

Zoossmann-Diskin, Avshalom, and Raphi Blustein. 1999. Challenges to Circumcision in Israel: The Israeli Association against Genital Mutilation. In *Male and Female Circumcision: Medical, Legal, and Ethical Considerations in Pediatric Practice*, edited by G. C. Denniston, F. M. Hodges, and M. F. Milos, 343–50. New York: Kluwer Academic/Plenum.

Zoske, Joseph. 1998. Male Circumcision: A Gender Perspective. *Journal of Men's Studies* 6(2):189–208.

———. 1999. Celebrating Phallus: Healing Men and Culture. In *Male and Female Circumcision: Medical, Legal, and Ethical Considerations in Pediatric Practice*, edited by G. C. Denniston, F. M. Hodges, and M. F. Milos, 279–83. New York: Kluwer Academic/Plenum.

Zwang, Gérard. 1997. Functional and Erotic Consequences of Sexual Mutilations. In *Sexual Mutilations: A Human Tragedy*, edited by G. C. Denniston and M. F. Milos, 67–76. New York: Plenum.

———. 1999. Motivations for Modifications of the Human Body. In *Male and Female Circumcision: Medical, Legal, and Ethical Considerations in Pediatric Practice*, edited by G. C. Denniston, F. M. Hodges, and M. F. Milos, 201–7. New York: Kluwer Academic/Plenum.

Index

About the Author

Eric Kline Silverman is associate professor of anthropology at DePauw University.